WOMEN, GENDER,
AND
SOCIAL PSYCHOLOGY

WOMEN, GENDER, AND SOCIAL PSYCHOLOGY

Edited by

VIRGINIA E. O'LEARY
American Psychological Association

RHODA KESLER UNGER
Montclair State College

BARBARA STRUDLER WALLSTON
George Peabody College
of Vanderbilt University

LEA LAWRENCE ERLBAUM ASSOCIATES, PUBLISHERS
1985 Hillsdale, New Jersey   London

Lawrence Erlbaum Associates, Inc., Publishers
365 Broadway
Hillsdale, New Jersey 07642

Library of Congress Cataloging in Publication Data
Main entry under title:

Women, gender, and social psychology.

Includes bibliographies and index.
1. Women—Psychology.   2. Social psychology.
3. Sex role.   I. O'Leary, Virginia E., 1943–   .
II. Unger, Rhoda Kesler.   III. Wallston, Barbara S.
(Barbara Strudler)
HQ1206.W875   1985   305.4   84-23114
ISBN 0-89859-447-2

Printed in the United States of America
10   9   8   7   6   5   4   3   2   1

This book is dedicated to Carolyn Wood Sherif. She was a friend, mentor, and a role model for us. We learned a great deal from her and that learning continues through the legacy of written material she left. We miss her words and wisdom, her humor and her incisive analysis. Her life enriched our own, both personally and professionally.

Contents

Biographical Notes

Kenneth Dion, Professor of Psychology at the University of Toronto, is a social psychologist with interests in small groups, intergroup relations, and prejudice. His research and writing in these areas and service as former Consulting and Associate Editor with the *Journal of Experimental Social Psychology* represents a strong commitment to experimentally-oriented social psychology. His research on the phenomenology of prejudice in vulnerable target groups, including women, illustrates the power of the experimental method for understanding socially significant problems. His current chapter on gender and groups, like his other reviews of group research, focuses on critically evaluating theoretical viewpoints.

Alice Hendrickson Eagly is a social psychologist trained at the University of Michigan. At Purdue University, she teaches courses on attitudes, social influence, the psychology of women, and meta-analysis. One of her research areas is sex differences in social behavior; within this area, she is especially interested in understanding how people's ideas about sex differences—their stereotypes—relate to research findings on sex differences. As a feminist, she is committed to understanding the bases of gender prejudice and discrimination so that people can think more systematically about how such prejudice and discrimination might be eradicated. While she strives to do unbiased research, she believes that researchers' own gender often affects their research and scholarship. She therefore scrutinizes her own and others' work for signs of bias in favor of the researcher's own sex.

William P. Gaeddert recently earned his Ph.D. at Iowa State University and is currently an Assistant Professor of Psychology at SUNY–College at Plattsburgh.

His research has focused on the effects of sex and sex roles on small group behavior and on achievement behavior. He believes that the study of women can be liberating, not only with respect to his research, but his teaching and living as well.

Steven L. Gordon is Associate Professor of Sociology at California State University, Los Angeles. While studying for his doctorate at U.C.L.A., he became interested in the differentiation, socialization, and regulation of emotions in social interaction. His essay "The Sociology of Sentiments and Emotion" appeared in *Social Psychology: Sociological Perspectives,* edited by Morris Rosenberg and Ralph H. Turner (Basic Books, 1981). He is currently writing a book on the social construction of emotional experiences.

Kathleen E. Grady was trained as a social psychologist at the Graduate Center of the City University of New York from 1972–77 and as a feminist in the women's civil rights and health movements in New York City and Western New England from 1970–present. During a postdoctoral fellowship in health psychology (1977–79), she integrated both training experiences and now does research on the social psychology of health behavior, with a particular focus on women's health issues, at the University of Connecticut. Her work reflects her belief that science and feminism are historic and current allies in the effort to expose bias.

Ranald D. Hansen, a social psychologist, is Associate Professor of Psychology at Oakland University in Rochester, Michigan. He has spent the past eight years developing a "commonsense" theory of attribution. In addition to his interest in developing a theory of attribution, he has spent the past five years in collaboration with Virginia E. O'Leary attempting to elucidate the impact of differential attributions for women's and men's behaviors on the perpetuation of sex-based beliefs about the differential behavior of women and men.

Arnold S. Kahn, Administrative Officer for Social and Ethical Responsibility at the American Psychological Association, is currently on leave from his position as Professor of Psychology at Iowa State University. He has long been interested in justice in everyday interaction, in how perceptions of injustice affect interpersonal behavior, and in how sex and gender affect everyday social interaction.

Jacqueline Macaulay holds a B.A. in English from Stanford, a Ph.D. in social psychology from Wisconsin, and a recent law degree from that institution. In the years since she left graduate school she has had a variety of jobs, ranging from an assignment to find demographers to talk to reproductive physiologists about common interests, to assignments to review all the social science literature relevant to a practical social concern. Whatever paradigmatic loyalties she started with have been leached away by the necessity to comprehend all competitors. The genesis of her contribution to this volume is probably explained as well by this career history as by anything else, but not incidentally, she has also developed a feminist concern for the state of the social sciences. No degree was awarded for this.

Virginia E. O'Leary is President of Virginia E. O'Leary & Associates, Inc., a Washington-based consulting firm specializing in enhancing the public's understanding of the social and behavioral sciences. Her former positions include Deputy Executive Officer for Public Affairs of the American Psychological Association and Associate Professor of Psychology at Oakland University in Rochester, Michigan. She and co-author Ranald D. Hansen began their research collaboration on sex-determined attributions in the mid-seventies. Her interest in women and achievement was sparked in the late 1960s when she selected the work acculturation of hard-core unemployed women as her dissertation topic.

Letitia Anne Peplau is Associate Professor of Psychology at the University of California, Los Angeles. As a graduate student at Harvard, she first taught an undergraduate seminar on sex roles in 1970, and has continued to teach and do research on gender ever since. Her interest in the impact of gender on close relationships has led to studies of friendship, heterosexual dating, and homosexual relationships. She and co-author/husband Steven Gordon have recently become interested in the impact of gender on parent-child relationships—an interest sparked by the birth of their first child.

For the last fifteen years, **Jane Allyn Piliavin** has studied altruism and helping behavior, with an emphasis on helping in emergencies. She has also done some work on gender roles in small groups and as they are presented in the media. She has a distinct bias towards considering the role of physiological responses and affective states when attempting to analyze social behavior. Her current position in a Department of Sociology has sensitized her to the importance of also considering structural factors in society as determinants of interpersonal behavior.

Janet T. Spence is currently Ashbel Smith Professor of Psychology at the University of Texas at Austin and a member of the Department of Psychology's social psychology program, in which Spence's co-author **Linda L. Sawin** is an advanced doctoral student. In their empirical research and theoretical writings, the senior author and her colleagues have been wrestling with the meaning of self-concepts of masculinity and femininity for nearly a decade. In this volume, the authors present the outlines of a theoretical model based on the proposition that men and women in contemporary society are gripped by a powerful but primitive sense of gender-identity. The authors attempt to describe what is but stop short of trying to discern what may be possible in a more egalitarian world.

Elyse Sutherland received her Ph.D. in Personality Psychology from the University of Michigan in 1980. Her interests and research are in sex roles, achievement and power motivation, and motivation and career development. She is currently doing employee and consumer attitude research at Michigan Bell Telephone Company. Apart from her personological orientation, she does not see many biases—other than obvious ones (i.e. white, female, young)—that would influence her paper.

Rhoda Kesler Unger regards herself as having been marginal throughout her professional career. She was the only woman in her year in the Experimental Psychology program at Harvard from which she received her Ph.D. She is a Professor of Psychology at Montclair State College and an active researcher in a primarily teaching institution. She is a feminist married to her first and only husband, with whom she is rearing two teen-aged daughters. Her research interests include the social psychology of sex and gender (especially interpersonal perception), social power, helping behavior, and the effects of values on methodology and conceptualization in psychology. She believes that marginality explains her scholarly concerns as well as expanding their perspective.

As an undergraduate at Wesleyan, **Joseph Veroff** thought that his mentors' (D. C. McClelland and J. W. Atkinson) work on achievement motivation in men would translate neatly into parallel research on women. His honors thesis partially disabused him of that. It took research on three representative surveys at ISR—where he went after his Ph.D. at Michigan—some work on motives in children, and a number of thesis supervisions while on the faculty at Michigan, to completely undo his early assumption. His current bias is that while women emphasize kinds of achievement goals that men do not, they both share the same set of potential achievement orientations.

Barbara Strudler Wallston was trained as an experimental social psychologist during the era when the recent wave of feminism was coming to the fore (Ph.D., 1972, University of Wisconsin, Madison). Only after graduation did she try to bring her feminism into serious interplay with her role as a psychologist. With her Division 35 presidential address in 1979, she made her first serious foray into methodological issues from a feminist perspective. She has continued that interest and involvement with a variety of chapters and presentations. However, her early experimental bias is a strong force in her consideration of broader methodological perspectives.

Wendy Wood completed her graduate work in social psychology at the University of Massachusetts-Amherst and is now teaching at Texas A & M University. Her research interests include sex differences in social behavior, especially the areas of social influence and group interaction. She is particularly interested in the adequacy of social role explanations for sex differences as compared to personality-based explanations.

WOMEN, GENDER, AND
SOCIAL PSYCHOLOGY

Introduction

Virginia E. O'Leary
Rhoda K. Unger
Barbara S. Wallston

In the fall of 1977 we were approached by David Stang, who was then Editor of the Newsletter of the Society for the Advancement of Social Psychology, and asked to guest edit an issue of that newsletter relevant to women. We were pleased to accept his invitation and proposed a thematic issue. The first of what was eventually two issues under our editorship was the first SASP Newsletter devoted to a single theme.

We contacted a number of our colleagues in the field and invited them to contribute short pieces focusing on methodological issues, definitional problems, and new questions—both empirical and theoretical—that had been inspired by the social psychological study of women in the last decade. Not a single person contacted for a contribution turned us down. The material submitted was rich and varied, and offered an exciting "new look" at the current and potential contribution of the study of sex and gender to social psychology. Although each contributor developed his or her topic independently, it was interesting to note that some general concepts emerged. In a denotative sense, these concepts serve as a foundation for the exploration of biological sex (male or female) and gender orientation (masculine, feminine, or androgynous) as social variables. The response to the two issues (1978; 1979) was very positive. It was clear that our colleagues agreed that much of the recent research and theorizing ghettoized under the rubric of the "psychology of women" was relevant to the traditionally perceived pursuits of mainstream social psychologists who were interested in sex-related effects. Hundreds of reprint requests attested to this.

We were so gratified by the response that we decided to explore a book of original chapters. The ten chapters that follow evolved from this exploration. Recognizing that much of the recent research and theorizing in the psychology of women had the potential to revitalize mainstream social psychology by providing researchers with a fresh perspective from which new issues of social relevance might be addressed, we proposed to bring this work to the attention of social psychologists. Experts in a variety of substantive areas within social psychology were asked to contribute chapters prepared specifically for this purpose. Each contributor considered the ways in which the study of women and gender have enhanced theory and research in his or her area of expertise. Key questions addressed in each chapter include: What new methodological issues have been raised? What definitional questions have been refocused? What new questions— both empirical and theoretical—have been inspired? Finally, consideration has been given as to why it has taken psychology so long to recognize the importance of this "minority" for understanding human behavior.

Within the last decade, psychology as a discipline has been severely criticized on the grounds that it has tended to be male-dominated and male-oriented. Historically, psychologists advanced theories of human behavior and attempted to verify those theories empirically in studies using only male subjects. The exclusion of female subjects from research was justified on a variety of grounds including the greater variability of female responses, the practical difficulties of obtaining a sufficient number of subjects to allow the researchers to analyze sex differences, and the investigators' lack of interest in sex differences in areas where they had been demonstrated (or were assumed) to exist. Perhaps the best known example of the male bias in psychology is in the area of achievement motivation, where the existence of sex differences has long been recognized (McClelland, Atkinson, Clark, & Lowell, 1953) but, until recently, seldom explored. Even in those studies in which sex differences were investigated (legitimized under the rubric of differential psychology), the tendency to view male responses as normative and to explain female "differences" in terms of the "male model" was pervasive, as was the tendency to view such investigations as peripheral to mainstream social psychological and personality research. Some traditionally trained social psychologists continue to view sex as a variable to be controlled rather than investigated. However, the advent of the women's movement and the heightened consciousness of all segments of society regarding issues relevant to women and gender has, we believe, had an impact on the field.

Over the years, the field of social psychology has frequently been affected by its social context. For example, the critical need to persuade civilians in a wartime economy to serve less popular cuts of meat (e.g., lungs and liver) culminated in many years of research on attitude formation and change (Hovland, Janis, & Kelley, 1953). More recently, the desire to understand how 38 people could stand by and watch a woman being murdered provided the impetus for a great deal of research and theory regarding helping (Latane & Darley, 1970; Macaulay & Berkowitz, 1970). It is not surprising that the women's movement of the 60s and 70s has had a similar impact.

Research relevant to the psychology of women that has accumulated over the last fifteen years clearly indicates that there are some biological differences between the sexes (i.e., menstruation, pregnancy, lactation, and ejaculation), which result in psychological phenomena that must be regarded as sex-specific. However, most of the behaviors traditionally assumed to be more characteristic of one sex than the other reflect social learning and values. Within the confines of these values, the female experience differs from the male experience. However, the extent of the physiological similarities between the sexes suggests that these differences are not immutable. More importantly, the behavior of girls and boys and women and men cannot be adequately explained apart from the political-social context in which it occurs. Human beings are social beings and, as social psychologists have so long been aware, their behavior varies as a function of the social situation to which they are called upon to respond. The chapters in this volume attempt to explicate areas of importance to social psychology in terms of their study of women, sex, and gender. We briefly comment on each chapter below and will discuss the general themes that emerge more extensively in the epilogue.

Wallston and Grady—discussing question formulation, sample selection, design, operationalization, the social psychology of the research process, statistics, and interpretation—show how the addition of female researchers and feminist questions has broadened our conception of social psychology. They point out the narrowness and limitations of our research designs and the need, therefore, to value alternative approaches. The theories underlying our sample selection and the meaning of appropriate control groups are discussed. Wallston and Grady provide a feminist critique of methods in social psychology with the hope of developing a more scientific science.

Spence and Sawin review both traditional and feminist models describing the organization of masculine and feminine characteristics within the individual. They suggest that instrumentality and expressiveness are important dimensions for analyzing the behaviors of females and males, but that these characteristics are only weakly correlated with masculinity and femininity. They provide new data suggesting that masculinity and femininity are perceived differently for the self and others; for example, physical characteristics are used to organize perceptions about male and female others, whereas traits (for males) and roles (for females) are more often used in perceptions of one's own gender identity. Spence and Sawin indicate that social psychology has had difficulty operationalizing concepts involving sex and gender because the vast majority of individuals take these concepts for granted and are unable to specify the grounds on which they rest.

Sutherland and Veroff, in their integrative review of research on achievement motivation, posit the centrality of norms regarding sex roles. These norms influence the extent to which achievement motivation is aroused and how it is translated into behavior for both women and men. The effects of age, cohort, and historical differences on achievement motivation are also discussed, and the potential of behaviors beyond occupational and academic performance that reflect achievement motivation is stressed.

Hansen and O'Leary explore the attributional bases of the belief in sex differences, suggesting that these beliefs, so widely shared by women and men, may derive from perceived naive expectations regarding the potential cause of a given behavior, which differ as a function of the sex of the person performing that behavior. Citing studies from the literature relevant to both sex and other attributions, the authors conclude that the cognitive and perceptual mechanisms by which sex biases operate must be understood if real social change in the status of women (or men) is to be effected. Clearly, sex- and gender-linked expectancies mediate people's reactions to the behavior of both themselves and others.

Kahn and Gaeddert, using several recently postulated models of distributive justice, explore the extent to which women and men allocate rewards differently (equity versus equality). Interestingly, despite the intuitive appeal of the suggestion that men—who are agentically oriented—prefer equity, and women—who are communally oriented—prefer equality, this does not appear to be the case. Gender expectations do affect reward allocation, particularly when those allocations are public. However, when women and men allocate rewards privately the sex-stereotypic differences in their behavior disappear or even reverse, dramatically illustrating the impact of social context on behavior.

Piliavin and Unger, using a model of the determinants of responses to helping opportunities, explore differences in helping and being helped when males and females are in each role in the helper–helpee transaction. They note that sex or gender can have effects at every stage in the process. Gender expectations, in terms of what is appropriate, may confound or interact with other facets of the situation. Stimulus characteristics of persons (including status and physical attractiveness) may be confounded with sex in their influence on helping. One of the chapter's central themes is the importance of considering the interface between social systems and individual behaviors.

Macaulay argues that the addition of gender research is producing a revolutionary change in research on aggression. Male centrism is decreasing, and new topics, including rape, domestic violence, and the relationship between sexual arousal and violence, are appearing with some frequency. Aggression is starting to be viewed in the broader context of understanding responses to provocation. Work on conflict resolution, criminal violence, political violence, and cross-cultural research on aggression will also enhance and change our approaches.

Eagly and Wood's discussion of influenceability focuses on the importance of status differences between men and women and their impact on sex differences in influence and influenceability. The sex stereotype that women are easily influenced exists, in part, because men tend to hold higher status positions and thus possess more legitimate authority than women. This stereotype becomes a self-fulfilling prophecy, producing confirming behavior in situations where formal status differences do not exist. Eagly and Wood's analysis of sex differences in influenceability focuses on the perceived demands inherent in social roles and the impact of behavior on status-based expectancies.

Peplau and Gordon provide a review and integration of research on close heterosexual relationships. They focus on partner preferences, falling in love, communication, the division of labor within relationships, power and decision-making, and satisfaction and well-being. While focusing on sex differences and similarities, they note the need to understand the patterns in relationships. Typologies of relationships are a suggested approach whose central dimensions include power, role differentiation, and companionship. Peplau and Gordon recognize that the characteristics of individual partners, features of the dyad, and aspects of the social system must all be considered. Explorations of sex differences in relationships provide an avenue for an improved understanding of basic interaction processes.

Dion has provided an integrative review of current work on group processes, taking into account the multiple ways that sex and gender can influence behavior in and of groups. He focuses on the impact of the sex composition of the group on perception of the self and others, on explanations for sex-related differences in group interaction processes and leadership styles, and on whether membership in a group affects females and males differently. A particularly noteworthy contribution of this chapter is its exploration of the value of various theoretical models such as idiosyncrasy credit, status and expectation, and status congruence theories for the explanation of gender-characteristic behavior in group contexts. Dion suggests that different theoretical models may be useful for explaining differences in the way the sexes behave in groups. He also stresses that the group context may have very different implications for males and females because of their different positions in the social system.

As all of these chapters provide a wealth of detail that cannot be easily summarized, we would like to conclude this introduction with a discussion of some of the trends they seem to indicate for research about women and gender. First, it is clear that the study of sex and gender cannot entirely abandon the individual difference or intrapsychic approach. However, future research may be more willing to use additional social or trait characteristics either within a sex or in evaluating cross-sex differences. Also, androgyny may predict less consistently and more narrowly than was previously believed. The conditions under which sex-related differences do or do not appear will form an important base for typologies involving sex and gender in all content areas.

Researchers may have to focus on particular realities rather than assuming that there are general laws and relationships which apply to all human beings. One particular variable that is especially valuable is the view of the self, which was once abandoned in our search for a single "objective" reality (Sherif, 1980).

Replicability may also become less possible as we deal with the interface between who we are and what society tells us we are to be. Attitudes such as those involving equality between the sexes may represent particularly labile social phenomena. As social psychology studies increasingly diverse subject populations, it will have to take into account a phenomenon well known among those who study cross-cultural psychology, i.e., that the cultural processes that define psychological manipulations vary among different subject populations (Touhey, 1981). Generalizability may be possible only when we ignore historical and societal context.

As we become less concerned with objectivity and replicability as ends in themselves, social psychologists may be freer to explore new research strategies. Some of these may be generated by utilizing clinical interviewing practices (Sanford, 1982), whereas others may involve making the "subject" a more active participant in the research. For example, we have little information on the effect that experimental manipulations may have on the subject's awareness of changing social realities (Unger, 1983).

Future researchers will be more aware of the effect of their own place in society on their research practices. Biases may have been introduced by the nature of the problems chosen, beliefs about what is appropriate methodology, and limited theoretical perspectives. Thus, researchers may have to examine themselves explicitly, just as they have always been an implicit part of the research process. These developments are clearly consistent with the cognitive "revolution" within social psychology and within psychology as a whole.

REFERENCES

Hovland, C. I., Janis, I. L., & Kelley, H. (1953). *Communication and persuasion*. New Haven: Yale University Press.

Latane, B., & Darley, J. M. (1970) *The unresponsive bystander. Why doesn't he help?* New York: Appleton-Century-Crofts.

Macaulay, J., & Berkowitz, L. (Eds.). (1970). *Altruism and helping behavior*. New York: Academic Press.

McClelland, D. C., Atkinson, J. W., Clark, R. A., & Lowell, E. L. (1953). *The achievement motive*. Englewood Cliffs, N. J.: Prentice-Hall.

Sanford, N. (1982). Social psychology: Its place in personology. *American Psychologist, 37*, 896–903.

Sherif, C. W. (1980). Social values, attitudes, and involvement of the self. In H. Howe & M. Page (Eds.), *Values, attitudes and beliefs. The Nebraska Symposium*. Lincoln: University of Nebraska Press.

Touhey, J. C. (1981). Replication failures in personality and social psychology: Negative findings or mistaken assumptions? *Personality and Social Psychology Bulletin, 7*, 593–595.

Unger, R. K. (1983). Through the looking glass: No Wonderland yet! *Psychology of Women Quarterly, 8*, 9–32.

1 Integrating the Feminist Critique and the Crisis in Social Psychology: Another Look at Research Methods

Barbara Strudler Wallston
George Peabody College of Vanderbilt University

Kathleen E. Grady
University of Connecticut Health Center

The major issues raised by the study of women and gender (and social psychology) have been expounded independently but have much in common. The lack of cross-citation among these literatures is not surprising, given the narrow scope of most of our reading as well as the nature of the scientific enterprise with respect to citation (cf. Kuhn, 1970; Merton, 1968; Over, 1981). Thus, a number of discussions of problems in social psychology (e.g., Baumgardner, 1976; Buss, 1975; Sampson, 1977; Weissberg, 1976) stress the importance of the social context and its influence on the research process with no recognition of the parallel feminist critiques (e.g., Parlee, 1975; Sherif, 1979; Shields, 1975; Vaughter, 1976; Weisstein, 1970; Wittig, 1982). Engendering cross-fertilization for the benefit of methodology in social psychology and in the psychology of women is one of our goals in this chapter. However, we begin with a consideration of how the study of women and gender has contributed to the debate.

The study of women and gender has the potential for a dual effect on methods in social psychology. On the one hand, the numerous feminist critiques of sample selection, control groups, and interpretation of results can lead to a more careful application of existing methods. Thus, they can make our science more "scientific." At the same time, there is a clear call for a broadening of available methods, more intensive descriptive research, more attention to understudied issues (such as rape, parenting, paid and family work), and an increased awareness of the political and cultural context for research.

The increasing emphasis on descriptive and correlational methods by researchers addressing issues of sex and gender has generated a debate about "hard" vs. "soft" methods that has often used the unfortunate labels of "masculine" vs. "feminine" (Bernard, 1973; Carlson, 1972). We believe that the

7

gender of the researchers and the novelty of the questions asked are so badly confounded that it is impossible to assert that women researchers have affinity for particular methods. The scientifically sound use of observation and description to study relatively new questions with rigorous tests reserved for a more highly developed "state of the art" may better describe the current state of psychology research. In fact, some of our most distinguished colleagues have now, after a lifetime of rigorous empirical research, begun to employ more qualitative methods to address novel or intransigent questions (cf., Festinger, 1980; Schachter, 1982).

Although the potential for contribution in methodology is tremendous, the actual impact on the field of social psychology has been less than in more substantive areas. Sherif's (1979) excellent discussion of bias in psychology and, in particular, the issue of status hierarchies in psychology suggests some reasons why this may be the case. Sherif notes that social psychology was at the bottom of the status hierarchy in 1943 and that the improved status of social psychology has come about through "self-conscious efforts to be accepted as experimental social psychologists. . . .The way to respectability in this scheme has been the appearance of rigor and scientific inquiry, bolstered by highly restricted notions of what science is about" (p. 98). We believe this continued emphasis on narrowly defined experimentalism has been one of the reasons that feminist methodological innovations and critiques have not had a substantial impact on social psychology.

In this chapter we have organized methodological issues into question formulation, sample selection, design, operationalization, the social psychology of the research process, statistics, and interpretation. These areas overlap extensively, and some of the distinctions, as well as the topic order, are clearly arbitrary. Over the months we have spent writing this chapter, everything written about methods or feminism has at some point seemed relevant. The resulting selection of citations has consequently been somewhat arbitrary.

One major goal has been the attempt to integrate the perspectives of the feminist critique and the "crisis" literature. As will become clear, it is our opinion that social psychology is getting older *and* better. Rather than simply rehashing criticisms, we try to highlight ways in which the study of women and gender has contributed to this process.

Question Formulation

How do we derive questions? Few of our research courses focus on the issue and our textbooks give little attention to question derivation. In general, we undervalue question generation (cf. Wallston, 1981), which is part of the art of scientific inquiry. McGuire (1973) has brought this to our attention as the first of seven koan "the sound of one hand clapping. . . . and the wrong hand" (p. 450). He notes that hypothesis testing has received 90% of our attention, while hypothesis generation has been neglected, "probably due to the suspicion that so complex a creative process as hypothesis formation is something that cannot be taught" (pp. 450–451).

In an unusual vein, and one that we applaud, Wrightsman and Deaux (1981) devote three pages of the methods chapter in their recent text revision to question formulation, and they note this in the preface as an important change. Unlike the traditional coverage of this issue, which assumes that questions are logical derivations from theory, Wrightsman and Deaux note theory as only one source of questions. They also give examples of observations of phenomena outside of the laboratory from which ideas have developed which are then translated into questions (and possibly theory) that are testable.

Frequently our questions in psychology reflect areas that are important and/or problematic to us. It is more than coincidence, for example, that much dual career research has been developed by members of dual career couples (e.g., Bryson, Bryson, Licht, & Licht, 1976; Rapoport & Rapoport, 1978; Wallston, Foster, & Berger, 1978). In social psychology, the emphasis on research on achievement and the nature of the definition of achievement certainly reflect the background and interest of the researchers (see Sutherland & Veroff, this volume). On the other hand, competence and achievement in parenting, homemaking, and volunteer activities have not been studied (cf. Wallston & O'Leary, 1981). This emphasis reflects the general valuing of traditionally male achievement in our culture (cf. Lenney, 1977; Mednick, Tangri, & Hoffman, 1975; Unger, 1979) and the socialization of researchers (female and male) into this value perspective.

Experience is a good source of questions. It may provide the best insights and most creative ideas. Unger (1981b) has noted that personal experience leads to questioning assumptions that others take as self-evident. Thus, as long as most psychologists are white, middle-class males, many important questions will remain outside the experience of most psychologists. Samelson (1978), in an historical analysis, has suggested that the change in psychological focus from the study of race differences to the study of racial prejudice could be accounted for by the entry of ethnic minority group members into the psychological profession. Unger (1981b) points out an analogous shift from the study of sex differences to the study of sexism. Thus, there are scientific, in addition to justice, arguments for changing the racist, classist, and sexist procedures by which students are selected and socialized. For example, Sherwood and Nataupsky (1968) have shown that the biographical characteristics of investigators were predictive of their conclusions regarding race differences in intelligence. Changing the faces of our student body is a first step. Allowing them to ask questions of interest to them, even or especially when those questions are beyond our experience, may be even more important in broadening our understanding of human behavior.

McGuire's (1973) initial suggestions for hypothesis generation sources are worth reiteration: "case study, paradoxical incident, analogy, hypothetico deductive method, functional analysis, rules of thumb, conflicting results, accounting for exceptions, and straightening out complex relationships'' (p. 451). Wallston (1981) explicates three additional principles for question generation: (1) experience which can be expanded by observation and discussion with others is a rich source of questions; (2) public policy issues (cf. Tangri & Strasburg, 1979) should be a focus of research; (3) situational as well as personological factors must be considered as potential causes of behavior when generating questions.

Methods for expanding our experience are critical to the formulation of good questions. Vaughter (1976) has argued for a participatory model in which research subjects and the public become an integral part of the scientific enterprise. The work of Plas and her colleagues (Plas & Bellet, 1983) to develop measures of Indian children's value-attitude orientations exemplifies such an approach. The Anglo research team lived on an Indian reservation with Indian families in order to better understand the culture. Questions they developed for the scale were reviewed by elders of the tribe to check face validity for the relevant population. Although less extreme, the recent work by Azjen and Fishbein (1980) has stressed the importance of eliciting salient beliefs from a representative sample of the relevant population in order to evaluate attitudes. Ethnographers regularly validate their perceptions against those of research participants (cf. Corsaro, 1981, Leinhardt, 1978; Wallston, 1983).

Research on sex and gender particularly illustrates the failure to give sufficient consideration to situational factors (cf. Riger & Galligan, 1980; Wallston, 1978), although other areas (e.g., Caplan & Nelson, 1973) have shown this failure as well. Condry and Dyer (1976), for example, have presented an important reinterpretation of the fear of success literature from a situational rather than a motivational interpretation. Allen (1979) similarly notes that research on black women's attainment has focused on personal characteristics and background rather than scrutinizing institutional and societal practices that systematically deny equal opportunity to black women. In fact, Caplan and Nelson (1973) found that only 16% of the studies of blacks included in six issues of the 1970 *Psychological Abstracts* examined situational causes rather than taking a personological approach (cf. Unger, 1981b). This tendency on the part of psychologists may reflect observers' tendencies to overattribute the causes of women's behavior to personal factors and men's behavior to environmental factors (cf. Hansen & O'Leary, 1983; O'Leary & Hansen, this volume; Wallston & O'Leary, 1981). Not only have personal factors been overused to explicate female behavior, but sex (which is a personal factor) has been used as an explanatory variable, although it is frequently confounded with situational factors such as status or power (cf. Dion, this volume; Eagly & Wood, this volume; Henley, 1977; Miller & Zeitz, 1978; Piliavin & Unger, this volume; Unger, 1979).

To summarize, we have argued that questions and theory are undervalued in psychology. We have suggested some appropriate sources of good questions. Because a researcher's experience is often a source of questions, it is important to broaden the experiential base of future researchers. The study of women and gender illustrates how the addition of female researchers has broadened the nature of the questions that are asked. Minority researchers and those from other social class and ethnic backgrounds would similarly enhance our understanding of human experience.

Design

We have already argued that the design should reflect the question. This is not to imply that there is a single design appropriate to each question (cf. Wallston, 1983). In fact, we can draw the best conclusions when several different methodologies are used to test the same hypothesis. Such triangulation (cf. Jick, 1979; Wallston, 1983) helps confirm that our findings are not tied to the specific methodology used. The important point is that some methodologies are not inherently better than others (cf. Labouvie, 1975), although fads in our field tend to suggest that they are. As Glass and Ellett (1980) note in their discussion of evaluation research, the best design is a compromise between the possibilities afforded by the situation and the research goal. Although choosing the situation allows some flexibility, practical constraints are involved in all research design.

Most of us have been socialized to think in terms of 2×2 analysis of variance models (cf. Rucci & Tweney, 1980). This limited design does not allow the investigation of complex processes when more than two variables with two levels of each may be important. Thus, our ideas regarding design, particularly to the extent that they are narrow, limit the kinds of questions we ask.

As social psychologists, we have been trained to value the quantitative over the qualitative, and experimental (manipulation) over correlational (measurement only) designs (cf. Wallston, 1983). Higbee, Millard, and Folkman (1980) found that 74% of journal articles in four mainline social psychology journals in 1978–79 utilized experimental methodology. There are stages of knowledge where qualitative and observational techniques may be particularly appropriate (cf. Depner, 1981), especially when we are investigating a new area and need to develop appropriate questions. Although such restrictions of the use of methods may be too limiting (cf. Trend, 1978), if we move too quickly toward manipulating one or two experimental variables, we run the risk of ignoring the most important variables because we have not sufficiently described the phenomenon of interest.

Taking advantage of powerful effects in the real world that cannot be simulated in the laboratory may necessitate giving up some control (cf. Cook & Campbell, 1979; Ellsworth, 1977). In most research we must consider the trade-off between internal and external validity (cf. Labouvie, 1975). Correlational studies in which the relationship between variables is investigated without assuming directional causality may be more appropriate for some questions (cf. Wallston, 1983).

Frieze's (1979) important work on battered women demonstrates this problem. Investigating these important theoretical and applied issues is not possible using experimental methodology; thus, she cannot make definitive causal statements. However, this creative work also combines the more qualitative intensive interviews with structured questions to provide quantitative data. It is exemplary at fitting the method to the questions.

Wallston, Foster, and Berger's (1978) utilization of experimental methods in combination with questions about the real-life experience of dual-career couples illustrates how different methods may complement each other. In a survey study, in addition to their personal job-seeking experience, respondents were provided with job-seeking situations and asked what they would do. The sex of hypothetical job seekers was experimentally manipulated through different forms of the situations. The hypotheses generated on the basis of responses to these situations provided a different approach to the actual experiences of these dual-career couples, in which sex was confounded with factors such as age, experience, and the ability to obtain a job offer. Interpretations were possible that would have been unlikely without this combination of methods.

Grady, Kegeles, and Lund (1981) maintained a simple experimental design in a year-long field study while gathering extensive medical, experiential, and attitude data before and after the experimental manipulation. The resulting medical, sociological, and attitude data not only enrich the understanding of the experimental effects and generate new hypotheses for subsequent research, but also help to interpret the findings for researchers in public health and place them in an interdisciplinary context.

These three research examples show the value of combining methods and techniques. They illustrate the richness that is possible when we go beyond limited 2 × 2 laboratory experiments. They also show the value of fitting the design to the question and context of interest.

We spend a great deal of time teaching our students to understand the difference between an independent and a dependent variable. We fail to remember that the choice of which variable fits which category is frequently arbitrary, even with experimental designs. After a great deal of research concluding that "what is beautiful is good" (cf. Berscheid & Walster, 1974; Wallston & O'Leary, 1981), several researchers reversed the independent and dependent variables to show that our perceptions of beauty may vary depending on other characteristics of the individual (e.g., Gross & Crofton, 1977) and the situation (Unger, Hilderbrand, & Madar, 1982). These studies do not refute the initial ones; rather, they illustrate the complexities of human behavior and judgment where unidirectional causation of B by A rarely gives the full picture of the phenomenon. Our designs need to better reflect these complexities. Our focus should be on "how to accommodate the complexities and limitations of reality without trivializing the study" (Wachtel, 1980, p. 403).

Our experimental methods have been appropriately critiqued as context stripping (cf. Bronfenbrenner, 1977; Mishler, 1979; Parlee, 1979; Petronovich, 1979; Unger, 1981b; Wallston, 1983). The laboratory, as a context, has particularly been called into question and much has been made of the move from laboratory to field research. This is, however, frequently a false dichotomy or an oversimplification. Unger (1981a) suggests that whether or not subjects are aware of being studied may be the more important distinction. Tunnell (1977) defines several dimensions of naturalness—natural behavior, natural setting, and natural treatment—along which research varies. Each natural dimension adds to the external validity of our work, with the potentially concomitant loss of internal validity.

Unger (1981a) points out that more sex-of-subject effects are found in field than in laboratory studies. Several potential explanations are provided: (1) sex is more likely to be confounded with other factors in the field; (2) the awareness of being studied in the laboratory may create social desirability demands, which decrease sex effects; (3) the laboratory creates a norm of social objectivity, minimizing the operation of sex roles (Eagly, 1978). Clearly the context is important for all research (cf. Mishler, 1979), and we must expand our awareness of our laboratory context and how it influences the carrier variable, sex, in particular.

The study of women and gender has emphasized the narrowness and limitations of our research designs. As we have discussed, factorial designs may severely limit the number of variables we can study before such selection is appropriate. We need to recognize the value of correlational methods and of qualitative approaches to research. The experiment may be the ''crowning glory'' of our research methods (Sherif, 1981), but it can be used prematurely or inappropriately. We must pay increased attention to the contexts of our research. Triangulation of methods is a particularly fruitful, though costly, approach.

Sample Selection

The description of subjects included in research reports provides a starting point for explicating some of the issues in sampling procedures. The information contained in these descriptions may reflect mini-theories or hunches about which variables (other than those selected to be independent variables) influence the outcomes of the research. A perusal of recent issues of journals in experimental social psychology suggests that there is remarkable consistency in the variables mentioned. Three major descriptors occur repeatedly and often exclusively: undergraduate status, sex, and whether the participants were paid or volunteer. Before considering how the study of women and gender can broaden this rather narrow view of subject characteristics, it may be useful to speculate on why these three descriptors are so common.

The specification that subjects are college students suggests a recognition of the problems of generalizability from this population. Indeed, the most frequently reiterated criticism of subject selection in psychology in general is its reliance on undergraduates as subjects. As long ago as 1946, McNemar accused psychology of creating a "science of the behavior of sophomores" (p. 333). Twenty-three years later, Schultz (1969) criticized the practice of using college students enrolled in introductory psychology classes and documented its continued practice.

There are obvious difficulties in assuming that college students represent the population as a whole. In addition, descriptions also often proceed to specify the size of the college or university and the region of the country, and occasionally its public or private status, e.g., a large midwestern university, a small eastern private college. These descriptions imply an additional consensus that there may be problems in assuming that any one population of college students represents college students as a whole. The emphasis on size and region may indicate the existence of mini-theories about the quality of education, student intelligence, race, religion, traditionality, or social class of the students. Some reports give the specific name of the institution, allowing the reader to draw conclusions about what aspects of that institutional setting may have influenced the data.

The frequency with which the conditions under which subjects were recruited are mentioned is quite probably related to the traumatic ethical questions that raged throughout the sixties. The literature on differences between volunteer and nonvolunteer subjects (Ora, 1966; Rosenthal & Rosnow, 1969) may be remembered, or on a broader level, cognitive dissonance and related theories may have shaped the thinking of social psychologists at least to the extent of recognizing a potential difference between subjects who are paid or who volunteer.

The specification of the proportion of the subjects who are female or male suggests a set of amorphous assumptions about between-sex differences and within-sex similarities. The assumption that sex represents a meaningful difference, that women and men form groups within which the members are alike— an undifferentiated entity—is simply unlikely to be true, according to Parlee (1975). The assumption that merely selecting for equal numbers of female and male subjects will "control for" sex is also unlikely to be true (Parlee, 1981a). Our sampling takes place within particular societal institutions that are known to make numerous distinctions on the basis of sex (Grady, 1981). The resulting problems of sample representativeness and its relationship to the theory being tested are left to the reader to resolve with the passing mention of sex as a descriptor. In fact, Wallston (1983) suggests that studies that analyze sex as an independent variable must be considered quasi-experiments, because comparisons of males and females always involve nonequivalent control groups. All the attendant threats to validity must be considered in understanding any resultant sex differences.

Thus, the most common descriptors for sample populations are deceptively simple given the number of assumptions that may underlie them. Some may argue that these factors are mentioned out of mere convention, passed on during scientific training. It is our contention that the convention reflects theoretical considerations, the origins of which may be lost in the mists of history. Our speculations about their meaning can certainly be supplemented or replaced. In the search for universal truths, it is often easy to glide over the particularities of our sample.

Because sex is so often mentioned in subject descriptions, it has become possible (and quite popular) to do archival studies of the representation of female and male subjects in research. Most clearly apparent is the overrepresentation of male subjects found in several studies over two decades (Carlson & Carlson, 1960; Schultz, 1969; Schwabacher, 1972; Smart, 1966). In fact, Holmes and Jorgensen (1971) found that "males appear as subjects twice as often as females, a ratio even greater than that favoring college student subjects over non college student subjects" (p. 3).

Researchers interested in women and gender have quite reasonably asked why males are more numerous. There are many possible reasons, all of which threaten generalizability at least as much as does the use of college students. As O'Leary (1977) points out, sex is generally considered a "nuisance variable to be controlled, not investigated" (p. 3). Because there are large literatures on sex differences potentially related to almost any topic, many researchers avoid the tedious task of having to review them by studying their phenomena of interest using single-sex designs. Why they use single-sex designs of men and boys only is another question. Availability would seem a likely reason except that Holmes and Jorgensen (1971) found that the overrepresentation of male subjects was as great or even greater with non-college student subjects. Thus, it is not simply because men have been overrepresented in the past among college students or available subject pools.

The topics chosen for study seem to bear some relationship to the sex of the sample selected. McKenna and Kessler (1977), correcting for the standard male overrepresentation, found that in aggression studies more than the expected number used all male subjects and more than the expected number of interpersonal attraction studies used all female subjects. If many topics are sex linked in the mind of the researcher, one must still explain why more "male" topics are studied. The answer to this question may relate to our earlier point about basing research questions on the investigator's own experience.

Researchers may also have implicit theories about the nature of women and men that guide them to choose one or the other as subjects, either generally or because of the particular research method to be used. A quite famous and prolific researcher once explained in a colloquium that he used only female subjects (referred to in his research reports by the so-called generic "he") because they are more cooperative subjects and are more likely to keep their appointments. Researchers responding to Prescott and Foster (1974) about reasons for using single-sex designs expressed fastidiousness about the social desirability or etiquette of applying their techniques to women: ''I manipulated anxiety and I frankly couldn't bring myself to do this with college girls''; ''Cultural values regarding sex roles make it easier to expose males to aversive stimulation.'' These ''cultural values'' may make certain things easier, just as compliant subjects do, but they shape the field in subtle and important ways.

Another researcher bias that may account for overrepresentation of male subjects may be an assumption about representativeness or generalizability. Although Reardon and Prescott (1977) subsequently found some improvement, both Schwabacher (1972) and McKenna and Kessler (1977) found that researchers were more likely to specify the sex of the subjects in the abstracts of research reports if a female sample had been used. Further, the conclusions drawn from research using all male subjects, according to Schwabacher (1972), are more likely to be generalized and discussed as ''individuals are. . .'' whereas research based on female subjects is likely to be discussed as ''women/girls/females are. . .'' Dan and Beekman (1972) attribute these tendencies to widespread androcentric assumptions: ''The habit of mind which allows that males are more representative of the human race than females should be recognized as a potentially serious bias in our psychological research and theory'' (p. 1078).

Whatever the reasons for biases in sample selection in the past, the new questions being raised by researchers studying women and gender have to some extent required the study of new populations, not only more girls and women but specific subgroups. It was bound to happen, for example, that rape research would finally move out of the laboratory with its countless studies of college students' attributions of blame/guilt, attractiveness of the victim, etc., to field studies of women who had been raped (e.g., Janoff-Bulman, 1979), or of women who had been attacked but were successful in avoiding rape (Bart, 1981). The social problems and policy issues raised by the women's movement could quite clearly not be addressed through the exclusive use of college student populations. They create a press for more ''real world'' research. The novelty of the questions, as discussed earlier, also requires intensive description from people actually involved. A cursory review of subject descriptions suggests that field studies that use non-college populations generally provide a more thorough description of subjects, including at least age, race, and some socioeconomic variables. Thus, whatever pressures for field research have resulted from the study of women and gender may also have contributed to the pressure for more thorough descriptions of subjects.

Another critical issue of sample selection is the choice of an appropriate control group. In an excellent paper on this topic, Parlee (1981a) describes ways in which selection of control groups reflect the scientist's implicit theoretical framework. She illustrates her points by citing a controversy between biomedical and social scientists over which control group of women to add to an ongoing study of aging in a sample of highly educated, professionally successful men. The social scientists suggested a group of women "matched" on social status variables; the biomedical scientists suggested the sisters of the men already in the study to "match" on physiological characteristics. The results and conclusions about sex differences in aging would have been quite different depending on which control was used. Thus, although the topic of control groups is usually considered "only" a methodological issue, Parlee underlines its conceptual significance in defining "what phenomena are and are not of interest and about what types of explanation are sought and are permissible" (1981a, p. 639). The basic issues raised about control groups are, as she points out, long-standing concerns of philosophers and historians of science; her specific and practical statements about their implications for feminist psychology and the discipline as a whole, however, bring a new urgency to a consideration of their implications.

Overall, then, the study of women and gender has heightened awareness of how samples are selected beyond the standard criticism of the use of college students. The overrepresentation of male subjects has received considerable attention, and researchers have been asked to justify their selection by sex. However, the larger issues of the meaning of selection by sex and "controlling for" sex have barely been addressed and are potentially of far more significance for social psychology. Further, the public policy aspects of many of the issues raised by feminist psychologists have contributed to the press for more field studies based on affected populations.

Operationalization

Social psychologists are appropriately self-critical about construct validity and the operations we actually choose for testing what we want to test. Certainly, there has been plenty of room for criticism when automobile honking is called aggression and pressing a button is called control. However, a whole new set of issues has become apparent with the study of women and gender. A recognition of the pervasiveness of sex-based distinctions and experiences has led to a re-evaluation of the methods and materials of social psychology, along new dimensions.

The specific problem of sex-typing of messages, tasks, and materials is part of the larger problem of understanding what our operationalizations mean to respondents. In some cases, sex-typing of stimulus materials means the same to subjects of both sexes. This similarity of meaning has been confirmed repeatedly with the evaluation bias literature. When Phil Goldberg (1968) discovered that women undergraduates evaluated essays differently depending on whether they were attributed to a male or female author, he called the article "Are women prejudiced against women?" Subsequent research has indicated that both men and women are "prejudiced" against women to approximately the same degree.

A failure to recognize the power of this widely shared cultural reaction has led to a major misinterpretation of the first findings of "fear of success" (Horner, 1972). Because Horner gave her verbal cue "At the end of first term finals, John/Mary found him/herself at the top of the medical school class" matching sex of subject and sex of stimulus person, she was unable to untangle cultural reactions to the stimulus person's sex from personal ones based on the subject's sex. Subsequent research indicates that cultural reactions predominated and that both female and male subjects wrote bizarre explanations for Mary's success (Condry & Dyer, 1976; Monahan, Kuhn & Shaver, 1974). Based on this similarity of meaning, Kay Deaux and others have developed research programs to test attributions to sex-typed stimulus materials, resulting in substantial contributions both to attribution theory and to the psychology of women and gender (Deaux & Taynor, 1973; Taynor & Deaux, 1973).

There are occasions when the sex-typing of materials or tasks means different things to subjects of different sexes. Because of differences in experiences, training, and education, tasks may differ in complexity, novelty, or interest-level for female and male subjects. The NASA survival task, for example, may be experienced differently by people who were not Boy Scouts in the past than by people who were. If the researcher is not interested in sex differences, then this experiential difference becomes a serious confound. In a re-examination of areas in which sex differences had been touted, researchers found that "math ability" was being tested with problems that were sex-typed in interest and that different results could be obtained when the same concept was tested with a problem described as cookie-making rather than carpentry (Milton, 1959). Similarly, Sistrunk and McDavid (1971) found sex differences in conformity depending on whether the stimulus items were masculine or feminine, with no sex differences on neutral items. Although Eagly and Carli (1981) do not confirm that there was an overall preponderance of masculine items in influencability research, they also note that masculine topics tended to be associated with greater female persuasibility. They provide useful information about the sex-typing of messages that can help to explore these relationships further or to avoid the confound. Sandra Bem has used the sex-typing of tasks to advantage in her androgyny research. She has confirmed that such tasks as playing with a kitten, peer-counseling, and the standard Asch conformity situation were indeed sex-role-typed, evoking different behavior from individuals who described themselves differently on the Bem Sex Role Inventory (Bem, 1975; Bem, Martyna, & Watson, 1976).

Problems of sex bias introduced by response categories may be most easily demonstrated in the construction of questionnaires and interviews. Because the researcher and the respondent share a common culture, the categories constructed may fairly easily capture a shared meaning. Nonetheless, it is widely recognized that there is a serious threat to validity in imposing researcher-generated response categories on subjects' descriptions of their own behavior. The study of women and gender has further suggested that the researcher may be imposing categories limited by his or her own sex-biased expectations of male and female behavior. The particular wording of questions and the allowable response categories may reflect very narrow, stereotyped views of sex roles.

Bart (1971) provides an excellent example of an outrageously narrow view of sex roles in sexual behavior. In a study of pregnant women and "normals," researchers asked whether the respondent's role in sexual intercourse was "passive," "responsive," "resistant," aggressive," "deviant," or "other." Obviously, different results might have been obtained if the allowable response included at least "active" but perhaps also "encouraging," "playful," "creative," and so forth. It is quite clear that different categories would have been constructed had men constituted part of the sample.

The existence of sex bias in the researcher, charged by many feminist psychologists, does not preclude the possibility of sex bias in the respondent. Indeed, sexism and its effects are part of our shared culture. It may be that most of the women subjects in the example above would not describe their sexual role in any way other than the categories provided. However, that issue deserves to be resolved empirically.

McKenna and Kessler (1977) have uncovered a more subtle form of sex bias in operationalization, one that involves both the type of response and the type of experimental manipulation. One might assume that the simple choice of whether to use a paper and pencil dependent measure or another kind of behavioral measure would depend on a variety of theoretical and practical considerations. The sex of the subjects would seem an unlikely factor to take into account. Yet, in a review of over 50 studies of aggression and interpersonal attraction, they found that paper and pencil measures are used significantly more often with female subjects in both topic areas. In addition, they have found that in aggression studies, independent variables differ by subject sex. "Passive" manipulations, such as the content of the story, the sex of the other person, or the order of exposure to treatment conditions, are much more common with female subjects. In contrast, male subjects are more likely to be treated by others in a hostile manner, frustrated or threatened. McKenna and Kessler also note that in the interpersonal attraction literature they have found no studies in which "physical attraction of other" was an independent variable with all-female subjects.

In an article on sex bias in psychology, Carolyn Sherif asks, "Did someone believe that the psychology of the researcher and the psychology of the subject, both human beings, are altogether different?" (1979, p. 105). Even as we study labeling, we label. Ellsworth (1977), discussing research applications, says ". . . to conduct research on the unconsidered assumption that the name of the variable guarantees that it is the thing we are interested in is foolhardy at best" (p. 607). Sherif (1979) criticizes the practice of tranforming "a specific set of actions in a specific research situation . . . into the label for something that the person has, is, or possesses as a trait" (p. 115).

The study of the psychology of women has contributed to the ongoing "crisis" literature about the trivial nature of operationalizations and the sweeping generalizations that often result. Close examinations of both stimulus and response materials have revealed overt and subtle forms of sex bias that influence the results and their interpretation. The sex-typing of materials, often seen as a confound, has also led to the development of new areas of study. Overall, in our judgment, the psychology of women has contributed to the more relativist attributional approach in social psychology, in which the conditions under which people label are at least as interesting as the labels themselves. Further it has applied this approach to the conduct of the researchers as well as of the subjects.

The Social Psychology of the Research Process

The social psychology of the psychological experiment has received sporadic attention since the 1950s. The standard concerns include at least experimenter bias (particularly expectancy effects), the interference of the setting or equipment with experimental and mundane realism, order effects, the influence of other participants, and the effects of deception. Most of the criticisms or cautions articulated have been directed to laboratory research, but research outside the laboratory can be evaluated along these dimensions as well.

Herb Kelman (1968) once stated that the difference between observing a rock and a human being is that the rock can't observe back. Many research situations attempt to constrain the subject's behavior to be as rock-like as possible. Subjects are put in cubicles and given checklists or buttons to press. One particular aspect of their behavior in public situations is observed and all others ignored. A fixed set of "demographics" is collected in interviews without giving attention to other features of the subjects' life situations.

Another strategy is to make the experimenter's behavior as rock-like as possible, familiar in the use of tape recorders, pre-coded interviews, etc. In an experiment that Sherif (1979) describes, a computer presents the persuasive communications, a method the experimenters describe as resulting in "a desirably high degree of situational control and assurance that possible sources of experimenter bias are minimized" (p. 102). Sherif points out that the experimenters have arbitrarily selected the topics, presented them in certain orders, varied the contents of the screen, etc. The authors of the report fail to comment on how the use of this novel, mechanical device itself might have affected the research situation:

> In short, this experiment typifies the assumption in a great deal of experimentation that "general laws" about the relationship among variables can be obtained by comparing averages of the responses made by a sizable number of individuals, who are regarded as being without a background, personal history, or gender that might have anything to do with their response in the situation. In this case, the situation itself is described only in terms of the equipment, which is shown in a photograph.

Its duration appears to have been well within the academic hour (Sherif, 1979, p. 103).

Sherif argues that these forms of "control" ignore the social psychology of the research situation, although research is inevitably a social process. She concludes that the generation of more data of the same type, using less and less human contact in the methods in an effort to minimize the social context, is not going to resolve any of the complex—or even interesting—questions about human behavior.

Unger (1981b) also urges a direct confrontation regarding the social nature of human experimentation and deplores the view that the human element presents "procedural" difficulties: "Like increased blood clotting due to the 'pill,' the social relationship between experimenter and subject is seen as an 'unwanted side effect.' Like the blood clotting properties of estrogenic substances, however, such effects are intrinsic. They are side-effects only to the extent that they are not the ones desired" (p. 5).

Many points already made in this chapter relate to a recognition of the social psychology of the research process. Research on women and gender cannot easily ignore the biosocial aspects of experimenter and subject, and social psychological research in this area contributes somewhat to the trend away from the aspiration to transform experimenter and subject to inanimate objects. There is not much to add, but there are a couple of implications we would like to draw.

One implication for research includes increased attention to the most minute details of the research setting as well as to the total *gestalt* created. Many researchers conceptualize their research settings as a stage that must be "dressed" properly to create the desired impact. The scenery, the props, the lighting—all contribute to the overall effect. It is generally assumed that constancy in these features renders them unimportant. Even though some environmental psychologists are studying the effects of physical features of the environment on social interaction (see Evans, 1981), it is probably not necessary for every social psychological research report to provide information on temperature, humidity, noise level, color of the walls, etc. However, some description of the physical as well as social aspects of the situation—the "instrumentation" of social psychology in a larger sense—would be useful.

In addition, as described previously, we know that the background of the experimenter influences the kinds of questions asked and the results obtained, particularly that training in theory and methods influences the competence with particular techniques as well as questions asked and results obtained; that the experimenter as a stimulus person presents a certain demeanor that influences the process and outcome of research; and that all of these factors interact with the individual characteristics and behavior of subjects. Shouldn't the reader of the research report have access to these critical aspects of the research situation? Research reports could include a section describing the experimenter(s) comparable to the section on subject description, a suggestion also made by Lewis and Wehren (1981). Wallston (1982) provides a section of self-description in an evaluative review article in order to help the reader evaluate her evaluations. Such tradition-breaking intrusions of social psychological sensibilities begin to respond to the criticisms and concerns of decades.

Statistics

Although statistics are a tool and should be viewed as such, psychologists have a tendency to glorify them (cf. Meehl, 1978; Sherif, 1981). In fact, analysis of variance has become the statistic of choice for psychologists in general (cf. Edgington, 1974) and for social psychologists in particular.

Some researchers involved in the study of sex and gender have called for the inclusion of qualitative techniques to complement the use of quantitative approaches (cf. Wallston, 1983; Weiss, 1981). Moreover, this dichotomy may be less clear-cut than we like to believe (cf. Cook & Campbell, 1979; Wallston, 1983). Cook and Campbell (1979) note that all science involves qualitative judgment. Determining whether a given rival hypothesis will explain the data necessarily utilizes qualitative contextual information.

Wallston (1983) notes that "our belief or disbelief of our findings is frequently a subjective judgment which dictates continuing statistical analysis, the decision to attempt a replication or to publish" (p. 32). Our decision as to when a question is answered is clearly qualitative and subjective. Shields (1975) has illustrated this particularly well with her history of the study of sex differences in the brain. Whenever conclusions suggested female superiority, a new interpretation and further questions and research were generated, because the conclusions did not fit the bias or experiences of the male researchers. Researchers in sex and gender explicitly call for testing our findings against our own experience (Parlee, 1979) as well as that of the research participant (Kidder, 1981), but write-ups of studies rarely include such discussions. They are part of our informal, rather than our formal, science.

In fact, Koch's (1981) interesting discussion of psychology as science suggests that a distrust of one's own experience is part of our current "pathology" of knowledge. We have given up or ignored the criterion that knowledge should make sense. The study of sex and gender may help instigate a move back to this approach. Of course, testing knowledge against our experience if our perspective is sexist will lead to sexist knowledge, as the brain research described by Shields (1975) shows. This criterion alone, without the inclusion of feminist scientists, will not change the nature of our conclusions.

Glass and Ellett (1980) similarly note the qualitative nature of scientific judgments: "A large part of scientific judgment is knowing which circumstances are important and which are not. Such forms of knowing are largely tacit and qualitative . . . In these respects, the most hidebound quantitative and statistical scientist is like the naturalistic investigator'' (p. 224). Glass and Ellett further discuss generalization as a qualitative process. Statistics ignore the problem of populations that are ever changing: "Reasoning from 'some to all' lacks any sort of mathematical warrant . . . Samples are always characterized by innumerable specific circumstances" (p. 224). We have already discussed issues of sample selection. Others have discussed the need for selecting representative situations (cf. Petronovich, 1979; Tyler, 1981; Wallston, 1983). The point here is that decisions regarding external validity and construct validity are qualitative, while statistical conclusion validity (cf. Cook & Campbell, 1979) and internal validity involve judgments that can be informed by statistics.

When judgments can be informed by statistics, the nature of the statistic may restrict the nature of the question or the answer. In an historical analysis of the acceptance of analysis of variance (ANOVA) in psychology, Rucci and Tweney (1980) have shown that by 1952 ANOVA was fully established as the most frequent technique. Clearly, this choice of statistic influences design, and the influence is reciprocal. Rucci and Tweney (1980) note that factorial designs were used more after 1940 and one cannot ascertain whether ANOVA influenced the design choice or the use of factorial design influenced the ready adoption of ANOVA. At any rate, there is clear restriction on the types of questions we ask when ANOVA is our statistic of choice, although ANOVA may be used in nonexperimental research (cf. Goldstein, 1979; Wallston, 1983) when the number of variables is limited.

Highbee, Millard, and Folkman (1980) explored the use of analysis of variance in four social psychology journals (*Journal of Personality and Social Psychology, Journal of Experimental Social Psychology, Social Psychology Quarterly, Journal of Social Psychology*) in 1978–79. They contrasted their findings with Christie's (1965) review of *Journal of Abnormal and Social Psychology* for 1949 and 1959, and Higbee and Wells' (1972) data on *Journal of Personality and Social Psychology* in 1969. There was an increase in the use of analysis of variance from 1949 to 1969. The changes were differential by journal in 1978–79, but analysis of variance is clearly the most used statistic and is used nearly as much as all other statistics combined.[1] More than 60% of the articles included analysis of variance in contrast to the less than 40% that included some form of correlational analysis in 1978–79. Parametric directional tests (F and t) were used in more than 80% of the studies.

Thus, new correlational approaches that allow multiple variables and causal inferences (cf. Boruch, 1983) have not yet attained much popularity in social psychology. Whether these techniques are used more in studies of sex and gender, or in non-mainstream journals where such studies are published, is an empirical question (cf. Stein et al., 1984). There has been a broad call for the use

---

[1]Comparisons of percentages across years is somewhat difficult as articles use more than one statistic and the percentages, therefore, add up to more than 100% and are not comparable.

of such approaches (e.g., Cook, Dintzer & Mark, 1980; McGuire, 1973). Whether the journals reflect what research is being done or whether these mainstream journals effectively screen out alternate methods and statistics is not clear. Certainly there are numerous biases in the publication process (e.g., Lindsey, 1978; Miller & Zeitz, 1978) which could be operating.

The reification of statistics is also clear from the Higbee et al. (1980) analysis. Over time, more statistics were used per article. Moreover, the category "description only" was empty for the 1978–79 sample. There were no nonstatistical studies in 1978–79 in these four journals. Given our need for description (cf. Wallston, 1981) and the nonproductivity of statistics (Meehl, 1978), these may be unfortunate trends for the future development of psychology. In fact, Diamond and Morton (1978) found that empirical landmarks in social psychology were less likely to use analysis of variance techniques than has become common today.

The study of sex differences has also shown that statistics are formulated to test differences and not to investigate similarities (cf. Grady, 1979; Jacklin, 1979b). Jacklin (1979b) provides interesting illustrations of these issues from developmental psychology. DiPietro (1981) has found a relatively large difference between boys and girls in rough and tumble play, but from the alternative perspective, focusing on similarities, 80% of the boys were indistinguishable from 80–85% of the girls. The frequently cited sex difference in verbal ability accounts for only 1% of the variance (Plomin & Foch, 1981). Similarly, sex differences in influenceability account for only 1% of the variance (Eagly & Carli, 1981), while cognitive gender differences account for 1%–4% of the variance (Hyde, 1981). Deaux (1982) has suggested that 5% may prove to be the upper boundary for subject sex main effect size in social and cognitive behavior.

We need to develop means of discussing similarities. Unger (1981a) has suggested the label "sex comparison." Without a statistically significant difference, articles are less likely to be published, so the file drawer problem (Rosenthal, 1979) is particularly acute in research on sex differences. Moreover, Unger (1981a) notes that published literature finding no differences may be lost because of the nature of computer searches. Statistics once again constrain our questions.

For a more complete discussion of methodological issues relevant to sex difference research, see Jacklin (1979b). One further point she makes involves the failure to use statistics when they are appropriate. Separate analyses on male and female data are inappropriately used to draw conclusions regarding sex differences when statistically significant effects are found for one sex but not the other. Statistics comparing male and female data are necessary for such conclusions. Thus, when used appropriately, statistics can assist in drawing conclusions.

In an analysis of research articles in developmental psychology, Lewis and Wehren (1981) found that studies characterized as social were more likely to hypothesize sex differences, analyze for sex differences, and find significant differences compared to studies on non-social topics. Although sex differences were hypothesized in only 10% of the studies, there were analyses of sex differences in 28% of the studies. This finding may relate to the journal policy of *Developmental Psychology,* requesting tests of sex differences. However, Signorella, Vegega, and Mitchell (1981) have sampled articles from developmental and social psychology journals. They found that female first authors (20%) were more likely than male first authors (14%) to hypothesize sex-related differences. Also, authors in social journals (19%) were more likely than authors in developmental journals (14%) to propose such hypotheses. While only 16% of the articles hypothesized sex differences, an additional 39% analyzed for sex differences without theory or research based predictions. Such analyses were somewhat more likely in developmental (44%) than in social (32%) journals. Rather than reflecting increased attention to sex as a variable, Signorella et al. (1981) note, the increases represent increased reporting of routine analyses which are likely to yield more Type I errors.

Those statistics which have become popular, beyond focusing on differences, also emphasize whether a relationship exists and ignore the magnitude of the relationship (cf. Jacklin, 1979b; Parlee, 1981b).[2] Research on sex differences has helped to illustrate the importance of this distinction, since the magnitude of sex differences, as discussed above, is frequently quite small (Hyde, 1981; Jacklin, 1979b). In their chapter in this volume, Eagly and Wood illustrate the value of knowledge of effect size for drawing conclusions across studies. Meta-analysis is an important approach (cf. Cooper & Rosenthal, 1980; Glass, McGaw, & Smith, 1981) which may increase the reporting of effect size in research articles; research on sex and gender has helped stimulate interest in such techniques (e.g., Cooper, 1979; Eagly & Carli, 1981; Hall, 1978; Jacklin, 1979b; Plant, Southern, & Jacklin, 1977).

The distinction between significance and effect size parallels the difference between statistical and practical significance. Any size difference may be of some interest theoretically. When we are interested in the implications of our theories, we must take the practical significance into account (cf. Petronovich, 1979). We cannot gauge the importance of a finding from a test of statistical significance (Petronovich, 1979) or even from a knowledge of effect size. Although the latter takes us a step further, we do not know to what extent our control of variables in the laboratory has artificially restricted or enhanced effect size. Differential findings of sex differences in field and laboratory research (cf. Eagly & Wood, this volume; Unger, 1981a) illustrate this issue. Moreover, Yeaton and Sechrest (1981) note that the nature of the variable is important in determining the meaning of equivalent effect sizes. Petronovich (1979) notes that

[2]Howard Sandler, a methodologist who reviewed the chapter, commented that researchers have statistics of effect size and power available but we are lazy about using them.

a complete science will include statements regarding the probable importance of variables.

The study of women and gender has raised issues relating to the nature of statistics and their utilization. The consistent theme is the relation among the statistics we use, the questions we ask, and the inferences we draw. To the extent that statistics restrict our questions, we must work on the development of alternative statistics and the more adequate use of available statistics. We must overcome the tendency to overrely on the statistic with which we are the most comfortable, analysis of variance. We must also put statistics back in their proper perspective. They are a tool to assist our inferences from our research. Petronovich (1979) appropriately emphasizes that adequacy of inference is a function of how the data are produced (cf. Huck & Sandler, 1979), not how they are analyzed. Statistics are only one aspect of the research process, and they need to be viewed in that light.

Conclusions

Overall, then, what has the study of women and gender contributed to methodology in social psychology? Perhaps most noticeably, it has infused some passion into the field. It is possible that this passion has or will be a partial antidote for the "crisis in social psychology." Social psychology has always thrived on controversy. Some of the best questions and research effort have been inspired by awesome social questions or events: Nazism, Kitty Genovese, segregation and other aspects of racism, and now sexism. As phenomena have presented themselves, social psychology and its methods have tried to be responsive.

What happens to science in the midst of all this passion? Occasionally it suffers, and occasionally it benefits. If a result is going to be used to inform public policy, or if a result is interpreted in a way that is bound to be unpopular with a large group of people, then the methods had better be defensible, the statistics absolutely appropriate and of the highest quality, and the interpretation tight and circumscribed. The result may then be a press toward more technically adequate science. Certainly the critiques of social psychological methods from a feminist perspective that have been referred to in this chapter may contribute toward that end.

On the other hand, complete responsiveness to policymakers and a vested interest in outcomes can obviously produce bad science—even though such responsiveness may contribute to decent social policy. Some of the social questions that need to be resolved simply cannot be answered through the methods of social science. The gap between what is known and what needs to be known is often bridged with flawed research. The eagerness with which the public policy makers and the media embrace results interpreted (or misinterpreted) as relevant to controversial issues makes one shudder for science and yearn for a continuation of irrelevant research.

In addition to infusing passion, the study of women and gender can change social psychology in other ways. It has attracted new people to the field with new questions and perspectives. The novelty of these questions has increased attention to qualitative methods for exploratory research, broadening the scope of inquiry as well as its tools. The focus of those studying the psychology of women and gender tends to be on situational rather than personological factors—a focus that can enhance a truly social psychology. The "context-stripping" of social psychology, which has been widely criticized, may be repaired by some of the approaches offered by social psychologists studying the psychology of women: the inclusion of more qualitative data, the triangulation or combination of methods, and the efforts to make research relevant across disciplines and to the real-world situation of women. Social psychology is being forced to examine assumptions in question generation, design, subject selection, and methods of gathering and analyzing data. The result may be a more thoughtful and considered science of social behavior.

Although most of the current literature seems to indicate at best a divergence, and at worst an adversary relationship between "mainstream" social psychology and the study of women and gender, it is important to remember that feminism and science have been historical allies against king and church, superstition and dogma (Ehrenreich & English, 1979; Grady, 1981). Eighteenth century feminists eagerly turned to science as a means of discovering truth and furthering social change. They believed that the objectivity of the scientific method could overcome sex bias. Scientists believed that the objectivity of the scientific method was impervious to sex bias. The discovery of sex bias along with numerous other inadequacies and limitations in the methods themselves has raised serious questions about the meaning and usefulness of social science. In attempting to resolve these questions, the historical alliance may yet survive and function for the mutual benefit of science and feminism.

ACKNOWLEDGMENTS

We appreciate the comments of Jeanne Plas, Howard Sandler, and Rhoda Kesler Unger on an earlier version of this manuscript. Equal work was done on this chapter by both authors.

REFERENCES

Ajzen, I., & Fishbein, M. (1980). *Understanding attitudes and predicting social behavior.* Englewood Cliffs, N.J.: Prentice-Hall.

Allen, W. R. (1979). Family roles, occupational statuses, and achievement orientations among black women in the United States. *Signs, 4,* 670–686.

Baumgardner, S. R. (1976). Critical history and social psychology's "crisis." *Personality and Social Psychology Bulletin, 2,* 460–465.

Bart, P. B. (1971). Sexism and social science: From the gilded cage to the iron cage, or, the perils of Pauline. *Journal of Marriage and the Family, 33,* 734–735.

Bart, P. B. (1981). A study of women who both were raped and avoided rape. *Journal of Social Issues, 37*(4), 123–137.

Bem, S. L. (1975). Sex role adaptability: One consequence of psychological androgyny. *Journal of Personality and Social Psychology, 31*(4), 634–343.

Bem, S. L., Martyna, W., & Watson, C. (1976). Sex typing and androgyny: Further explorations of the expressive domain. *Journal of Personality and Social Psychology, 34*(5), 1016–1023.

Bernard, J. (1973). My four revolutions: An autobiographical history of the ASA. *American Journal of Sociology, 78,* 773–791.

Berscheid, E., & Walster, E. (1974). Physical attractiveness. In L. Berkowitz (Ed.), *Advances in experimental social psychology* (Vol. 7). New York: Academic Press.

Boruch, R. F. (1983). Causal models: Their import and their triviality. In B. L. Richardson & J. Wirtenberg (Eds.) *Sex role research: Measuring social change.* New York: Praeger.

Bronfenbrenner, U. (1977). Toward an experimental ecology of human development. *American Psychologist, 32,* 513–531.

Bryson, R. B., Bryson, J. B., Licht, M. H., & Licht, B. G. (1976). The professional pair: Husband and wife psychologists. *American Psychologist, 31,* 10–16.

Buss, A. R. (1975). The emerging field of the sociology of psychological knowledge. *American Psychologist, 30,* 988–1002.

Caplan, N., & Nelson, S. D. (1973). On being useful: The nature and consequences of psychological research on social problems. *American Psychologist, 28,* 199–211.

Carlson, R. (1972). Understanding women: Implications for personality theory and research. *Journal of Social Issues, 28*(2), 17–32.

Carlson, E. R., & Carlson, R. (1960). Male and female subjects in personality research. *Journal of Abnormal and Social Psychology, 61*(3), 482–483.

Christie, R. (1965). Some implications of research trends in social psychology. In O. Klineberg & R. Christie (Eds.), *Perspectives in social psychology.* New York: Holt, Rinehart, & Winston.

Condry, J. C., & Dyer, S. L. (1976). Fear of success: Attribution of cause to the victim. *Journal of Social Issues, 32,* 63–83.

Cook, T. D., & Campbell, D. J. (1979). *Quasi-experimentation: Design and analysis issues for field settings.* Chicago: Rand McNally.

Cook, T. D., Dintzer, L., & Mark, M. M. (1980). The causal analysis of concomitant time series. In L. Bickman (Ed.) *Applied social psychology annual* (Vol. 1). Beverly Hills, Calif.: Sage.

Cooper, H. M. (1976). Statistically combining independent studies: A meta-analysis of sex differences in conformity research. *Journal of Personality and Social Psychology, 37,* 131–146.

Cooper, H. M., & Rosenthal, R. (1980). Statistical versus traditional procedures for summarizing research findings. *Psychological Bulletin, 87,* 422–449.

Corsaro, W. A. (1981). Entering the child's world—Research strategies for field entry and data collection in a preschool setting. In J. L. Green & C. Wallat (Eds.), *Ethnography and language in educational settings.* Norwood, N.J.: Ablex.

Dan, A. J., & Beekman, S. (1972). Male versus female representation in psychological research. *American Psychologist,* 1078.

Deaux, K. (1982, May). *From individual differences to social categories: Analysis of a decade's research on gender.* Presidential address, Midwestern Psychological Association, Minneapolis.

Deaux, K., & Taynor, J. (1973). Evaluation of male and female ability: Bias works boths ways. *Psychological Reports, 32,* 261–262.

Depner, C. (1981, March). *Toward the further development of feminist psychology.* Paper presented at the annual meeting of the Association for Women in Psychology, Boston.

Diamond, S. S., & Morton, D. R. (1978). Empirical landmarks in social psychology. *Personality and Social Psychology Bulletin, 4,* 217–221.

DiPietro, J. A. (1981). Rough and tumble play: A function of gender. *Developmental Psychology, 17,* 50–58.

Eagly, A. H. (1978). Sex differences in influenceability. *Psychological Bulletin, 85,* 86–116.

Eagly, A. H., & Carli, L. L. (1981). Sex of researchers and sex-typed communications as determinants of sex differences in influenceability: A meta-analysis of social influence studies. *Psychological Bulletin, 90*(1), 1–20.

Edgington, E. S. (1974). A new tabulation of statistical procedures used in APA Journals. *American Psychologist, 29,* 25–26.

Ehrenreich, B., & English, D. (1979). *For her own good.* Garden City, N.Y.: Anchor Books.

Ellsworth, P. C. (1977). From abstract ideas to concrete instances: Some guidelines for choosing natural research settings. *American Psychologist, 32,* 604–615.

Etaugh, C., & Spandikow, D. B. (1979). Attention to sex in psychological research as related to journal policy and author sex. *Psychology of Women Quarterly, 4*(2), 175–184.

Evans, G. W. (Ed.) (1981). Environmental stress. *Journal of Social Issues, 37*(1), whole issue.

Festinger, L. (1980). *Can the science of psychology address the question of human nature?* Invited address at the annual meeting of the American Psychological Association, Montreal, Canada.

Frieze, I. H. (1979). Perceptions of battered wives. In I. H. Frieze, D. Bar-Tal, & J. S. Carroll (Eds.), *New approaches to social problems: Applications of attribution theory.* San Francisco: Jossey-Bass.

Glass, G. V., & Ellett, F. S. (1980). Evaluation research. In M. R. Rosenzweig & L. W. Porter (Eds.), *Annual review of psychology, Volume 31.* Palo Alto, Calif.: Annual Reviews, Inc., 211–228.

Glass, G. V., McGaw, B., & Smith, M. L. (1981). *Meta-analysis in social research.* Beverly Hills: Sage.

Goldberg, P. (1968). Are women prejudiced against women? *Transaction, 5,* 28–30.

Goldstein, E. (1979). Effect of same-sex and cross-sex role models on the subsequent academic productivity of scholars. *American Psychologist, 34,* 407–410.

Grady, K. E. (1979). Androgyny reconsidered. In J. H. Williams (Ed.), *Psychology of women: Selected readings.* New York: Norton.

Grady, K. E. (1981). Sex bias in research design. *Psychology of Women Quarterly, 5*(4), 628–636.

Grady, K. E., Kegeles, S. S., & Lund, A. K. (1982). Experimental studies to increase BSE—Preliminary findings. In C. Mettlin & G. P. Murphy (Eds.), *Issues in cancer screening and communications.* New York: Alan R. Liss, Inc..

Gross, A. E., & Crofton, C. (1977). What is good is beautiful. *Sociometry, 40,* 85–90.

Hall, J. A. (1978). Gender effects in decoding nonverbal cues. *Psychological Bulletin, 85,* 845–857.

Hansen, R. D., & O'Leary, V. E. (1983). Actresses and actors: The effects of sex on causal attributions. *Basic and Applied Social Psychology, 4*(3), 209–230.

Henley, N. M. (1979). *Body politics: Power, sex, and nonverbal communication.* Englewood Cliffs, N.J.: Prentice-Hall.

Higbee, K. L., Millard, R. J., & Folkman, J. R. (1980). *Four decades of research methods in social psychology.* Paper presented at the meeting of the Western Psychological Association.

Higbee, K. I., & Wells, M. G. (1972). Some research trends in social psychology during the 1960s. *American Psychologist, 27,* 963–966.

Holmes, D. S., & Jorgensen, B. W. (1971). Do personality and social psychologists study men more than women? *Representative Research in Social Psychology, 2,* 71–76.

Horner, M. S. (1972). Toward an understanding of achievement-related conflicts in women. *Journal of Social Issues, 28,* 157–176.

Huck, H. W., & Sandler, H. M. (1979). *Rival hypotheses: Alternative interpretations of data based conclusions.* New York: Harper & Row.

Hyde, J. S. (1981). How large are cognitive gender differences? A meta-analysis using ω^2 and d. *American Psychologist, 36,* 892–901.

Jacklin, C. N. (1979a). Epilogue. In M. A. Wittig & A. C. Petersen (Eds.), *Sex-related differences in cognitive functioning: Developmental issues.* New York: Academic Press.

Jacklin, C. N. (1979b). *Methodological issues in the study of sex-related differences.* Paper presented as Master Lecture, Annual Meeting of American Psychological Association, New York City.

Janoff-Bulman, R. (1979). Characterological versus behavioral self-blame: Inquiries into depression and rape. *Journal of Personality and Social Psychology, 37,* 1798–1809.

Jick, J. (1979). Mixing qualitative and quantitative methods: Triangulation in action. *Administrative Sciences Quarterly, 24,* 601–611.

Kelman, H. C. (1968). *A time to speak: On human values and social research.* San Francisco: Jossey-Bass.

Kidder, L. H. (1981). Face validity from multiple perspectives. In D. Brinberg & L. H. Kidder (Eds.), *New directions for methodology of social and behavioral science: Forms of validity.* New York: Jossey-Bass.

Koch, S. (1981). The nature and limits of psychological knowledge: Lessons of a century qua "science." *American Psychologist, 36,* 257–269.

Kuhn, T. S. (1970). *The structure of scientific revolutions* (2nd ed.). Chicago: University of Chicago Press.

Labouvie, E. W. (1975). The dialectical nature of measurement activities in the behavioral sciences. *Human Development, 18,* 396–403.

Leinhardt, G. (1978). Coming out of the laboratory closet. In D. Bar-Tal & L. Saxe (Eds.), *Social psychology of education.* Washington, D.C.: Hemisphere.

Lenney, E. (1977). Women's self-confidence in achievement settings. *Psychological Bulletin, 84,* 1–13.

Lewis, M., & Wehren, A. (1981). *Implicit rule systems in developmental research.* Unpublished manuscript.

Lindsey, D. (1978). *The scientific publication system in social science.* San Francisco: Jossey-Bass.

McGuire, W. J. (1973). The yin and yang of progress in social psychology: Seven koan. *Journal of Personality and Social Psychology, 26,* 446–456.

McKenna, W., & Kessler, S. J. (1977). Experimental design as a source of sex bias in social psychology. *Sex Roles, 3*(2), 117–128.

McNemar, Q. (1946). Opinion–attitude methodology. *Psychological Bulletin, 43,* 289–374.

Mednick, M. T. S., Tangri, S. S., & Hoffman, L. W. (Eds.). (1975). *Women and achievement: Social and motivational analyses.* Washington, D.C.: Hemisphere.

Meehl, P. E. (1978). Theoretical risks and tabular asterisks: Sir Karl, Sir Ronald, and the slow progress of soft psychology. *Journal of Consulting and Clinical Psychology, 46,* 806–834.

Merton, R. K. (1968). The Matthew Effect in science. *Science, 69,* 56–63.

Miller, F. D., & Zeitz, B. (1978). A woman's place is in the footnotes. *Personality and Social Psychology Bulletin, 4,* 511–514.

Milton, G. (1959). Sex differences in problem solving as a function of role appropriateness of the problem content. *Psychological Reports, 5,* 705–708.

Mishler, E. G. (1979). Meaning in context: Is there any other kind? *Harvard Educational Review, 49,* 1–19.

Monahan, L., Kuhn, D., & Shaver, P. (1974). Intrapsychic vs. cultural explanations of the "fear of success" motive. *Journal of Personality and Social Psychology, 29,* 60–64.

O'Leary, V. E. (1977). *Toward understanding women*. Monterey, Calif.: Brooks/Cole Publishing Company.

Ora, J. P. (1966). *Personality characteristics of college freshman volunteers for psychological experiments*. Unpublished master's thesis, Vanderbilt University.

Over, R. (1981). Research impact of men and women social psychologists. *Personality and Social Psychology Bulletin, 7,* 596–599.

Parlee, M. B. (1975). Review essay: Psychology. *Signs, 1,* 119–138.

Parlee, M. B. (1979). Psychology and women. *Signs, 5,* 121–133.

Parlee, M. B. (1981a). Appropriate control groups in feminist research. *Psychology of Women Quarterly, 5*(4), 637–644.

Parlee, M. B. (1981b). *Issues of construct validity in social processes research*. Paper presented for the National Institute of Education.

Petronovich, L. (1979). Probabilistic functionalism: A conception of research method. *American Psychologist, 34,* 373–390.

Plant, W. T., Southern, M. L., & Jacklin, C. N. (1977, February). *Statistically significant sex differences in attitude, interest, and personality measures: Much ado about very little!* Paper presented at the meeting of the Western Association for Women in Psychology, San Jose, California.

Plas, J. M., & Bellet, W. (1983). Assessment of the value-attitude orientations of American Indian children. *Journal of School Psychology, 4,* 57–64.

Plomin, R., & Foch, T. T. (1981). Sex differences and individual differences. *Child Development, 52,* 383–385.

Prescott, S., & Foster, K. (1974). *Why researchers don't study women: The responses of 67 researchers*. Paper delivered at the Eighty-Second Annual Meeting of the American Psychological Association.

Rapoport, R., & Rapoport, R. N. (Eds.) (1978). *Working couples*. London: Routledge & Kegan Paul.

Reardon, P., & Prescott, S. (1977). Sex as reported in a recent sample of psychological research. *Psychology of Women Quarterly, 2*(2), 157–161.

Riger, S., & Galligan, P. (1980). Women in management: An exploration of competing paradigms. *American Psychologist, 35,* 902–910.

Rosenthal, R. (1979). The "file drawer problem" and tolerance for null results. *Psychological Bulletin, 86,* 638–641.

Rosenthal, R., & Rosnow, R. L. (1969). The volunteer subject. In R. Rosenthal & R. L. Rosnow (Eds.), *Artifact in behavioral research*. New York: Academic Press, 59–118.

Rucci, A. J., & Tweney, R. D. (1980). Analysis of variance and the "second discipline" of scientific psychology: A historical account. *Psychological Bulletin, 87,* 166–184.

Samelson, F. (1978). From "race psychology" to "studies in prejudice": Some observations on the thematic reversal in social psychology. *Journal of the History of the Behavioral Sciences, 14,* 65–78.

Sampson, E. E. (1977). Psychology and the American ideal. *Journal of Personality and Social Psychology, 35,* 767–782.

Schachter, S. (1982). Recidivism and self-cure of smoking and obesity. *American Psychologist, 37,* 436–444.

Schultz, D. P. (1969). The human subject in psychological research. *Psychological Bulletin, 72*(3), 214–228.

Schwabacker, S. (1972). Male vs. female representation in psychological research: An examination of the *Journal of Personality and Social Psychology, 1970, 1971. Catalogue of Selected Documents in Psychology, 2,* 20–21.

Sherif, C. W. (1979). Bias in psychology. In J. A. Sherman & E. T. Beck (Eds.), *The prism of sex: Essays in the sociology of knowledge*. Madison, Wis.: University of Wisconsin Press.

Sherif, C. W. (1981). *What do we do about bias in psychology?* Paper presented at the Annual Meeting of the Association for Women in Psychology, Boston.

Sherwood, J. J., & Nataupsky, M. (1968). Predicting the conclusions of Negro-White intelligence research from biographical characteristics of the investigator. *Journal of Personality and Social Psychology, 8*, 53–58.

Shields, S. A. (1975). Functionalism, Darwinism, and the psychology of women: A study in social myth. *American Psychologist, 10*, 739–754.

Signorella, M. L., Vegega, M. E., & Mitchell, M. E. (1981). Subject selection and analyses for sex-related differences: 1968–1970 and 1975–1977. *American Psychologist, 36*(9), 988–990.

Sistrunk, F., & McDavid, J. W. (1971). Sex variable and conformity behavior. *Journal of Personality and Social Psychology, 17*, 200–207.

Smart, R. (1966). Subject selection bias in psychological research. *Canadian Psychologist, 19*, 1183–1187.

Stein, M. J., Rog, D. J., Shapiro, E., Wallston, B. S., Hillsinger, L. B., Forsberg, P., & Dandridge, B. A. (1984). Emergent journals: A response to social psychology's crisis. Manuscript submitted for publication.

Tangri, S. S., & Strasburg, G. L. (1979). Can research on women be more effective in shaping policy? *Psychology of Women Quarterly, 3*, 321–343.

Taynor, J., & Deaux, K. (1973). When women are more deserving than men: Equity, attribution, and perceived sex differences. *Journal of Personality and Social Psychology, 28*(3), 360–367.

Trend, M. G. (1978). On the reconciliation of qualitative and quantitative analysis: A case study. *Human Organization, 37*, 345–354.

Tunnell, G. B. (1977). Three dimensions of naturalness: An expanded definition of field research. *Psychological Bulletin, 84*, 426–437.

Tyler, L. E. (1981). More stately mansions—psychology extends its boundaries. In M. R. Rosenzweig & L. W. Porter (Eds.), *Annual review of psychology, 32*, 1–20.

Unger, R. K. (1979). *Female and male: Psychological perspectives.* New York: Harper & Row.

Unger, R. K. (1981a). Sex as a social reality: Field and laboratory research. *Psychology of Women Quarterly, 5*, 645–653.

Unger, R. K. (1981b). *Through the looking glass: No wonderland yet!* Presidential address to Division 35, American Psychological Association, Los Angeles.

Unger, R. K., Hilderbrand, M., & Madar, T. (1982). Physical attractiveness and assumptions about social deviance: Some sex-by-sex comparisons. *Personality and Social Psychology Bulletin, 8*, 293–301.

Vaughter, R. M. (1976). Review essay: Psychology, *Signs, 2*, 120–146.

Wachtel, P. L. (1980). Investigation and its discontents: Some constraints on progress in psychological research. *American Psychologist, 35*, 399–408.

Wallston, B. S. (1978). *Situation vs. person variables in research on women and employment.* Paper presented at the meeting of the American Psychological Assocation, Toronto, Canada.

Wallston, B. S. (1981). What are the questions in psychology of women? A feminist approach to research. *Psychology of Women Quarterly, 5*, 597–617.

Wallston, B. S. (1983). Overview of research methods. In J. Writenberg & B. L. Richardson (Eds.), Sex role research: Measuring social change. New York: Praeger.

Wallston, B. S., Foster, M. A., & Berger, M. (1978). I will follow him: Myth, reality, or forced choice—Job seeking experiences of dual-career couples. *Psychology of Women Quarterly, 3*, 9–21.

Wallston, B. S., & O'Leary, V. E. (1981). Sex makes a difference: Differential perceptions of women and men. In L. Wheeler (Ed.), *Review of personality and social psychology: 2.* Beverly Hills, Calif.: Sage.

Weiss, H. B. (1981). *The contribution of qualitative methods to the feminist research process.* Paper presented at the Annual Meeting of the Association for Women in Psychology, Boston.

Weissberg, N. C. (1976). Methodology or substance? A response to Helmreich. *Personality and Social Psychology Bulletin, 2,* 119–121.

Weisstein, N. (1970). Kinder, Kuche, Kirche as scientific law: Psychology constructs the female. In R. Morgan (Ed.), *Sisterhood is powerful.* New York: Vintage.

Wittig, M. (1982). *Value-fact-intervention dilemmas in the psychology of women.* Presidential Address, American Psychological Association, Washington, D.C.

Wrightsman, L. S., & Deaux, K. (1981). *Social psychology in the 80's.* Monterey, Calif.: Brooks/Cole.

Yeaton, W. H., & Sechrest, L. (1981). Meaningful measures of effect. *Journal of Consulting and Clinical Psychology, 49,* 766–767.

2 Images of Masculinity and Femininity: A Reconceptualization

Janet T. Spence
Linda L. Sawin
University of Texas at Austin

Although sex-role standards in this country have been modified and liberalized over the past decades, men and women continue to be distinguished by a diverse array of attributes, attitudes, and behaviors, and are assigned primary responsibility for different societal tasks. In the initial section of this chapter, we briefly examine some of the psychological models that have been concerned with describing and explaining the relationships among these "masculine" and "feminine" attributes and behaviors. This discussion sets the stage for the second section, which presents a set of data that explores individuals' images of masculinity and femininity from a different perspective than has typically been employed. In the final section, a theoretical reconceptualization of the masculinity and femininity concepts is outlined.

MODELS OF MASCULINITY, FEMININITY, AND GENDER-ROLE IDENTIFICATION

A number of theoretical and empirical models have been devised to describe the organization of masculine and feminine characteristics and behaviors within the individual, and how they develop and are maintained over the lifespan. Although they differ in their comprehensiveness and in their details, most of these models have been predicated on a common set of overarching assumptions. Two key propositions can be identified (Constantinople, 1973). First, it has traditionally been tacitly assumed that the socially desirable qualities and behaviors that normatively distinguish the genders are substantially correlated so that information about the degree to which individuals exhibit one type of masculine or feminine attribute permits an inference to be made about their standing with respect to other types of gender-differentiating attributes. This proposition leads directly to the second: Masculinity and femininity can be elevated to the status of general theoretical constructs that form the endpoints of a single bipolar continuum along which individuals of both genders can be assigned a position. Taken together, these propositions imply that individuals' places on the masculinity–femininity continuum can be measured or diagnosed by assessing the degree to which they exhibit or report specific gender-linked qualities and behaviors.

In some models of masculinity–femininity, these behaviors and attributes are apparently presumed to be equally diagnostic. For example, in traditional masculinity–femininity tests, no rationale for selection of items, beyond their empirical capacity to distinguish between the genders was provided by the tests' originators; understandably, item content varies widely among, and often within, the different instruments. Other models imply that certain classes of attributes should be given special weight or define the "essence" of masculinity and femininity. What have come to be called instrumental or agentic personality traits and expressive or communal personality traits have most often been accorded this special status (e.g., Bakan, 1966; Bem, 1974; Block, 1973). Reflecting the pivotal position assigned to these clusters of personality characteristics, a number of recently developed instruments used in investigations of gender-related phenomena contain a heavy, if not exclusive, load of desirable instrumental and expressive traits (e.g., Bem, 1974; Spence, Helmreich, & Stapp, 1974).

In a number of theories, the masculinity–femininity construct and such parallel concepts as sex-role orientation, sex-role identification, or gender schema, take on more dynamic overtones, implying a set of processes that are responsible for both the acquisition and the maintenance of societally prescribed patterns of attributes and behaviors. In subsequent discussion, this family of dynamic constructs will be referred to by the generic label *gender-role identification,* because it is their common features that concern us here. According to these theories, children desire to be like, and attempt to model themselves after, their same-sex parent or other members of their own sex. In this way, it is hypothesized, children acquire the characteristics, attitudes, and behaviors that are regarded as appropriate for their gender. Simultaneously, they develop self-images of their own masculinity or femininity (or gender-role identity) that lead them to evaluate and monitor their own and others' behavior according to its gender-appropriateness (e.g., Bem, 1981b; Heilbrun, 1973; Kohlberg, 1966).

Most theorists who postulate this type of dynamic construct, involving a conception of the self, also assume that individuals vary in the strength of their gender-role identity and in the direction in which it is oriented. One end of this hypothetical continuum is occupied by sex-typed individuals, males and females who strongly identify with their own gender and are therefore highly masculine or highly feminine in their attributes, attitudes, and behaviors. Located at the other extreme are cross-typed individuals, who identify with the other gender and resemble its characteristics. The midpoint of this hypothetical continuum marks the zero point, which designates the absence of gender-role identification, implying that the individual has either failed to develop this type of self-identity or else has transcended it (e.g., Hefner, Rebecca, & Olefshanky, 1975).[1]

Although theoretically richer in their details and implications, gender-role identity constructs share with the more purely descriptive bipolar conception of masculinity and femininity the two presuppositions that were mentioned earlier. It is therefore possible to assess the degree to which individuals exhibit particular classes of behaviors or attributes (e.g., gender-differentiating personality traits) and to infer from this assessment the degree to which an individual is gender-role identified.

Until quite recently, psychological theorists, along with the community at large, tacitly accepted the legitimacy of gender-related divisions of labor. The task of parents and other adults, therefore, was to encourage children to develop a firm sense of gender-role identity and so to develop those attributes and behaviors that would presumably allow them to take their expected places in adult society. This imperative had as its corollary the assumption that individuals who failed to develop a strong gender-role identification, or who rebelled against society's normative expectations for their gender, were likely to be neurotic misfits. Over the past decade, however, ideological shifts concerning women's status and roles have been reflected in the thinking of many psychologists. One feminist position, for which Bem (1974, 1981b) has been the most articulate spokesperson, has proposed the creation of a society in which gender-role distinctions are abolished and members of both sexes are free to develop according to their individual natures and predilections. Bem and others gave scientific

[1]Although it is apparent that those with weak or absent role-identities are postulated to evaluate and guide their behaviors by other standards than those linked to gender, the behavioral consequences of a low degree of gender-role identity are less clear than has been presumed. Such individuals, it is typically implied, exhibit both masculine and feminine attributes and behaviors equally but it seems more reasonable to assume that, collectively, they would exhibit all possible admixtures. That is, even in a (hypothetical) society in which gender-role distinctions are nonexistent and characteristics and behaviors that presently differentiate men and women no longer do so, individual differences in these qualities would still be expected to occur for reasons unrelated to sex. This creates a problem for those investigators who operationally define degree of gender-role identification by assessing the degree to which individuals manifest specific gender-differentiating attributes (e.g., instrumental and expressive qualities), without simultaneously assessing their "meaning" to the individual or their developmental histories. Introducing the latter procedures would be tantamount to introducing a new method of measuring role identification and denies the simple isomorphism that has been proposed between the presence or absence of gender-related characteristics and the identity construct. Although Bem (1981 a and b) has recently intimated that such a procedure is necessary, she has yet to suggest the form it would take.

legitimacy to this ideological stance through several proposals that contradicted some of the presumptions of prior theories (themselves doubtless influenced by ideological considerations). First, they proposed that weak rather than strong gender-role identity is associated with better mental health (Bem, 1974, 1981b) or a more advanced stage of ego development (Block, 1973).

The classic bipolar view of masculinity and femininity was also disputed. Bem (1974), among others, proposed instead that masculinity and femininity constitute two independent dimensions or aspects of the self-concept. This formulation suggests that observable gender-related attributes and behaviors can be divided into two conceptually and statistically independent classes. Although the components within each of these classes are presumed to be correlated within each gender, the two classes are said to be orthogonal. Thus, the degree to which individuals exhibit or admit to possessing feminine properties (or any given type of feminine property) is presumed to be indicative of their underlying femininity, and the degree to which they exhibit or admit to possessing masculine properties is indicative of their underlying masculinity. By proposing that masculinity and femininity can coexist, Bem cleared the psychological way for a society in which men and women, freed of gender expectations, would each be able to exhibit the characteristics that contemporary society defines as "masculine" and "feminine."

Several self-report measures containing separate "masculinity" and "femininity" scales have been used in investigations of these hypothetical concepts (Baucom, 1976; Bem, 1974; Berzins, Welling, & Wetter, 1978; Heilbrun, 1976; Spence, Helmreich, & Stapp, 1974). The two most popular measures are the Bem Sex Role Inventory (BSRI; Bem, 1974) and the Personal Attributes Questionnaire (PAQ; Spence & Helmreich, 1978; Spence, Helmreich & Stapp, 1974), the latter exclusively and the former largely containing descriptors of socially desirable instrumental personality traits and expressive personality traits on their "masculinity" and "femininity" scales, respectively. In the wake of demonstrations with both instruments that correlations between the two gender-related scales were close to zero in both sexes, many investigators explicitly renounced the bipolar conception of masculinity–femininity and accepted a dualistic conception of these theoretical constructs in its place. This rapid switch in allegiance appears to have been based more on the attractive ideological package in which the dualistic conception was wrapped than on the persuasiveness of the empirical data (beyond those provided by the BSRI and PAQ). Furthermore, renunciation of the unidimensional bipolar model in favor of the bidimensional one has turned out to be more apparent than real.

In her theorizing, Bem (1974, 1977, 1981b) has not only stated that scores on the BSRI and other similar instruments operationally define the two independent self-concepts, masculinity and femininity, but has simultaneously implied that scores on the two scales are measures of a unidimensional construct that many investigators label sex-role orientation or identification. In her most recent theory, Bem (1981b) equates this orientation with "gender schema." Thus, individuals classified as sex-typed on the BSRI or PAQ (men high in their "masculinity" scores and low in their "femininity" scores, and women with the reverse pattern) have been assumed to be strong in gender-role identification and highly gender schematic in their processing of information; as such, sex-typed individuals presumably develop and manifest only the characteristics associated with their own sex, as well as viewing others through the lens of gender. Although there has been some confusion and mind-changing about how it is to be done, individuals exhibiting other constellations of "masculinity" and "femininity" scores can presumably be arranged elsewhere along the dimension of gender-role identification or saliency of gender schema.

The hypothesis that the BSRI and PAQ are measures of a unidimensional construct, namely gender-role identification, has been endorsed by many investigators who simultaneously embrace the concept of masculinity and femininity as independent dimensions, thus implying that the two notions are compatible. However, as has been discussed elsewhere (Spence, 1984; Spence & Helmreich, 1981), these sets of concepts, when operationally defined by the same measure, are inherently contradictory and cannot be logically reconciled. In practice, many investigators appear to be nominally advocating the dualistic model while testing the implications of the old bipolar model (under the guise of "sex-role orientation" or the like).

Putting aside questions related to the association between gender-linked attributes and behaviors and indices of mental health and to the desirability of abolishing gender-role distinctions, both the unidimensional and two-dimensional models described above have testable implications that permit their scientific utility to be assessed. In the case of the bipolar model, substantial correlations are expected between the various categories of gender-differentiating attributes and behaviors that go to make up the total class of masculine and feminine phenomena.

On the other hand, the dualistic model suggests, first, that all gender-related phenomena can be conceptually separated into two noncontradictory categories, an effort that is often but not always feasible. Secondly, it suggests that the attributes and behaviors within each category contribute to a single factor, but that the masculine factor and the feminine factor are uncorrelated. Neither set of expectations has been confirmed. For example, correlations among masculinity–femininity tests (whether or not their items are divided into two scales) are often low—sometimes even negative—and factor analyses have indicated multidimensionality among and often within these instruments (e.g., Coffman & Levy, 1972; Wakefield, Sasek, Friedman, & Bowden, 1976), rather than a single factor or two independent factors that account for most of the variance.

In light of the prominence of desirable instrumental and expressive traits in psychological theories of masculinity, femininity, and gender-role identification, and the popularity of the BSRI and PAQ, both essentially measures of these trait domains, particular mention should be made of data obtained with these instruments. Factor and other types of analyses suggest that desirable instrumental and expressive characteristics do form orthogonal, unifactorial dimensions (e.g., Helmreich, Spence, & Wilhelm, 1981). If instrumentality and expressiveness have special status as indicators of role-related attitudes and behaviors, one would expect substantial relationships between measures of these personality characteristics and various gender-role indices not directly influenced by instrumental and expressive skills. Many investigations employing the PAQ or BSRI have been conducted to explore this possibility, e.g., studies of sex-role attitudes (Orlofsky, Aslin, & Ginsburg, 1977; Spence & Helmreich, 1978; Spence, Helmreich, & Stapp, 1975); self-reported sex-role behaviors (Orlofsky, 1981; Spence, Helmreich, & Sawin, 1980); choice of or comfort in performing mundane tasks that are stereotypically masculine or feminine (Bem & Lenney, 1976; Helmreich, Spence & Holahan, 1979; Spence et al., 1980); and the use of gender schema in processing information (Bem, 1981b; Mills & Tyrrell, 1983). At best, the relationships have been small. Furthermore, even when differences occur, variable patterns of results have been found with respect to which profile of scores (sex-typed, cross-typed, etc.) produces the most or least congruence with traditional gender-role standards in attitudes, preferences, and behaviors. The data also suggest that the developmental course of instrumental and expressive characteristics is affected by a different constellation of factors than are other gender-differentiating qualities (e.g., Baumrind, 1967; Spence & Helmreich, 1978). In short, theories that propose that individuals have self-images of their masculinity–femininity (single factor model), or of their masculinity and femininity (two factor model) that lead them to develop and exhibit the full constellation of characteristics and behaviors normatively expected of their gender, lack empirical support.

Direct Assessment of Masculine and Feminine Self-images

The presumption that self-images of masculinity and femininity are tightly linked to gender-differentiating attributes, as we have noted, has almost universally led investigators to operationally define these self-images indirectly, inferring their strength from measures of particular sets of such attributes. However, it is also possible to assess these self-images directly, most simply by asking individuals to rate themselves on the two adjectives "masculine" and "feminine." These two trait descriptors are included among the items on the BSRI and data concerning them are found in factor analyses of the BSRI provided by Pedhazur and Tetenbaum (1979). These investigators reported that, in both sexes, "masculine" and "feminine" constitute a separate, 2-item bipolar scale that is weakly related to other BSRI factors. Similar results have been reported by Storms (1980). One additional finding reported by Pedhazur and Tetenbaum (1979) should also be noted here. Although scores on the 2-item masculinity–femininity factor showed some variability within each sex, there was little overlap in the two distributions; men clustered at the masculine pole and women at the feminine pole. A discriminant function analysis indicated that over 90% of the cases were correctly classified as to gender on the basis of responses to these two items alone.

The presently available evidence, then, suggests that men and women can be reliably differentiated on the basis of their perceptions of their own masculinity and femininity; that these two global self-assessments are negatively correlated, forming a single bipolar continuum; and that within each sex, these self-images have little or no relationship with individuals' perceptions of their instrumental and expressive characteristics.

The latter findings constitute still another refutation of theories of gender-role identification. They leave us, however, with a critical question. On what basis *do* individuals "diagnose" or reach their judgments about their masculinity or femininity?

Attempts to answer this question could take the form of assessing self-images directly, e.g., by obtaining self-ratings or ratings of others on the adjectives "masculine" and "feminine," and to continue the search for the correlates of these measures. This approach is fundamentally quantitative, seeking to determine the sources of individual differences in self-perception and perceptions of others. In its simplest form, it would involve a search for a single model (or a single model for each gender) that would specify the specific gender-differentiating attributes that contribute to assessments of masculinity and femininity and the relative weights of each. Another possible tack would be to address the issue less obliquely, and more qualitatively, by asking individuals to specify what properties determine their sense of their own masculinity or femininity or their judgment of these qualities in others.

In the study described in the following section, we elected to follow the second alternative, both because it represented a fresh approach and because of our conviction that men and women and, within each sex, *individual* men and women, would differ in their conceptions of masculinity and femininity, both in themselves and in others.

CONCEPTIONS OF MASCULINITY AND FEMININITY:
AN INTERVIEW STUDY

In what must be frankly acknowledged as an exploratory investigation, we set out to interview men and women about their conceptions of masculinity and femininity. At the time the interviews were undertaken, our expectations were as expressed in the following quotation:

Masculinity and femininity can . . . be regarded as global aspects of the self-concept that men and women directly identify in these or equivalent terms (such as being a ''real man'' or a ''real woman''). Individuals . . . have organized belief systems . . . about the psychosocial meaning of being ''a man'' or ''a woman'' and can be expected to have incorporated these beliefs into their sense of self. These belief systems, our observations suggest, are compounded of many elements: assumptions about appropriate sex roles, characteristics of the self such as personality attributes and cognitive abilities, physique and physical appearance, styles of speech and body movement, sexual behavior, and so forth.

One can expect that individuals belonging to the same culture or subculture will be reasonably similar in identifying the factors contributing to masculinity and femininity in themselves and others in the sense that they will be drawn from a common pool and will not be completely idiosyncratic. Individuals' definitions of masculinity and femininity, however, are likely to be based on complexly weighted sets of indicators that not only vary from one person to another but also change with age and may even differ when individuals are assessing themselves as opposed to others. . . .

The forging of a self-concept permitting an adequate sense of self-worth may often necessitate efforts to integrate contradictory elements or perceived lacks within a personal belief system. . . [M]en or women who possess cross-sex characteristics, or who lack a sufficient degree of stereotypically appropriate ones, may variously relabel these characteristics under neutral headings, deny them, or consider them as irrelevant, basing their judgments of their own masculinity or femininity on those conventionally acceptable characteristics they do possess. . .

If, as we suspect, there is substantial variability among men and women in the constellations of sex-typed characteristics they possess, differences among individuals in the nature of their self-definitions of masculinity or femininity are the inevitable consequence, even though the majority of men and women may consider themselves as acceptable members of their sex (Spence & Helmreich, 1978, pp. 116–117).

In essence, we originally hypothesized that men and women possess what Markus (1980) and Bem (1981a) have referred to as gender schema. Unlike these theorists, however, we anticipated that individuals may have developed different schemas for themselves and for others. Further, we predicted that across individuals, the structure of these schemas would be variable, rather than varying only along a strength dimension.

Participants

The participants, residents of communities in the greater Austin, Texas area, were drawn from a group of married couples who were the parents of a first- or second-grade child and who were taking part in a larger study of white, middle class families. One of the purposes of that study was to relate husbands' and wives' instrumental and expressive personality characteristics, as measured by the Personal Attributes Questionnaire (PAQ; Spence & Helmreich, 1978) to a number of variables such as their child-rearing practices. Accordingly, the initial selection of couples who were invited to participate in the larger study was aimed at obtaining certain commonly occurring or theoretically interesting couple types with respect to the husband's and the wife's profile of scores on the PAQ. For this purpose, each parent was classified, according to the median split method, into one of four cells. We have in the past labeled these four cells Androgynous, Masculine, Feminine, and Undifferentiated to call attention to gender differences on the particular trait clusters measured by the PAQ. To avoid unwanted and unintended connotations, we use here a more literally descriptive label for the four groups: high Instrumental and Expressive (above the median on both scales); Instrumental (above the median on instrumentality and below on expressiveness); Expressive (below the median on instrumentality and above on expressiveness); and low Instrumental and Expressive (below the median on both scales).

Out of the larger sample, 42 men and 41 women took part in the interview; 40 of each sex were married to one another. With respect to PAQ category, 7 of the 42 men were classified as high Instrumental and Expressive, 21 as Instrumental, 8 as Expressive, and 6 as low Instrumental and Expressive. The corresponding numbers for the 41 women were 11 high Instrumental and Expressive, 4 Instrumental, 15 Expressive, and 11 low Instrumental and Expressive. These distributions are not representative of same-age peers. For example, cross-typed individuals (Expressive males, Instrumental females) are overrepresented. These distortions were the result of our deliberate recruitment of specified couple types, including couples with a cross-typed husband and/or wife for the larger study of families.

The mean age of the men was 38 years (R: 31–54). Thirty-five percent were native Texans. In religion, 58% were Protestant, 20% Catholic, and 3% Jewish, the remaining indicating no religious affiliation; 43% reported attending church regularly, 12% occasionally, and the remainder infrequently or never. In education, 35% had postbaccalaureate training, 28% were college graduates, 30% had attended college, and 7% were high school graduates. Twenty percent held higher-level professional or executive positions, 47% were middle-level managers or owners of small businesses, and 32% were in sales or skilled crafts. Only 3% worked less than full time.

Among the women, 45% of whom were born in Texas, the mean age was 36 years (R: 30–45). In religion, 68% were Protestant, 11% Catholic, 3% Jewish, and 13% reported no religion; 45% attended church regularly, 21% occasionally, and the rest infrequently or never. Five percent had postbaccalaureate training, 29% were college graduates, 37% had attended college, and 21% were high school graduates. Forty-five percent were currently employed full time and 16% part-time; 39% were fulltime housewives. Of those who currently were employed outside the home, 4% held upper level professional or executive positions, 37% lower level professional or managerial positions, 46% were in sales and clerical-secretarial positions, and 13% held semi-skilled positions.

The interviews, which were semi-structured in form, were conducted in the participants' home by a same-sex interviewer. These sessions took place after other scheduled home visits, in which the interviewer had taken part, had been concluded. The first half of the interview explored the person's conceptions of masculinity and femininity and related topics. (The second half, data from which will not be reported here, went on to explore other matters.) Three major questions were asked of the respondents, the first of which asked, in the case of men, their conception of femininity in women or, in the case of women, their conception of masculinity in men:

> People often talk about ("femininity" in women) ("masculinity" in men). Not all (women) (men) are equally (feminine) (masculine), of course. Some (women) (men) are extremely (feminine) (masculine), and some are not (feminine) (masculine) at all. As far as you are concerned, when you think of a very (feminine woman) (masculine man), what kind of characteristics does it bring to mind?

The second major question asked men about their conceptions of masculinity in men and women about their conception of femininity in women. The third inquired into their views of themselves:

> When you think in terms of (being a man and your own masculinity) (being a woman and your own femininity), what defines your (manhood) (womanhood) as far as your own self-image is concerned?

Following each of these open-ended questions, the respondents were given one or more probes in an attempt to elicit information about types of attributes (physical appearance, interests, personality characteristics) the respondent had not spontaneously mentioned in the initial answer (e.g., "Some people mention physical appearance or ways of moving or speaking. Are any of these things part of a [woman's femininity] [man's masculinity] as far as you are concerned?") Several follow-up questions were also asked following each of the major queries. These questions will be mentioned at a later point.

The Findings

Responses to the three major questions were classified in two ways. First, every individual's first response to each open-ended question was assigned to a content category. All additional responses to that question were then categorized, without regard to whether they occurred spontaneously in the course of individuals' answers to the initial question, or in response to a follow-up probe. Some individuals mentioned multiple attributes falling into a single category (e.g., a masculine man is tall, handsome, and muscular, all examples of physical characteristics); others offered only a single exemplar. For data reduction purposes, individuals' number of responses in each category was ignored; only the number of categories each individual employed was determined. Special mention should be made of the category, "Don't know/Question," used in coding first responses. Throughout the interview, a number of respondents expressed confusion or an inability to answer, asking for clarification or explanation, saying they didn't know, couldn't think of anything, or had never thought about the question. When this type of response occurred to an initial open-ended question and the individual required prompting from the interviewer before essaying a substantive answer, the first response was assigned to the "Don't Know/Question" category.

Femininity in Women. Listed in Table 2.1 are the categories to which answers were assigned in response to the questions about women's femininity (with the exception of Don't Know/Question), along with a list of examples. In the occasional instance in which men and women tend to mention different attributes within the same general category, sample responses of the two genders are listed separately.

Table 2.2 reports, first, the percentage of men and of women whose first response fell into each category. (For economy of presentation, some subcategories in Table 2.1 were combined before conducting the analyses reported in Table 2.2). As each individual is represented once, the column total is 100. Also, for each category the percentage of individuals who gave one or more instances falling into this category in their subsequent responses is reported. Individuals often repeated or gave an additional instance of the category mentioned in their first response; these were included in the count of subsequent responses. In analyzing the data, separate counts were made for individuals assigned to the four PAQ categories. These results have not been tabled because the groups were typically comparable. The occasional difference will be reported informally in the text.

An inspection of Table 2.2 reveals that 45% (rounded figure) of the men first mentioned a physical characteristic. About 9% specified that femininity was marked by an absence of masculine attributes; the remainder of the substantive replies were scattered among other categories. Fourteen percent of the initial responses fell into the "Don't Know/Question" category. In their subsequent answers, 64% mentioned physical attributes. Several other categories are also worth mention. Sixty percent of the men gave responses falling into one or more of the three role categories: being a good wife and mother, having home-oriented interests, and/or behaving socially in a ladylike fashion. At the same time, over 30% denied some aspect of the stereotype; most specified that a woman could have "masculine" interests and still be feminine, but others denied that femininity was associated with motherhood, being a housewife, and so forth. Expressive characteristics were mentioned by almost 10% of the men, all of whom were

TABLE 2.1
Categories of Responses to Questions about Femininity in Women
and Examples of Each

Physical Attributes
  General appearance. Physical appearance, looks, looks like a lady, physical characteristics.
  Movements and speech. Graceful, how she walks and talks, carriage, soft voice.
  Dress and care of appearance. Way they dress, frilly dresses, cares about appearance, pretty hair-do, neat, clean, china doll look.
  Physical characteristics. Men: Petite, shapely, slim, attractive, cute, dainty, delicate, not physically strong, long hair, soft body, can reproduce. Women: not obese, soft body.
Personality Characteristics
  Expressive. Quiet, tender, gentle, kind, supportive, empathetic, caring, sensitive to people, selfless in service to their family and community, emotional.
  Noninstrumental. Submissive, nonaggressive, dependent, not domineering, on the passive side, not outgoing, unassertive, less demanding.
  Instrumental. Nonsubservient, assertive, self-assured.
  Miscellaneous. Happy, good personality, responsible, good outlook, makes the best of what God gave them, good conversationalist, good sense of humor, well-rounded, predictable, silly, not serious.
Cognitive Characteristics. Intelligent, good head on their shoulders.
Roles and Social Behavior
  Wife and mother. Mother image, main concern is family, good mother, good wife, children come first.
  Domestic activities and feminine interests. Does housework, bakes bread, likes cooking, good housewife, home decorating, interested in the home and not world of employment, bridge, organizing charity ball, sewing, knitting, dancing, art lessons, interested in flowers and crafts.
  Sexual. Seductive, sexy.
  Ladylike behavior. Old fashioned (classic) lady, ladylike, conducts self like a lady, lets (expects) men to hold open the door, has men be gentlemen.
  Social interactions and language. Wants man to do hard things for her, you push her car, how she acts around people, doesn't try to push men around, defers to men too much, you treat her like a woman, not profane, doesn't let people see the ugly side of themselves, able to meet the public.
Absence of Masculine Characteristics. Not masculine, not like men, doesn't (wouldn't) do man's work, not business-oriented, doesn't go for sports or hunting, doesn't look (dress) like a man.
Denial of Stereotype. Unrelated to being motherly (housewife, sex symbol, looks, how she dresses). Feminine women could also: enjoy anything, be an athlete, do male-dominated things, be goal-oriented, be intelligent, have a job.
Vague. Something that makes you you (have an impression about), the whole woman, acts like a woman, attitudes toward things.

---

classified as Expressive on the PAQ. Both the presence and absence of instrumental characteristics were also mentioned by several men (not always with approval), all but one of whom were classified as Instrumental. Personality characteristics that are not ordinarily regarded as stereotypically feminine were mentioned more often than expressive or instrumental characteristics, in a context that suggested that the men were describing the kind of woman they liked, rather than what was necessarily "feminine." In this connection, several men

TABLE 2.2
Femininity in Women:
Percentage of First Responses in Each Category
and Percentage of Individuals Utilizing Each Category
in Later Responses

Category	Men		Women	
	First R	Later Rs	First R	Later Rs
Physical Attributes	45.2	64.3	53.7	82.9
Personality				
Expressive	7.1	9.5	7.3	43.9
Noninstrumental	2.4	0.0	2.4	24.4
Instrumental	4.8	7.1	2.4	2.4
Miscellaneous	2.4	26.2	0.0	24.4
Cognitive	2.4	11.9	0.0	0.0
Roles, etc.				
Wife/Mother	2.4	16.7	9.8	39.0
Domestic/interests	2.4	16.7	0.0	29.3
Ladylike and social beh.	4.8	26.2	2.4	22.0
Sex	0.0	0.0	0.0	4.9
Non-masculine	9.5	19.1	0.0	4.9
Denial of stereotype	0.0	31.0	7.3	24.4
Vague	7.1	4.8	9.8	9.8
Don't Know/Questions	14.3	—	4.9	—

Note: Only percentages of first responses total 100.

also described intelligence as desirable. Finally, attention is called to the "non-masculine" category. Some 19% of the men specified that femininity was associated with the absence of qualities associated with men.

Women were more forthcoming than men in describing the characteristics associated with femininity. Thus, only 5% of the women were unable to respond without prompting to the initial question. In their first responses, 54% referred to the physical attributes of the feminine women; 10% nominated the role of wife or mother, and an additional 10% gave global, vague responses (e.g., "The whole woman"). In their subsequent responses, 83% appealed to physical characteristics. A substantial number also mentioned other types of qualities: the presence of expressive characteristics (44%), being a wife and/or mother (39%), having domestic and other feminine interests (29%), ladylike social behavior (22%), and (discouragingly) the absence of instrumental characteristics (24%). Almost a quarter of the women, however, denied the significance of some aspect of the female stereotype. Like men, most of these women stated that women could have any interests they wanted, including "masculine" ones, and still be feminine. A substantial number (24%) mentioned characteristics that are not ordinarily considered gender-differentiating, again suggesting that some women were ticking off qualities they generally valued, rather than those that were specifically related to femininity.

In two follow-up questions, the participants were asked what they liked most and least about feminine women. One man said he liked everything about feminine women, a second that he liked nothing about them (because femininity implied passivity and catering to men) and 11 (26%) replied they didn't know or couldn't think of anything in particular. Of those who nominated specific positive attributes, 42% mentioned physical appearance—shapeliness, clothing styles, and neatness—and 9% referred to women's sexual charms. Twenty-three percent described family role relationships: their liking of women's caring for the home and children, or to the positive feelings and boost in self-esteem they themselves gained from being the protector of, or from being deferred to by, women. Twenty percent described women's expressive characteristics: their sensitivity, concern, and compassion for others. Eighteen percent found women's instrumental qualities attractive, e.g., willingness to speak up and express their views, not being subservient; all but one of these men were themselves high in instrumentality. As observed above, whereas some men were trying to describe what they perceived as feminine qualities—which they did not necessarily like— others were describing what they liked in women (and, most probably, in men as well).

The impression that some men were describing women, or what they liked or disliked in women, rather than femininity was furthered by some of their descriptions in response to the question about what characteristics of feminine women they liked the least. One quarter did not nominate any characteristic or specified that all feminine characteristics were positive, whereas 7% said they did not like women to act or appear "masculine," and 5% objected to unladylike behavior. The latter suggestions, of course, were nonresponsive to the question. Somewhat more relevant were the 5% who objected to too much make-up, provocative clothes, or excessive concern with appearance; 14% were upset by egotism, playing hard to get, or materialism. More psychologically interesting was the fact that 37% of the men nominated lack of instrumentality: helplessness, too much dependence on men, an inability to make decisions, an inability to do things by themselves. Twenty percent objected to role-playing: women feigning helplessness or using their femininity to manipulate men or as an excuse to avoid responsibilities. The ambivalence of many men is apparent. As reflected in their replies to other questions, men value their sense of superiority and their role of protector as long as too many demands are not made of them and the women they "protect" are capable of functioning on their own. Similar findings have been reported by Komarovsky (1979).

When the women were asked about what they liked most about feminine women, 8% said they disliked or liked nothing about feminine women (reasons unspecified), and 26% said they didn't know. Forty percent specified that feminine women's appearance and dress were appealing, and 30% mentioned their general conduct: ladylike, gracious, not trying to dominate. Fifteen percent nominated women's interpersonal sensitivity. These responses were similar to the men's. As was also found with men, quite a few women referred to socially desirable characteristics that are not stereotypically feminine: e.g., self-acceptance, self-confidence, cheerfulness, ability to command respect. A particularly interesting reaction (exhibited by 18% of the women) was that one felt comfortable or could relate to or identify with feminine women.

Asked what they disliked, 20% said they didn't know and 10% that there was nothing they disliked about feminine women. As with the men, a number of women (26%) objected to lack of instrumental characteristics—too passive, dependent, indecisive—and others (18%) to women pretending to be helpless or dumb to play up to men and/or to get men to do things for them. Twenty-three percent pointed to egocentricity: showing off, arrogance, conceit, thinking of themselves as God's gift to men. A scattering of others of women's sins also surfaced: catty, too nosey, little girl voices, etc. Once more, the distinction between women and femininity often appeared to be lost.

Masculinity in Men. Table 2.3 shows the categories into which responses to the series of questions about men's masculinity were classified; Table 2.4 reveals the results of this classification. More women than men (29% vs. 10%) failed to respond to the initial open-ended question without prompting. This outcome paralleled the results with the question about femininity, in which men were more uncertain than women.

When women did reply substantively, their most frequent first response (given by 37%) concerned physical attributes. The second most frequent response (12%), however, rejected the masculine stereotype, particularly the conception of the masculine man as the muscular jock. In later responses, 68% specified physical attributes, many making explicit that their first impression of men was their looks. Forty-six percent evoked men's instrumental characteristics (their mental strength, assertiveness, ability to assume responsibilities), and 34% specified masculine interests, these latter nominations arising most frequently in response to a direct probe rather than spontaneously. Almost one-quarter mentioned that masculine men were not gay or effeminate, thus defining masculinity through the absence of its presumed opposite. Twenty-four percent continued to deny some aspect of the macho stereotype, about half of these objecting to men's constant need to prove themselves or their masculinity.

Men's most frequent first response (given by 29%) also referred to physical characteristics. However, an almost equal number (24%) first described the masculine man's instrumental qualities: leadership ability, assertiveness, decisiveness, and so forth. A fair number (14%) evoked a miscellaneous set of nonstereotyped characteristics, e.g., honesty and being an adult. In subsequent responses, references to qualities falling into each of these three categories almost doubled. A substantial number of responses fell into several additional

TABLE 2.3
Categories of Responses to Questions about Masculinity in Men
and Examples of Each

Physical Attributes
  General appearance. Physical appearance, looks like a man, way they look, Marlboro commercial.
  Movements and speech. Speech, talk, gruff, deep voice, way he shakes hands, way they carry
    themselves.
  Physical characteristics. Tall, well-built, muscular, broad shoulders, strong, handsome, athletic,
    large frame, not short or obese, always in shape, healthy, plumbing.
Personality Characteristics
  Expressive. Men: sympathetic, understanding, sensitivity towards female needs, gentle. Women:
    sentimental, sheds tears, warmth, compassion, can be upset, not afraid to show emotion,
    considerate, unselfish.
  Nonexpressive. Men: not emotional, doesn't show weakness.
  Instrumental. Men: strong leadership capacity, successful, able to take care of self without depend-
    ing on others, assertive, self-assured, makes decisions, action-oriented, take charge, in control,
    strong ego, authority. Women: firm but gentle, inner strength, mentally strong, ability to make
    decisions (handle situations), sure of self, takes responsibility, knows what he wants of life,
    stubborn.
  Miscellaneous. Predictable, honest with self and others, gives guidance in right direction, keeps
    his word, being an adult, polite and well-mannered.
Cognitive. Intellectual ability, intelligence.
Roles and Social Behavior
  Roles in family. Men: ability to provide (take responsibility for) family, primary wage earner,
    looks out for women and children, give children direction, kind to his woman, stabilize his
    family. Women: plays with his children, good father, sense of responsibility to his family.
  Social behavior. A man: keeps women under his thumb. Women: opens doors, knows how to treat
    a woman.
  Interests. Hunting, fishing, likes (good at) athletics (sports), outdoor activities, watch football,
    likes politics (philosophy, business), has beer with the boys.
Lack of Feminine Characteristics. Not feminine in appearance (speech and gestures, interests), not
    effeminate, not gay.
Denial of Stereotype. Nothing to do with being muscular (looks), stereotype about traits are wrong.
    Women: Doesn't worry about being feminine, doesn't have to prove he's masculine, doesn't
    have to compete, not overbearing.
Vague. As complete a person as possible, a role you have to play, there's an aura, knows he's a man.

---

categories: 26% mentioned family responsibilities, 24% masculine interests (as in women, usually in response to a probe) and 17% the absence of homosexuality or effeminate characteristics. One third of the men denied that being big and muscular was necessary to masculinity.

In follow-up questions about what they liked most and least about masculine men, a quarter of the women were unable to specify what they liked most. Twenty-nine percent referred to men's physical characteristics. An equal percentage described men's instrumental traits—their sureness in themselves and capacity to handle situations. Relatedly, 19% described feeling protected and

TABLE 2.4
Masculinity in Men:
Percentage of First Responses in Each Category
and Percentage of Individuals Utilizing Each Category
in Later Responses

Category	Men		Women	
	First R	Later Rs	First R	Later Rs
Physical Attributes	28.6	59.5	36.6	68.3
Personality				
Expressive	0.0	4.8	2.4	4.8
Nonexpressive	0.0	4.8	0.0	4.8
Instrumental	23.8	40.5	4.8	46.3
Miscellaneous	14.3	26.2	7.3	14.6
Cognitive	0.0	2.4	0.0	0.0
Family roles	4.8	20.2	0.0	4.8
Social behavior	4.8	9.5	0.0	0.0
Interests	2.4	23.8	2.4	34.1
Sex	2.4	4.8	0.0	4.9
Non-feminine	0.0	16.7	0.0	24.4
Denial of stereotype	7.1	33.3	12.2	24.4
Vague	2.4	2.4	2.4	2.4
Don't know/questions	9.5	—	29.3	—

having someone who can take charge and on whom they can be dependent. Fifteen percent described real masculinity in a man as self-confidence in his manhood without having to prove it or expressing concern about it, and 7% as a man's ability to express his emotions and concern with others without fear of being thought effeminate.

A greater proportion of the women had something to say about what they disliked in masculine men than what they liked, only 12% saying they didn't know or denying that masculine men had any undesirable characteristics. Thirty-five percent nominated the macho, super-masculine male (using these terms) and the man who considered himself God's gift to women. Fifty-six percent described what have been labeled undesirable agentic characteristics (Spence, Helmreich, & Holahan, 1979): overbearing, domineering, egotistical, conceited, stubborn, obnoxious, and so forth; 12% of the women (all of whom were married to Instrumental men) specifically complained about lack of expressive, communal qualities: cold, cruel, few feelings, or an inability to express emotion. Twenty-two percent objected to men's treatment of women: belittling them, inability to see women as persons, or treating them as lacking in sense. Ten percent disliked men's assumption of the freedom to do what they wanted while restricting women's alternatives and choices.

Only one man, when asked what he liked most about masculine men, said that he didn't know. Twenty-six percent described physical qualities: healthy, physically fit, athletically inclined. An even higher proportion (31%) nominated such instrumental qualities and roles as knowing how to handle situations, being a problem solver, determination, or being in charge, and one third nominated such characteristics as maturity, honesty, and personal integrity.

Reflecting the same gender chauvinism exhibited by women in their reactions to femininity in women, men were less often able to describe what they disliked in masculine men than what they liked: 19% said they didn't know what they disliked and 10% claimed that there was nothing they disliked. As in women, the characteristics that were mentioned most often referred to undesirable, agentic qualities (33% mentioned such attributes as overbearing, self-centered, all-knowing, and overly aggressive) or to the macho image (31%): men who had to prove their masculinity, were male chauvinists, pushed women around, and thought of themselves as God's gift to women. Ten percent disliked masculine men's inability to express tender emotions or their lack of concern for others (which is implicit, however, in negative agentic qualities).

Men's Self-images of Masculinity.   Table 2.5 lists the categories used to code men's responses to the questions about their own masculinity and Table 2.6 summarizes the outcome. A comparison of Table 2.6 with Table 2.4 indicates that descriptions of masculinity in other men vs. the self varied in several significant respects. Looking at first responses, 24% of the men were unable to respond without prompting (vs. 10% in describing others' masculinity) and 10% responded by simply asserting they were masculine or were self-confident about their masculinity. Whereas references to physical attributes were most frequent and references to family/provider roles were made by few in describing other men, this imbalance was reversed in self-description: only 5% referred to a physical characteristic in themselves, whereas 26% mentioned their role as the family leader and provider, and an additional 5% their status as a parent. Successful job performance, almost never mentioned in descriptions of others, was nominated by 7%. Thus, 38% located their sense of masculinity in their family or vocational roles. Instrumental traits or roles were important to 12%, half the proportion who first listed such qualities in describing men in general. However, in their later responses, more men (24%) described instrumental qualities and roles, but family and parental roles were also high (26% and 19%), as was job performance (17%). Except as family responsibilities implied kindness toward women and children, none of the men mentioned an expressive characteristic.

Two follow-up questions inquired about what they liked most and least about being men (as opposed to being masculine). Only two men (5%) could think of nothing to say and an equal number said "everything." In those giving concrete answers, the qualities popularly suggested as most liked paralleled those that the men had listed as defining their personal sense of masculinity. Thus, 38% nomi-

TABLE 2.5
Categories of Men's Responses to Questions about Self-images of Masculinity

Instrumental Characteristics and Roles. Ability to get point across, proud, strong-willed, convince people I'm right, control my own life, being a leader, problem-solver, assertive, making decisions, rugged individual, my authority, I'm the boss, take charge, am independent, don't let myself be pushed around.

Job Performance. Being successful, how I work, my profession (job, career), good in business, being a good salesman, compete in business, excell in what I do.

Household-provider Roles. Provide (care, support, responsible) for family, head of household, good husband image, wife doesn't have to work, won't do my wife's work in the house, family leader, enforce discipline at home, looked up to at home.

Parenting. Having (raising, spending time with) children, being a good father, want sons to accept me as a leader, tender and understanding with children.

Physical Characteristics. Doing physical things, size, shave every day, wouldn't want to be a little fellow, looks, I have an X and Y chromosome.

Sex. Sexually a man, sex needs, male role in sex.

Interests. Athletic, interested in sports, keeping physically fit, sportsman, building things, working with hands.

Statement about Masculinity. I consider myself masculine, am as much a man as anybody, am confident about myself as a man, never had a problem with masculinity.

Denial of Stereotype. I don't fit the stereotype, try not to distinguish between masculine and feminine roles with my kids, try not to be domineering. Masculinity is unrelated to: going to work, being muscular, being a lady killer, sports, masculine or feminine interests, household duties, my car.

Miscellaneous. Honest, sincere, open-minded, fair, live up to my word, responsible person, real person, good communicator and diplomat.

TABLE 2.6
Men's and Women's Self-images: Percentage of First Responses in Each Category and Percentage of Individuals Utilizing Each Category in Later Responses

Category	Men		Category	Women	
	First R	Later Rs		First R	Later Rs
Instrumental	11.9	23.8	Instrumental	0.0	17.0
Job Performance	7.4	16.7	Emot. Depend.	4.8	17.0
Provider role	26.2	26.2	Expressive	0.0	19.5
Parenting	4.8	19.0	Wife/Mother	46.3	19.5
Physical Char.	4.8	14.3	Dress & Appear.	7.3	19.5
Sex	4.8	11.9	Sex	2.4	0.0
Interests	2.4	11.9	Interests	0.0	2.4
Masc. Statement	9.5	7.4	Fem. Statement	7.3	9.7
Denial of stereotype	0.0	16.7	Denial of stereotype	0.0	14.6
Misc.	4.8	21.4	Self-acceptance	0.0	7.3
Don't know/question	23.8	—	Non-femininity	7.3	7.3
			Misc.	2.4	4.2
			Don't know/question	22.0	—

nated their role as family provider and leader, and an additional 10% the plea-sures of being a parent. Thirty-one percent mentioned job-related factors—their ability to pursue a career and their greater opportunity and freedom, in com-parison to women, to accomplish something; an additional 14% described their pleasure at being the leader or boss at work. Other responses—each suggested by about 10% of the men—were sex, stereotypically masculine activities such as hunting, fishing, and contact sports, and not having to do what women do, such as housework or having babies.

Twenty-three percent of the men said they didn't know what they disliked most about being a man or that there was nothing they disliked. Aside from a scattering of men who described such irritations as shaving every day or doing menial household chores such as taking out the garbage, 36% of the men men-tioned the burdens of their work—the 9 to 5 grind, having to shoulder so much responsibility, the pressures to be successful, and the feeling they had to work for their entire lives. Twenty-three percent complained of the responsibility of being the family breadwinner and feeling limited or trapped by their family obligations. The men who described the negative features of having demanding work and family responsibilities were sometimes the same men who nominated these roles as being the most liked aspects of being a man. Of special interest was the response of one man, classified as Expressive in personality, who indicated that what he liked least was being deprived of the experience of having a baby.

Women's Self-images of Femininity.   Data obtained from women are re-ported in Tables 2.6 and 2.7. As in the case of men, a higher percentage of

TABLE 2.7
Categories of Women's Responses to Questions
about Self-images of Femininity

Emotional Dependency. Need (want) someone to love (lean on, take care of me, protect me, shoulder to cry on), don't want to make all the decisions (have all the responsibility).

Expressive Characteristics and Roles. Selfless spirit, give myself to my family, need (want) to nurture (please, make people happy, be helpful).

Wife/Mother Roles. Being a mother (wife), taking care of the housework, fulfilling my duties as wife and mother, home oriented, not the breadwinner.

Interests. Cooking, sewing, needlework, poetry, taking care of flowers.

Self-acceptance. I like me, feel good about myself, like myself as I am.

Sex. Sexuality.

Dress and Physical Appearance. Look feminine, dress to please husband, dressing the part, like to look nice, fix my hair, make-up, perfume, keep trim, not let myself go to pot.

Statements about Femininity. I feel (am) feminine, enjoy being a woman, wouldn't want to be a man, I'm a woman and always have been.

Instrumentality. Could take care of myself if I had to; can stand up for myself, try to be (value) independent, don't like being dependent on my husband.

---

women initially said they didn't know when asked about their own femininity, as opposed to that of women in general (22% vs. 5%); 17% merely described themselves as being a woman or as being feminine. Also parallel to men, the plurality (46%) described their role as wife and mother as the basis of their sense of femininity. In subsequent responses, 20% specified expressive characteristics and roles and an equal percentage their emotional dependency—their need to be loved and protected and to have someone to assume responsibilities. At the same time, 17% valued their independence and capacity to take care of themselves if need be (a sense of personhood, it would appear, rather than femininity per se). A substantial number (20%) referred to keeping themselves slim or dressing up as important to their sense of femininity. One additional category is notable. Some 7% of the women (all high in instrumentality) described characteristics in themselves that they identified as nonfeminine (rather than as nonstereotypic, but irrelevant to femininity): independent, pushy and aggressive, etc. However, 15% explicitly rejected some aspect of the female stereotype as relevant to their sense of femininity.

Asked what they liked most about being a woman, one woman said nothing, 3 said everything, and 7 (17%) said that they didn't know. Thirty-two percent elected their status as wife and mother, and an equal percentage cited their relationship with men: being protected and pampered by them and not having to be the leader or boss. Correlatively, 24% described freedom from career pressures and responsibilities and a life-time of work; 12% described women as having fewer role demands and more freedom or options than men to do what they enjoyed. Ten percent liked being able to dress up and feel feminine, and 7% liked sex.

On the negative side of being a woman, 7% said there was nothing they disliked; 5% said that they didn't know. Twenty-two percent complained about routine housework, which their husbands expected them to do simply because they were women, and 15% mentioned reproductive functions: pregnancy, having babies, and menstruation. Twenty-seven percent were unhappy about job conditions: low pay, slow advancement, or lack of vocational direction; 22% complained of being looked down on by men as less competent or important, or as being expected to cater to men's egos; 12% saw themselves as having fewer options or less control over their lives than men.

Overall, conventional masculine roles and conventional feminine roles were perceived as having costs as well as rewards, with the two sets of roles tending to be mirror images with respect to these outcomes. Men enjoy their positions of leadership and authority in their vocational and family lives but simultaneously find that being tied to these roles and the pressures of their responsibilities are burdensome. Women rejoice in being free from such stresses and in having someone to lean on emotionally, but they also resent the loss of status that often accompanies subordinate roles and more mundanely, being stuck with routine household drudgery.

Additional Analyses.   A count was made for each individual of the number of substantive categories employed in his or her total responses to the three major questions. Analyses of these data revealed that in both sexes, fewer categories were employed in self-descriptions than in descriptions of others' masculinity and femininity (for men, a mean of 2.7 for self vs. 3.4 for others, and for women, means of 2.4 and 3.5). Additionally, individuals of both sexes who were low in both Expressiveness and Instrumentality utilized fewer categories than individuals in the other three categorical groups, means of 2.8 vs. 3.2 for men and of 2.7 vs. 3.4 for women.

Other Questions.   An additional question asked the men and women to rate their own masculinity or femininity on a scale of 1–10. Except for one man and one women who stated they thought of themselves only as people and gave 0 as their response, everyone gave numbers in the upper half of the scale, an outcome congruent with other studies (e.g., Pedhazur & Tetenbaum, 1979). An inspection of the interview data and participants' PAQ scores did not reveal any promising leads to the variability within each gender.

Several questions were aimed at instrumental and expressive qualities and behaviors, which were prefaced by a statement describing these characteristics and the common belief that they differentiate the genders. One question asked whether the individual ever had a problem reconciling these two aspects of his or herself. The women uniformly denied that they did, although two (both high in instrumentality) indicated that they had encountered trouble when acting assertively and speaking their minds in (mixed-sex) situations in which they were expected to keep quiet and act submissive. This question, however, elicited more informative responses from the men. Most of the men spontaneously mentioned that when their jobs called upon them to make decisions that hurt others, they went ahead with the decision but attempted to implement it in a sympathetic, compassionate fashion. However, 63% of the men said these job decisions caused them discomfort. This statement was made by 87% of the men scoring high in expressiveness, as opposed to 30% of the low scoring men. Conflict was especially intense in the men classified as Expressive, who felt they had to be assertive in their jobs (but were often not as forceful as they wished), yet felt guilty about making harsh decisions or (in the case of two salesmen) in persuading people to do things that were not necessarily in their best interests.

TOWARD A RECONCEPTUALIZATION:
THE SIGNIFICANCE OF GENDER IDENTITY

Although we had predicted variability within each gender in their conceptions of masculinity or femininity for themselves and others, we had also expected that, for any given individual, the interviews would yield clues to fairly stable, well-

organized belief systems or gender schemas. However, our reading of the protocols, combined with the mounting evidence that, at the level of the individual,
gender-related phenomena show little tendency to cluster together, has led us to a
more radical conceptualization of the concepts of masculinity and femininity.
Before outlining these hypotheses, we will review some of the features of the
interview data that were influential in leading us to them.

In other parts of the interview devoted to such topics as husband–wife role
relations, personal goals and aspirations, and child-rearing, this group of mature,
middle-class men and women were often articulate and perceptive in their comments. A reading of their responses to questions about their conceptions of
masculinity and femininity yielded a very different impression, even more stark
than the summary data we have presented. Although no attempt was made here
to report such responses beyond the individuals' initial replies to a new topic, the
protocols were shot through with "don't know," "don't understand," "never
thought it," "please repeat the question," and "I can't think of anything"; with
demands that the interviewer specify what masculinity or femininity meant so
that these individual would know how to respond; and with complaints—which
sometimes verged on the resentful—about how difficult or peculiar the questions
were. Substantive responses tended to be brief, impoverished, and exquisitely
banal. Direct probes into categories of gender-related attributes not mentioned
spontaneously often elicited no new information; the respondents said they could
think of nothing or simply repeated what they had said earlier, as though it were
responsive to the probe when in fact it was not. These men and women were
obviously aware of gender stereotypes and often endorsed their reality in the
sense of acknowledging the existence of gender differences. Yet even here, a
number of individuals explicitly denied that these characteristics were related to
masculinity and femininity. In mentioning these qualities, it was as though they
were running through a checklist of gender differences, eliminating those that
were irrelevant ("a woman can like to go hunting and still be feminine," "my
husband isn't big and muscular but he's very masculine"); they could specify
what masculinity and femininity are not but had problems specifying what they
are. In describing others, both men and women tended to focus on the most
conspicuous differences between men and women—their physical characteristics
and appearance. In describing themselves, what became most salient for many
was their current roles and the characteristics they perceived to be demanded by
those roles. Although the respondents appeared to make a sincere effort to
answer the questions, it seemed that they often lost track of masculinity and
femininity, describing instead the kinds of characteristics they liked in men or
women (or both) or valued in themselves. In contrast, the respondents had no
problems rating their own masculinity or femininity numerically, all of the
individuals (except for the two who rejected the whole notion) assigning themselves numbers in the upper half of the scale. However, no relationship could be
discerned between these ratings and their self-descriptions, e.g., individuals who

described their lack of a number of stereotyped characteristics rated themselves as high as those who admitted to them. And finally, despite the pivotal role assigned to instrumental and expressive characteristics in many psychological theories of masculinity, femininity, and gender-role identification, few differences were found among either men or women assigned to the four PAQ categories, and those that were found were directly related to these personality characteristics, per se.

Ironically, these same men and women, who had such difficulty in specifying what constituted masculinity and femininity, quite often used these terms spontaneously later in the interview when describing a family member. What particular characteristics or behaviors they were indicating by use of these descriptors could seldom be discerned because they were not used to qualify particular behaviors or attributes. (Popular articles and essays in which "masculine" and "feminine" appear can be similarly characterized.) It would seem that, as with good art, people can not say what femininity or masculinity is, but they know it when they see it.

It could be argued that, however well-educated, the layperson could not be expected to be articulate about such abstractions as masculinity and femininity without having given them a great deal of thought. One might expect better from psychologists, who are not only trained to define their theoretical terms but typically offer such definitions as a matter of routine. However, an examination of articles and textbooks, including books on the psychology of women, is of little help. Like Sherlock Holmes' dog who didn't bark, what is remarkable here is the absence of definitions.

The enigma of masculinity and femininity deepens when one considers the empirical data and psychologists' reactions to them. Except for a lonely few, investigators have ignored evidence disconfirming theories presupposing that the diverse categories of attributes and behaviors normatively expected of men and women can be subsumed under a single superordinate dimension or even a pair of dimensions, and that subsets of these attributes are reliable indicators of individuals' self-images of masculinity and femininity. Psychologists are ordinarily highly respectful of data and tend to reach their theoretical statements inductively. Yet in this instance, we seem to have been caught up in an overpowering mindset that has made us almost hysterically blind to the evidence and has caused us to cling to our hypothetical constructs as if they were revealed truths, invulnerable to empirical disconfirmation. This uncharacteristic behavior adds to the mystery.

It cannot be denied that masculinity and femininity are meaningful concepts to ordinary men and women (and not merely to psychologists) and that gender and gender-related expectations shape in profound ways the lives of individuals and the structure of the society of which they are members. We are thus faced with a puzzle: masculinity and femininity are everywhere, yet they are nowhere in particular.

A Way Out

We propose a bit of radical surgery—that the class of monolithic concepts that include masculinity–femininity, gender-role identity, gender schema, and the like, as they have traditionally been formulated, be excised and discarded. In their place, we substitute the concept of *gender identity,* a more primitive notion that, following Green (1974), we define as a basic, existential conviction that one is male or female.

The gender identity concept has been employed by Green (1974), Stoller (1968), Money (1968), and others in their work with individuals experiencing severe problems with this aspect of their self-concept. The American Psychiatric Association's *Diagnostic and Statistic Manual III* also formally recognizes disturbances of gender identity, listing two major disorders: transsexualism and disorders of childhood. Transsexuals are individuals who express the belief— whose origins they typically trace back to early childhood—that they are psychically "normal" individuals of one sex who have the misfortune to have the body of the other sex. Children exhibiting disturbances of gender identity are boys and girls who express the literal desire to be a member of the other sex or insist that they have or will grow up to have the anatomical characteristics of the other sex, and simultaneously manifest a strong proclivity toward cross-sex behaviors in dress, physical mannerisms, play activities, and choice of sex of playmates. It is made explicit that these disorders are rare and do not merely reflect rejection of expected role-related behaviors, such as occurs in the girl who is a "tomboy," or the boy who is considered a "sissy" because he avoids sports or physically rough activities. Although some children who exhibit marked disturbances in their sense of maleness or femaleness grow up to be homosexuals, most homosexuals do not have a childhood history of gender identity problems and, unlike transsexuals, they are content with their biological sex.

The development of an adequate sense of gender identity is thus all but universal. Green (1974) and others further suggest that this psychological sense of maleness or femaleness is established early in life—by age 2 or 3—and as such, even precedes the age at which children have matured sufficiently to grasp the cognitive notion of gender constancy, i.e., the fact that biological sex is inborn and unchanging (e.g., Slaby & Fry, 1975).

The gender identity concept has been mentioned by only a few psychological theorists interested in normal development. In describing her feminist vision of society, Bem (1978), for example, advocated that gender-role identification (or more recently, gender schematization, Bem, 1981b) be abolished, with all that implies for behavior, and that a sexual preference for one's own or the other gender should be a matter of individual choice, but that men and women retain their sense of gender identity—a quiet pride in their bodies and their part in the reproductive process. She did not elaborate, however, beyond this simple statement. Spence and Helmreich (1978) specified that gender identification is one of the four critical domains into which gender-releated phenomena can be divided (the others being sexual orientation, sex-role attitudes and behaviors, and personality characteristics), and even though they noted the deficiencies of the concept of gender role identification, they failed to exploit the gender identity concept further.

Several reasons can be found to explain why this concept has been overlooked. Except for the unfortunate few, gender identity is nonproblematic and would therefore appear to be of value as an explanatory construct only to investigators whose interests are in the occasional developmental failure. The very vagueness of the gender identity construct—a "sense" without any concrete references—would also seem to invite its dismissal. But, in our view, herein lies its significance.

Gender is an important factor in the processing of information about the self and others, but according to our conception, it operates in a different fashion than proposed by other investigators. When they encounter another, men and women make a rapid, automatic assessment, using whatever data are available, whose aim is to assign the person to a gender category and to determine whether that person exhibits, in quantitative sense, an adequate number of gender-appropriate characteristics. This process is likely to reach the level of awareness only when judgments become problematic or when the person being assessed falls below a threshold of acceptability. The only information that is likely to be available in brief exposures to strangers is physical appearance: body build, hairstyle, dress, and stylistics mannerisms (speech and body movements). If the data are ambiguous, one is likely to strive consciously to determine whether the person is male or female, often to the point of taking a second look to determine fine details or of asking for information ("My, what a cute baby; is it a boy or a girl?"). In the case of adults, who are expected to exhibit visible signs identifying their gender, the very indefiniteness of the information is likely to throw one into a suspect position with respect to one's own masculinity or femininity or to evoke a sense of irritation. (The hue and cry that arose a decade ago against men with long hair or women in blue jeans and other "mannish" garb may have been based in part on discomfort at having the significance of previously reliable clues to people's sex diminish.)

Highly conspicuous characteristics are also likely to be prominent in abstract judgments about men and women in general i.e., the "masculine" man and the "feminine" woman. As more information about a particular individual becomes known, these new data are added into the equation for assessing masculinity/femininity. As implied above, we suspect that these calculations result in a rough sort, in which most individuals reach a threshold value, falling into an "acceptable" category, and a lesser number fall into "doubtful" or "unacceptable" categories.

Individuals differ, we suggest, in the particular diagnostic indicators, along with their weights and signs, that they enter into this calculus. Such factors as individuals' perceptiveness, their values and personal tastes, their liking (on other grounds) of the person being judged, the age or life circumstance of that person, and their implicit personality theories (what signals what) are likely to be influential. Situational factors that increase or decrease the saliency of gender also affect this appraisal.

Although there is ample room for variability between and within genders, some commonality doubtless exists, particularly among those with the same cultural standards. Physical characteristics and sexual orientation are probably given the heaviest weight by most (heterosexual) men and women, but even here the equation is not a simple one. A man whose physical appearance and mannerisms are effeminate, for example, is likely to be judged unmasculine, in part because these characteristics are often presumed to be associated with homosexuality; to the extent that such a man is known to be heterosexually active and vigorous, his effeminancy is likely to be discounted. Whether one refers to men and women in general or to particular individuals, people are unlikely to use a single equation to evaluate others. As a consequence, no specific diagnostic indicator, or set of indicators, is likely to be the sine qua non that confirms the presence of masculinity in men or of femininity in women. In fact, the absence of stereotypic characteristics associated with the other sex is likely in many instances to assume a near equal importance with the presence of gender-congruent characteristics.

Turning to self-assessments, most men and women, having achieved an adequate sense of gender identity, could be expected to judge themselves as masculine or as feminine. Although some variability could be expected when individuals are asked to rate themselves on a masculinity–femininity continuum, the distributions for each sex would as a consequence be highly skewed, with most men clustering at the masculine pole and most women at the feminine pole. Because masculinity–femininity (in its gender identity sense) is a bipolar continuum, separate self-ratings of masculinity and femininity should produce responses that are strongly correlated in a negative direction. The empirical data bear out these implications.

The characteristics of self that men and women use to confirm their sense of their own gender identity focus on those attributes and behaviors they manifest, value, or are called upon to possess at their particular stage of life development, and may often be quite different than those that they employ in assessing others, even those of the same sex and age. What counts is the outcome of the arithmetic, not the individual components. Based on the evidence—which includes the interview data reported here, as well as commonsense observation—it seems to us unlikely that the vast majority of adult men and women, having passed the gender test in their own eyes and the eyes of others, are concerned with their gender identity; they more or less take it for granted and are unable to specify, when asked, on what grounds their sense of maleness or femaleness rests. Complaints heard during the interviews that masculinity and femininity are matters they had never thought or concerned themselves about, and the profusion of "don't knows" now appear to us to have a firm basis in psychological reality. The equal inability of psychologists to define masculinity, femininity, and other similar terms, and to comprehend the significance of data relevant to their implicit theories also becomes understandable.

Seemingly superficial statements that occurred in the interviews take on new significance in the light of these hypotheses. For example, the statement by a number of women in our sample, who are ordinarily busy doing grubby housework and chasing after children, that they "feel feminine" when they dress themselves up and have men open doors for them or otherwise dance in attendance, says less about where they locate their sense of femininity than about the conditions under which their gender becomes salient.

This is not to say that once gender identity becomes established, one's masculinity or femininity never becomes problematic. Undoubtedly, there are stressful periods in some individuals' lives when they become preoccupied with or full of self-doubt about their masculinity or femininity, as in the case of men who are unable to support their families. Adolescents, concerned with their emerging sexuality and with establishing their autonomy, are particularly prone to such stresses, as are homosexuals. The latter may have particular difficulties in reconciling their sense of maleness or femaleness with their contradiction of what society at large considers a major (if not *the* major) consequence of appropriate gender identification.

Developmental psychologists have typically appealed to gender-role identification or other similar constructs to explain the initial acquisition of gender-related attributes and behaviors by children, as well as the continued acquisition of gender-appropriate attributes throughout the lifecycle. Although theorists differ in their detailed descriptions of the acquisition process, they are similar in implying that children indiscriminately tend to acquire all gender-related attributes by the same set of processes. This tendency is purportedly reinforced by parents and other standard-bearers who are assumed in their own behaviors and their expectations for their children to include the total package of gender-related phenomena. These assumptions imply that (beyond a certain age) at whatever developmental stage one taps into gender-related phenomena, all the behaviors and attributes expected at that stage occur together.

We disagree with these theoretical accounts on several grounds. It does seem likely that gender identification will motivate children quite directly to adopt some types of gender-appropriate characteristics. However, reasoning backwards, it is known that the various categories of gender-related attributes and gender-role attitudes are not strongly correlated at the level of the individual in older males and females. The child is therefore exposed to many models of males and females who, although they are all acceptably masculine or feminine in their aggregated characteristics, are quite diverse in their individual properties, values, and attitudes. Thus, the attributes that children acquire as a quite direct consequence of gender identification may be confined to those that are concrete, obvious, or made highly salient by their parents, older peers, and other standard bearers. For example, boys learn that wearing dresses and experimenting with their mother's make-up is inappropriate, and girls that they are expected not to engage in fist fights; both sexes appreciate at an early age the kinds of toys that they are expected to enjoy and those they are expected to avoid. On the other hand, other gender-differentiating variables, such as instrumental and expressive characteristics, are more subtle and less likely to be self-consciously sought after. The child, then, is exposed to multiple influences and may acquire—or fail to acquire—various gender-related behaviors through diverse and relatively independent routes.

Even though a child may turn out to resemble the stereotypic member of his or her own sex in many respects, the etiology of particular attributes may be quite independent of gender considerations. For example, the development of instrumental and expressive characteristics in both sexes appears to be influenced by parental child-rearing practices, such as degree of warmth and acceptance, that are quite independent of the parents' sex-role behaviors and expectations for their male or female offspring (e.g., Spence & Helmreich, 1978). (It is thus not surprising that at all age levels, gender differences in these trait domains are small in comparison to the variability within each gender.) As with the older individual, the child is rarely under any internal or external compulsion to search out and slavishly emulate some abstract model that incorporates all the cultural stereotypes of his or her own gender. From the perspective of both the child and the child's peers and caretakers, the child, like the adult, is allowed considerable latitude in his or her behaviors without eliciting censure from others and disturbing his or her own sense of gender identity.

CONCLUSIONS

The theory of gender identity, whose outlines we have sketched here, allows gender as a psychological construction to retain its paramount importance in human affairs and, at the same time, encompasses the evidence showing that gender-related phenomena are multidimensional and often independent of each other. The capacity to account for extant data is, of course, the prime requisite of any concept.

The permissiveness and elasticity of the concept, however, render our theoretical and empirical tasks more difficult rather than easier. The positive implications of the concept are less obvious and straightforward than those in gender-role identification theories and are likely to be realized more slowly. It is clear that gender identity is a less imperalistic concept than notions of gender-role identity. At the level of the individual, it leaves us with the challenge of identifying and devising methods to assess the variety of attitudes, preferences, cognitive schemas, values, and other personal qualities that differentiate the sexes and that contribute to gender-related behavior. Further, multiple theories will have to be developed to account for their etiology and their implications for other attributes and behaviors. Greater attention must also be paid to the contribution of situational factors and to their interactions with person variables. As Sherif (1982) has reminded us, gender roles belong to situations and the social structure; a person is not a role but instead occupies or plays out a role. Steps in all these directions are already being taken (see, e.g., Spence, Deaux & Helmreich, 1984). The renunciation of current theories of gender-role identification and the substitution of the gender identity concept in their stead should hasten these theoretical and empirical advances.

ACKNOWLEDGMENTS

Preparation of this chapter was supported in part by National Science Foundation Grant 3NS78-08911 and National Institute of Mental Health Grant 32066 to Janet T. Spence and Robert L. Helmreich, principal investigators. Thanks are due to Robert L. Helmreich for his reading of the manuscript.

REFERENCES

Bakan, D. (1966). *The duality of human existence*. Chicago: Rand McNally.

Baucom, D. (1976). Independent Masculinity and Femininity scales on the California Psychological Inventory. *Journal of Consulting and Clinical Psychology, 44* (5), 876.

Baumrind, D. (1967). Child care practices anteceding three patterns of preschool behavior. *Genetic Psychology Monographs, 75,* 43–88.

Bem, S. L. (1974). The measurement of psychological androgyny. *Journal of Consulting and Clinical Psychology. 42,* 155–162.

Bem, S. L. (1977). On the utility of alternate procedures for assessing psychological androgyny. *Journal of Consulting and Clinical Psychology, 45,* 196–205.

Bem, S. L. (1978). Beyond androgyny: Some presumptuous prescriptions for a liberated sexual identity. In J. A. Sherman & F. L. Denmark (Eds.), *The Psychology of women: Future directions in research*. New York: Psychological Dimensions.

Bem, S. L. (1981). The BSRI and gender schema: A reply to Spence and Helmreich. *Psychological Review, 88,* 369–371. (a)

Bem, S. L. (1981). Gender schema theory. A cognitive account of sex typing. *Psychological Review, 88,* 354–364. (b)

Bem, S. L. & Lenney, E. (1976). Sex-typing and the avoidance of cross-sex behavior. *Journal of Personality and Social Psychology, 33,* 48–54.

Berzins, J. I., Welling, M. A., & Wetter, R. E. (1978). A new measure of psychological androgyny based on the Personality Research Form. *Journal of Consulting and Clinical Psychology, 46,* 126–138.

Block, J. H. (1973). Conceptions of sex roles: Some cross-cultural and longitudinal perspectives. *American Psychologist. 28,* 512–527.

Coffman, R. N., & Levy, B. I. (1972). The dimensions implicit in psychological masculinity–femininity. *Educational and Psychological Measurement, 32,* 975–985.

Constantinople, A. (1973). Masculinity–femininity: An exception to the famous dictum? *Psychological Bulletin, 80,* 389–407.

Green, R. (1974). *Sexual identity conflict in children and adults.* New York: Basic Books.

Hefner, R., Rebecca, M. & Olefshansky, B. (1975). Development of sexual transcendence. *Human Development, 18,* 143–158.

Heilbrun, A. B., Jr. (1973). Parent identification and filial sex-role behavior: The importance of biological context. In J. K. Cole & R. Dienstbier (Eds.), *Nebraska Symposium on Motivation* (Vol. 21). Lincoln: University of Nebraska Press.

Heilbrun, A. B., Jr. (1976). Measurement of masculine and feminine sex-role identities as independent dimensions. *Journal of Consulting and Clinical Psychology, 44,* 183–190.

Helmreich, R. L., Spence, J. T., & Holahan, C. K. (1979). Psychological androgyny and sex-role flexibility: A test of two hypotheses. *Journal of Personality and Social Psychology, 37,* 1631–1644.

Helmreich, R. L., Spence, J. T., & Wilhelm, J. A. (1981). A psychometric analysis of the Personal Attributes Questionnaire. *Sex Roles, 7,* 1097–1108.

Helmreich, R. & Stapp, J. (1974). Short forms of the Texas Social Behavior Inventory (TSBI), an objective measure of self-esteem. *Bulletin of the Psychonomic Society, 4,* 473–475.

Kohlberg, L. A. (1966). Cognitive-developmental analysis of children's sex-role concepts and attitudes. In E. E. Maccoby (Ed.), *The development of sex differences.* Stanford: Stanford University Press.

Komarovsky, M. (1979). Dilemmas of masculinity in a changing world. In J. E. Gullahorn (Ed.), *Psychology and women: In transition.* V. H. Winston & Sons, Washington, D.C.

Markus, H. (1980). The self in thought and memory. In D. M. Wegner & R. R. Vallacher (Eds.), *The self in social psychology.* New York: Oxford University Press.

Mills, C. J., & Tyrrell, D. J. (1983). Sex-stereotypic encoding and release from proactive inhibition. *Journal of Personality and Social Psychology, 45,* 772–781.

Money, J. (1968). *Sex errors of the body.* Baltimore: The Johns Hopkins Press.

Orlofsky, J. L. (1981). Relationship between sex role attitudes and personality traits and the Sex Role Behavior Scale-1: A new measure of masculine and feminine role behaviors and interests. *Journal of Personality and Social Psychology, 40,* 927–940.

Orlofsky, J., Aslin, A. L., & Ginsburg, S. D. (1977). Differential effectiveness of two classification procedures on *The Bem Sex Role Inventory. Journal of Personality Assessment, 41,* 414–416.

Pedhazur, E. J. & Tetenbaum, T. J. (1979). Bem Sex Role Inventory: A theoretical and methodological critique. *Journal of Personality and Social Psychology, 37,* 996–1016.

Slaby, R. G. & Frey, K. S. (1975). Development of gender constancy and selective attention to same-sex models. *Child Development, 47,* 849–856.

Sherif, C. (1982). Needed concepts in the study of gender identity. *Psychology of Women Quarterly, 6,* 375–398.

Spence, J. T. (1984). Masculinity, femininity and gender-related traits: A conceptual analysis and critique of current research. In B. A. Maher & W. B. Maher (Eds.), *Progress in experimental research* (Volume 13). New York: Academic Press.

Spence, J. T., Deaux, K., & Helmreich, R. L. (in press). Sex Roles in Contemporary American Society. In G. Lindzey & E. Aronson (Eds.), *Handbook of social psychology,* Third Edition. Reading, Mass.: Addison-Wesley.

Spence, J. T. & Helmreich, R. L. (1978). *Maculinity and femininity: Their psychological dimensions, correlates, and antecedents.* Austin: University of Texas Press.

Spence, J. T. & Helmreich, R. L. (1981). Androgyny vs. gender: A comment on Bem's gender schema theory. *Psychological Review, 88,* 365–368.

Spence, J. T., Helmreich, R. L., & Holahan, C. K. (1979). Negative and positive components of psychological masculinity and femininity and their relationships to self-reports of neurotic and acting out behaviors. *Journal of Personality and Social Psychology, 37,* 1673–1682.

Spence, J. T., Helmreich, R. L., & Sawin, L. L. (1980). The Male–Female Relations Questionnaire: A self-report inventory of sex-role behaviors and preferences and its relationships to masculine and feminine personality traits, sex role attitudes, and other measures. *JSAS Selected Documents in Psychology, 10,* 87, MS 2123.

Spence, J. T., Helmreich, R., & Stapp, J. (1974). The Personal Attributes Questionnaire: A measure of sex-role stereotypes and masculinity–femininity. JSAS *Catalog of Selected Documents in Psychology, 4,* 43–44, MS 617.

Spence, J. T., Helmreich, R., & Stapp, J. (1975). Likability, sex-role congruence of interests, and competence: It all depends on how you ask. *Journal of Applied Social Psychology, 5,* 93–109.

Stoller, R. (1968). *Sex and gender: On the development of masculinity and femininity.* New York: Science House.

Storms, M. (1980). Theories of sex-role identity. *Journal of Personality and Social Psychology, 38,* 783–792.

Wakefield, J. A., Jr., Sasek, J., Friedman, A. F., & Bowden, J. D. (1976). Androgyny and other measures of masculinity–femininity. *Journal of Consulting and Clinical Psychology, 44,* 766–770.

3 Sex-Determined Attributions

Ranald D. Hansen
Oakland University

Virginia E. O'Leary
American Psychological Association

The existence of sex biases favoring men have been amply documented across both centuries and cultures (cf. Broverman, Vogel, Broverman, Clarkson, & Rosenkrantz, 1982; Fernberger, 1948; McKee & Sherrifs, 1959; Rosaldo & Lamphere, 1974; Steinman & Fox, 1966). More importantly, the existence of sex biases have been found to affect differentially the outcomes received by women and men in a variety of laboratory settings (cf. Deaux & Emswiller, 1974; Feldman-Summers & Kiesler, 1974; Heilman & Guzzo, 1978; Kahn, O'Leary, Lamm, & Krulewitz, 1980; Rosen & Jerdee, 1974a,b; Unger, 1979), in the economic marketplace (cf. Brown, 1979; Kanter, 1977; O'Leary, 1974; Terborg, 1977), and in clinical practice (Abramowitz & Dokecki, 1977).

As Unger (1979) has observed, the results obtained in a number of studies using no stimulus materials other than "female" and "male" or "Anne" and "John" indicate that sex plays an important role in determining the criteria for mental health (Broverman, Broverman, Clarkson, Rosenkrantz, & Vogel, 1970), the evaluation of the artistic merit of paintings (Pheterson, Kiesler & Goldberg, 1971), and of the qualifications of student applicants for a foreign study program. Empirical evidence published during the last decade clearly suggests that the behavioral similarities between women and men are substantially greater than the differences (cf. Deaux, 1976; Eagly, 1978; Maccoby & Jacklin, 1974; O'Leary, 1977; Unger, 1979). Yet the belief in sex differences persists and is evidenced by the predilection of perceivers (both men and women) to attribute differentially traits, behavioral characteristics, and even causes for identical performances as a function of the sex of the performer (Wallston & O'Leary, 1981).

No domain has been studied as extensively for evidence indicating perceived rather than actual sex differences than performance and achievement evaluation. The evidence is abundant and, with a few exceptions we will note, argues for a pervasive devaluation of women's performance relative to men's performance (Nieva & Gutek, 1980). The documentation of the impact of sex on the evaluation of performance in organizational settings has been of great interest. Dipboye and colleagues (Dipboye, Arvey, & Terpstra, 1977; Dipboye, Fromkin, & Wiback, 1975) have shown a clear male advantage over women in hiring practices, and in the initial salaries of employees. Women were rated lower than men in spite of the fact that the employees' records were identical. Many studies show a bias toward hiring men over equally qualified women in many different domains (Fidell, 1970; Gutek & Stevens, 1979; Haefner, 1977; Rosen & Jerdee, 1974a,b, & c; Rosen, Jerdee & Prestwich, 1975). In one exception to this trend, Terborg and Ilgen (1975), found that a woman was no less likely than a man to be hired. But, they also reported that the woman was assigned a substantially lower salary. Although this study perhaps should not be classified as an exception to the undervaluing of women's performance, clear exceptions do exist.

Some researchers have reported a reversal of the devaluation trend (Abramson, Goldberg, Greenberg & Abramson, 1977; Jacobson & Effertz, 1974): Women were advantaged over similarly performing men. Abramson et al. have labelled this the "talking platypus phenomenon," suggesting that the women's advantage derived from the surprise value of their success. This, a context effect, implies that women's high performance against a context of expected low performance may, on occasion, lead to the higher valuation of women's performance. Other researchers have reported finding no sex differences (cf. Hall & Hall, 1977). With these exceptions, however, there is a clear trend: Women are disadvantaged in the evaluation of their performance and achievement. We seek here to explore one line of thought suggesting an explanation for when and how sex mediates evaluation.

SEX-DETERMINED ATTRIBUTIONS

Attribution theorists contend that perceivers understand behavior in terms of its cause (Heider, 1958; Jones & Davis, 1965; Jones & McGillis, 1976; Kelley, 1967, 1971a,b; Weiner, 1979; Weiner, Freize, Kukla, Reed, Rest, & Rosenbaum, 1971). Logically, then, the social and psychological consequences of behavior should be mediated by the perceived causes for that behavior. The same behavior attributed to different causes may be perceived quite differently and result in quite different evaluations by the perceiver (cf. Heilman & Guzzo, 1978). If sex determines attributions, sex would also influence the consequences of behavior. Ample evidence can be found indicating that sex does influence perceivers' causal explanation for behavior, particularly achievement–performance behaviors. But, before becoming too enthusiastic about the potential of sex determined attributions for explaining the devaluation of women's performance, we should note that some research is discouraging. A number of studies appear to question the potency of attributionally mediated sex differences in evaluation (Chaikin, 1971; Frieze, Whitley, Hanusa, & McHugh, 1982; Lefcourt, Hogg, Struthers, & Holmes, 1975; Zuckerman, 1979). However, accepting the null hypothesis with regard to the impact of sex on attributions does not seem warranted in the face of some meta-analytic evidence that methodological factors may account for some of these failures to obtain effects (cf. Whitley & Frieze, 1981). These experiments do highlight the need for more precise specification of domains within which sex-determined attributions can be expected and the nature of the attributional inferences on which sex bears more heavily.

Common Sense Explanations

Most research has focused on everyday or common sense explanations of performance. This tradition (Heider, 1983/1958) has led to intensive inquiries into perceivers' use of four common explanations for achievement performance behavior: ability, effort, task difficulty, and luck. These four causes were identified by Heider and later by Weiner (Weiner et al., 1971) as often invoked by perceivers to explain their own and others' performance. They have become central to the discovery of the dramatic impact of sex on attributions. It is not surprising, given the general finding that women are judged less competent than equally performing men (Deaux, 1972; Dipboye et al., 1977; Dipboye et al., 1975; Linsenmeier & Wortman, 1979; Wallston & O'Leary, 1981; Zickmund, Hitt, & Pickens, 1978), that perceivers' use of ability to explain performance has been of greatest interest. Two points must be made about the evolving theoretical sense of perceivers' attributions to these four causal factors. First, sex-determined attributions to these factors have often been shown as interacting with situational and sex-role determined variables. Second, the four causes are not psychologically independent within the common sense understanding of cause. The second point becomes important when interpreting the first. We will deal with each in turn as we look at the evidence indicating that sex influences causal attributions for performance.

A few researchers have reported that women attribute their own achievement performance to different factors than do men. Bar-Tal and Frieze (1976, 1977), Feather (1969), and Simon and Feather (1973) found that women attribute their performance more to task difficulty levels (easy task upon success) and luck (good luck upon success) than do men. But these are the exceptional studies. More often, the different attributions of women and men are qualified by other variables. The pattern of attributions made by women and men is influenced by the level of performance achieved.

Performance Variables.   Men attribute their success to their (high) ability and their (great) effort. They attribute their failure to the (difficult) task and (bad) luck. Although women tend to show this same attributional pattern, it is much less pronounced (Feather & Simon, 1975; Levine, Reis, Sue, & Turner, 1976; Nicholls, 1975). This phenomenon is further qualified by the nature of the task on which the person is acting, but research has established a general tendency to make different attributions for women's and men's performance. Of particular interest is the finding that women's performance is attributed to ability much less than men's. That is, women's high performance, unlike men's, is not seen as diagnostic of high ability. This pattern is further complicated by the sex-typing of the task on which performance is measured. Masculine tasks render a different pattern of sex-determined attributions than do feminine tasks.

Role-Defined Task Variables.   Deaux and her colleagues (Deaux & Emswiller, 1974; Deaux & Farris, 1977; Deaux & Taynor, 1973; Taynor & Deaux, 1975) have amply documented the impact of task sex-typing on attributions. When a woman was perceived as performing as well as a man on a masculine task, her high level of performance was attributed to luck. The man's high level of achievement was attributed to ability. Cash, Gillen, and Burns (1977) reported similar findings in their research. Here, however, effect of performance in feminine tasks on attributions was strikingly different. The anticipated reciprocal pattern—women's ability accounting for their success and men's luck for theirs—was not found. Women's high performance on a feminine task did not garner inferences of their higher ability over equally performing men. Rather, it seemed that a woman's performance was attributed to luck regardless of the sex-typing of the task (Deaux & Farris, 1977). This research can be summarized as follows: An inference of a man's high ability derived from his high performance level is augmented by his achievement on masculine tasks. A woman's high performance on either feminine or masculine tasks is not seen as diagnostic of her high ability. We hesitate to argue that a woman's high performance augments an inference of her good fortune. A number of researchers have found that a woman's high performance is seen as indicating high levels of effort (Etaugh & Brown, 1975; Feldman-Summers & Keisler, 1974; Taynor & Deaux, 1975). Yet other researchers have reported that a woman's high performance was seen as attributable to task ease (Feather & Simon, 1975; Rosenfield & Stephan, 1978). In each of these experiments, a man's high performance led to inferences of his high ability but a woman's did not. A woman's high performance was attributed to anything but high ability. Although these findings describe sex-determined attributions, their explication requires an understanding of how these causal factors relate to one another within perceivers' common sense theories of behavior.

The Meaning of Common Sense Explanations

Attribution theory clearly specifies the logic underlying these common sense explanations and allows us to offer some meaning to the pattern of sex-determined attributions described above. Ability is perceived as compensatory to effort with regard to performance outcome (Heider, 1958; Kelley, 1971a,b; O'Leary & Hansen, 1983a,b). Both ability and effort are seen as facilitating high performance (Anderson & Butzin, 1974; O'Leary & Hansen, 1983a,b). Research has shown that an increase in one or the other or both results in estimates that performance level will increase. The common sense corollary to this multiple compensatory principle has been termed "compensatory cause" (Kelley, 1971b). If performance level is held constant and one of the facilitative factors is known to increase, the other is perceived as decreasing. Thus, if two people achieve the same level of performance, the person who exerts more effort to achieve that level will be judged as having less ability. The compensatory relationship of ability to effort has been demonstrated by a number of experimenters (cf. Anderson & Butzin, 1974; Hansen & Hall, 1983; O'Leary & Hansen, 1983a,b). The results reported by O'Leary and Hansen indicate that the positive acceleration of perceived ability induced by increasing performance level exceeds that induced by decreasing effort level while holding performance constant. Thus, we contend that ability inferences are *anchored* on performance level and inversely *adjusted* for effort. To put this in different terms, the *information value* of performance level is greater than that of effort level for inferences of the performer's ability level. We speculate that this might be the case because the relationship of ability to effort is negative (often termed augmentation in attribution theory), whereas the relationship of ability to performance is positive (often termed covariation in attribution theory). Ample evidence is available to assert that perceivers overlook the important information value of negative instances (cf. Nisbett & Ross, 1980).

The same type of logical relationship holds between the facilitative forces of ability and effort within the task difficulty level. As originally noted by Heider (1958) performance, and hence ability, is defined within common sense understanding in terms of the difficulty of the task. The task represents the context within which performance becomes meaningful. Ability is defined with reference to the task. As such, task ease discounts high performance as diagnostic of high effort and/or ability. Task difficulty discounts low performance levels as diagnostic of low effort and/or low ability. Task ease augments an inference of low ability and/or low effort from low performance. Task difficulty augments an inference of high ability and/or high effort from high performance. Thus, an inference of high ability is likely when high performance is achieved on a difficult task with minimal effort. An inference of high ability is least likely when low performance is achieved on an easy task with high effort.

It is important to note here the asymmetrical effects of augmentation and discounting on inferences. That is, high performance achieved in the presence of inhibitory forces (e.g., difficult task) yields considerable information regarding ability level. High or low performance achieved in the presence of facilitative forces (e.g., high effort/easy task facilitative of high performance or low effort/difficult task facilitative of low performance) does not yield much information about ability level. Performance achieved in the face of inhibitory forces renders performance level highly diagnostic of ability: High performance translates into high ability and low performance translates into low ability. Performance achieved in the presence of facilitative forces discounts performance level as diagnostic of ability: High performance does not translate into high ability and low performance does not translate into low ability.

The common sense view of performance as it relates to ability, effort, and task difficulty is one of multiple compensatory causes. Within this view, performance may or may not yield information about any one of these causes as a function of the others. Into this view we must inject the factor of luck. We contend that luck is a residual cause that typically is invoked only to account for performance that is not readily explained by the other factors. This would be most likely when the performance level is not interpretable in terms of other forces—it is not expected. Luck (good or bad) is, in a sense, perceivers' attributional magic. It can be facilitative of any performance level. It is most likely to be used as a causal explanation for performance when other causal factors are perceived as inhibiting the observed outcome or as insufficient to explain it. Thus, luck would be likely to be used to explain the success of an unskilled person who exerts little effort but succeeds on a difficult task. It is also likely to be invoked to explain the failure of a competent person who exerts a great deal of effort on an easy task. With this in mind, the pattern of sex-determined attributions obtained in studies of attributions made for performance attain some level of theoretical explanation.

Performance Variables.   It should be obvious at this point that effort, task ease, and luck are used as compensatory causes to discount women's but not men's successful performance as indicative of high ability. Whence these effects derive is not so obvious. The easiest explanation would be that perceivers assume that women try harder, work on easier tasks, and have better luck than their successful male counterparts. As such, these women become disadvantaged because their performance is not used to infer their high ability level. However, others have argued that the process may be reversed. Women may be expected to have low ability and low performance levels (cf. Deaux, 1976). As a result, the observation of a woman performing well on a task leads to the search for facilitative causes to account for her success. The possibility that the perceiver's original assumption of low ability may not be correct remains unchallenged as these additional causes are used to maintain the belief in women's and men's differential abilities. This view is consistent with some models of attribution (cf. Hansen, 1980) that argue for perceivers' selective search for only information supporting (or at least not contradicting) their common sense understanding of behavior. In either case, the inferential result is the same: High performance outcomes help men but not women.

Thus far, we have taken the position that a man's successful performance is more likely than a woman's to be attributed to ability. But what of failure? Some of the research we have reported supports Deaux's contention that perceivers expect men to succeed and women to fail. This position, you will recall, argues that upon encountering an unexpected outcome (e.g., a man's failure or a woman's success) the search for compensatory causes begins. The man's failure comes to be attributed to his bad luck, his low effort, or a difficult task. The woman's success comes to be attributed to her great effort, her good luck, or an easy task. But other research—including our own—argues for a different view for success and failure. Our research (O'Leary and Hansen, 1983a,b) suggests that men's performance is attributed more strongly to their abilities than is women's, across a number of performance levels. That is, a man's performance is more diagnostic of ability level than is a woman's. We have found that a man's high performance is seen as resulting from his level of ability. While the same result is obtained in response to a woman's differential success, the impact of performance on a woman's perceived ability level is not as dramatic. A woman is never considered as competent as a man following success or as incompetent as a man following failure. Similar conclusions have been drawn by others (Heneman, 1977; Nieva & Gutek, 1980; Rosen & Jerdee, 1974a,b). We presume that this effect is bound by a number of conditions, including the unavailability of other causal factors such as low effort and/or bad luck. Although we do not wish to make a blanket statement about the impact of sex on attributions to ability, if we did it would read: Men's performance is attributed more than women's to ability; as a result, perceivers' estimates of a man's ability are more influenced than are their estimates of a woman's ability by performance outcome. A man is more advantaged by success, and more disadvantaged by failure, than is a woman.

Role-Defined Task Variables.   Research has evidenced the consistent impact of role-defined tasks on sex-determined attributions. Men's success results in inferences of their greater ability compared to equally successful women only on masculine tasks. On feminine tasks, the inferred ability level of successful men does not exceed that of equally successful women. We contend that this is obtained because perceivers judge that ability can only be diagnosed from performance on a masculine task. Why? Some research suggests that role-defined tasks may differ on their perceived difficulty or status (Geis, 1983; Geis, Brown,

Jennings, & Corrado-Taylor, 1981; Porter & Geis, 1981). If this is the case, the pattern of effects obtained on ability attributions as a function of task gender is understandable. The ease of feminine tasks discounts ability inferences from performance. On feminine tasks, success does not result in inferences of high ability. This results in a common sense tautology maintaining the belief in sex differences in ability: Women who, more than men, work and succeed on feminine tasks are judged as having low ability. Success by a less able performer leads to an inference of task ease. Success on an easy task discounts high ability inferences.

GOING BEYOND SEX-DETERMINED ATTRIBUTIONS

Recognizing the compensatory relationship among these common sense explanations for achievement lends greater clarity to the findings of sex-determined attributions. However, a conceptual analysis of the meaning of these explanations requires that we go beyond sex-determined attributions.

Weiner et al. (1971) have presented these four causes in the context of a conceptual taxonomy. Following in the tradition of Heider (1958), Weiner (Weiner, 1979; Weiner et al., 1971; Weiner, Nirenberg, & Goldstein, 1976; Weiner, Russell, & Lerman, 1979) has taken the position that the theoretical understanding of perceivers' common sense explanations for behavior must take into account the meaning of perceivers' causal statements. The common sense explanations are the "raw material" of this analysis of their underlying meaning. The full implications of these causal explanations can be understood only at a more embedded level of inference.

As originally presented, these common sense explanations were described as having meaning on two dimensions. These dimensions were termed *locus* of cause and *stability* of cause. Weiner and his colleagues have argued that the location of the cause internal or external to the performer, and as stable or unstable over time and circumstance, are critical to perceivers' understanding of behavior. Since the time of the original presentation (1971), a number of additional dimensions of meaning have been added to the formulation (cf. Wimer & Kelley, 1982). The most researched of these additional dimensions is that of controlability (can the causal force be seen as under the intentional control of the performer). However, the original intent of Weiner's taxonomy of causes seems to have been partially lost to some researchers.

The taxonomy was not intended to describe the meaning of the common sense explanations for achievement, but merely to point out the necessity of capturing the underlying meaning of these causes. A number of researchers have used the taxonomic placement of the causes inappropriately to transform common sense explanations into derived scores in order to place perceivers' explanations onto the stability and locus dimensions (Arkin & Maruyama, 1979; Bernstein, Stephan, & Davis, 1979; Luginbuhl, Crowe, & Kahan, 1975; Rosenfield & Stephan, 1978; Stephan, Rosenfield, & Stephan, 1976; Zuckerman, Larrance, Porac, & Blanck, 1980). These researchers, then, have assumed that: (a) ability is stable and internal; (b) effort is external and unstable; (c) task difficulty is stable and external; and (d) luck is external and unstable. A fair amount of research is now available indicating that these assumptions are not warranted (Covington & Omelich, 1979; Meyer, 1980; Hansen, Ronis, & O'Leary, 1980). The meaning of the common sense explanations for performance cannot always be derived from the theoretical taxonomy. Effort can be perceived as stable or unstable (Elig & Frieze, 1979; Ostrove, 1978; Weiner, 1979). Luck can be either internal or external as a function of the context in which the performance occurs (Meyer, 1980; Weiner et al. 1976). Task difficulty can be either stable or unstable (Valle & Frieze, 1976). A conclusion from the sex-determined attribution literature that women's performance is attributed to external and/or unstable causes, while men's performance is attributed to internal and stable causes, is not warranted. Where does this leave us? It suggests that a theoretical analysis of perceivers' explanations for performance must go beyond common sense explanations for women's and men's performance to specify the underlying meaning of these explanations and how they might differ as a function of the performer's sex.

Beyond Effort

We have chosen effort to illustrate the efficacy of adopting Weiner's focus on the underlying meaning of causal explanations for a number of reasons. First, research indicates that effort may be the primary mediator of organizational rewards contingent on performance (Green & Mitchell, 1979). Second, effort has been shown to be perceived as both stable and unstable (Elig & Frieze, 1979) and internal as well as external (Weiner et al., 1976). Third, effort can be observed; hence, it is not as "embedded" in the inference process as are more abstract causal forces such as luck, task difficulty, and—particularly—ability. Finally, a great deal of research has been focused on the meaning of effort and the implications of the meaning of effort for sex-determined attributions.

The issue of the meaning of effort has been dealt with extensively by those testing Deci's (1975) theory of intrinsic motivation. Paradoxically, the theory of intrinsic motivation has a much clearer conceptualization of extrinsic motivating causes than of intrinsic motivating causes. The theory does make it clear that intrinsic forces are compensatory to extrinsic forces with regard to effort level. Intrinsic motivation is typically treated as a residual force compensating for different levels of effort given constant levels of extrinsic forces, or for constant levels of effort given different levels of extrinsic force. Extrinsic forces—i.e., those extrinsic to the task itself—are typically reinforcements that are contingent upon success or completion of the task. We might construe intrinsic forces to be the performer's interest in the task as well as such psychological factors as *Nach* (cf. McClelland, 1958; McClelland, Atkinson, Clark, & Lowell, 1953).

The compensatory nature of internal and external facilitative forces perceived as acting on effort have been demonstrated clearly and repeatedly. In general, effort has been conceptualized as persistence on a task. The research indicates that equally persistent performance yields different inferences of intrinsic motivation as a function of different levels of reinforcement (Deci, 1975). Likewise, different levels of persistence in performance yields different inferences of intrinsic motivation if reinforcement is held constant. Thus, if two people are seen performing under the same reinforcement contingency, the person who exerts greater effort will be judged more intrinsically motivated. The differential meaning of these forces in terms of locus of cause is obvious. We also contend that these forces have different meanings in terms of their stability. Intrinsic motivation is seen as more stable than extrinsic motivation, which is tied to the availability of reinforcement in the environment. We could stretch the dissonance findings in the domain of forced compliance to support this contention (Festinger & Carlsmith, 1959). As a reminder, lest we think of extrinsic motivation as constant, Lawler (1973) has noted that the reinforcement effect on behavior tends to diminish over time, necessitating the increased potency of the reinforcement. Nevertheless, we argue that extrinsic motivation is perceived as predominantly external and unstable.

Effort is an interesting factor also because it can be seen as intended. Effort is considered to be under the control of the performer (Heider, 1958). It has been noted that perceivers hold performers more accountable for their effortfully produced outcomes because they connote intent (Jones & Davis, 1965). Intent is usually described in terms of the performer's desire to obtain some effect. These effects have been described in the achievement literature as ranging from an attempt to obtain an external reward through maintaining the impression of competence, to a concern with compliance with social norms (cf. Veroff, 1977; Veroff, McClelland, & Ruhland, 1975). Again, as we have noted, the locus of these effects in the environment or within the person, and the stability of these effects can drastically alter the meaning of a common sense explanation of performance as it is attributable to effort.

Sex-Determined Effort

Some evidence can be found to support the contention that women's effort is less likely than men's to be seen as extrinsically motivated. Hansen and O'Leary (in press) have conducted a series of experiments demonstrating that perceivers attribute men's behavior more to environmental factors, but not necessarily less to personal factors, than women's behavior. Although this research was conducted using measures of attributions to personal and environmental facilitative forces rather than measures of perceivers' inferences regarding the locus of cause for effort, the implication of the research is apparent. Effort, which can be seen as internal or external, may have a different meaning for the perceiver as a function of the performer's sex. Men's effort is more likely than women's to be seen as intended to produce an environmental effect—for example, obtaining an organizational reward.

This yields a rather intriguing view of sex-determined attributions. Women's performance is more likely to be attributed to effort than is men's (Etaugh & Brown, 1975; Feldman-Summers & Kiesler, 1974). Women are judged as having exerted greater effort than men who achieve the same level of performance (O'Leary & Hansen, 1983a,b). Women's (greater) effort is more likely than men's to be seen as intrinsically caused (Hansen & O'Leary, in press). Taking the most pessimistic view of these findings we arrive at an image of a woman exerting great effort on an—intrinsically motivated—easy (i.e., feminine) task in order to compensate for her lack of ability. A less pessimistic view would be an image of a woman whose effort is not commensurate with the difficulty of the task (i.e., high effort on an easy task), which is explained in terms of her higher level of intrinsic motivation.

This analysis of effort illustrates the importance of recognizing that perceivers' common sense explanations for achievement acquire meaning at a more embedded level of understanding. The full implications of sex-determined attributions can be conceptually derived only by taking into account the dimensions of meaning that underlie common sense explanations. We should avoid a priori assumptions based on a conceptual scheme such as Weiner's (Weiner et al., 1971) taxonomy. To assume, for example, that effort is both unstable and internal, as is implied by the taxonomy, would be to overlook some of the more important implications of sex-determined attributions.

WHY DOES SEX DETERMINE ATTRIBUTIONS?

The literature we have reviewed here makes a compelling case for the impact of sex on causal attributions. This leads to the compelling question of why women's and men's behaviors should be explained differently. Three categories of explanation for these effects are available. First, there may be a "kernel of truth" in these sex-determined attributions. Women and men may, in fact, achieve similar performance levels through different means and for different reasons. Women may try harder than men for reasons less related to extrinsic rewards. That is, sex-determined attributions may reflect behavioral reality. Second, these phenomena may reflect another, perhaps broader, cognitive process. A number of cognitive processes have been suggested as the culprit, including self-serving biases, fundamental attribution errors, and automatic processing. Third, these attributions may serve the socio-political and economic goals of maintaining women's lower status. That is, attributions are explicitly driven by conscious processing oriented toward the status quo. We focus on the first two explanations (without prejudice toward the third).

Kernel of Truth

A number of researchers have reported that women do exert more effort than men when placed in the same environmental contingency (Callahan-Levy & Messe, 1979; Kahn, O'Leary, Krulewitz, & Lamm, 1980; Major & McFarlin, 1982; Major & Vanderslice, 1982). In one study, for example, women who were paid an equal amount to men for working on a task worked significantly longer on that task than did the men. Given the analysis of the meaning of effort, this behavioral difference would be expected to lead to two attributional conclusions: Women require effort to compensate for lower ability and women are more intrinsically motivated than are men. This research implies that some portion of the sex-determined attribution pattern may match behavioral reality. Two approaches have been taken by researchers that could explain this apparent behavioral difference. One of these, essentially psychological, suggests that women and men may actually achieve for different reasons. The second argues that the behavioral difference is a result of a social comparison process.

Achievement theorists have recently articulated a number of achievement orientations (Spence & Helmreich, 1978; Veroff, 1977; Veroff, McClelland & Ruhland, 1975). They have suggested that women have a "process orientation," meaning that women are motivated to achieve out of concern for the process of achievement itself: It's not whether you win or lose that's important, but how you play the game (Kidd & Woodman, 1975; Veroff, 1977; Zander, Fuller, & Armstrong, 1972). The process orientation has been described in terms of the criteria used by the achiever to evaluate self-achievement as reflecting three achievement themes: (a) autonomous achievement or a concern for achievement, (b) a concern for trying as hard as the task—or the external evaluators—requires, and (c) competence achievement or a concern with building competence. Men, on the other hand, have been characterized as having an "impact orientation," meaning that they are concerned not so much with how the game is played but whether they win or lose. The impact orientation has also been described in terms of three themes: (a) Power achievement, or a concern with having an impact on the environment; (b) competitive achievement, or a concern for doing as well as or better than others in the same domain; and (c) task achievement, or a concern that the task has been successfully completed. To the extent that women define success in terms of process and men in terms of environmental impact, their psychological orientations to achievement would match perceivers' view of women as more intrinsically motivated and less extrinsically motivated than men. Indeed, men may be more sensitive to environmental demands than are women.

A number of researchers have argued that men and women have different orientations to success and therefore value different outcomes (Crosby, in press;

Kahn et al., 1980). They have suggested that men value and are motivated to maximize their—publicly obtained—environmental gains. Women were portrayed as motivated by interpersonal gains. Other researchers have argued that the phenomena of women exerting more effort than men for equal reward or paying themselves less for equal effort (cf. Major & McFarlin, 1982) can be explained by social processes. They suggest that women and men tend to use same-sexed comparison to others to generate reward expectations (Chesler & Goodman, 1976; Major & Deaux, 1982). Because women are paid less than men for equivalent work, their use of comparison to others would result in lower reward expectations, supporting the behavioral self-fulfilling prophecy of rendering more effort for equal reward or equal work for less reward. This, of course, would have the appearance of making women seem more intrinsically motivated than men.

Both the psychological—achievement orientation—and the social comparison explanations can account for women's greater effort. Which of these explanations has more merit is not of concern here. What is important is that research suggesting that women may try harder than men under the same environmental conditions on the same task does exist. To the extent that sex-determined attributions reflect this behavioral reality, there may be a kernel of truth to perceivers' perceptions that women exert more effort than men. The fact that effort results in the discounting of ability implies that the harder women try the less likely their high performance is to result in perceived high ability. The implications of greater effort leading to the perception of greater intrinsic motivation are equally devastating, particularly if both of the explanations offered above to account for this effort are more or less veridical. Research in intrinsic motivation suggests that performers who exert equal effort for less money or more effort for equal money, come to perceive themselves as more intrinsically motivated (Arnold, 1976; Calder & Staw, 1975; Deci, 1975). Women may see themselves as more intrinsically motivated than men. Further, women's process orientation of achievement may lead them to find the lower levels of extrinsic reward more satisfactory than would men, who are more concerned with the impact of their achievements on the environment. It would seem hard to believe that women would enjoy working harder for less money, but the theoretical approaches discussed here imply that this may well be the case. At the very least, they imply that women would be less dissatisfied with this state of affairs than would men.

Self-Serving Biases

Attribution researchers have long argued that attribution can be used by perceivers to enhance or maintain self-esteem (Jones & Nisbett, 1971). This can be accomplished by attributing praiseworthy behaviors to personal factors and blameworthy behaviors to environmental factors. This has been demonstrated experimentally a number of times (cf. Hansen & Lowe, 1976; Nicholls, 1975). A number of explanations have been offered to account for the cognitive operations that underlie this effect (Miller & Ross, 1975). Of particular interest here is the suggestion that this pattern of attributions may result from perceivers' expectations of success. In general, perceivers judge positive outcomes as more probable than negative outcomes—although highly positive outcomes may be judged somewhat less probable than highly negative outcomes (Parducci, 1963, 1965, 1968). Research has also indicated that perceivers are more likely to attribute expected, rather than unexpected outcomes to personal cause. For example, they are less likely to attribute expected outcomes to luck (Feather, 1969). Thus, as noted by Zuckerman (1979), Ross and Miller's explanation of self-serving biases located the ego-enhancing component in perceivers' expectations of success. This is an important point because, to the perceiver with inflated expectations of success—relative to some independent assessment of the probability of success—personal attributions made for success are not likely to appear ego-enhancing.

Research has shown that women generally have lower expectations of success than do men (cf. Lenney, 1977). This, together with the suggestion that perceivers attribute expected outcomes to personal causes, has led Deaux (1976) to conclude that men may evidence a greater tendency to make self-serving attributions for success. We might anticipate that such an effect would be more exaggerated on masculine than on feminine tasks. This allows for the interpretation of the finding that men attribute their success more to ability and that women attribute their success more to luck. It also allows for an interpretation of the finding that these effects are most pronounced—or are only obtained—on masculine tasks. Men, more than women, expect to succeed and attribute this expected outcome to personal factors. Women, more than men, expect to fail and attribute this expected outcome to personal factors such as lack of ability.

Zuckerman (1979) has made a careful analysis of these findings and comes to a different conclusion from Deaux (1976). Zuckerman notes that research had shown a sex effect on both expectancies of success and on attributions for success, but no direct relationship between these two categories of inference. Some research has shown no relationship between expectancies and attributions (cf. Nicholls, 1975). Zuckerman (1979) also notes that Rosenfield and Stephan (1978) had reported that when expectancies were partialled out in an analysis of covariance, sex effects on attributions were still obtained. But, when Rosenfield and Stephan removed ego-involvement in the task as a covariate, sex effects were not obtained. Zuckerman (1979) and Rosenfield and Stephan (1978) have defined ego-involvement as a self-reported measure of the importance of "doing well on the task." Thus, Zuckerman concludes that "the motivation to do well is a more important determinant of sex differences in attribution than is the expectancy to do well "(1979, p. 265). Zuckerman argues that the sex-differences obtained on self-serving biases in attribution are related to the performer's need to do well. We presume that men feel a greater need to do well on masculine rather than feminine tasks while women feel a lesser need to do well on masculine rather than feminine tasks. This hypothesis would predict the obtained sex-determined attributions. The careful reader will also note the parallel of Zuckerman's "doing well" hypothesis with the position taken by achievement motivation theorists on sex differences in achievement orientation. Males should have a greater need to do well; hence, they should evidence a greater tendency to make what appear to be self-serving attributions. They do just that.

It Might Be Gender Not Sex

Gender has been shown to have potent effects on many different types of behavior (cf. Bem, 1977; Bem & Lenney, 1976; Spence & Helmreich, 1978). Alagna (1982) sought to extend the investigation of gender effects to attributions for performance. She chose to investigate these effects in a competitive achievement environment for a number of reasons. Androgynous and masculine persons have been shown to be more motivated by competitive achievement situations than are feminine persons (note the parallel with the work we reported above as linked to sex). Alagna (1982) also speculated that because masculine and androgynous persons are more interested in competitive achievement situations they may have a higher expectancy of success than do feminine persons.

In the experiment, groups of subjects were required to solve problems and were told that in order to win a prize they would have to best the others' performances. The subjects were also provided with a normative statement regarding the value of competition. Half were told that a large sample of students reported valuing and approving competition while the rest were told that the sample did not value and disapproved of competition. We might construe this manipulation in terms of the achievement orientations discussed above as reflecting concern with process. That is, we would anticipate from the achievement findings (e.g., Depner, 1975; Kipnis, 1974; Veroff, 1977) that such a manipulation would have a greater impact on women than on men. Alagna (1982) anticipated that the manipulation would have a greater impact on feminine than masculine or androgynous persons, although the prior research led her to equivocate on this prediction.

After working on the task during an initial portion of the experiment, subjects were given false feedback indicating that they had placed second and were asked to make attributions for their performance. Masculine and androgynous persons attributed their performance more to ability than did feminine persons, although this effect was only significant for masculine persons. Feminine persons attributed their performance more to luck than did masculine persons. No effects were obtained on attributions to task difficulty or to effort. An examination of the experimental method, however, led us to question whether the absence of effects on effort might have been artifactual resulting from instructions prominently featuring statements about trying. Obviously, these effects obtained by Alagna (1982) parallel the sex-determined effects reported in other research. Further, Alagna measured expectations of success and found that masculine and androgynous persons had higher expectations than did feminine persons. The parallel of these findings with the position taken by Zuckerman (1979) is also obvious: More self-serving attributions (to ability) were made by masculine and androgynous persons.

Attributions to ability were influenced by normative sanctions voiced for or against competition as well. Women attributed their performance more to ability when normative sanctions had been voiced in favor of competition rather than against competition. No such effect was seen on men's attributions to ability. It should also be noted that this same interactive pattern was evidenced on the actual measured performance of the subjects. These findings, then, conform to the achievement-orientation predictions with regard to women's greater concern with process. In summary, with the exception of this last reported sex-determined effect, Alagna (1982) has obtained a pattern of attributions that could be anticipated from sex using gender. Thus, Alagna's research would tend to suggest that in previous studies not assessing gender identity, gender effects (given the distribution of masculinity and femininity across the sexes) may have been mistaken for sex effects. In the laboratory, gender becomes sex. We contend that for the perceiver in the "real world"—again, given the distribution of masculinity and femininity across the sexes—gender probably becomes sex. Feminine persons, who are more probably female, attribute their success to luck; masculine persons, who are probably male, attribute their success to ability. Whether the locus of the attribution effects we have been discussing lies in gender or in sex has yet to be determined.

A Fundamental Attribution Error

Geis (1983) has hypothesized that a number of effects usually perceived as linked to the sex of people may, in fact, be a function of sex roles. She has pointed out that women are typically assigned to lower status roles than are men (Porter & Geis, 1981). She also notes with interest that the stereotypically assigned characteristics of high status roles (e.g., independent, dominant, rational, ambitious) read suspiciously like those stereotypically assigned to men. Similarly, stereotypically assigned characteristics of low status roles (e.g., dependent, submissive, emotional, contented) are more than vaguely similar to traits stereotypically assigned to women. In an experiment conducted to answer the obvious question (Geis, Brown, Jennings & Corrado-Taylor, 1981), subjects were asked to assign traits to a man or a woman who was described as filling a high or low status role. The experiments report that traits tended to follow role and not sex. Geis (1983) concludes that the typical placement of women into lower-status roles may constitute a self-fulfilling prophecy whereby men and women acquire traits as a function of role status.

This phenomenon can be analyzed further. Ross, Amabile, and Steinmetz (1977) conducted an experiment that bears on the point made by Geis (1983).

Ross et al. brought pairs of subjects into the laboratory and assigned one the role of quizmaster and the other that of contestant. The quizmaster was instructed to make up a trivia test that would be taken by the contestant. The quizmasters, selecting their most obscure knowledge, inevitably were able to stump the contestants. At the conclusion of the quiz game, both the contestant and the quizmaster were asked to estimate their own and the other's knowledge of trivia. The quizmasters, cognizant of the power of their role and knowing that they had selected their most trivial knowledge, estimated that their own knowledge of trivia was about the same as that of the contestant. The contestants, apparently ignoring their role-produced power disadvantage, estimated that the quizmaster had much greater knowledge than they themselves possessed.

The subjects who had been role-disadvantaged did not take the power of the social environment into account when judging the power-advantaged other. The social role should have discounted the quizmasters' performance as diagnostic of knowledge. It did so for the advantaged but not the disadvantaged person. The phenomenon of overlooking the power of the environment to influence behavior has been termed the fundamental attribution error (Ross et al., 1977). This suggests an explanation for the role-based effects described by Geis. Perceivers may overlook the power of role to influence behavior and, as a result, attribute role-constrained behavior to personal characteristics. If, as suggested by Geis, self-perceivers make the same error, a self-fulfilling prophecy follows. Women are seen as possessing the characteristics stereotypically associated with low status roles and men are seen as possessing the characteristics stereotypically associated with high status roles. Further, if the data reported by Ross et al. (1977) are to be believed, women (the disadvantaged) are more likely than men (the advantaged) to attribute their own performance to personal attributes. Men are more likely to attribute their (role-advantaged) behavior to the environment. The work of Geis (1983) along with the research demonstrating the fundamental attribution error provides yet another explanation for the origin of sex-determined attributes.

Mindless Attributional Facts

A great deal of attention has been focused recently on the concept of automatic processing (Bargh, 1984; Bargh & Cerny, 1983; Bargh & Pietromonaco, 1982; Hastie & Kumar, 1979; Higgins, King & Marvin, 1982). Automatic processing has been described in many facets. Of particular interest has been the notion that because it occurs at a level not requiring awareness it can be described as "mindless" (cf. Langer, 1982). The perceiver's lack of awareness of automatic processing has a number of interesting implications. First, automatically processed information arrives at the level of conscious processing without the perceiver knowing that it has been processed. It arrives more or less as a sensory input without *apparent* screening or mediation and would have the appearance of completeness, of fact. Second, because the perceiver is unaware of the process, its correctness cannot be monitored. This has led to the speculation that automatic processing may become rigid or sloppy without the perceiver's knowledge (Langer & Imbner, 1979). Thus, perceivers are not aware of what they knew before it was automatically processed, and they don't know how they know what they know (Higgins, Rhodes, & Jones, 1977).

Beyond this criteria, a number of others have been offered to place a process into the category of automatic (cf. Bargh, 1984). We are less interested in the theoretical explication of automatic processing than in its implications for attributions. It has been proposed that automatic processing serves the function of screening, and/or categorizing, and/or distilling information prior to conscious processing, which has limited capacity. As such, automatic processing results in some information being lost to conscious processing and other information being emphasized. Most researchers, for example, would contend that the activation of a *schema* or category in automatic processing tends to favor information consistent with that schema (Higgins, King, & Mavin, 1982; Higgins, Rhodes, & Jones, 1977; Markus, 1977; Markus & Smith, 1981).

The view of the attribution process to emerge from the consideration of both conscious and automatic processing (Bargh, 1984) is one in which automatic processing results in aspects of the available information becoming enhanced relative to other information, making its use in subsequent conscious processing more probable. Bargh (1984), for example, argues that the often documented greater impact of salient information is not a result of a completely automatic process, but the result of this enhancement effect. We wish to argue that this plays a role in sex-determined attributions.

A number of studies suggest that the observation of a man performing a behavior is more likely than the observation of a woman performing the same behavior to activate a stimulus-cause schema (Kelley, 1972b). Perceivers in these studies (O'Leary & Hansen, 1983a,b) were given verbal reports or videotaped vignettes of either women or men behaving in the presence of clearly defined stimuli. For example, each of a number of women or men were described as working on different tasks. Each of the men or women had a different outcome on the task they attempted. In this instance of multiple causation (each person was working on a different task), the perceivers tended to explain the variance in behavior in different terms as a function of the performer's sex. Variance in men's performance was explained more in terms of differences among the tasks on which the men worked than in terms of differences among the men's skills. Variance in women's performance, on the other hand, was explained more in terms of differences among the women's skills than in differences among the tasks on which they worked. This research, along with a number of other studies documenting a tendency for perceivers to attribute a man's behavior more than a woman's to stimulus factors, have led to the hypothesis (O'Leary & Hansen, 1983b) that stimulus factors are more likely to be emphasized—perhaps through the result of automatic processing—when perceivers are explaining a man's, rather than a woman's, behavior. If so, the greater contribution of stimulus cause to men's behavior would probably be viewed by perceivers as an attributional fact. For example, perceivers may be more likely to detect a convariation of men's behavior with extrinsic motivating factors over a similar covariation of women's behavior with extrinsic factors. This would also argue that a woman's sex is more likely than a man's to be used as an explanation for behavior, per se.

If we maintain, as does Bargh (1984), that mindlessness refers to instances in which relevant information is overlooked or not used in optimal fashion, another manifestation of this phenomenon can be documented. A number of researchers and theorists have maintained that perceivers seek or remember information consistent with their explanation of a behavior (cf. Hansen, 1980) or their stereotypic schema for a class of events or people (cf. Higgins et al., 1982; Yarkin, Harvey, & Bloxom, 1981). Darley and Gross (1983) have shown this effect with stereotypes based on socioeconomic status. Teachers were shown videotapes of a girl taking an oral achievement test. The videotapes were constructed so that the girl's behavior on some occasions indicated that she was an attentive, interested, and achievement-oriented person. At other points, her behavior was inattentive, disinterested and indicated that she was not an achievement-oriented person. At the conclusion of the videotape presentation, teachers were asked for their opinions about the girl's probable level of performance, as well as for instances recalled from the film to support their estimates. Prior to showing the film, the experimenters led half of the subjects to believe that the girl was from a lower-class background (i.e., a stereotypically low achiever) and half were led to believe that the girl was from a middleclass background (i.e., stereotypically higher in achievement). Darley and Gross (1983) report that the teachers' expectations of the girl's performance were consistent with their initial stereotypes. Of even greater interest is their finding that teachers were much more likely to recall instances in the videotape presentation that were consistent with their evaluations. Again, it is important to note that the selective recall of the information was anything but selective to the teachers. The translation of stereotypes, be they based on status, sex, or socioeconomic status into selective recall of consistent information can be classified as mindless. The contribution of "mindless" attributional facts to the phenomenon of sex-determined attributions has not been established. That the possibility exists that mindlessness characterizes some aspect of the process—automatic or conscious—implies that sex-determined attributions favoring men over women in the domain of performance are likely to be relatively impervious to change.

CONSEQUENCES OF SEX-DETERMINED ATTRIBUTIONS

Sex-determined attributions have implications for the self-perceiver who is explaining her or his own performance. Sex-determined attributions also have implications for women and men as a function of the invocation by an evaluator explaining success or failure. A performer's affective reaction to success or failure, for example, is influenced by the causal explanation used by the person to explain her/his own performance (Weiner, Russell, & Lerman, 1978). Affective reaction to performance outcome has been implicated in the performer's subsequent achievement behavior (Weiner, 1974). Beyond affective reactions, the meaning of performance for expectations regarding future levels of performance and the evaluation of performance by another have been shown to be dramatically influenced by attributions for current performance (Heilman & Guzzo, 1978; Ronis, Hansen & O'Leary, 1983).

Affective Reactions to Success and Failure

Weiner, Russell, and Lerman (1978, 1979) have presented a good deal of data and have extensively theorized on the affective consequences of performance outcome. They have suggested that performance-related affect is influenced at three levels. First, they argue for outcome-dependent affect. One component of the affective reaction is a function of the person's perception of success or failure regardless of its cause. Not surprisingly, happiness was the affect reported as associated with success regardless of cause. Confidence also was consistently associated with success, with the exception of success seen as having been caused by luck. Confidence, then, may also be independent of attribution while dependent on outcome. Weiner et al. (1978) have indicated that frustration and upset were failure-dependent emotions not associated with any particular causal attribution. Weiner et al. (1979) found that depression, disappointment, disgust, and anger were also commonly associated with failure regardless of perceived cause. In discussing these outcome-dependent emotions, Weiner et al. (1979) suggest that performers experience a positive reaction to success and a negative reaction to failure and assign some label consistent with the valence of the reaction. They also suggest that these reactions are immediate or automatic and are relatively short-lived, although intense.

Coming close to prescribing a sequential model of affect, Weiner et al. suggest that these intense emotional experiences are antecedent to the ascription of the performance to a cause. The attribution, then, modifies or changes the emotional experience. The researchers document the manner in which a number of attributions for success or failure discriminate among affective reactions to outcome. Without cataloging their findings here, a few observations are of particular interest. Weiner et al. (1978, 1979) have found that success and failure lead to reciprocal affect when performance has been attributed to ability. Success caused by ability results in feelings of competence, while failure due to ability leads to feelings of incompetence. But in other cases, the affective consequence of an attribution for success and failure seems to have no relationship. For example, success attributed to stable effort has led to relief, while failure attributed to the same factor has led to anger. And in yet another case, luck, success and failure have resulted in the same affective reaction: Surprise. One final interesting emotional consequence of attributions should be noted. In one instance, success attributed to luck, success has resulted in the expression of a negative affective state: Guilt.

Weiner et al. (1978, 1979) have gone on to suggest that the longest-term emotional reactions to performance outcome are mediated at the level of the dimensions underlying their taxonomy. They present data indicating that locus of cause may have a bearing on the long term affective consequences of performance. These data show that emotions such as pride, competence, and satisfaction are linked to success attributed to internal cause, while emotions such as gratitude, thankfulness, modesty, and guilt are linked to success attributed to external causes. Failure attributed to internal causes is most likely to result in emotions such as guilt, resignation, and regret. Failure attributed to external causes is most likely to result in an experience of anger and surprise. Weiner et al. (1978) have demonstrated that the stability dimension of attributions also predicts affective consequence.

In summary, Weiner et al. have theorized and presented data suggesting that the affective consequences of performance derive from three factors: (a) success or failure, (b) the discriminating effects of common sense explanations for outcomes, and (c) the meaning of common sense explanations on the dimensions—at least—of stability and locus. They have argued that these effects might be sequential with outcome-dependent affect being immediate, intense, and short-lived and dimension-dependent affect being more reflective, less intense, but longer-lived.

Folding sex-determined attributions into this framework implies different affective consequences for men and women who attribute their performance to different causes. Going much beyond the data, we could speculate that men, who attribute their success to ability, are more likely to feel competent following success than are women, who do not. Women, on the other hand, might experience guilt following success if they attribute their performance to luck (cf. Fontain, 1975). In any case, the approach taken by Weiner clearly indicates that sex-determined attributions will result in different affective consequences for men and women who achieve the same performance outcome. The potential for women to experience a negative affective state following success, and for men to experience a positive affective state following success is a reasonable prediction within this framework.

An interesting sidelight to the impact of sex-determined attributions is offered by an intriguing study reported by Weiner et al. (1979, Experiment 2). In this study, they provided perceivers with the performance outcome of a person (success or failure) and provided them with information about the performer's affective reaction to the outcome. In general, the perceivers had little trouble diagnosing the performer's attributions from their emotional reactions. This may indicate that sex-determined attributions for one's own performance can be translated by another into a causal inference. This may also suggest one more way in which sex-determined attributions can influence the evaluation by another of one's own performance outcome and result in a self-fulfilling prophecy.

Expectations of Future Performance

Attributions for performance have implications both for the performer's own expectations regarding future performance, and for another's expectations of the performer's future performance. We deal with the implications of a perceiver's attributions for another's performance before dealing with the issues related to self attribution.

A number of recent studies present findings indicating that attributions for performance are not a particularly potent influence on expectation for the future success of the performer (Bernstein, Stephan, & Davis, 1979; Covington & Omelich, 1979; Davis & Stephan, 1980). In each of these studies, correlations between attributions of ability, effort, task difficulty, and luck with expectations of future success were not significant. Ronis, Hansen and O'Leary (1983) report a similar failure of correlations between common sense explanations for performance and expectations for future performance. However, Meyer (1980) reports a significant relationship between the stability of attributions and expected future success. Meyer's findings derive from a three-mode factor analysis of attributions and not from the a priori assumption of ability and task difficulty as stable factors with effort and luck as unstable factors. Ronis, Hansen, and O'Leary (1983) have had similar success with a measure of stability that was not tied to the taxonomy (Weiner et al. 1971). These findings, then, indicate that current success or failure has an impact on expectations of future success only when the current success has been attributed to stable cause. The attribution of current performance to unstable cause discounts current performance as indicative of future performance. Given what we know about the pattern of sex-determined attributions, and guessing about their meaning on the stability dimension, we could speculate about the consequences of sex-determined attribution for perceivers' expectations of the performer's future success.

A man's success, attributed to his ability (stable), should result in an expectation of continued success. A woman's success, attributed to her luck (unstable), should discount her current success as indicative of future success. A woman's failure, which is more likely than a man's to be attributed to lack of ability (stable), is more likely to lead to an expectation of future failure. The consequences of an attribution of performance to effort are not clear-cut. If a man's effort is seen as extrinsically motivated, future performance would be predicted from current performance only if extrinsic motivation remains constant. If a woman's effort is seen as intrinsically motivated (stable), current performance is likely to be seen as diagnostic of future performance. But what of the self-attributor's expectations for future success?

We might speculate that, with the exception of the affective consequences of attributions for performance, the self-attributor's expectations for future performance based on current outcome are influenced in more or less the same fashion by attributions as are the expectations of the other attributor. However, the self-attributor may behave very differently in subsequent achievement situations as a function of attributions for current performance. This is spoken to most directly by those conducting research on the phenomenon of learned helplessness (Seligman, 1975). In this instance, researchers have demonstrated that an important dimension of meaning is controllability. People exposed to uncontrollable outcomes stop trying to influence them (Hiroto, 1974; Hiroto & Seligman, 1975; Maier & Seligman, 1976). A particular focus in this research has been the attribution of performance to luck. Because luck is perceived as an uncontrollable cause, success or failure attributed to luck results in a tendency for the performer to stop exerting effort. This is of particular interest when the attributor has made an error and has attributed a skill or effort-determined outcome to luck. In the case of success misattributed to luck, the subsequent lack of effort would undoubtedly result in the performer reattributing performance outcome to effort or ability and the reinstitution of effort. However, in the case of failure, the misattribution of failure to luck and the resultant lack of effort virtually guarantees future failure. This misattribution is unlikely to be discovered (Koller & Kaplan, 1978) and the attribution becomes an apparent self-fulfilling prophecy of future performance.

Although it might be assumed that learned helplessness may be more characteristic of women than of men, the research we have reviewed here on sex-determined attributions does not suggest this conclusion. In fact, the research we have reviewed implies that men are more likely than women to attribute their failures to luck. Learned helplessness may refer less to the attributional consequences for expectations of future performance than to the attributional consequences related to affect. Such a sex-determined effect could only be anticipated if women were more likely than men to attribute their failure to lack of ability, which is also considered beyond the control of the individual. This finding, however, is not well-established.

Performance Evaluation

Heilman and Guzzo (1978) have conducted an experiment to test the consequences of attributions for performance evaluation. MBA students were given descriptions of a number of fictitious successful employees and were asked to indicate the appropriateness of two organizational rewards, pay raises and promotions. The descriptions of the equally successful employees included a statement about the reasons for the employee's success. The causes for success, not surprisingly, were ability, effort, task ease, and good luck. Neither of the organizational rewards were seen as preferable to no action when success had been attributed to luck or task ease. Pay raises were seen as equally appropriate for success attributed to ability and success attributed to effort. Promotions, however, were reserved only for those employees whose success had been attributed to ability. This is particularly significant because promotions are the most highly valued organizational rewards.

This pattern of effects is meaningful, given acceptance of the placement of these causes in the Weiner taxonomy. In order for the application of reward to be considered, the person must have participated in causing success. Rewards were not considered appropriate for success caused by luck and by task ease. Heilman & Guzzo's results could be interpreted in terms of the attributional mediation of current performance to expectations for future performance. Success, when attributed to ability, is viewed as diagnostic of future success. Success, when attributed to effort—if effort is unstable—is not diagnostic of future performance. Effort-caused success may have resulted in pay raises out of the subjects' recognition that the employee's effort may have been extrinsically caused. The application of a pay raise may have been intended to ensure the continuation of the person's effort and, hence, of their success.

Heilman and Guzzo's (1978) findings have interesting implications within the framework of sex-determined attributions. If men's success is more likely than women's to be attributed to high ability, men are more likely than women to receive promotions for success. But are women, whose success is more likely than men's to be attributed to effort, just as likely as men to receive pay raises? Clearly, the fact that women receive about 40% less remuneration than their male counterparts for their performance would seem to argue against this position. The reconciliation of Heilman and Guzzo's findings and the prevalence of women's lower pay may lie in the way in which women's and men's effort is viewed—if, as we have suggested, women's effort is less likely than men's to be seen as extrinsically caused. A supervisor—even as role-played by MBA students—must make decisions about the allocation of limited organizational resources with the goals of maximizing productivity or effort. Under such circumstances, the allocation of a pay raise to someone (i.e., a woman) whose effort is intrinsically motivated—not reflecting an intent to obtain extrinsic rewards—may be viewed as foolish given the necessity of maintaining the efforts of those employees (i.e., men) whose efforts are extrinsically motivated. Intrinsically motivated people will exert effort regardless of extrinsic reward contingencies; extrinsically motivated people will not. In short, women, who are perceived as less extrinsically motivated, are less likely than men to receive organizational rewards.

For Women

The research exploring sex-determined attributions has offered some hints as to why women are disadvantaged in the domain of achievement performance. The fact that women are disadvantaged is not particularly newsworthy. That attributions may play a role in the disadvantaging of women does have implications for change. Women and men agree on differential causal perceptions of women and men (including their own). The sex-determined attribution literature implies that successful change will require an intervention in the self- and other-attribution of both women and men. So long as women's success is attributed to luck, effort, task ease, or other compensatory factors, their achievements will not be recognized as reflecting their competence. So long as women's effort is interpreted in terms of intrinsic motivation, and as compensatory to their ability, they will be disadvantaged in performance evaluation.

The probability of an attributional intervention—if it can be accomplished—resulting in a change in the differential status of women and men is not known. On the one hand, the suggestion that sex may become an attributional fact through automatic processing would argue that the differential causal perception of women and men is fundamental and rather impervious to change. Perceivers do not have access to automatic processing events. However, cognitive theorists maintain that conscious processing can override automatic processing phenomenon (cf. Bargh, 1984). For example, data inconsistent with the schema used to process information automatically is not likely to be retained or made salient. In conscious processing, however, inconsistent information is likely to attract a great deal of attention (cf. Fiske, 1980). One key to a change in the attributions made for women's and men's behavior is to force automatically processed information into conscious processing.

Cognitive psychologists are beginning to develop more sophisticated views of automatic and conscious processing. As they do, these developments should be scanned for suggestions whereby automatic processing can be defeated.

At least two experiments provide encouraging data to attempts at changing mindless attribution processes. First, Darley and Gross (1983) reported that the priming of an attributional set can alter attributions and consequent performance evaluation. They found that when teachers are primed to think about environmental differences between lower-class and middle-class settings, their tendency to view a lower-class child as having less ability than a middle-class child diminished dramatically. Their estimates of performance also changed as a result. One mechanism for altering sex-determined attributions may be to focus perceivers' attention on women's environments. Second, Heilman and Guzzo (1978) include the sex of the employee as a factor in their experiment. They have found that the sex of the employee has no effect on perceivers' allocation of organizational rewards or their assessments of the employee's management potential. The provision of explicit attributions for performance may override sex-determined attributions for performance.

Finally, the research and theory we have reviewed suggests that an "attributional fix" should also involve an intervention in women's attributions for their own performance. Of particular importance would be the reattribution of success to ability as well as other personal factors falling into the category of personal and controllable causes. Recent work in this area (Wilson & Linville, 1982) indicates the efficacy of reattributing one's own performance on affect and future performance levels. Their work also implies that a reattribution intervention may not be as time consuming or as difficult as it would seem at first blush.

For Social Psychology

It would be easy to contend that sex-determined attributions demonstrated in the social psychological literature are not particularly important, either because they are not robust or because they are overshadowed by other sex-linked effects (Ilgen, 1983). Such a conclusion might seem warranted from the current literature, which is a patchwork of methodologies and findings.

Conflict in the appearance and nature of sex-determined attributions seems to abound. We, however, are not discouraged by this literature. We maintain that the research available is but a beginning. Most of this work has focused on common sense explanations for performance or behavior without regard to the meaning of these explanations for perceivers. Researchers have just begun to grasp the importance of exploring the underlying meaning of common sense explanations. We contend that it is at this deeper level of analysis that sex-determined attributional phenomena have a potent impact that can be theoretically explicated and exploited.

Most attribution literature focuses on the locus dimension by defining causes as personal or environmental. The first small step away from the one-dimensional view of attributional meaning was taken by Weiner and his associates (cf. Weiner et al., 1971) by including a second dimension: Stability. This was slightly expanded by Rosenbaum (1972), who suggested the third dimension of intentionality. Most of the research on sex-determined attributions has remained at this level of development. More recent developments imply further research and potential for explicating the effect of sex on attributions.

Weiner (1979) and Meyer (1980) have found that controllability of cause may be important to understanding perceivers' attributions for achievement. Abramson, Seligman, and Teasdale (1978) have suggested that globality (a dimension describing the domain of effects produced by a cause), along with locus and stability are important to understanding the phenomenon of learned helplessness. They contend that learned helplessness derives from attributions for failure to internal, stable, and global causes. Wimer and Kelley (1982) have made what is perhaps the biggest leap thus far in this literature by suggesting about ten dimensions in which attributions have meaning. This work, and the growing general recognition that common sense explanations for behavior have meaning on a number of different dimensions, is exciting. It implies the imprecision of previous research in attributions—including sex-determined attributions—and suggests great potential for future exploration. We believe that, once attribution theorists and researchers begin to explore this world of meaning, the impact of sex on attributions will be recognized for the pervasive and fundamental phenomenon we believe it to be.

REFERENCES

Abramowitz, C. V., & Dodecki, P. R. (1977). The politics of clinical judgment: Early empirical returns. *Psychological Bulletin, 84,* 460–476.

Abramson, P. R., Goldberg, P. A., Greenberg, J. H., & Abramson, L. M. (1977). The talking platypus phenomenon: Competency ratings as a function of sex and professional status. *Psychology of Women Quarterly, 2*(2), 114–124.

Abramson, P. R., Seligman, M. E. P., & Teasdale, J. (1978). Learned helplessness in humans: Critique and reformulation. *Journal of Abnormal Psychology, 87,* 49–74.

Alagna, S. W. (1982). Sex-role identity peer evaluation of competition and the responses of women and men in a competitive situation. *Journal of Personality and Social Psychology, 43,* 546–554.

Anderson, R. H. & Butzin, C. A. (1974). Performance=motivation and ability. An integration=theoretical analysis. *Journal of Personality and Social Psychology, 30*(5), 598–604.

Arkin, R. M. & Maruyama, G. M. (1979). Attribution, affect, and college exam performance. *Journal of Educational Psychology, 71,* 85–93.

Arnold, H. J. (1976). Effects of performance feedback and extrinsic reward on high intrinsic motivation. *Organizational Behavior and Human Performance, 17,* 275–288.

Bargh, J. A. (1984). Automatic and conscious processing of social information. In R. S. Wyer, & T. K. Srull (Eds.), *Handbook of social cognition* (Vol. 3). Hillsdale, N.J.: Lawrence Erlbaum Associates, 1984.

Bargh, J. A. & Cerney, R. (1983). *Automatic and conscious processes in impression formation.* Unpublished manuscript, New York University.

Bargh, J. A. & Peitromonaco, P. (1982). Automatic information processing and social perception: The influence of trait information presented outside of conscious awareness on impression formation. *Journal of Personality and Social Psychology, 43,* 437–440.

Bar-Tal, D. & Freize, I. H. (1976). Attributions for success and failure for actors and observers. *Journal of Research in Personality. 10,* 256–265.

Bar-Tal, D. & Frieze, I. H. (1977). Achievement motivation formula for males and females as a determinant of attributions for success and failure. *Sex Roles, 3,* 301–313.

Bem, S. L., & Lenny, E. (1976). Sex typing and the avoidance of cross-sex behavior. *Journal of Personality and Social Psychology, 33,* 48–54.

Bernstein, W. M., Stephan, W. G. & Davis, M. H. (1979). Explaining attributions for achievement: A path-analytic approach. *Journal of Personality and Social Psychology, 37*(1), 1810–1821.

Broverman, S. K., Broverman, D. M., Clarkson, F. E., Rosenkrantz, P. S. & Vogel, S. R. (1970). Sex-role stereotypes and clinical judgements of mental health. *Journal of Consulting and Clinical Psychology, 34,* 1–7.

Broverman, I., Vogel, S. R., Broverman, D., Clarkson, F. E. & Rosenkrantz, P. S. (1972). Sex role stereotypes: A current appraisal. *Social Issues, 28,* 59–78.

Brown, S. H. (1979). Male versus female leaders: A comparison of empirical studies. *Sex Roles, 5,* 595–612.

Calder, B. J. & Staw, B. M. (1975). Self-perception of intrinsic and extrinsic motivation. *Journal of Personality and Social Psychology, 31*(4), 599–605.

Callahan-Levy, C. M. & Messe, L. A. (1979). Sex differences in the allocation of pay. *Journal of Personality and Social Psychology, 37,* 433–446.

Cash, T. F., Gillen, B. & Burns, D. S. (1977). Sexism and beautyism in personnel consultant decision making. *Journal of Applied Psychology, 62,* 301–310.

Chaikin, A. L. (1971). The effects of four outcome schedules on persistence liking for the task and attributions of causality. *Journal of Personality, 39,* 512–526.

Chesler, P. & Goodman, E. J. (1976). *Women, money, and power.* New York: Marrow.

Covington, M. V. & Omelich, C. L. (1979). Are causal attributions causal? A path analysis of the cognitive model of achievement motivation. *Journal of Personality and Social Psychology, 37*(9), 1487–1504.

Crosby, F. (in press). *Relative deprivation and working women.* London: Oxford University Press.

Darley, J. M. & Gross, P. H. (1983). A hypothesis-confirming bias in labeling effects. *Journal of Personality and Social Psychology, 44,* 20–33.

Davis, M. H. & Stephan, W. G. (1980). Attributions for exam performance. *Journal of Applied Social Psychology, 10,* 235–248.

Deaux, K. (1972). To err is humanizing: But sex makes a difference. *Representative Research in Psychology, 3,* 20–28.

Deaux, K. (1976). Sex and the attribution process. In J. H. Harvey, W. J. Ickes, & R. F. Kidd (Eds.), *New directions in attribution research* (Vol. 1). New York: Wiley.

Deaux, K. & Emswiller, T. (1974). Explanations of successful performance on sex-linked tasks: What's skill for the male is luck for the female. *Journal of Personality and Social Psychology, 29,* 80–85.

Deaux, K. & Farris, E. (1977). Attributing causes for one's own performance: The effect of sex, norms, and outcome. *Journal of Research in Personality, 11,* 59–72.

Deaux, K. & Taynor, J. (1973). Evaluation of male and female ability: Bias works two ways. *Psychological Reports, 32,* 261–262a.

Deci, E. L. (1975). *Intrinsic motivation.* New York: Plenum Press.

Depner, C. E. (1975). *An analysis of motivational factors which contribute to sex differences in expression of achievement motivation.* Unpublished manuscript, University of Michigan.

Dipboye, R. L., Arvey, R. D., & Terpstra, D. E. (1977). Sex and physical attractiveness of raters and applicants as determinants of resume evaluations. *Journal of Applied Psychology, 62* 228–294.

Dipboye, R. L., Fromkin, H. L., & Wiback, K. (1975). Relative importance of applicant sex, attractiveness, and scholastic standing in evaluations of job applicant resumes. *Journal of Applied Psychology, 60,* 39–43.

Eagly, A. H. (1978). Sex differences in influence ability. *Psychological Bulletin, 85,* 86–116.

Elig, T. W. & Frieze, I. H. (1979). Measuring causal attributions for success and failure. *Journal of Personality and Social Psychology, 37,* 621–634.

Etaugh, C. & Brown, B. (1975). Perceiving the causes of success and failure of male and female performers. *Developmental Psychology, 11,* 103.

Feather, N. T. (1969). Attribution of responsibility and valence of success and failure in relation to initial confidence and perceived locus of control. *Journal of Personality and Social Psychology, 13,* 129–144.

Feather, N. T. & Simon, J. G. (1975). Reactions to male and female success and failure in sex-linked occupations: Impressions of personality, causal attribution and perceived likelihood of difference consequences. *Journal of Personality and Social Psychology, 31,* 20–31.

Feldman-Summers, S. & Kiesler, S. B. (1974). Those who are number two try harder: The effect of sex on attributions of causality. *Journal of Personality and Social Psychology, 30,* 846–855.

Fernberger, S. W. (1948). Persistence of stereotypes concerning sex differences. *Journal of Abnormal and Social Psychology, 43,* 97–101.

Festinger, L. & Carlsmith, J. M. (1959). Cognitive consequences of forced compliance. *Journal of Abnormal and Social Psychology, 58,* 203–210.

Fidell, L. S. (1970). Empirical verification of sex discrimination in hiring practices in psychology. *American Psychologist, 25,* 1094–1098.

Fiske, S. T. (1980). Attention and weight in person perception: The impact of negative and extreme behavior. *Journal of Personality and Social Psychology, 38,* 889–906.

Fontain, G. (1975). Causal attribution in stimulated vs. real situations: When people are logical, when are they not? *Journal of Personality and Social Psychology, 32*(6), 1021–1029.

Frieze, I. H., Whitley, B. E., Jr., Hanusa, B. H., & McHugh, M. C. (1982). Assessing the theoretical models for sex differences in causal attributions for success and failure. *Sex Roles, 8*(4), 333–357.

Geis, F. L. (1983, April). *Women, sex-roles and achievement: The self-fulfilling prophecy.* Paper presented at the annual meetings of the Eastern Psychological Association, Philadelphia.

Geis, F. L., Brown, V., Jennings, J., & Corrado-Taylor, D. (1981). *Sex vs. status in sex associated stereotypes.* Unpublished manuscript, University of Delaware.

Green, S. G. & Mitchell, T. R. (1979). Attributional processes of leaders in leader–member interactions. *Organizational behavior and human performance, 23,* 429–458.

Gutek, B. A. & Stevens, D. A. (1979). Differential responses of males and females to work situations which evoke sex-role stereotypes. *Journal of Vocational Behavior, 14,* 23–32.

Haefner, J. E. (1977). Sources of discrimination among employees: A survey investigation. *Journal of Applied Psychology, 52, 265 070.*

Hall, F. S. & Hall, T. D. (1977). *The two-career couple.* Reading, Mass.: Addison-Wesley.

Hall, S. F. & Hall, D. T. (1976). Effects of job incumbents' race and sex on evaluations of managerial performance. *Academy of Management Journal, 19,* 476–481.

Hansen, R. D. (1980). Common sense attribution. *Journal of Personality and Social Psychology, 39*(6), 996–1009.

Hansen, R. D. & Hall, C. A. (1983). *Discounting and augmenting causal forces: The winner takes almost all.* Unpublished manuscript, Yale University.

Hansen, R. D. & Lowe, C. A. (1976). Distinctiveness and consensus: The influence of behavioral information on actors' and observers' attributions. *Journal of Personality and Social Psychology, 34*(3), 425–433.

Hansen, R. D. & O'Leary, V. E. (1983). Actresses and actors: The effects of sex on causal attributions. *Basic and Applied Social Psychology, 4,* 209–230.

Hansen, R. D., Ronis, D. L. & O'Leary, V. E. (1980). *The stability of meaning: A test of the validity of Weiner's taxonomy.* Unpublished manuscript, Oakland University.

Hastie, R. & Kuman, P. A. (1979). Person memory: Personality traits as organizing principles in memory for behaviors. *Journal of Personality and Social Psychology, 37,* 25–38.

Heider, F. (1983). *The psychology of interpersonal relations.* Hillsdale, N.J.: Lawrence Erlbaum Associates. Originally published 1958.

Heilman, M. E. & Guzzo, R. A. (1978). The perceived cause of work success as a mediator of sex discrimination in organizations. *Organizational Behavior and Human Performance, 21*(3), 346–357.

Henemann, H. G. (1977). Impact of test information and applicant sex on applicant evaluations in a selection simulation. *Journal of Applied Psychology, 62,* 524–526.

Higgins, E. T., King, G. A., & Mavin, G. H. (1982). Individual construct accessibility and subjective impressions and recall. *Journal of Personality and Social Psychology, 43,* 35–47.

Higgins, E. T., Rhodes, W. S., & Jones, C. R. (1977). Category accessibility and impression formation. *Journal of Experimental Social Psychology, 13,* 141–154.

Hiroto, D. S. (1974). Locus of control and learned helplessness. *Journal of Experimental Psychology, 102,* 187–193.

Hiroto, D. S. & Seligman, M. E. P. (1975). Generality of learned helplessness in man. *Journal of Personality and Social Psychology, 31,* 311–327.

Ilgen, D. R. (1983). Gender issues in performance appraisal: A discussion of O'Leary and Hansen. In F. Landy, S. Zedeck & J. Cleveland (Eds.) *Performance measurement and theory.* Hillsdale, N.J.: Lawrence Erlbaum Associates.

Jacobson, M. B. & Effertz, J. (1974). Sex roles and leadership: Perception of the leaders and the led. *Organizational Behavior and Human Performance, 12,* 383–396.

Jones, E. E., & Davis, K. E. (1965). From acts to dispositions: The attribution process in person perception. In L. Berkowitz (Ed.) *Advances in experimental social psychology* (Vol. 2). New York: Academic Press.

Jones, E. E., & McGillis, D. (1976). Correspondent inferences and the attribution cube: a comparative reappraisal. In J. H. Harvey, W. Ickes, & R. F. Kidd (Eds.), *New directions in attribution research* (Vol. 1). Hillsadle, N.J.: Lawrence Erlbaum Associates.

Jones, E. E. & Nisbett, R. E. (1971). The actor and the observer: Divergent perceptions of the causes of behavior. In E. E. Jones, et al. (Eds.), *Attribution: Perceiving the causes of behavior.* Morristown, N.J.: General Learning Press.

Kahn, A. S., O'Leary, V. E., Krulewitz, J. E., & Lamm, H. (1980). Equity and equality: Male and female means to a just end. *Basic and Applied Social Psychology, 1,* 173–194.

Kanter, R. M. (1977). *Men and women of the corporation.* New York: Basic Books.

Kelley, H. H. (1967). Attribution theory in social psychology. In D. Levine (Ed.) *Nebraska symposium on motivation.* Lincoln: University of Nebraska Press.

Kelley, H. H. (1972a). Attribution in social interaction. In E. E. Jones, et al. (Eds.), *Attribution: Perceiving the causes of behavior.* Morristown, N.J.: General Learning Press.

Kelley, H. H. (1972b). Causal schemata and the attribution process. In E. E. Jones, et al. (Eds.), *Attribution: Perceiving the causes of behavior.* Morristown, N.J.: General Learning Press.

Kidd, T. R. & Woodman, W. F. (1975). Sex and orientations toward winning in sports. *Research Quarterly, 46*(4), 476–483.

Kipnis, D. M. (1974). Inner direction, other direction and achievement motivation. *Human Development, 17*(5), 321–343.

Koller, P. S. & Kaplan, R. M. (1978). A two-process theory of learned helplessness. *Journal of Personality and Social Psychology, 36,* 1177–1183.

Langer, E. J. (1982). *Minding matters: The mindlessness/mindfulness theory of cognitive activity.* Paper presented at the meetings of the Society for Experimental Social Psychology, Nashville, Indiana.

Langer, E. J. & Imber, L. G. (1979). When practice makes imperfect: Debilitating effects of overlearning. *Journal of Personality and Social Psychology, 37,* 2014–2024.

Lawler, E. E., III. (1973). *Motivation in work organizations.* Monterey, Calif.: Brooks/Cole.

Lefcourt, H. M., Hogg, E., Struthers, S., & Holmes, C. (1975). Causal attributions as a function of locus of control, initial confidence and performance outcomes. *Journal of Personality and Social Psychology, 32,* 391–397.

Lenney, E. (1977). Women's self-confidence in achievement settings. *Psychological Bulletin, 84,* 1–13.

Levine, R., Reis, H. T., Sue, E., & Turner, G. (1976). Fear of failure in males: A more salient factor than fear of success in males? *Sex Roles, 2,* 389–398.

Linsenmeier, J. A. W. & Wortman, C. B. (1979). Attitudes toward workers and toward their work: More evidence that sex makes a difference. *Journal of Applied Social Psychology, 4,* 326–334.

Lowe, C. A., & Hansen, R. D. (1976). Motivational influence of behavioral desirability on actors' and observers' attributions. *Social Behavior and Personality, 4,* 17–25.

Luginbuhl, J. E. R., Crowe, D. H., & Kahan, J. P. (1975). Causal attributions for success and failure. *Journal of Personality and Social Psychology, 31,* 89–93.

Maccoby, E. E., & Jacklin, C. N. (1974). *The psychology of sex differences.* Stanford, Calif.: Stanford University Press.

Maier, S. F. & Seligman, M. E. P. (1976). Learned helplessness: Theory and evidence. *Journal of Experimental Psychology: General, 105,* 3–146.

Major, B. & Deaux, K. (1982). Individual differences in justice behavior. In J. Greenberg & R. L. Cohen (Eds.), *Equity and justice in social behavior.* New York: Academic Press.

Major, B., & McFarlin, D. (1982). *Impression management and gender differences in perceptions of fair performance for pay.* Unpublished manuscript, State University of New York at Buffalo.

Major, B., & Vanderslice, V. (1982). *Effects of pay expected in pay received: The self-confirming nature of initial expectations.* Unpublished manuscript, State University of New York at Buffalo.

Markus, H. (1977). Self-schemata and processing information about the self. *Journal of Personality and Social Psychology, 35,* 63–78.

Markus, H., & Smith, J. M. (1981). The influence of self-schemas on the perception of others. In N. Cantor & J. F. Kihlstrom (Eds.), *Personality, cognition, and social interaction.* Hillsdale, N.J.: Lawrence Erlbaum Associates.

McClelland, D. C. (1958). Risk-taking and children with high and low need for achievement. In J. W. Atkinson (Ed.), *Motives in fantasy, action and society.* Princeton: Van Nostrand.

McClelland, D. C., Atkinson, J. W., Clark, R. A. & Lowell, E. L. (1953). *The achievement motive.* New York: Appelton-Century-Crofts.

McKee, J. P., & Sherrifs, A. C. (1959). Men's and women's beliefs, ideals, and self concepts. *American Journal of Sociology, 65,* 356–363.

Meyer, J. P. (1980). Causal attributions for success and failure: A multivariate investigation of dimensionality, formation, and consequences. *Journal of Personality and Social Psychology, 38*(5), 704–718.

Miller, D. T. & Ross, M. (1975). Self-serving biases in the attribution of causality: Fact or fiction? *Psychological Bulletin, 82,* 213–225.

Nicholls, J. G. (1975). Causal attributions and other achievement related cognitions: Effects of task outcome, attainment value, and sex. *Journal of Personality and Social Psychology, 32,* 1111–1118.

Nieva, V. F. & Gutek, B. A. (1980). Sex effects on evaluation. *The Academy of Management Review, 5*(2), 267–276.

Nisbett, R. & Ross, L. (1980). *Human inference: Strategies and shortcomings of social judgment.* Englewood Cliffs, N.J.: Prentice-Hall.

Ostrove, N. (1978). Expectations for success on effort-determined tasks as a function of incentive and performance feedback. *Journal of Personality and Social Psychology, 36,* 909–916.

O'Leary, V. E. (1974). Some attitudinal barriers to occupational aspirations in women. *Psychology Bulletin, 81*(11), 809–816.

O'Leary, V. E. (1977). *Androgynous men: The best of both worlds?* Paper presented at the American Psychological Association, San Francisco.

O'Leary, V. E. & Hansen, R. D. (1983a). Trying hurts women, helps men: The meaning of effort. In H. J. Bernardin (Ed.), *Women in the workforce.* New York: Lexington.

O'Leary, V. E. & Hansen, R. D. (1983b). Performance evaluation: A social psychological perspective. In F. Landy, S. Zedeck, & J. Cleveland (Eds.) *Performance measurement and theory.* Hillsdale, N.J.: Lawrence Erlbaum Associates, 199–218.

Parducci, A. (1963). Range-frequency compromise in judgment. *Psychological Monographs, 77,* (2 Whole No. 565).

Parducci, A. (1965). Category judgment: A range-frequency model. *Psychological Review, 72,* 407–418.

Parducci, A. (1968). The relativism of absolute judgments. *Scientific American, 219,* 84–90.

Pheterson, G. I., Kiesler, S. B., & Goldberg, P. A. (1971). Evaluation of the performance of women as a function of their sex, achievement, and personal history. *Journal of Personality and Social Psychology, 19,* 114–118.

Porter, N., & Geis, F. L. (1981). *Androgyny and leadership in mixed-sex discussion groups.* Unpublished manuscript, University of Delaware.

Ronis, D. L., Hansen, R. D., & O'Leary, V. E. (1983). Understanding the meaning of achievement attributions: A test of derived locus and stability scores. *Journal of Personality and Social Psychology, 44,* 702–711.

Rosaldo, M. Z., & Lamphere, L. (1974). *Women, culture and society.* Stanford, Calif.: Stanford University Press.

Rosen, B., & Jerdee, T. H. (1974a). Influence of sex-role stereotypes on personnel decisions. *Journal of Applied Psychology, 59,* 9–14.

Rosen, B., & Jerdee, T. H. (1974b). Perceived sex differences in managerially relevant characteristics. *Sex Roles, 4,* 837–844.

Rosen, B., & Jerdee, T. H. (1974). Sex stereotyping in the executive suite. *Harvard Business Review, 52,* 45–58.

Rosen, B., Jerdee, T., & Prestwich, T. (1975). Dual career marital adjustment: Potential effects of discriminatory managerial activities. *Journal of Marriage and the Family, 37,* 565–572.

Rosenbaum, R. M. A. (1972). *A dimensional analysis of the perceived causes of success and failure.* Unpublished doctoral dissertation, University of California, Los Angeles.

Rosenfield, D. & Stephan, W. G. (1978). Sex differences in attributions for sex-typed tasks. *Journal of Personality, 46*(2), 244–259.

Ross, L. D., Amabile, T. M., & Steinmetz, J. L. (1977). Social roles, social control and biases in social-perception processes. *Journal of Personality and Social Psychology, 35,* 485–494.

Seligman, M. E. P. (1975). *Helplessness: On depression, development, and death.* San Francisco: Freeman.

Simon, J. G. & Feather, N. T. (1973). Causal attributions for success and failure at university examinations. *Journal of Educational Psychology, 64,* 46–56.

Spence, J. T. & Helmreich, R. L. (1978). *Masculinity and femininity.* Austin, Tex.: University of Texas Press.

Steinmann, A. & Fox, D. J. (1966). Male–female perceptions of the female role in the United States. *Journal of Psychology, 64,* 265–276.

Stephan, W. S., Rosenfield, D. & Stephan, C. (1976). Egotism in males and females. *Journal of Personality and Social Psychology, 34,* 1161–1167.

Taynor, J. & Deaux, K. (1975). Equity and perceived sex differences: Role behavior as defined by the task, the mode, and the actor. *Journal of Personality and Social Psychology, 32,* 381–390.

Terborg, J. R. (1977). Women in management: A research review. *Journal of Applied Psychology, 62,* 647–664.

Terborg, J. R., & Ilgen, D. R. (1975). A theoretical approach to sex discrimination in traditionally masculine occupations. *Organizational behavior and human performance, 13,* 352–376.

Unger, R. K. (1979). Toward a redefinition of sex and gender. *American Psychologist, 11,* 1085–1094.

Valle, V. A., & Frieze, I. H. (1976). Stability of causal attribution as a mediator for changing expectations for success. *Journal of Personality and Social Psychology, 33,* 579–587.

Veroff, J. (1977). Process vs. impact on men's and women's achievement motivation. *Psychology of Women Quarterly, 1*(3), 283–293.

Veroff, J., McClelland, L., & Ruhland, D. (1975). Varieties of achievement motivation. In M. T. S. Mednick, S. S. Tangri, & L. W. Hoffman (Eds.), *Women and achievement.* New York: Wiley, 172–205.

Wallston, B. S., & O'Leary, V. E. (1981). Sex makes a difference: Differential perceptions of women and men. In L. Wheeler (Ed.) *Review of Personality and Social Psychology,* Vol. 2, 9–41.

Weiner, B. (1974). *Achievement motivation and attribution theory.* Morristown, N.J.: General Learning Press.

Weiner, B. (1979). A theory of motivation for some classroom experiences. *Journal of Educational Psychology, 71,* 3–25.

Weiner, B., Frieze, I. H., Kukla, A., Reed, L., Rest, S., & Rosenbaum, R. M. (1971). *Perceiving the causes of success and failure.* Morristown, N.J.: General Learning Press.

Weiner, B., Nierenberg, R., & Goldstein, M. (1976). Social learning (locus of control) interpretations of expectancy of success. *Journal of Personality and Social Psychology, 44*, 52–68.

Weiner, B., Russell, D., & Lerman, D. (1978). Affective consequences of causal ascriptions. In J. H. Harvey, W. J. Ickes, & R. F. Kidd (Eds.), *New directions in attribution research* (Vol. 2). Hillsdale, N.J.: Lawrence Erlbaum Associates

Weiner, B., Russell, D., & Lerman, D. (1979). The cognitive-emotive process in achievement-related contexts. *Journal of Personality and Social Psychology, 37*(7), 1211–1220.

Whitley, B. E., Jr., & Frieze, I. H. (1981). *The effects of question wording and situational context on success and failure attributions: A meta-analysis.* Manuscript submitted for publication, University of Pittsburgh.

Wimer, S., & Kelley, H. H. (1982). An investigation of the dimensions of causal attribution. *Journal of Personality and Social Psychology, 43*, 1142–1162.

Wilson, G. D., & Linville, P. W. (1982). Improving the academic performance of college freshmen: Attribution therapy revisited. *Journal of Personality and Social Psychology, 42*, 367–376.

Yarkin, K. L., Harvey, J. H., & Bloxom, B. M. (1981). Cognitive sito, attribution and overt behavior. *Journal of Personality and Social Psychology, 41*, 243–252.

Zander, A., Fuller, R., & Armstrong, W. (1972). Attributed pride or shame in a group and self. *Journal of Personality and Social Psychology, 23*(3), 346–352.

Zickmund, W. C., Hitt, M. A., & Pickens, B. A. (1978). Influence of sex and scholastic performance on reactions to job applicant resumes. *Journal of Applied Psychology, 63*, 252–255.

Zuckerman, M. (1979). Attribution of success and failure revisited, or: The motivational bias is alive and well in attribution theory. *Journal of Personality, 47*(2), 245–285.

Zuckerman, M., Larrance, D. T., Porac, J. F. A., & Blanck, P. D. (1980). Effects of fear of success on intrinsic motivation, causal attributions, and choice behavior. *Journal of Personality and Social Psychology, 39*, 503–513.

4 Achievement Motivation and Sex Roles

Elyse Sutherland
Michigan Bell Telephone Company

Joseph Veroff
University of Michigan

Systematic research on the projective assessment of achievement motivation has received much attention in the scholarly and popular literature since its introduction more than 30 years ago. Researchers have shown that the level of achievement motivation significantly relates to many different types of behaviors and attitudes. In working out these findings, some systematic theories have been generated (e.g., Atkinson & Feather, 1966) and the measurement procedure used has proven valuable.

This ambitious undertaking did not clarify or confirm all aspects of the structure of achievement motivation, of course. Many questions concerning race, age, and social class differences in achievement motivation; the development of motives; the relation between motives; and even the exact nature and operation of motives are still left unanswered. One critical question that still haunts researchers in this area, which has been much studied but never solved, is that of sex differences. The experimental procedures designed to heighten the level of achievement motivation have been found valid only for males. More accurately, these arousal procedures have been validated only for the white, middle class males used in most studies. Further, many studies on the relationship between achievement motivation and behavior did not find the expected results for females, but did for males. Some researchers simply opted for more reliable, all-male samples. Others, however, tried to account for the different results of males and females, and in doing so contributed much information about the nature and operation of achievement motivation.

This chapter first reviews the history of achievement motivation research, focusing on possible reasons for sex differences. It then takes this research one step further. By integrating results that point to differences in the achievement

101

strivings of men and women, we generate a framework for thinking about achievement motivation that can be applied to both sexes.

REVIEW OF RESEARCH ON ACHIEVEMENT MOTIVATION

Achievement motivation was originally defined as a concern with excellence (McClelland et al., 1953). People are said to learn this orientation in childhood if they are taught to find satisfaction in achievement behavior, and to associate achievement cues with pleasant affective experiences. When such learning occurs, striving for success against a standard of excellence becomes a goal orientation. This internalized concern is thought to be a dispositional aspect of the personality, a motive that is latent until aroused by the appropriate environmental cues. A state of motivation exists when the motive is engaged by the expectation that some behavior will result in the attainment of a motive-related goal (Atkinson, 1950). Thus, motivation is determined by the interaction between personal and environmental cues.

Using this theoretical framework, McClelland and his colleagues set out to assess achievement motivation and detail its impact on behavior. Because Murray's (1938) system of needs (from which achievement motivation theory was derived) specified that motives were unconscious, projective tests were thought to be the best means of assessment. In the early validation studies a projective test based on the Thematic Apperception Test was administered in two conditions—neutral and aroused—to college students. The arousal procedure consisted of instructions highlighting the competitive nature of the task, in an effort to engage the latent achievement motive. Imagery that reflected the differences between conditions became the basis of a scoring system which was used to derive nAchievement scores.[1] Males' nAchievement scores increased from the neutral to the aroused condition. Females' scores did not.

A second component of the validation studies was performance. Subjects were asked to perform timed achievement tasks, such as unscrambling words or arithmetic problems. The nAchievement scores of males were found to relate to performance in a theoretically consistent manner—males with a high need for achievement initiated tasks faster, displayed more effort, and performed at a higher level than male subjects with a low nAchievement score. One early study (Veroff, Wilcox & Atkinson, 1953) confirmed the relationship between nAchievement scores and performance for women.

These and later studies have contributed to the overwhelming evidence of the construct validity and reliability of the basic theory and measurement system for

---

[1]The nAchievement score refers to the sum of the categories used to assess achievement motivation through thematic apperception. We will hereafter use the term nAchievement to refer to that score.

males. The theory was later expanded to include a fear of failure motive, which was thought to inhibit achievement motivation and behavior (Atkinson, 1958), and a measure of it was subtracted from the nAchievement score to derive a resultant score. Other studies have shown that, in addition to the findings mentioned above, males with a high resultant nAchievement score persisted longer at an achievement task after failure (Feather, 1966), preferred moderate risks (Atkinson, 1958; Litwin, 1966; Moulton, 1966), and preferred consecutively more difficult tasks after success (Feather, 1963). Again, these results were not found with females.

EXPLANATIONS FOR SEX DIFFERENCES IN THE STUDY OF ACHIEVEMENT MOTIVATION

Four major explanations of sex differences in experimental findings have been proposed. These are the following:

1. Females are at their peak level of achievement motivation in the neutral condition, so experimental procedures cannot possibly heighten that level.
2. Females have complex, sometimes conflicting, responses to themes of women in achievement situations, which interfere with the straightforward use of pictures of women to elicit achievement imagery.
3. Females are motivated for achievement by social approval and the need for affiliation, so the experimental procedures used failed to engage their achievement motivation.
4. Females, more often than males, fear success, which inhibits the expression of achievement motivation in behavior.

Each of these somewhat interrelated explanations has been the subject of much research, but none has been shown to explain the "problem" of women and traditional achievement behavior conclusively. The following section reviews research related to each explanation.

Females at Their Peak nAchievement Level in the Neutral Condition

Not only was the nAchievement level of females equal in both the relaxed and aroused conditions, their scores in the neutral condition were found to be higher than the scores for males in the *aroused* condition (Veroff, Wilcox & Atkinson, 1953). One early explanation of these results was that females are hypersensitive to achievement cues in the environment and so the neutral condition is, for them, similar to arousal condition. Females, if they are at their highest level of nAchievement in the neutral condition, would of course be unable to increase those scores in an arousal condition.

Attempts were made to decrease the achievement cues within the experimental situation. Veroff, Wilcox, and Atkinson (1953) purposely attempted to set up a very relaxed atmosphere for the neutral condition, and still found no increase in nAchievement scores from that to the traditional aroused condition. They found that the projective stories of the females had equivalent themes in both conditions, implying that these conditions were virtually equal in evoking achievement imagery for them.

The experiments of Field (1951), Lesser, Krawitz, and Packard (1963), and French and Lesser (1964) discussed below replicated Veroff, Wilcox, and Atkinson's (1953) finding that females' nAchievement scores were much higher in the neutral condition than those of their male counterparts.

Complex Responses to Male and Female Cues

The early validation studies showed that female-cued cards tended to elicit less achievement imagery for both sexes than did male-cued cards. In fact, the achievement motivation scores of males as well as of females did not increase under arousal to female-cued pictures (Veroff, Wilcox & Atkinson, 1953).

These findings served as fairly good evidence that neither sex considered achievement within the realm of women's role and so were unable to imagine females in achievement situations. This seemed particularly ominous for female subjects. Because the response to projective cues involves some measure of identification with the cue character, it appeared that women subjects were either unable to project their own achievement desires onto the female cue characters, or that they had none to project.

It was felt that perhaps the response to female-cued pictures was moderated by the achievement orientations of the women. Lesser, Krawitz, and Packard (1963) matched females who were low achievers and high achievers in school on IQ, and measured nAchievement under neutral and aroused conditions to *both* male and female pictures. High achievers increased to female pictures only. The high achievers also had higher nAchievement scores than did the underachievers.

Although Lesser, Krawitz, and Packard (1963) have suggested that only high achievers considered achievement relevant to the feminine role, and so only they could identify with the females in achievement situations, this did not really justify why they did not increase to male pictures as well (Horner, 1968). Nor does their argument explain the variation in overall nAchievement scores according to the sex of the cue character. They were ignoring the fact that female cue characters were shown in homemaking situations more often than in career settings in this and most other studies, which may account, in part, for the lower nAchievement imagery to female-cued pictures.

French and Lesser (1964) continued in the same tradition with their study of the impact of personal value orientations on nAchievement scores in women. Females were divided into those who valued traditional feminine pursuits, those who valued intellectual, achievement-oriented goals, and those who valued both equal-ly.[2] They assessed *n*Achievement to male- and female-cued pictures under conditions of achievement arousal and feminine role arousal. Higher levels of achievement motivation were found for male-cued pictures under intellectual arousal and for female-cued pictures under feminine role arousal. Also, *n*Achievement scores increased in intellectual and feminine role arousal conditions as compared to neutral conditions, but only for women who valued the appropriate goal orientation. Personal value orientation related to overall *n*Achievement only for those women who valued both intellectual and feminine goals. These women did not show as much achievement imagery to female-cued pictures under any condition. Finally, *n*Achievement scores for female-cued pictures predicted performance data better than scores for male-cued pictures for all subjects except those who valued both orientations.

This study was important in that it showed that projective cues with female characters could elicit more achievement imagery than male-cued pictures under certain conditions, that the *n*Achievement scores of women could increase under arousal, and that the *n*Achievement scores from female-cued pictures were more reliable predictors of behavior for most subjects than were scores from male-cued pictures.

Women have thus been shown to be reluctant to write achievement-oriented stories to female-cued pictures unless conditions suggest that achievement is consistent with the feminine role. Further, the lower *n*Achievement scores derived from female-cued pictures for both men and women suggest that both sexes have difficulty thinking of women as desiring achievement and striving for achievement goals, both in imagination and in real life.

Females' Achievement as Motivated by Affiliative Needs

One intriguing result of the French and Lesser (1964) study was the increase in *n*Achievement scores to female cues under feminine role arousal. This experimental procedure in effect told women that achievement could be attained within the feminine domain (e.g., excellence in social skills). Many years earlier, Field (1951) had shown that women's *n*Achievement scores increased under similar conditions, when excellence would guarantee social approval.

---

[2]We are aware that the normative connotation for the term ''achievement'' embodies traditionally masculine actions and desires. While a person should be able to ''achieve'' while cooking, caring for a child, house-cleaning—i.e., doing traditionally feminine activities—French and Lesser and other authors define achievement as the pursuit of excellence in academic, occupational and socially competitive arenas. For the most part, we will use the term ''achievement'' as it has been used traditionally, realizing that excellence can be pursued through diverse activities. It is excellence in the occupational and social-competitive fields which have eluded women for many years and which this chapter will emphasize.

A persistent theory in the field has been that females are primarily concerned with affiliation and so construe achievement in terms of its effects on affiliative success. In fact, there is reason to believe that nAffiliation (a score parallel to nAchievement, used to assess affiliation motivation; see Atkinson, Heyns & Veroff, 1954) may be related to the achievement behavior of women (Hoffman, 1972). Females have also been shown to have higher nAffiliation scores than males (e.g., Romer, 1974).

The literature shows that the only increase in nAchievement scores for women has been found under conditions linking affiliative and achievement concerns, presumably bringing competition and achievement behavior within the feminine role. It would be very tempting to assume a relationship between achievement motivation and affiliation motivation for women, as Hoffman (1972) implies.

There has been virtually no work done on this relationship, but Atkinson and Reitman (1958) did study males with different combinations of high and low nAchievement and nAffiliation. They found that high levels of nAffiliation decreased the relationship between nAchievement and performance, the multiplicity of incentives increasing subjects' total motivation level past that which is optimal for performance. This finding suggests that if women are highly affiliation oriented, the addition of a need for affiliation may obstruct their achievement behavior: Achievement, for them, may always entail multiple incentives. Women's psychological resolution may be to make their achievement desires subservient to those of affiliation.

The relationship between affiliation motivation and achievement-oriented behavior was later clarified by Atkinson and O'Connor (1966). They showed that strong affiliation motivation enhanced the level of performance at an achievement task when the experimental situation implied social approval for excellence. In people for whom affiliation is an important need, incentives such as social approval or affection would offset the effects of low or inhibited achievement motivation.

It is an important assumption here that only a moderate level of nAffiliation be elicited, however, since extreme levels of arousal have been shown to inhibit performance (Atkinson & Litwin, 1960). A situation implying social *dis*approval for excellence might elicit such extreme levels of affiliation motivation. This could be the situation in which many females find themselves, both in experiments and in real life. Whether in an overt or subtle manner, women may receive the message that either they risk jeopardizing social approval for outstanding achievement, or they can be guaranteed social approval for low achievement, particularly when competing against another person (Horner, 1968). Although their affiliative needs may place females in such a situation when the major incentive for achievement is social approval, these same needs at a more moderate level may promote achievement behavior. This may explain, as Hoffman (1972) suggests, the superior achievement of females as compared with males in elementary school, and the drastic reversal in high school and college. Elementary school girls' affiliation motivation may be moderate, but it could get even higher in high school. As their affiliation incentives change, so might their total motivational level for achievement. Thus, the affiliation motive in females is important in determining the meaning and operation of their achievement

Fear of Success

By far the most elaborate and enticing explanation of women's "problem" with achievement is Horner's (1968) theory of the fear of success. This theory provides important insights because it focuses on theory rather than methodology, and thus analyzes some fundamental issues directly. Horner found that the theory of achievement motivation was unable to account for the experimental results with women and for women's lower achievement.

Horner has thus extended achievement motivation theory by postulating a motive to avoid success. This motive characterizes people who expect negative consequences from success, most frequently affiliative loss, and so avoid achievement. Like all motives, the fear of success was considered a stable personality characteristic that was learned in early childhood. Horner claimed that the motive should be found more frequently in women; that it should be aroused in competitive situations; and that it should characterize achievement-oriented women while inhibiting their achievement behavior.

Fear of success was assessed by having subjects write a story to the following cue:

> After first term finals, Anne (John) finds herself (himself) at the top of her (his) medical school class.

Horner's study found that 62% of the female subjects and 10% of the male subjects wrote stories concerning the negative consequences of Anne's or John's success. Females with fear of success performed an achievement task better when working alone than when competing against a male. No parallel relationships could be tested for males, since there were too few of them with fear of success to conduct performance trials. It thus seemed as if the fear of success could be one factor inhibiting the achievement behavior of females.

The theory of fear of success has inspired much research and, consequently, much criticism as well. Before reviewing the research which studied the minutiae of fear of success theory and methodology, it is important to note the contributions made by Horner which have been overlooked in the literature.

Apart from the great contribution in swinging the focus of research on women's achievement back to the analysis of basic theory, Horner has helped to clarify the nature of the achievement situation. She distinguishes two aspects of such situations: competition against a standard of excellence and competition against other people. It is with the latter that people with fear of success are presumed to have problems. This distinction would seem to be a critical one for those researchers studying women's motivation, as it is well known that females tend to be more attentive to the interpersonal/affiliative concerns within a situation than are males. This, in fact, is Horner's explanation of the higher incidence of fear of success in women.

Secondly, Horner has proposed ways in which females' socialization engenders fear of success. She claims that fear of success is a result of sex-role training, through which females come to acknowledge societal restrictions on their achievement, and the consequences of violating these restrictions. This is important not only because it recognizes societal impact on personality development, but also because it implies that societal standards are internalized and thus come to have motivational significance.

Another of Horner's major contributions is her suggestion of relationships between motives. Fear of success theory makes sense out of the studies linking affiliative arousal and achievement behavior by showing how a perceived threat to affiliative goals inhibits performance. Horner has also assumed a relationship between fear of success and the need for achievement. Other motives were thought to be independent of the achievement motive, but the motive to avoid success was assumed to be at least partially dependent on the achievement orientation of the individual. Unfortunately, Horner has been vague about this aspect of fear of success. In fact, she claims that fear of success is at once related to a high need for achievement, because it characterizes achievement-oriented people, and to a low need for achievement, because it inhibits achievement motivation and behavior. Regardless of the lack of precision in Horner's description, she has stimulated a fertile area of inquiry because the hypothesis of a relationship between motives had rarely before been considered.

The above contributions, in spite of their significance to the field of motivation, have been neglected in favor of concentration on the most socially relevant issue raised by the theory—do women inhibit their achievement strivings because of a disposition to avoid success? As the sum of findings has accrued, however, the value of the theory in fully explaining the problems concerning women and achievement has diminished.

Tresemer (1976, 1977) has recently reviewed the research on fear of success that has accumulated since Horner's (1968) original statement. Several paths of research and thought are notable. One major research question has been whether fear of success imagery is a reflection of motivation or merely the predictably stereotyped response to a woman's success given the status of women in American society and its lack of encouragement (and even active discouragement) of their achievement. A flurry of studies has tested whether fear of success is a function of the sex of the stimulus figure. Depending on the study and the reviewer, the gender of the cue character does and does not have an impact on the frequency of fear of success imagery. In general, more fear of success imagery is written by females to the "Anne" cue than to the "John" cue (Condry & Dyer, 1976; Monahan, Kuhn, & Shaver, 1974; Tresemer, 1976, 1977; Zuckerman & Wheeler, 1975). This is not true for males. Obviously, if fear of success is simply a response to a stereotype, males as well as females should write more fear of success stories to the Anne cue. Thus, the fear of success cannot be seen as completely determined by stereotypical responses, but the sex of the cue character does have some effect on females. One explanation of this may be the greater identification with a same-sexed cue character for females, in conjunction with their greater willingness to express negative affect.

Most studies have shown fear of success to be valid and meaningful only for females. As predicted by Horner, fear of success has been shown to increase in frequency with age in females only up to young adulthood (Horner & Rhoem, 1972), and functions as a motive in adolescence (Romer, 1974; Sutherland, 1980), a developmental sequence that parallels the acquisition of sex-role attitudes and behaviors. Also, fear of success has been generally found to be more frequent in females (Tresemer, 1976, 1977), but never to the extent found by Horner in her original study. In addition, Hoffman (1974, 1977), Romer (1974), and Sutherland (1980) have also found the content of fear of success to be different for males and females, as has Tresemer in his review of many studies. The modal theme of women's stories seems to be affiliative loss—the fear of losing the affection of friends, lovers, husbands. Males most often question the value of success, writing stories that depict the uselessness and folly of achievement pursuits. Because this divergence in content may parallel a divergence in the operation of fear of success in males and females, this finding may explain why the fear of success has never been validated for males and has never proven a useful variable in predicting their achievement behavior. Fear of success for females may be indicative of a conflict between achievement and affiliative needs, probably resulting from their sex-role socialization (Horner, 1968; Romer, 1974). Males may have no such conflict, but they may experience disillusionment with both the idea and reality of success, due to the pressures on them to succeed and/or the negative modelling of "successful" male adults in their lives (e.g., their fathers, brothers, etc.).

The scoring system for fear of success has also presented a problem for researchers. All other motive scoring systems first code for imagery and then code for subcategories, so there is agreement on the general theme of stories coded as "high" in any one motive. This is not so for fear of success. The presence of any number of themes can be coded for imagery, and so the content of fear of success may be qualitatively different from person to person. This is dangerous in research on sex differences when, despite greatly different thematic content in the stories of men and women, each qualifies as evidence of fear of success. Fear of success is treated in theory and in research as if it were a unitary construct, yet an analysis of the scoring system indicates it is multi-dimensional.

In spite of all these problems, one can still be impressed with the construct validity of the measure of fear of success. Unlike most of the research on the relationship of nAchievement to behavior, studies of fear of success have frequently gone outside the laboratory situation to find the consequences of the motive on real-life behaviors. Most notable are Hoffman's (1977) findings that fear of success in certain women predicts an earlier marriage, marriage to an older man, and more children as compared to women without fear of success. Most interestingly, Hoffman has also found that fear of success predicted an unplanned pregnancy on the eve of a long-awaited success. Moore (1974) has found that females with fear of success have more children than those without fear of success. Sutherland (1980) has found that both males and females with fear of success value having friends more highly than doing well in school, and fear of success was found to relate to poor relationships with the same-sex parent. Thus, fear of success has been found to have important behavioral consequences in both the achievement and affiliative domains.

Fear of success is an important contribution to the theory of achievement motivation. Research on it has been inadequate and has provided conflicting reports of its meaningfulness and validity in the prediction of laboratory behavior in males and females, but much of this can be attributed to the unsystematic and fad-oriented sequence of studies. Fear of success theory helps to illuminate many grey areas within achievement motivation theory and it shows great promise as a predictor of real-life behavior in women.

Summary.   Although we have explored a number of different explanations for the researchers' difficulties in establishing the validity of the objective assessment of achievement motivation for women in American society, a common theme seems to underlie the various explanations. Because of the symbolic meaning of women achieving in a man's world, conflicts, new societal incentives, and inhibitions have emerged that interfere both with the straightforward expression of achievement fantasies and the straightforward connection between the level of motivation aroused and its expression in behavior. To state it simply, women's sex-role expectations may be incompatible with achieving. Accounting for their roles may thus help us understand their interpretations and expressions of achievement motivation.

In the rest of this chapter we expand on this theme; we demonstrate that women's sex-role expectations color the way in which achievement information is acknowledged, interpreted, and acted upon in women's strivings. But we also go one step further, and apply the same idea to men. We suggest that men's sex-role expectations also color the way in which achievement information is acknowledged, interpreted, and acted upon in their strivings. Accounting for sex-role expectations only gives us new ways of thinking not only about women's achievement motivation, but also about men's.

SEX ROLES AND THE THEORY OF ACHIEVEMENT MOTIVATION

Although the impact of sex roles has been considered a determining factor in the connection of achievement motivation to the achievement behavior of women (see especially Alper, 1974), this idea has never really been extended to include men. In this section we discuss the moderate risk-taking and competitive behaviors that characterize masculine achievement motivation as consistent with the male-assertive role: being superior in comparison with others.

The remainder of this chapter pursues the impact of sex roles as mediators between achievement incentives and behavior. To do this, we reconsider some previous research and also present some results on achievement motivation that have not yet been presented. Our analysis of sex roles and achievement motivation will be grouped into six major topics: (1) the relationship of the achievement motive to other motives; (2) the expression of achievement motivation in occupational and family role behaviors; (3) the combined significance of achievement motivation when it is linked to other social concerns; (4) dimensions of achievement motivation; (5) continuities and discontinuities of achievement motivation across the life-span; (6) the socio-historical context for achievement motivation. For each analysis we consider the impact of both male and female sex roles on the topic.

Relationships between the Achievement and Other Motives

Motivational dispositions have long been considered independent of one another, both statistically and conceptually. Our review of the literature indicates that this view should be reevaluated. Sex roles appear to influence these relationships, since females' achievement concerns seem linked with affiliative concerns and, as we will discuss, males' appear linked with the power-oriented concerns of social impact and competition.

There has been little research testing for any kind of relationship between achievement and other motives. Studies on the correlation of achievement with other motives have been the most frequent. For males, these have shown a *negative* correlation between nAchievement and nAffiliation (Sutherland, 1980; Veroff, 1983), nAchievement and fear of success (Romer, 1974; Sutherland, 1980; Tresemer, 1977), and nAchievement and fear of weakness or Veroff nPower (Veroff, 1983). NAchievement is negatively correlated with test anxiety and fear of success for females (e.g., Sutherland, 1980; Tresemer, 1977); the motive is *positively* correlated with nAffiliation (Romer, 1976; Sutherland, 1980; Veroff, 1980) and also with hope for power or Winter nPower (Veroff, 1983) for them.

This pattern of results can be seen as influenced by traditional sex roles. Males and females with high nAchievement seem to be following stereotypic male or female roles: the strong, competent male; the socially concerned, nurturant female. Highly achievement-oriented males are unconcerned with the social anxieties of failing (low Text Anxiety), making friends (low nAffiliation), or appearing weak (low in nPower). Females with high nAchievement, however are those most concerned with pleasing others (high nAffiliation) and having status in the eyes of others (high *n*Power). Veroff (1983), in fact, has found that males and females with high *n*Achievement conform most to their sex roles and, therefore, are considered the most socially adjusted. These results imply that both males and females who are achievement-oriented learn their lessons in sex roles well. Some further evidence of this is described in the next section.

Thus, the pattern of results also suggests that achievement motivation may have very different meaning for males and females. Perhaps the most interesting is the difference in how *n*Achievement is related to *n*Affiliation among males and females. As discussed earlier, many researchers have speculated that achievement and affiliative concerns are fused in women. Women, perhaps, cannot feel successful unless *both* their affiliative and achievement needs are met. This, of course, is one explanation of fear of success in women. Women, it is speculated, are often in the position of having to choose between success and love or friendship. The feminine role traditionally precludes competitive success; females desiring success risk social ostracism. A female with high achievement and affiliative needs might be in an especially precarious position. The outcome of this situation might indeed be fear of success, as Horner (1968) suggests. Another outcome may be a press on women to refine the meaning and operation of achievement for themselves, so that these would be consistent with the feminine sex role.

Similar reasoning can be applied to the situation of males. The traditional masculine sex role calls for excellence in comparison with set social standards: competition. Certainly, over-concern with making or keeping friends would interfere with competition. As males are not traditionally taught the value of, or skills in, social interaction to the same degree as females, and thus typically have lower *n*Affiliation scores, males may have to disengage from the social concerns of an achievement situation to succeed. Also, because males in particular are taught the value of appearing strong in the eyes of society, only those males with a relatively low fear of weakness may be able to take the necessary risks involved in striving for success.

Although the results indicate that sex roles influence the relationships between motives, we get further evidence for these speculations when we look at results that contrast the behaviors connected to achievement motivation for men and women. Some of these results are briefly presented in the next section.

The Differential Relationship of Achievement Motivation and Behavior in Men and Women

We have already discussed many of the results relating achievement motivation and behavior for males and females; in fact, it is the disparity in the two sets of results that has spurred the present investigation. Males with high *n*Achievement perform faster and more competently than males with low *n*Achievement, although no such relationship exists for females. Why?

The explanation we have posited is that for women the stereotyped sex role interferes with the connection between achievement motivation and the behavior studied. Such interference would also exist for men if achievement behaviors atypical of men were to be examined. While the interfering impact of sex roles is not obvious in the results of Atkinson, McClelland, and other early researchers—largely because they did not often use female subjects—later studies of the effect of nAchievement on real-life behavior show compelling evidence of the influence of sex roles. Much of this, too, has been discussed. But the most comprehensive study of motives and behavior comes from Veroff and his colleagues, in two national sample surveys from 1957 to 1976.

In the earlier study, Veroff and Feld (1970) found that a high need for achievement related to marital and parental behaviors for women, but not for men. Achievement motivation was quite tied to work behaviors and attitudes for men, though, primarily relating to "disquiet" or "dissatisfaction" due to the ever escalating need for challenge that high nAchievement demands. Working women were not analyzed in that study.

The later survey (Veroff, 1983) replicated much of what had been found, but went several steps further. The new study showed that high nAchievement in both men and women is related to sex-role consistent activities and attitudes. Again, nAchievement was found to relate to work for males: Men with high nAchievement saw work as fulfilling their major life values, found their jobs interesting and held prestigious positions. Achievement motivation was thus found to be facilitative of work adjustment for males. More importantly, males with high nAchievement also showed signs of greater well-being than males with low nAchievement: They were happier and more satisfied with their lives.

Although achievement motivation was not found to be related to work for females, it was highly related to leisure-time activities and family attitudes and behaviors for them—which may, in fact, constitute "achievement" for them. Females with high nAchievement seemed more concerned with their families and their civic responsibilities than did other women. Like the men, women with high nAchievement also showed evidence of greater well-being.

These results suggest that males and females with high nAchievement may conform more to sex-role demands than those who are less achievement-motivated. Because there is little divergence between their attitudes or behaviors and those prescribed by their sex roles, men and women with high nAchievement show greater social adjustment and general well-being.

These findings further reinforce our interpretation of the large body of research results on nAchievement: The disparity in results with males and females is due in no small part to the influence of normative sex-role expectations. Males and females with high nAchievement behave in sex-stereotypic ways; females with high nAchievement behave differently from males because stereotypic sex roles prescribe different behavior and attitudes. Moreover, social science has, for the most part, perpetuated the view that achievement is defined by traditional masculine attitudes and behaviors.

The Combined Significance of Achievement Motivation and Social Orientation

As researchers in achievement motivation have tried to encompass more varied situations and more heterogeneous populations in the data that they examine, it has become clear that studying the motive to achieve in combination with critical social orientations of men and women will give researchers a more complete understanding of the dynamics of achievement strivings. This insight reflects the general position we are adopting in this paper: sex-role orientations in both men and women interact with their motive structure to determine behavior. Stein and Bailey (1973) and Hoffman (1972) have emphasized that the affiliative component to achievement may be the crucial basis for women's achievement strivings. Indirectly, this same idea propels the insights offered by the fear of success research on women. We think the idea should be extended to include men.

No study better demonstrates this viewpoint than Walker and Heyns' (1962) use of both achievement and affiliation motives to understand conformity. They have found that those women high in nAchievement but low in affiliation motivation tend to ignore a personal friend's request to lower their own performance levels in order to help their friend's performance. By contrast, those women low in achievement motivation but high in affiliation motivation would comply with their friend's pleas. Men, no matter what their pattern of motive scores were, do not comply. One might argue that most men are expected to be more concerned with achievement than affiliation, even if their social concerns are strong. The pattern of results for both sexes fits nicely into our speculation that achievement motivation predicts behavior only when one accounts for each of the sex-role ideals—males as competitive individuated people, and females as competent but socially concerned individuals.

More recent results of a longitudinal study conducted by Sutherland (1980) give further credence to the idea that patterns of achievement and affiliation motivation are particularly critical to consider in the study of female achievement strivings. Sutherland conducted a follow-up study of the research that Romer (1974) initiated with children aged 9 through 16. In 1979, Sutherland interviewed 60 males and 54 females who had participated in the original study. Romer had measured achievement and affiliation motivation in 1972; Sutherland also measured these motivations, along with other measures. Sutherland found, in relating both achievement and affiliation motivation to achievement-related behaviors and antecedents, that only in combination with low nAffiliation was the use of achievement motive scores predictive of achievement-related phenomena for females. For the males, however, the achievement motive scores alone related to achievement-oriented behaviors and attitudes. Males, therefore, would seem to have a more singular, unconflicted involvement with achievement; women appear to have social concerns that interfere with that involvement.

Men, however, are not always unconflicted about individualistic achievement. Indeed, Atkinson's powerful achievement motivation theory and research findings (Atkinson & Feather, 1966) hinge on isolating a group of men who are high in achievement motive but low in fear of failure. The usual measure of fear of failure in Atkinson's research is the Test Anxiety Scale, a measure its originators (Sarason et al., 1960) claim reflects an unconscious *dependency* on others. One can interpret the pattern of men high in achievement and low in fear of failure as the true masculine ideal. By contrast, those who are low in the achievement motive but high in test anxiety may very well be the most unmasculine, in stereotypic terms. It is this contrast between the high achievement–low test anxiety and the low achievement–high test anxiety for which most of Atkinson's critical results emerge. Thus, one may argue the Atkinson has implicitly acknowledged the need to study the achievement motive in combination with measures of social concern. In this work, the most masculine role extreme is pitted against the most unmasculine role extreme in order to attain results that differentiate men's achievement strivings. Men who are achievement-motivated but free of test anxiety lack social conflict. Thus, they should have the most realistic risk orientation, the most motivated and persistent behaviors, perhaps because they are the ones least involved with the social concerns that both increase anxiety about failure and impede appropriate achievement choices and optimal performance.

Thus, taking account of social concerns along with achievement motivation helps us understand how achievement motivation translates into behavior for both men and women. Social concerns can at times interfere with the expression of individualistically oriented achievement desires. These social concerns seem to be *affiliative* for women but are best represented as *fear of failure* for men. For women, affiliative concerns seem to be positive competing orientations, ones that direct women to make other choices in lieu of achieving; for men, fear-of-failure concerns seem to be negative, inhibitory orientations, ones that press men away from achievement to avoid failure, or dampen their performance.

Dimensions of Achievement Motivation

As work on achievement motivation has expanded, it has naturally begun to differentiate types of situations that do not elicit achievement incentives from those that do. It is now clear that certain types of achievement situations may be especially central to men, and others expecially central to women. If incentives are sex-specific, we suggest the following: Men are more likely to rely on certain standards of excellence that fit into male roles and women are more likely to rely on other standards of excellence that fit into female roles. This type of reasoning has led a number of theorists (Helmreich, et al., 1980; Kipnis, 1974; Veroff, 1977; Veroff, McClelland, & Ruhland, 1975) to differentiate types of achievement motivation that may be more characteristic of one sex or the other, but are clearly relevant to both sexes.

From this work, we derive the following propositions: For men, the power-mastery and the social comparison aspects of achieving are critical for their individuation as men in our society; for women, intrinsic aspects of doing well and autonomous standards of excellence are critical to the female role. Thus, power-mastery and social comparison definitions of achievement should be more typical of men's strivings; intrinsic or autonomous orientations to achievement should be more typical of women's strivings. We examine these assertions in some detail, because in some ways they are counter to the stereotypes that one has about the nature of peculiarly feminine achievement styles. They also get at the heart of our thesis that achievement motivation has to be assessed in the context of each sex role.

For a long while (see Crandall, 1963), theorists have been exploring different dimensions of achievement orientations. This work is detailed in Veroff, Mc-Clelland, and Ruhland (1975) and Veroff and Veroff (1980) but has gotten its most lively examination in recent work by Helmreich, Spence and their colleagues (1980). Two somewhat independent bipolar dimensions to achievement can be posited.

The first dimension contrasts motivation for achievement that requires social impact with motivation that is intrinsically oriented to task accomplishment. This is an important differentiation. Although people can be equally oriented toward excellence in task performance, their interpretation of excellence can be different to the extent that they also fuse power with accomplishment. If a person thinks about task accomplishment as also having social impact (power), his/her orientation to work, to success, or to failure might be quite different than as if he/she were to think of accomplishment without that added social impact. One can argue quite easily that men's orientation to task accomplishment contains many elements of power while women's orientation to task accomplishment is much more centered around their intrinsic orientation to the task. This differentiation is in keeping with traditional stereotypes of sex roles. Men, in traditional terms, are interested in being assertive and having social impact; task accomplishment that has social impact will thus be very attractive to them. Women, in traditional terms, may be more modest, involved in doing something for its own sake without public display or recognition.

Such a distinction may also play some part in the continued findings showing some discrepancy between men and women's predictions about their own success or failure at tasks (e.g., Crandall, 1969). Men are more likely to exaggerate their own success; women are more likely to be modest. While these results have been interpreted as saying that men are more achievement motivated, we would now interpret them to mean that men select the social impact side of achievement more quickly than do women, and women select the more intrinsic orientation to achievement more quickly than do men.

In the same way, we can look at some of the results about sex differences in attribution about success and failure (e.g., Denmark, Tangri, & McCandless, 1975; Hansen & O'Leary, this volume). Compared to women, men are more quick to attribute success to themselves and failure to a task. If men were more involved with the social impact of their task accomplishments or failures they would attribute their own success to the world. If women were more involved with the intrinsic aspects of task accomplishment they would be less anxious than men about seeing their own involvements with failure on a task.

A second bipolar dimension can be introduced to think about still other types of achievement orientations which, again, may implicate sex roles differently. Kipnis (1974) has convincingly argued that men, more so than women, rely on peer comparisons to evaluate success; women, on the other hand, seem more oriented to their own autonomous improvement in performance, or their own internal relationship to a task. Kipnis argues that this may have occurred because, unlike men, women learn achievement standards in close connection with their parents' or teachers' standards—standards that they internalize early. Boys are shunted off into peer attachments more quickly and thus become more oriented to social comparisons as a way to establish what success or failure is about. This is a very insightful set of ideas. While women may be very concerned about pleasing others, they are theorized to be *less* concerned than men about their performance with others. It is true that women may choose affiliative or communal types of goals over achievement goals more than men, but when women *do* orient themselves to achievement, this line of argument suggests that they are *more* likely than men to be *internal* in their conception of excellence. Kipnis' persuasive argument is that men, by contrast, are more persistently involved in peer comparisons.

In the two bipolar dimensions suggested, men and women can be differentiated in the following ways: Men are more involved in having social impact through task accomplishment and more involved in social comparison in evaluating excellence; women are more involved in the intrinsic aspects of task accomplishment and have more autonomous standards for judging excellence in performance. It is important to point out that men's orientation to mastery through either impact or social comparison evaluations should not be characterized as simply a desire for *competitive* mastery. Social comparison or social impact can be the basis of setting standards, or arriving at goals, that may have nothing to do with winning or beating other people out. Social impact can come about through noncompetitive means. And social comparison does not necessarily entail being competitive with other people; social comparison can give people means of establishing what excellence is all about. It should also be pointed out that there is little evidence in any research that the projective measure of achievement motivation primarily reflects a strong competitive orientation (see Veroff, McClelland, & Ruhland, 1975). Rather, it reflects mastery or social comparison orientations, which, as we have said, may not necessarily be competitive. Very recent research by Helmreich et al. (1980) suggests that, although mastery and power orientation to achievement are important in predicting accomplishments among students and scientists, a strictly competitive orientation is, if anything, a *negative* predictor of performance.

Women's intrinsic or autonomous orientations to excellence may have been considerably ignored in research on women's achievement orientation. Women's obvious overriding affiliative orientations are more readily documented. Nevertheless, intrinsic or autonomous achievement orientations often crop up in women's behavior. Consider the intrinsic pleasures of accomplishment that must occur in household tasks (cooking, cleaning) that rarely get recognized because they so often need replacement each day in daily routines. Also consider such observations found in systematic research. Veroff (1969) has found that among elementary school aged girls there is *more* achievement orientation to improvement in performance than there is among boys. When trying to master their own skills, girls are less likely than boys to take extreme risks, the kinds of risks that Atkinson (1958) labels as indicative of fear of failure. House (1972) has also found that college women, compared to college men, are much more likely to select achievement-motivated preferences for autonomous tasks, but are just as likely to select motivated preferences in social comparison settings. In Helmreich et al's (1980) work, women were higher than men in a work orientation to achievement. Depner and Veroff (1979) have shown that women are more responsive than men to achievement imagery in response to cues about a person trying to accomplish a task by her/himself. Thus, both casual observation and systematic research point to the fact that women are more intrinsically and autonomously oriented to their achievement than are men.

As society moves toward a greater idealization of androgyny perhaps these distinctions in types of achievement motivation that are coordinated with traditional masculinity and femininity will be less critical. For now, it is best to recognize that a variety of dimensions do exist and that certain dimensions are more relevant to one sex or another because they fit traditionally stereotypic sex roles. Nevertheless, all dimensions represent achievement orientations to which everyone is exposed, and which, in one way or another, everyone activates in their achievement strivings.

Continuities and Discontinuities in Achievement Orientation Across the Life-Span

In what way can we interpret developmental continuities and discontinuities in achievement orientations as related to the major thesis of this paper, that sex-role orientations interact with achievement strivings for both men and women? Our analysis is divided into two related questions: (1) Is there evidence for stability in the achievement orientations of men and women across the life-span? (2) Are there any indications of specific age differences within men's or women's orientation to achievement?

Evidence of Stability of Achievement Orientation.   Considerable research has now been devoted to the question of how persistent achievement orientations are for people. By and large, these results have been confined to the examination of the childhood, adolescent, and early adult stages of life. Kagan and Moss (1958) found achievement orientations to be stable in both boys and girls over 3-year intervals during childhood. Feld (1960) found achievement to be stable in boys over a 6-year period from childhood through adolescence, and Moss and Kagan (1961) found stability for males and females from adolescence through adulthood. Hoffman (1977) found stability in both nAchievement and fear of success for females from college years to the late 20s. Sutherland (1980) has more recently shown that although scores from adolescence through young adulthood were slightly more stable, there is virtually no stability in achievement scores from childhood through adolescence for boys. Girls show very little stability in achievement scores. In sum, even though there has been some inconsistency, considerable stability in assessments of achievement orientations across childhood and adolescent periods exists. Only two studies go much beyond late adolescence, and these two are inconsistent with one another.

The stability in the early stages of life is not surprising when we consider issues of sex roles. Family socialization for both achievement and sex roles is likely to be fairly consistent across the early developmental period. While adolescent peer socialization may introduce discrepancies from family socialization, the results suggest that family socialization prevails. This is not unlike Conger's (1978) resumé of the sources of adolescent socialization of most orientations.

Sutherland's results perhaps indicate that recent late adolescent socialization may in fact be very powerful in undoing the stability that family socialization may have once produced in achievement orientation. Nesselroade and Baltes (1974), in their analysis of personality data, have shown that adolescence is a critical time, when the experiences of socio-historical events could make a deep and lasting impression on adolescents that may counteract early socialization of personal characteristics. We have some evidence that this is occurring in the achievement domain with the Sutherland data.

The question of stability of achievement orientations across the *adult* life-span has not been closely examined. The major data we can use to discuss this phenomenon come from two national surveys, one done in 1957 and one in 1976, where one can examine cohort continuities of mean levels of nAchievement. Veroff, Reuman, and Feld (in press) report little evidence that there is cohort continuity in the mean level of achievement orientation. We should be aware, however, that while the entire cohort goes up and down in mean level, individual differences *within* a cohort may remain stable. By looking at mean levels of motive scores alone, our conclusions about stability and continuity in achievement orientations in cohorts of men and women across life-spans must be tentative. Nevertheless, the lack of stability in the cohort suggests that motivations shift over the life-span. We would argue that as men and women enter and have experience with work and family roles, there could be very dramatic changes in their level of achievement orientation.

Elsewhere, Veroff, Feld, and Gurin (1962) have argued that certain groups of men have particularly high achievement orientations during midlife because it is a time when there is extraordinary family pressure on them to be providers. The elevation of Catholic men's achievement orientation during midlife has been interpreted as that group's particular reaction to family pressures. That group, we would argue, has had their adequacy as males called into question; hence, their achievement orientation was exacerbated. In the same way, women, once they raise children, can have their achievement orientations raised as they consider outside employment. This seems to have been the case for women in the 1976 national sample who were 40-50 years old. This was not true for the same group of women, in cohort terms, when they were younger. Thus we can see how fluctuations in sex roles, or changes in family integration patterns can enormously affect the achievement orientations of men and women, both in cohort and in individual terms. It is for this reason that there may not be much evidence for the stability of achievement orientations across the life-span.

Age Differences in Achievement Orientations.   Another approach to the study of developmental differences in achievement orientations is to note at what point in the life-cycle men and women are particularly high or particularly low in various types of achievement orientations. Studies of achievement orientations in both men and women rarely focus on an absolute level of scores. People who do research on nAchievement usually divide a group at the median or into thirds and talk about relatively high, relatively moderate, or relatively low scores, and to what these arbitrary levels are related. If one wants to examine age differences in achievement orientation, the absolute level of achievement orientation becomes critical. Rarely has this been the focus of achievement motivation research.

In one large-scale study, Veroff (1969) found that there was a rise in social comparison achievement orientation in middle childhood, which then plateaued. The autonomous achievement orientation plateaued relatively early in children's lives (around 6 or 7).[3]

Projective assessments of children's orientations were also taken in the Veroff (1969) study; boys' and girls' achievement orientation as measured through projective assessment rose throughout childhood. Boys' and girls' levels could not be compared directly because different pictures were used.

Sutherland's (1980) study can also be used to compare absolute levels of achievement orientation. For the purpose of age and birth cohort analyses, subjects in the study were divided into two groups: Those born from 1956 through

---

[3]It should be noted, however, that girls continue to rise in autonomous achievement orientation, a bit beyond boys in middle childhood. This age effect is quite in keeping with our sense that girls are more involved in autonomous orientations, and hence continue this involvement through childhood at a higher intensity, while boys are more likely to turn to social comparison orientations to achievement as a way to fulfill the masculine ideals.

TABLE 4.1
Mean *n*Achievement Scores in 1972 and 1979
for Earlier and Later Birth Cohorts (by Sex)

Year	Males		Females	
	Earlier Cohort	Later Cohort	Earlier Cohort	Later Cohort
1972	2.61 (N = 18)	2.73 (N = 26)	2.50 (N = 22)	2.52 (N = 27)
1979	2.35 (N = 28)	1.47 (N = 30)	1.50 (N = 26)	3.21 (N = 24)

1959 (13–16 years old in 1972 and 19–22 years old in 1979) were in the earlier cohort group; those born from 1960 to 1962 (9–12 years old in 1972 and 13–16 years old in 1979) were in the later cohort. Thus, the ages of the subjects ranged from 9 years old in 1972 to 22 years old in 1979. The mean level of achievement motive scores are presented in Table 4.1. The pattern is quite interesting. The mean level for males who went from childhood to adolescence show a considerable decline, while the mean for those who went from adolescence to adulthood is relatively stable. The mean achievement scores of each cohort group when at the same age range are also quite different: 2.61 in 1972 and 1.47 in 1979. Clearly, the socio-historical period had more of an effect than did the age of the subjects. The opposite is true for the females. The birth cohort that went from childhood to adolescence increased in achievement orientation; the cohort that went from adolescence to adulthood seemed to decrease. The later cohort group has a much higher mean score in 1979, when that group was adolescent, than did the earlier cohort group in 1972, when they were in the same age range. Again, social history may be the most important factor.

These results are not easily understandable, but they suggest that something very critical happened during the 70s that changed achievement orientations in adolescent boys and girls, perhaps in ways that had not been seen before. We can observe that during that time discussion of sex roles was often heard in school settings, as well as in the mass media. More explicit attention to androgyny as a value was occurring. These phenomena undoubtedly had historical effects on boys' and girls' achievement orientations during their adolescence.

Exciting data concerning age differences in achievement orientations among American adults are available in the comparison of the aforementioned 1957 and 1976 national surveys of *n*Achievement. These data are summarized in Figures 4.1 and 4.2. Figure 4.1 presents the results of plotting mean level of achievement motivation score for each 5-year interval of age separately for men in 1957 and in 1976. The mean scores are residualized scores, based on the elimination of the correlation of motive scores with story length. The mean for the total distribution

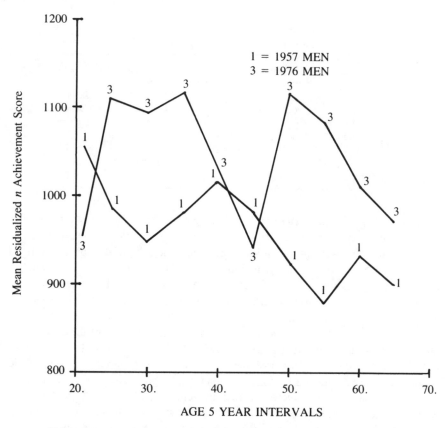

FIG. 4.1. Age Differences in Men's nAchievement in a 1957 and a 1976 National Sample Survey.

is 1,000 in both figures. Figure 4.2 presents the parallel data for women. What is remarkable about these figures, particularly for men, is the lack of any parallel patterns relating motive score to age. Although Fig. 4.1 indicates that men over 60 in both years tend to have relative low achievement motive scores, these results are not very significant. Also exciting are some clear reversals in these data.

Let us examine the results for men first. The peak in achievement motivation in 1957 was either at the very youngest age (21–25) or at midlife (between 35 and 45). The peak in 1976 is certainly no longer between the ages of 21 and 25, but occurs at the ages of 25–35 or 45–55. In no way do these results demonstrate any cohort effects. What do they demonstrate? They seem to reflect certain historical circumstances that affect why certain ages are particularly strong in achievement orientation. One can build a case for the very strong orientations to achievement in the very young (21–25) men in 1957 because the male sex role was so predominantly achievement-oriented at that time. As these young men were becoming particularly acclimated to work orientations in society at that time, it was quite natural for strong achievement orientations to be elicited. Similarly, in 1957 one can argue that the peak of achievement orientations was perhaps at midlife, between 40 and 45, when men presumably were coming into the peak of their social impact at work. In the 1950s it took some time to develop seniority and supervisory responsibility in work. Each of these situations was perhaps not so much the case in 1976. The 21–25 year olds in 1976 were undoubtedly experiencing some conflict about achievement. Considerable questioning of the male sex role and its emphasis on achievement had occurred. Twenty-one to 25-year-old men in 1976 were not the highest, but were among the lowest in nAchievement. The men between the ages 40 and 45, were also among the lowest in 1976. The achievement orientations for men at midlife were

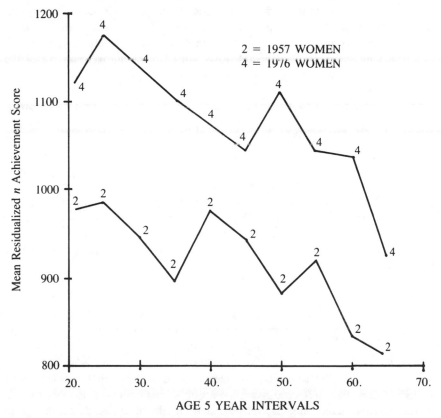

FIG. 4.2.   Age Differences in Women's nAchievement in a 1957 and a 1976 National Sample Survey.

called in question in the 1970s, and were evidently not in the 1950s. The midlife crisis was a 1970s phenomenon. With this reasoning, one would have to say that the men who were about 50 in 1976 were immune to the effects of pressures to change sex roles in our society. Their scores on nAchievement were still high.

If we look at the nAchievement results for women, we find that in both 1957 and 1976 younger women are generally higher in nAchievement than are older women. These results are significant in our analyses. More in evidence are the somewhat different curves in 1957 and 1976 for the different age periods between the youngest and oldest groups. The peaking of achievement orientation occurred for the 40–45-year-old women in 1957, but for the 50–55-year-old women in 1976. Why is this so? One way to read the results is to suggest that some revitalization of achievement motivation occurs for women when their children are out of the house. This explanation makes sense if we realize that women who were 40–45 in 1957 perhaps thought that their jobs as mothers were relatively complete, at least more so than women of a similar age in 1976. The 50–60-year-old women in 1976 were mothers during the baby boom. They had more children over a longer period of their child-bearing lives. Hence, their responsibilities as mothers were perhaps more prolonged. Another interpretation of the peaking of the 50–55-year-old women in 1976 is that this group may have been the one most susceptible to the pressures of the feminine demystification of the mother/wife role.

At any rate, Figures 4.1 and 4.2 clearly indicate that one cannot talk about achievement motivation as being consistently tied to one age group or another, especially for men. There is some tendency for it to be more tied to the younger groups of women and less tied to the older groups of women, but even within women the specific peaking of achievement orientation seems to come at slightly different ages. Thus, these graphs, based on the national studies, indicate that age differences are not consistent. They are best interpreted by understanding the particular historical context in which adults exist as younger or older members of our society. One critical aspect of each historical context is the particular orientation to sex roles that are relevant to people of a particular age in a particular historical time.

Historical Effects on Achievement Motives

The results just discussed make us aware of how much social history affects the achievement motivation of men and women in different ages. Although we have very little evidence that historical influences are laid down systematically at adolescence (as Baltes suggests), we clearly have evidence that historical time periods differentially affect a given age group's orientations. It is clear that all women at all ages have higher nAchievement in 1976 than do parallel groups in 1957 (see Fig. 4.2).

Examining the results in Figures 4.1 and 4.2 in cohort terms we find no clear evidence of cohort phenomena. A group that was particularly high in 1957 is not particularly high in 1976 for both males and females. We are thus in firm belief that the effects of historical circumstances will be peculiar to each major age group in the life-cycle. Particular historical periods interpret the relevance of achievement at a particular age for both men and women.

Our generalizations also seem pertinent to understanding Sutherland's (1980) data, discussed earlier. In her study, the later birth cohort of females' nAchievement scores had more evidence of construct validity than did the earlier birth cohort. Furthermore, the web of results relating achievement motive to other achievement-related factors for the later birth cohort was very similar to the result patterns for the males. Results for the earlier cohort of females thus seemed to account for the majority of the theory discrepant results. Furthermore, a within-cohort analysis for males showed that almost all of the results found to validate the construct of achievement motivation were found in the earlier birth cohort. The result patterns for both males and females were therefore similar, in that the later cohort groups of each sex deviated from the patterns created by the earlier, more traditional, cohort groups. The later birth cohorts showed result patterns similar to those of the opposite sex in the earlier cohort group. Whether this means that the younger generation is becoming androgynous with respect to achievement motivation is unclear. Certainly it is a hypothesis that bears examining in future research. We may very well be at a transition period, when results for younger females may look more like the older male pattern and results for younger males may look like the older female pattern. Once we pass this transitional point, when the expectations for both men and women in their roles will be truly parallel, perhaps the results for both men and women will be similar.

CONCLUSION

We have attempted to integrate our review of research on measuring achievement motivation of women, and the impact it has had on thinking about achievement motivation in general, by positing that sex roles influence how much achievement motivation is aroused and how it is translated into behavior. This conclusion would seem to be very obvious when considering the results for women, especially as the findings from using the fear of success instrument have come to play a role in research. Nevertheless, the conclusion seems as appropriate with regard to men's data as it is to women's. We have reviewed how this hypothesis may operate in the analysis of achievement motivation data for both sexes. We have found it useful in thinking about how motives are related to each other; how motives are translated into behavioral choices for both men and women; how the motive for achievement and social orientations in combination seem to be effective in thinking about the dynamics of behavior; how different types of dimensions to achievement seem to have sprung up in conceptualizing achievement motivation; and how age, cohort, and historical differences affect the achievement motive in both men and women. We have not thought of the effect of sex-role orientation on the dynamics of achievement motivation in terms of individual differences. While each person may have a peculiar orientation to his/her sex role that may affect his/her behavior, we have emphasized sex roles as general societal norms that are available to all men and all women in our society and the way they affect personal interpretations of achievement circumstances. This analysis of the nature of achievement motivation in men and women has also alerted us to new ways of measuring achievement motivation: contrasting autonomous vs. social comparison orientation to achievement as well as social impact vs. intrinsic orientations to achievement. Finally, our analyses have alerted us to taking the absolute level of motive scores more seriously, and to thinking about behaviors that reflect achievement orientations over and above occupational or academic performance. We hope that these insights will help promote new kinds of research on achievement motivation for both men and women.

ACKNOWLEDGMENTS

The authors wish to acknowledge the general valuable consulation offered by members of an NIMH training program in Mental Health and Social Roles (MH 14613). Some of the research reported in this paper was supported by a grant from NIMH (MH 26006) and from the Henry Murray Research Center, Radcliffe College.

REFERENCES

Alper, T. (1974). Achievement motivation in college women: A now-you-see-it-now-you-don't phenomenon. *Journal of Personality and Social Psychology, 29* 194–203.

Atkinson, J. (1950). *Studies in projective measurement of achievement motivation.* Unpublished doctoral dissertation, University of Michigan.

Atkinson, J. (1958). Determinants of risk-taking behavior. *Psychological Review, 64,* 359–372.

Atkinson, J. & Feather, N. (1966). *A theory of achievement motivation.* New York: Wiley.

Atkinson, J. W., Heyns, R. W., & Veroff, J. (1954). The effect of experimental arousal of the affiliation motive on thematic apperception. *Journal of Abnormal and Social Psychology, 49,* 405–410.

Atkinson, J. & Litwin, G. (1960). Achievement motivation and test anxiety conceived as motive to approach success and motive to avoid failure. *Journal of Abnormal and Social Psychology, 60,* 52–63.

Atkinson, J. & O'Connor, P. (1966). Neglected factors in studies of achievement-oriented performance: Social approval as an incentive and performance decrement. In J. Atkinson & N. Feather (Eds.), *A theory of achievement motivation.* New York: Wiley.

Atkinson, J. & Reitman, W. (1958). Performance as a function of motive strength and expectancy of goal attainment. In J. Atkinson (Ed.), *Motives in fantasy, action, and society.* Princeton, N.J.: D. Van Nostrand Company, Inc., 278–287.

Condry, J. & Dyer, S. (1976). Fear of success: Attribution of cause to the victim. *Journal of Social Issues, 32*(3), 63–83.

Conger, J. (1978). Adolescence: A time for becoming. In M. Lamb (Ed.), *Social and personality development*. New York: Holt, Rinehart & Winston.

Crandall, V. J. (1963). Achievement. In H. Stevenson (Ed.), *Child psychology, the sixty-second yearbook of the NSSE*. Chicago: NSSE.

Crandall, V. J. (1969). Sex differences in expectancy of intellectual and academic reinforcement. In C. Smith (Ed.), *Achievement-related motives in children*. New York: Russell Sage.

Denmark, F., Tangri, S., & McCandless, S. (1975). *Affiliation, achievement and power: A new look*. Draft of paper for New Directions for Research on Women conference, Madison, Wisconson.

Depner, C. & Veroff, J. (1979). Investigating Veroff's taxonomy of achievement motivation. *Journal of Social Psychology, 107,* 283–284.

Entwistle, D. (1972). To dispel fantasies about fantasy-based measures of achievement motivation. *Psychological Bulletin, 77,* 377–391.

Feather, N. (1963). Persistence at a difficult task with an alternative task of intermediate difficulty. *Journal of Abnormal and Social Psychology, 66, 604–609.*

Feather, N. (1966). The study of persistence. In J. Atkinson and N. Feather (Eds.), *A theory of achievement motivation*. New York: Wiley, 49–74.

Feld, S. (1960). *Studies in origins of achievement strivings*. Unpublished doctoral dissertation, University of Michigan.

Field, W. (1951). *The effects of thematic apperception upon certain experimentally aroused needs*. Unpublished doctoral dissertation, University of Maryland.

French, E., & Lesser, G. (1964). Some characteristics of achievement motivation in women. *Journal of Abnormal and Social Psychology, 68,* 119–128.

Helmreich, R. L., Spence, J. T., Beane, W. T., Lucker, G. W., & Matthews, K. A. (1980). Making it in academic psychology: Demographic and personality correlates of attainment. *Journal of Personality and Social Psychology, 39,* 896–908.

Hoffman, L. (1972). Early childhood experiences and women's achievement motivation. *Journal of Social Issues, 28,* 129–155.

Hoffman, L. (1974). Fear of success in males and females: 1965 and 1972. *Journal of Consulting and Clinical Psychology, 42,* 353–358.

Hoffman, L. (1977). Fear of success in 1965 and 1974: A follow-up study. *Journal of Consulting and Clinical Psychology, 44,* 310–321.

Horner, M. (1968). *Sex differences in achievement motivation and performance in competitive and non-competitive situations*. Unpublished doctoral dissertation, University of Michigan.

Horner, M. S. & Rhoem, W. (1972). *The motive to avoid success as a function of age, occupation, and progress at school*. Unpublished manuscript, University of Michigan, 1968. Reported in M. S. Horner, Toward an understanding of achievement-related conflicts in women. *Journal of Social Issues, 28,* 157–175.

House, G. (1972). *Orientations to achievement: Autonomous, social comparison, and external*. Unpublished doctoral dissertation, University of Michigan.

Kagan, J. & Moss, H. (1958). Stability and validity of achievement fantasy. *Journal of Abnormal and Social Psychology, 58,* 357–364.

Kipnis, D. (1974). Inner direction, other direction, and achievement motivations. *Human Development, 17,* 321–343.

Lesser, G., Krawitz, R., & Packard, R. (1963). Experimental arousal of achievement motivation in adolescent girls. *Journal of Abnormal and Social Psychology, 66,* 59–66.

Litwin, G. (1966). Achievement motivation, expectancy of success, and risk taking behavior. In J. Atkinson & N. Feather (Eds.), *A theory of achievement motivation*. New York: Wiley, 103–116.

McClelland, D., Atkinson, J., Clark, R., & Lowell, E. (1953). *The achievement motive*. New York: Appleton-Century-Crofts, Inc.

Monahan, L., Kuhn, D., & Shaver, P. (1974). Intrapsychic versus cultural explanations of the fear of success motive. *Journal of Personality and Social Psychology*, 60–64.

Moss, J. & Kagan, J. (1961). Stability of achievement and recognition-seeking behaviors from early childhood through adulthood. *Journal of Abnormal and Social Psychology, 62*, 504–513.

Moore, K. (1974). *Fear of success: The distribution correlates, reliability and consequences for fertility of fear of success among respondents in a metropolitan survey population*. Paper presented at the American Psychological Association Conference, New Orleans.

Moulton, R. (1966). Effects of success and failure on level of aspiration as related to achievement motives. In J. Atkinson and N. Feather (Eds.), *A theory of achievement motivation*. New York: Wiley, 147–159.

Murray, H. (1938). *Explorations of personality*. New York: Oxford University Press, 36–141.

Nesselroade, J. & Baltes, P. (1974). Adolescent personality development and historical change: 1970–1972. *Monographs for the Society for Research in Child Development, 39*(1).

Romer, N. (1974). *Sex differences in the development of achievement-related motives, sex role identity, and performance*. Unpublished doctoral dissertation, University of Michigan.

Sarason, S. G., Davidson, K. S., Lighthall, F. F., Waite, R. K., & Roebuck, B. K. (1960). *Anxiety in elementary school children*. New York: Wiley.

Stein, A. & Bailey, M. (1973). The socialization of achievement orientation in females. *Psychological Bulletin, 80*, 343–366.

Sutherland (Ratliff), E. (1980). *A follow-up study on achievement-related motivation and behavior*. Unpublished doctoral dissertation, University of Michigan.

Tresemer, D. (1976). The cumulative record of research on "fear of success." *Sex Roles, 2*, 217–236.

Tresemer, D. (1977). *Fear of success*. New York: Plenum Press.

Veroff, J. (1969). Social comparison and the development of achievement motivation. In C. Smith (Ed.), *Achievement-related motives in children*. New York: Russell Sage.

Veroff, J. (1977). Process vs. impact in men's and women's achievement motivation. *Psychology of Women Quarterly, 1*, 228–293.

Veroff, J. (1983). Assertive motivation: Achievement vs. power. In A. Stewart (Ed.), *Motivation and society*. San Francisco: Jossey-Bass.

Veroff, J. & Feld, S. C. (1970). *Marriage and work in America*. New York: Van Nostrand-Reinhold.

Veroff, J., Feld, S. C., & Gurin, G. (1962). Achievement motivation and religious background. *American Sociological Review, 27*, 205–217.

Veroff, J., McClelland, D., & Ruhland, D. (1975). Varieties of achievement motivation. In M. Mednick, S. Tangri, & L. Hoffman (Eds.), *Women and Achievement*. New York: 175–205.

Veroff, J., Reuman, D., & Feld, S. (in press). Motives in American men and women across the adult lifespan. *Developmental Psychology*.

Veroff, J., & Veroff, J. B. (1980). *Social Incentives*. New York: Academic Press.

Veroff, J., Wilcox, S., & Atkinson, J. (1953). The achievement motive in high school and college age women. *Journal of Abnormal and Social Psychology, 48*, 108–119.

Walker, E. L. & Heyns, R. W. (1962). *An Anatomy for Conformity*. Englewood Cliffs, N.J.: Prentice-Hall.

Zuckerman, M. & Wheeler, L. (1975). To dispel fantasies about the fantasy-based measure of fear of success. *Psychological Bulletin, 82*, 932–946.

5

From Theories of Equity to Theories of Justice: The Liberating Consequences of Studying Women

Arnold S. Kahn
American Psychological Association

William P. Gaeddert
State University of New York at Plattsburgh

THE DISTRIBUTION PROBLEM

Problems of distributive justice abound daily. On what basis should the teacher distribute grades? How should the winning team allocate its championship earnings? How should one divide his or her paycheck among the many who request parts of it? What is your *fair share* to be given to the United Way?

Solutions to the distribution problem are not trivial. Children fight, colleagues complain, group members resign, tempers flare, and nations battle over issues of fairness. As parents, employers, teachers, and presidents know, the most frequent response to an allocation decision is "not fair."

An area as important to interpersonal relations as fairness has not escaped social psychologists' theories and laboratories. Distribution rules have been proposed and tested, and theories have been advanced for how people actually allocate and how people should allocate. In the process of testing, it has become evident that women and men at least some of the time prefer and adopt different solutions to the distribution problem. This chapter is an attempt to explore the implications of such sex differences. It is, first of all, an examination of the body of research on the effects of sex and gender on solutions to the distribution problem. Secondly, and perhaps more importantly, it is an investigation of how social psychologists interpret sex and gender differences when they occur, how these interpretations shape the theories of justice they expound, and how interpretation affects public policy recommendations.

129

Equity as a Solution to the Distribution Problem

Research on justice and fairness (the two terms are used synonymously in this paper) was slow to develop in social psychology. In the middle part of the twentieth century, together with the concept of status consistency (e.g., Sampson, 1969), came the notion that people believe they are entitled to receive valued outcome or rewards in proportion to what they have invested. Thus, if an individual has put in a number of years of service, acquired a goodly number of skills, "paid one's dues" so to speak, that individual is entitled to more money, respect, status, and other valued commodities than another person who is new to the job. Justice was seen as a proportionality of ratios, whereby a person's outcomes (e.g., pay, respect, status, etc.) relative to his or her inputs (i.e., task contributions, experience, skills, tools, etc.) should equal the comparable ratio for others in the group: The more one has, the more one should get; the more one gives, the more one should receive. Furthermore, as Homans (1961, 1974) and Sampson (1969) conceived it, one's relative ranking across a number of dimensions should remain constant—status consistency. If A is older than B, A should have more experience, make more contributions, be better liked than B, and get more in pay. Homans (1961, 1974) termed this proportionality "distributive justice"; Adams (1965) labeled it "equity."

Equity is presumed to produce satisfaction and lead to high performance; inequity to lead to unhappiness and dissatisfaction. When one's outcome/input ratio is greater than another's, the individual feels guilty—he or she has received more than is deserved; when one's ratio is less than another's, anger is experienced—one has been deprived. The experience of inequity motivates a person to attempt to reduce the dissatisfaction and to restore equity.

Research undertaken to verify the predictions derived from equity theory met with remarkable initial success. Homans (1961) showed how data collected with clerical workers (Homans, 1953) could be understood in terms of distributive justice, and Adams and his coworkers (Adams & Jacobsen, 1964; Adams & Rosenbaum, 1962) showed that workers would change their work patterns in an attempt to reduce inequity. Leventhal and his colleagues (Leventhal & Anderson, 1970; Leventhal & Michaels, 1969; Levanthal, Weiss, & Long, 1969) took the lead in demonstrating that people allocated rewards to themselves and to others in an equitable manner, and Walster, Berscheid, and Walster (1973) expanded equity theory to include exploitative, helping, and intimate relationships. Equity theory was quickly elevated to the status of a general theory of social behavior (e.g., Berkowitz & Walster, 1976; Walster, Walster, & Berscheid, 1978).

Equity, Men, and Masculinity

A number of theorists have pointed out that equity is a theory based on status, power, and hierarchies. It assumes that people are unequal and that inequalities should be maintained. The person who works the hardest, has the most skill, the better training, the most tools is entitled to reap the greatest benefits, and justice only occurs when this is so. As Deutsch (1975), Kahn, O'Leary, Krulewitz, and Lamm (1980), Leventhal (1976), and Sampson (1975) have pointed out, equity as a social norm reinforces competition, ambition, dominance, hard work, and aggressiveness. One would expect that equity would be most strongly endorsed by individuals who are concerned with maximizing their own outcomes, winning, doing things better than others, and who feel most comfortable knowing how good each person is and where in the social system each person fits. After all, in a group in which equitable allocations prevail, status distinctions become known and recognized, and people are classified on the basis of their contributions. In such groups, communication is often restricted to others of the same status level (Hurwitz, Zander & Hymovitz, 1960), and everyone knows his or her place.

These traits and behaviors fostered by equity are linked quite clearly to the stereotypic male in Western society (e.g., Broverman, Vogel, Broverman, Clarkson, & Rosenkrantz, 1972), and research has amply documented that men do, in fact, operate in this manner, rewarding the ambitious, hardworking achiever with status, power, and prestige, while rejecting low achievers (cf., Berkowitz, Levy, & Harvey, 1957; Shaw & Gilchrist, 1955). Aries (1976) has shown that all-male discussion groups quickly form into hierarchies, with competition and status enhancement as their main concerns. This traditional male behavior pattern resembles Bakan's (1966) concept of agency, Veroff's (1977) notion of an impact orientation, and Kelley and Thibaut's (1978) concept of an egotistical orientation. Sampson (1975) has also pointed out that it is a theory congruent with capitalism: It is a behavior pattern that promotes the individual and glorifies and rewards individual achievement, separating the individual from the group and making him or her distinctive. Because equity, with its emphasis on input and outcome differences, fits so well with this agentic, impactful, egotistical, masculine formulation, it should come as no surprise that men would be more likely to behave consistently with equity predictions than would women.

Women and Equity

That equity would emerge as the initial rule of justice and solution to the distribution problem is understandable in a society in which male is normative, most researchers are themselves male, and most subjects of research are male (e.g., Carlson, 1972). The theory's meteoric rise to the position of a general theory of social behavior can also be understood within this same context.

One of the consequences of taking women seriously is that it frequently upsets conceptions of what is and what should be. From the beginning, the data from female subjects served as a problem for equity proponents. Leventhal and Anderson (1970) found that while boys took more for themselves when they outperformed another boy and less for themselves when they were outperformed by another boy, girls took equal amounts for themselves in both conditions. Leventhal and Lane (1970) found that women took less for themselves than did men both when outperforming and when outperformed by their partner. Leventhal, Popp, and Sawyer (1973) found that when rewarding others, boys allocated rewards more equitably than girls, who were more equal in their allocations. Similar findings have been reported by others (e.g., Benton, 1971). There has now accumulated a large body of literature, reviewed by Kahn, O'Leary, Kruleweitz, and Lamm (1980) and Major and Deaux (1981) to suggest that women more frequently deviate from equity predictions than do men. Generally, the allocation behavior of women is more generous and less selfish than that of men, and it is frequently more in line with what would be predicted by justice as equality.[1]

Equality, Women, and Femininity

Equality is, to a large extent, the antithesis of equity. Whereas equity implies input considerations should be prime in determining the allocations of outcomes, equality states that inputs should be entirely ignored. Whereas equity theory was derived to explain inconsistencies between measures of outcome and satisfaction (e.g., Adams, 1965; Homans, 1961; Stouffer, Suchman, DeVinney, Star, & Williams, 1949), equality seems to have emerged more as an empirical fact in research designed to test equity theory (e.g., Kahn, 1972; Lerner, 1974; Mikula, 1974).

Sampson (1975) and others (e.g., Kahn, O'Leary et al., 1980) have summarized much of the initial research supporting equality as a solution to the distribution problem and have pointed out the advantages of equality over equity. Sampson has also demonstrated the link between stereotypically feminine concerns with interpersonal harmony and equality in allocations. According to his argument, equal distributions of rewards remove status differentiation and competition, thus maintaining harmonious interpersonal relationships.

In a group or society in which rewards are allocated equally there is little basis for competition, few barriers to open communication, slight room for individuality or selfishness. Communal rather than individual concerns dominate under such circumstances, with group welfare, equal participation, and a focus on openness and union with others rather than separation and uniqueness the norm. A number of authors from diverse disciplines within psychology were quick to note the relationship between equality, a communal life pattern, and the stereotypic female in Western society (e.g., Bakan, 1966; Carlson, 1972;

---

[1]When an allocator's inputs are higher than one's partner, women tend to allocate equally; when an allocator's inputs are lower than one's partner, equality is also selfishness. Hence, women do not allocate equally when they have low inputs, but take even less for themselves than predicted by equity, and less than do men.

Sampson, 1975; Stein & Bailey, 1973). Evidence, particularly from the area of achievement, suggests that compared with males, females are less concerned with winning competition, focus more on the process of achieving (Spence & Helmreich, 1978; Veroff, 1977), and strive to achieve in areas such as social skills and affiliation (Stein & Bailey, 1973). Equity, with its emphasis on social comparison and differentiation, would be inconsistent with the traditional conception of femininity.

THE LOCUS OF SEX AND GENDER EFFECTS

That females and males differ frequently in their allocation patterns is not a matter of dispute. Two recent reviews (Kahn, O'Leary et al., 1980; Major & Deaux, 1981) amply document such effects. Males appear more likely to allocate rewards equitably than females, and females are more likely than males to take less for themselves than predicted by equity, and to minimize the differences among outcomes when allocating to others only. Generally, it can be said that males are more likely to opt for equity and females for equality, except when the female allocator has low inputs, in which case choosing equality would indicate selfishness.

Why these sex effects occur and the conditions which produce them are matters of some debate. This is, at least in part, a political question as well as a scientific one, for our conceptions of why women and men differ determine what we examine, what we manipulate in experiments, and what variables we control (cf. Parlee, 1981).

At least four loci for sex differences in reward allocation have been advanced. Each of these positions implies differences in research procedures; differences in how we consider sex and gender; differences in what we mean by fairness, justice, and equity; and differences in how we apply the knowledge gained from this research. The first position suggests that there is only one rule of justice, equity, and that sex and gender differences merely reflect different perceptions of relevant inputs and outcomes. The second position views sex and gender effects as caused by the nature of women and men: Males and females are different people who have different goals and are motivated by different concerns. The third position sees sex and gender as a stimulus variable (Grady, 1979; Hansen & O'Leary, 1983). Women and men do not necessarily have different conceptions of how to solve the distribution problem, but all people solve the problem differently when they interact with women than when they interact with men. Sex and gender differences occur because past research has been primarily limited to all-female and all-male groups. The final position is that sex and gender per se is not the important issue; rather, sex and gender are highly correlated with status and power (Unger, 1976; 1978), and status and power affect reward allocations and norm preference.

Each of these positions will be reviewed, their research support evaluated, and their implications assessed. It should be indicated at the outset that space considerations do not allow for an exhaustive, definitive research review. The purpose of this article is not to determine which position is correct, but to investigate how social scientists' views of women and men affect their research and theories of justice and fairness.

Sex and Gender as Trivial

One conception of sex and gender is that it is trivial when considering justice. Proponents of this position believe there is only a single rule of justice, equity, for all people, women and men (Homans, 1974, 1976; Walster & Walster, 1975). When sex and gender differences are found empirically they are attributed to differences in what are considered relevant inputs and outcomes. For example, men may be more likely to consider effort and skill relevant inputs, and because these differ across individuals, they allocate equitably; women may be more likely to consider participation as the most relevant input, and because this is equal for all individuals (at least in most laboratory experiments), they allocate equally. Because inputs and outcomes must be perceived and deemed relevant to be entered into one's outcome/input ratio, sex and gender differences merely reflect gender preferences that are independent of the rule of justice.

The following quotations illustrate this perspective:

> In spite of the fact that most theorists seem to feel that equality and proportionality are markedly different types of justice, we would argue that . . . [these] examples fit nicely within equity theory. In the view of equity theorists . . . [they are] simply describing two different collections of situations. In the first, participants assume that only relevant input is a person's humanity. Since all possess equal humanity, all are entitled to equal outcomes. In the second collection of situations, participants assume that the relevant inputs are ones on which people vary . . . Thus, they conclude, different people deserve different amounts of reward (Walster & Walster, 1975, p. 29).

> As I have pointed out . . . Most of the action in justice occurs not over the generalized rule of distributive justice (equity) but over what dimensions for comparing the contributions and rewards of different individuals and groups shall be used in applying the formula (Homans, 1976, p. 237).

In one sense, this view does not deny sex and gender as important, per se, but only that it is not important to the area of reward distribution. Clearly, there must be a reason why the sexes would differ in their perceived relevance of various inputs and outcomes, and this is probably a worthy endeavor in its own right, but it is not relevant to the study of justice: Justice is equity.

In another sense, this position represents a partriarchal bias. It is men, after all, whose behavior most clearly supports equity. When the inputs are manipulated it is men who pay the greatest attention to them. Thus, explaining the behavior of women in terms of a theory that is most strongly supported by data collected on men is a clear case of using men as the norm and explaining women in terms of deviation from that norm (cf. Shields, 1975).

It is also men who most benefit from equity. In a society where men are presumed to have greater skills and to produce items of greater value (Goldberg, 1968; Pheterson, Kiesler, & Goldberg, 1971), it will be men who will reap the greater rewards. Evidence of salary discrimination, for example, reflects this male bias. To choose to ignore the data from women, which suggests that equality might be a viable allocation norm, and to interpret those data as actually supporting equity, is a political decision, not a scientific one. It is a decision that can be construed to imply that women's lower pay and generally lower status is due, at least in part, to women's failure to act or at least evaluate like men.[2]

There is no direct evidence to support this sex-as-artifact position. Investigators who believe equity is the only rule of justice have been primarily concerned with expanding the scope of the theory and testing its limits (e.g., Walster, Berscheid, & Walster, 1973; Walster, Walster, & Berscheid, 1978), not with differences in sex and gender.

Sex and Gender as Real Variables

By far the most popular explanation in social psychology for the observed differences between men and women is that women and men are different types of humans who strive for different goals and social relationships. From this perspective, women are more communal than men and seek to establish and maintain relationships in which affiliation, emotional expression, group identity, and interpersonal harmony are the prime goals; men are more agentic than women, interested in promoting relationships in which dominance, individuality, achievement, and problem-solving play a preeminent role. Numerous authors have espoused this view (e.g., Deaux, 1976; Kahn, O'Leary et al., 1980; Leventhal, 1973; Sampson, 1975; Vinacke, 1959). This position holds that sex and gender effects are not artifacts, but real phenomena that, either through nature or nurture, produce two different kinds of people. Most adherents to this interaction goals position make vague reference to the fact that socialization patterns produce this difference, without specifying the precise nature of these patterns or how they lead to preferences of equality or equity. However, the developmental literature provides some support for this perspective (e.g., Huston-Stein & Higgins-Trent, 1978; Kipnis, 1974; Stein & Bailey, 1973).

Rather strong indirect evidence for women and men's different interaction goals comes from two directions. First, there is a sizable literature showing that

[2]We do not intend to imply that those adhering to this perspective necessarily maintain such beliefs.

women behave in a more communal and men in a more agentic manner. For example, women are more likely than men to avoid status hierarchies (Anderson, 1961; Aries, 1976); allocate coalition rewards equally (Komorita & Moore, 1976; Vinacke et al., 1974; Whata, 1972); communicate about interpersonal rather than task concerns (Hottes & Kahn, 1974); disclose more intimate information to others (Cozby, 1973; Jourard, 1968; Morgan, 1976); and change their behavior as the nature of other participants change (Kahn, Hottes & Davis, 1971).

Second, there is rather strong evidence that equality is used by allocators to promote interpersonal harmony, while equity is used by allocators to elicit and maintain maximal performance. Leventhal (1976, 1979) has reviewed this literature and suggests that equitable allocations are used to reward those who have performed well in order to encourage them to continue their high level of performance. Furthermore, equitable allocations can be used to encourage low performers to improve or leave the group ("shape up, or ship out"). However, equal allocations are used, according to Leventhal, when cooperation and interdependence are important for group success. Thus, equal allocations are used to reduce competition and conflict in order to promote cooperation and harmony.

Unfortunately, the fact that sex is associated with norm preference (females prefer equality; males prefer equity), and these preferences are associated with interaction goals (equal divisions promote harmony; equitable divisions promote competition), does not demonstrate that females and males have different interaction goals. More direct, empirical demonstrations are called for, and an examination of the literature suggests such evidence is not robust. The ideal study would simultaneously manipulate sex of subject as well as some aspect of the situation. For example, one could manipulate the extent to which the situation contained interpersonal or status elements. Research of this type has been rare, although some recent investigations are suggestive.

Austin and McGinn (1977) had subjects allocate a reward to two others, one who had high inputs and one who had low inputs. Some subjects anticipated future interaction with the high input other, some anticipated interaction with the low input other, and some did not anticipate any future interaction. Both females and males allocated generously, using equity when anticipating interaction with the high input other, and equality when anticipating interaction with the low input other. However, when no future interaction was anticipated, males used equity whereas females tended to compromise with an allocation between equity and equality. Similar data have been provided by Sagan, Pondel, and Wittig (1981). These findings suggest that people of both genders are sensitive to situational constraints, but when those constraints are absent, females and males have different preferences, which are consistent with the hypothesis of different interaction goals. Further support for this supposition comes from questionnaire data provided by Austin and McGinn. Males were more likely to justify their allocations in terms of cost considerations (e.g., to avoid conflict), while females explained their allocations in terms of reward aspects (e.g., increase friendliness). Other research (e.g., Bowden & Zanna, 1978; Greenberg, 1978) has also found that both sexes respond similarly when situational demands are strong, but diverge in the expected manner in the "control" conditions in which the manipulations are absent. Also consistent with the interaction goal explanation is the finding that although both females and males prefer a generous to a stingy allocator, the female preference is stronger (Kahn, Lamm, & Nelson, 1977; Watts & Messe, 1982).

Perhaps even stronger support comes from recent investigations by Carles and Carver (1979) and Watts, Messe, and Vallacher (1982). Carles and Carver found that females were more generous with their allocations when they had knowledge about the identity and personal attributes of their partner (person-salient) than as if such personalizing information were absent (role salient), while males were less generous when their partner was person-salient. Questionnaire data revealed that males felt more competitive when their partner was person-salient, while females felt less competitive under these conditions. That a close relationship with another would bring forth cooperative concerns from females and competitive concerns from males is consistent with the interaction goals hypothesis.

Watts, Messe, and Vallacher (1982) reasoned, in line with the interaction goal hypothesis, that if women and men were preselected on an agency-communion measure such that they were comparable, then agency-communion would be related to allocation behavior, rather than sex and gender. They found that high agency people took more of a reward for themselves than persons low in agency, but, surprisingly, that females still took less for themselves than males.

Finally, we note two additional lines of research that suggest that females and males are basically different, not so much in interpersonal orientation per se, but in the way they perceive and evaluate events, and that these differences account for sex and gender effects in reward allocation. Messe and his colleagues (Messe & Callahan-Levy, 1979; Messe & Watts, 1980) have demonstrated that women pay themselves less than men do, women rely more than men on external cues to determine how much to pay themselves, and that women feel more discomfort about paying themselves. That men take more for themselves and feel good about doing so is consistent with an agentic orientation.

The data from these and other studies suggest that given the opportunity, males will interpret an allocation situation as one of potential conflict and will react competitively, while females will interpret that same situation as an opportunity for a relationship and cooperation. It is but a small step to the assumption that women seek cooperation and affiliation whereas men seek competition.

It is but an additional small step to suggest that men and women might be best suited for different work environments, different social organizations, and different family and societal roles. After all, a good society is one that maximizes individual pleasure, and it appears that different things please most women and most men.

This position also blames women for their low status in society, for it suggests that women lack the agentic qualities necessary for success in our society. If we want to improve women's lot, we must make women more like men.

Yet, before one jumps on the interpersonal orientation bandwagon, we must consider some additional evidence. There is substantial evidence that women and men do not have different interpersonal orientations. For example, in a recent study, Gaeddert (1981) had college students write essays concerning their own successes and failures. These essays were then edited to remove any gender-relevant cues and were rated by trained observers across a number of dimensions. No gender effects were found for either the agency or the communal dimensions, and although a factor-analysis of all the dimensions revealed a strong agency/task mastery versus communal/affiliative factor, gender was unrelated to it.

In addition, a number of recent studies have shown that whether one allocates equally or equitably depends on the nature of the situation and how one interprets that situation. For example, Wittig and her colleagues (Wittig, Marks, & Jones, 1980; Sagan, Pondel, & Wittig, 1981) have demonstrated that when the causes for task performance are clear women and men do not differ in their allocations. For example, when task performance is clearly due to effort, both sexes allocate equitably; when performance is clearly due to luck, men as well as women allocate equally. Kidder, Bellettirie, and Cohn (1977) found that whether allocations were public or private strongly influenced the allocation behavior of both women and men, and Reis and Jackson (1981) showed that whether a task is masculine or feminine strongly influences allocation behavior. Finally, both Kahn, Nelson, and Gaeddert (1980) and Reis and Jackson (1981) have noted that most allocation research has confounded subject sex with sex of partner by using only same-sex dyads to study allocation behavior. As pointed out elsewhere in this volume by O'Leary and Hansen, sex often operates as a stronger stimulus variable than subject variable. What may appear to be a sex of subject preference for allocation norm may actually be a sex of recipient preference.

Sex Differences as a Belief

Research by Grady (1979) has clearly shown that gender is important to people. It is the thing we most want to know about one another, and the first piece of information we are likely to transmit about another person. Furthermore, as Hansen and O'Leary (1983) have shown, people have strong expectations about what motivates the behavior of women and men, with both genders agreeing, for example, that men are more reactive to the environment and that women behave for dispositional reasons. In addition, there is a growing body of literature suggesting that what appear to be gender differences in social behavior are, in fact, artifactual. That is, most of the research that has examined sex has done so in same-sex situations. Dabbs (1977) has shown that what appear to be sex differences in eye contact and reaction to being crowded are often due to both sexes avoiding eye contact and feeling greater discomfort with males. Because much of the research reviewed in this paper has used situations in which males allocate to males and females allocate to females, it may well be that the obtained sex effects are due to the sex of the individual to whom one is allocating, rather than the sex of the allocator. It may be that the presence of men in a group serves as a stimulus to both women and men that status, competition, ambition, and other agentic qualities are relevant, while the presence of women informs one that social, affiliative, and other communal qualities are important. That is, sex operates as a stimulus variable rather than as a subject variable.

The most direct test of the sex as stimulus variable position would be to manipulate both sex of subject and sex of partner factorially. Strongest support would be if only sex of partner effects were obtained. A number of studies have now been reported in the literature that have manipulated both sex of subject and sex of other, but the results, although they are suggestive of the importance of sex of stimulus person, are not as clearcut as adherents of this position would prefer.

Two studies, reported by Callahan-Levy and Messe (1979) and Messe and Callahan-Levy (1979), showed that subjects of both sexes distributed more money to females than males, and that this pattern obtains for children as young as in the first grade. Mikula (1974) found a tendency for males (but not females) to allocate more to females than to other males.

Kahn, Nelson, and Gaeddert (1980) examined the allocation behavior of females and males in triads. They found that allocations made by males (but not females) depended upon the sex of the low-input group member. Males allocated more equally when a female was the low-input group member, but more equitably when a male was the low-input member. Consistent with this finding, the presence of at least one male in the group led subjects to perceive that they had worked harder.

These studies suggest that both females and males are frequently more generous and more equal in their allocations to females than they are to males. However, research by Reis and Jackson (1981) shows that the pattern is more complex. Reis and Jackson have found that males allocate equitably and females equally on a stereotypically masculine task when they are allocating to same-sex partners. However, this pattern did not obtain on stereotypically feminine tasks or when allocating to a cross-sex partner.

Although it has yet to fall into a coherent pattern, the research cited above shows that men are not inextricably linked to equity, nor are women compelled to allocate equally. Rather, whether one chooses equity, equality, or some other mode of distribution depends strongly on how one perceives the nature of the situation, including expectations about the sex of those with whom one is making the allocation. Locating the cause for sex differences in reward allocations in the beliefs and expectations people hold about the nature of women and men is a perspective that neither ignores sex and gender nor blames women, which is true of the other positions discussed thus far. This position further highlights a point all-too-frequently ignored in sex and gender research: Research that relies solely on same-sex groups and finds sex differences in reward allocations cannot be taken, prima facie, as evidence of a sex of subject effect.

Sex and Gender as Status Variables

In recent years there has been a growing realization by social scientists that men have higher status than women and that the behavior of men is frequently identical to that of high-status actors, while the behavior of women is often congruent with that of low-status actors. A swelling list of authors have pointed out that what appear to be sex and gender differences in social behavior may be better described as differences due to status and power (e.g., Eagly & Wood, 1982; Frieze & Ramey, 1975; Henley, 1977; Lockheed & Hall, 1976; Meeker & Weitzel-O'Neill, 1977; Unger, 1976; 1978). Men behave in a more high-status fashion by having a more relaxed posture that takes up much physical space, maintaining little eye contact, touching women more frequently than they are touched by women, disclosing less personal information but talking more in groups, showing less argument in interaction, and engaging in more dominant behavior.

Meeker & Weitzel-O'Neill[3] (1977) have provided the most cogent analysis to date of the effects of sex and gender on social interaction when gender is considered a status variable. They point out, in line with expectation states theory (Berger, Cohen, & Zelditch, 1972), that people expect high-status individuals to take the lead in group participation. If a low-status actor participates at a high rate it will be seen as illegitimate and self-serving. Hence, if a low-status actor is to engage in a high level of task behavior and gain acceptance for it, he or she must first demonstrate that he or she is both competent and well-intentioned. Given that women are generally considered low-status individuals (e.g., Henley, 1977) by both men and other women (e.g., Lott, 1983), their behavior in groups is a result of their low status.

Although status per se has not been the focus of much reward allocation research, one would expect a low-status individual to be reluctant to take a high proportion of a group reward for him or herself, for to do so would appear to be self-serving and illegitimate, whereas the same behavior by a high-status individual would be considered normative, since greater activity, task participation, and expertise are expected from high-status actors (e.g., Sampson, 1963, 1969). From this perspective, then, the frequently observed generosity of women when

[3]We wish to thank Wendy Harrod for pointing out this position.

in both high- and low- input positions is due not so much to communal desires as to a desire to behave congruently with their low status. By acting generously, women can demonstrate group rather than selfish concerns and provide legitimacy for future task-relevant behaviors (cf. Meeker & Weitzel-O'Neill, 1977, p. 97). Likewise, the less generous allocations of men, especially in same-sex groups, can be construed as an indication of a status struggle in a group of uniformly high-status members.

The ideal study to test the sex and gender as status position would be to manipulate both status and sex independently and determine their effects on reward allocations. No such study has yet been conducted in the area of reward allocation, although such an approach has proven useful in other areas (e.g., Denmark, 1977, Eagly & Wood, 1982). An alternative route would be to investigate the effects of status on allocation behavior in groups of both women and men separately. Two attempts to manipulate status (Kahn, 1972; Parcel & Cook, 1977) have not, however, provided support for this theoretical position. In both studies status was manipulated in terms of perceived ability among otherwise equal-status individuals. Sex and gender, while having implications for ability (e.g., Deaux & Emswiller, 1974; Lott, 1983), encompasses a wide variety of expectations and attributions (e.g., Deaux, 1976). Manipulations of a single ability may not be strong enough to establish strong, stable expectation states.

Although it has yet to be adequately tested in the area of reward allocation, this position has been gaining wide support from researchers in a number of areas. The appeal of interpreting differences in sex and gender in terms of status is that it locates the cause of these differences out of individual actors into the social structure. In our society, men and women do have different status, and it is the status of women that must be improved if sex differences are to disappear, and this will not be accomplished by changing perceptions or making women act more like men. From this perspective, the stereotypes are a reflection of the status differences, and making women act more like men will frequently lead them to be perceived as selfish and uppity.

SUMMARY AND CONCLUSIONS

The Consequences of Studying Women for Theories of Justice

The research reviewed in this paper has demonstrated that as long as researchers studied how males allocated rewards to other males there was good reason to believe that the terms equity and justice were synonymous. A major consequence of including women as subjects in justice research has been to expand and complicate the meaning of the term justice. Taking into account the research conducted over the past decade, with female as well as male subjects, forces one to acknowledge that equity is but one conception of justice upon which people rely when allocating rewards; equality and various compromises between equity and equality are as common, if not more frequent, than equity alone when both sexes and a variety of circumstances are employed in research.

However, the inclusion of women into the research on justice has had additional implications, including the burden of interpreting the causes for such differences. We have found four major explanations for the sex differences in the literature:

1. Sex differences are due to women and men differing in their perceptions of relevant inputs and outcomes, and when these differences in perception are taken into account we find no sex difference in justice behavior. Justice is equity for men and women.

2. Sex differences are due to the fact that women and men, either through biology or socialization, develop different interaction goals, which lead men to strive for equity and women to attempt to achieve equality. Equity is justice for male actors; equality is justice for female actors.

3. Sex differences are due to the fact that all people hold different expectations for beliefs about women and men. The presence of women elicits beliefs that equality is appropriate allocation norm, while the presence of men leads people to believe that equity is appropriate. Equity is the manner people allocate to men; equality is the manner people allocate to women.

4. Sex differences due to the fact that women and men typically hold different status levels in our society, and high and low status people are expected to act differently and are treated differently. Equity is the way high-status people behave and are treated; equality is the way low-status people behave and are treated.

These different explanations are shown in Table 5.1.

Although the research reviewed here has pointed out the strengths and weaknesses of each of these four explanations, it is not the purpose of this paper to show the superiority of any one explanation. Indeed, sufficient research has not yet been conducted to allow such a determination. Future research and scholarship will likely produce additional theoretical explanations. However, if pressed we would argue that the effects of sex and gender are so pervasive that no single explanation yet proposed is sufficient to account for sex and gender affects in reward allocation or any other social behavior.

Social psychologists tend toward theoretical chauvinism, with each theorist attempting to show not only the validity of his or her own theory, but the invalidity of all other theories. While not denying that some of the theories thus far proposed are more valid than others, it seems absurd to attempt to place the locus of sex and gender effects solely at the level of biology, socialization, perceptions by women and men, perceptions of women and men, or the status of

TABLE 5.1

Implications of Various Theories for Sex and Gender Differences in Reward Allocation

View of Sex and Gender	View of Equity	View of Equality	Causes of Sex and Gender Differences	Causes of the Inequality Between Women and Men
Trivial Variable	A general principle applicable to all	Equity when inputs and outcomes are equal	Differential evaluation of relevant inputs and outcomes	Women, since they do not view the world in the way men do
Real Variable	Justice held by men	Justice held by women	Through biology and/or socialization, sexes have different interaction goals	Women, since they do not have the same goals possessed by men
Belief or Stimulus Variable	How people allocate to men	How people allocate to women	Stereotypic beliefs and expectations held by men and women	Women and men, since both share sex and gender stereotypes
Status Variable	Justice for high status actors	Justice for low status actors	Different status levels of women and men in society	Men, since they control access to status

women and men. We live in a society in which sex and gender are central and pervasive. As such, sex and gender operates on multiple levels and any attempt to confine their effects to a single level will necessarily be incomplete. We suspect the best theory will be one that merges the effects of biology, socialization, stereotypes, and status.

The Politics of Explanations of Sex and Gender Differences

We have also tried to show that the explanation one adopts for sex and gender differences in reward allocation has implications for social policy considerations (See Table 5.1). To assert that male behavior is indicative of justice (i.e., equity), and then to interpret female behavior to show that it is a special case of male behavior, is to do what we have always done—view men as normative and women as incomplete or inappropriate men. This position suggests that the inequality of women is due to women's not acting like men. Women need to act like men if they are to reap the rewards traditionally reserved for men.

To attribute differences in sex and gender to the different needs and goals of women and men acknowledges that the needs and goals of women and the behaviors of women are at least as important as those of men. However, such an explanation also blames women for their low status in society. Like the first explanation, it leads to the conclusion that for women to be valued and treated with the deference given to men they must learn to have the same desires and goals. In terms of public policy implications, both theories suggest that for women to gain equality, women must change their behavior.

The third explanation for the sex and gender differences in reward allocation—that people treat women and men differently—has the advantage of not blaming women for their low status. From this perspective, both women and men are to blame for holding sex-role stereotypic beliefs about the nature of men and women and acting upon them. To improve the status of women both men and women will have to change their perceptions of women and men.

The fourth explanation takes the blame for the low position of women in our society out of the heads of individual actors and into the social structure of our society. Women and men allocate differently because women and men occupy different status levels, with men having higher status than women. In order to have women equal to men we must, as a society, place greater value on the roles and behaviors of women and view women as being as valuable as men. Like the third explanation above, both women and men will have to change their beliefs about sex and gender, but unlike that position, men who have higher status and power in society and thereby control the institutions which confer status are the ones most to blame and most responsible for initiating change (Kahn, 1984).

Social psychology, like the other social sciences, has found that the inclusion of women as well as men into its domain has led to a more complex consideration of the forces that cause behavior. The simple explanations of the past such as equity can no longer be maintained as the sole theory to explain all relevant behavior. The inclusion of women into social psychology has also led to a greater sensitivity regarding the policy implications of research. It has forced us to recognize that the way we attribute the causes of sex and gender differences has direct implications for the necessary changes in society to produce equality.

As a final note, we wish to add that there is nothing inherent in the study of women that has these liberating consequences for a science like social psychology. Were social psychologists to now expand their research to include lesbians and gays, the physically handicapped, ethnic minorities, and others who have been neglected, the complexities of research and theory and the liberation from a narrow, white male dominated perspective would be of equal measure.

REFERENCES

Adams, J. S. (1965). Inequity in social exchange. In L. Berkowitz (Ed.), *Advances in experimental social psychology* (Vol. 2). New York: Academic Press.

Adams, J. S., & Jacobsen, P. R. (1964). Effects of wage inequities on work quality. *Journal of Abnormal and Social Psychology, 69,* 19–25.

Adams, J. S., & Rosenbaum, W. E. (1962). The relationship of worker productivity to cognitive dissonance about wage inequity. *Journal of Applied Psychology, 46,* 161–164.

Anderson, N. H. (1961). Group performance in an anagram task. *Journal of Abnormal and Social Psychology, 55,* 67–75.

Aries, E. (1976).Interaction patterns and themes of male, female, and mixed groups. *Small Group Behavior, 7,* 7–18.

Austin, W., & McGinn, N. C. (1976). Sex differences in choice of distribution rules. *Journal of Personality, 45,* 379–394.

Bakan, D. (1966). *The duality of human existence.* Chicago: Rand McNally.

Benton, A. A. (1971). Productivity, distributive justice, and bargaining among children. *Journal of Personality and Social Psychology, 18,* 68–78.

Berger, J., Cohen, B. P., & Zelditch, Jr., M. (1977). Status characteristics and social interaction. *American Sociological Review, 37,* 241–255.

Berkowitz, L., Levy, B., & Harvey, A. (1957). Effects of performance evaluation on group integration and motivation. *Human Relations, 10,* 195–208.

Berkowitz, L., & Walster, E. (1976). *Equity theory: Toward a general theory of social interaction* (Vol. 9). *Advances in experimental social psychology.* New York: Academic Press.

Bowden, M., & Zanna, M. P. (1978, September). *Perceived relationship, sex-role orientation, and gender differences in reward allocation.* Paper presented at the meeting of the American Psychological Association, Toronto, Canada.

Broverman, I. K., Vogel, S. R., Broverman, D. M., Clarkson, F. E., & Rosenkrantz, P. S. (1972). Sex-role stereotypes: A current appraisal. *Journal of Social Issues, 28,* 59–78.

Callahan-Levy, C. M., & Messe, L. A. (1979). Sex differences in the allocation of pay. *Journal of Personality and Social Psychology, 37,* 433–446.

Carles, E. M., & Carver, C. S. (1979). Effects of person salience versus role salience on reward allocations in a dyad. *Journal of Personality and Social Psychology, 1979, 37,* 2071–2080.

Carlson, R. (1972). Understanding Women: Implications for personality theory and research. *Journal of Social Issues, 28* 17–32.

Cozby, P. C. (1973). Self-disclosure: A literature review. *Psychological Bulletin, 79,* 73–91.

Dabbs, J. M., Jr. (1977). Does reaction to crowding depend upon sex of subject or sex of subject's partner? *Journal of Personality and Social Psychology, 35,* 343–344.

Deaux, K. (1976). *The behavior of women and men.* Monterey, Cal.: Brooks/Cole.

Deaux, K., & Emswiller, T. (1974). Explanations of successful performance on sex-linked tasks: What is skill for the male is luck for the female. *Journal of Personality and Social Psychology, 29,* 80–85.

Denmark, F. L. (1977). Styles of leadership. *Psychology of Women Quarterly, 2,* 99–113.

Deutsch, M. (1975). Equity, equality, and need: What determines which value will be used as the basis of distributive justice? *Journal of Social Issues, 31,* 137–149.

Eagly, A. H., & Wood, W. (1982). Inferred sex differences in status as a determinant of gender stereotypes about social influence. *Journal of Personality and Social Psychology, 43,* 915–928.

Frieze, I. H., & Ramey, S. J. (1976). Nonverbal maintenance of traditional sex roles. *Journal of Social Issues, 32,* 133–141.

Gaeddert, W. P. (1981). *Sex differences in achievement strivings: An examination and application of four models.* Unpublished doctoral dissertation. Iowa State University.

Goldberg, P. (1968). Are women prejudiced against women? *Trans-action, 5,* 28–30.

Grady, K. E. (1979). Androgyny reconsidered. In J. H. Williams (Ed.), *Psychology of women: Selected readings.* New York: Norton.

Greenberg, J. (1978). Effects of reward value and retaliative power on allocation decisions: Justice generosity, or greed? *Journal of Personality and Social Psychology, 36,* 367–379.

Hansen, R. D., & O'Leary, V. E. (1983). Actresses and actors: The effects of sex on causal attributions. *Basic and Applied Social Psychology,* (4), 209–230.

Henley, N. M. (1977). *Body politics: Power, sex, and nonverbal communication.* Englewood Cliffs, N.J.: Prentice-Hall.

Homans, G. C. (1953). Status among clerical workers. *Human Organization, 12,* 5–10.

Homans, G. C. (1961). *Social behavior: Its elementary forms.* Harcourt, Brace & World.

Homas, G. C. (1974). *Social behavior: Its elementary forms* (rev. ed.). New York: Harcourt, Brace & World.

Homans, G. C. (1976). Commentary. In L. Berkowitz & E. Walster (Eds.), *Advances in experimental social psychology.* Vol. 9. New York: Academic Press.

Hottes, J., & Kahn, A. (1974). Sex differences in a mixed-motive conflict situation. *Journal of Personality, 42,* 260–275.

Hurwitz, J. E., Zander, A. F., & Hymovitz, B. (1960). Some effects of power on the relations among group members. In D. Cartwright & A. Zander (Eds.), *Group dynamics: Research and theory* (2nd ed.). Evanston, Ill.: Row, Peterson.

Huston-Stein, A., & Higgens-Trent, A. (1978). The development of females: Career and feminine role orientations. In P. B. Baltes (Ed.), *Life-span development and behavior* (Vol. 1). New York: Academic Press.

Jourard, S. J. (1968). *Disclosing man to himself.* Princeton, N.J.: Van Nostrand.

Kahn, A. (1972). Reactions to the generosity or stinginess of an intelligent or stupid work partner: A test of equity theory in a direct exchange relationship. *Journal of Personality and Social Psychology, 21,* 116–123.

Kahn, A. (1984). The power war: Male response to power loss under equality. *Psychology of Women Quarterly, 8,* 234–247.

Kahn, A., Hottes, J., & Davis, W. L. (1971). Cooperation and optimal responding in the Prisoner's Dilemma Game: The effects of sex and physical attractiveness. *Journal of Personality and Social Psychology, 17,* 267–279.

Kahn, A., Lamm, H., & Nelson, R. E. (1977). Perferences for an equal or equitable allocator. *Journal of Personality and Social Psychology, 35,* 837–844.

Kahn, A., Nelson, R. E., & Gaeddert, W. P. (1980). Sex of subject and sex composition of the group as determinants of reward allocation. *Journal of Personality and Social Psychology, 38,* 737–750.

Kahn, A., O'Leary, V. E., Krulewitz, J. E., & Lamm, H. (1980). Equity and equality: Male and female means to a just end. *Basic and Applied Social Psychology, 1*, 173–197.

Kelley, H. H., & Thibaut, J. W. (1978). *Interpersonal relations: A theory of interdependence.* New York: Wiley.

Kidder, L. H., Bellettirie, G., & Cohn, E. S. (1977). Secret ambitions and public performances. *Journal of Experimental Social Psychology, 13*, 70–80.

Kipnis, D. M. (1974). Inner direction, other direction and achievement motivation. *Human Development, 17*, 321–343.

Komorita, S. S., & Moore, D. (1976). Theories and processes of coalition formation. *Journal of Personality and Social Psychology, 33*, 371–381.

Lerner, M. J. (1974). The justice motive: "Equity" and "parity" among children. *Journal of Personality and Social Psychology, 29*, 539–350.

Leventhal, G. S. (1973, August). *Reward allocation by males and females.* Paper presented at the meeting of the American Psychological Association, Montreal, Canada.

Leventhal, G. S. (1976). The distribution of rewards and resources in groups and organizations. In E. Walster & L. Berkowitz (Eds.), *Advances in experimental social psychology* (Vol. 9). New York: Academic Press.

Leventhal, G. S. (1979). Effects of external conflict on resource allocation and fairness within groups and organizations. In W. G. Austin & S. Worchel (Eds.), *The social psychology of intergroup relations.* Monterey, Calif.: Brooks/Cole.

Leventhal, G. S., & Anderson, D. (1970). Self-interest and the maintenance of equity. *Journal of Personality and Social Psychology, 15*, 57–62.

Leventhal, G. S., & Lane, D. W. (1970). Sex, age, and equity behavior. *Journal of Personality and Social Psychology, 15*, 312–316.

Leventhal, G. S., & Michaels, J. W. (1969). Extending the equity model: Perceptions of inputs and allocation of reward as a function of duration and quantity of performance. *Journal of Personality and Social Psychology, 12*, 303–309.

Leventhal, G. S., Popp. A. L., & Sawyer, L. (1973). Equity or equality in children's allocation of reward to other persons? *Child Development, 44*, 753–763.

Leventhal, G. S., Weiss, T., & Long, G. (1969). Equity, reciprocity, and reallocating rewards in the dyad. *Journal of Personality and Social Psychology, 13*, 300–305.

Lockheed, M. E., & Hall, K. P. (1976). Conceptualizing sex as a status characteristic: Applications to leadership training strategies. *Journal of Social Issues, 32*, 111–124.

Lott, B. (1983). *The devaluation of women's competence.* Unpublished manuscript, Department of Psychology, University of Rhode Island.

Major, B., & Deaux, K. (1981). Individual differences in justice behavior. In J. Greenberg & R. L. Cohen (Eds.), *Equity and justice in social behavior.* New York: Academic Press.

Meeker, B. F., & Weitzel-O'Neill, P. A. (1977). Sex roles and interpersonal behavior in task-oriented groups. *American Sociological Review, 42*, 91–105.

Messe, L. A., & Callahan-Levy, C. M. (1979). Sex and message effects on reward allocation behavior. *Academic Psychology Bulletin, 1*, 129–133.

Messe, L. A., & Watts, B. (1980). Self-pay behavior: Sex differences in reliance on external cues and feelings of comfort. *Academic Psychology Bulletin, 2*, 83–88.

Mikula, G. (1974). Nationality, performance, and sex as determinants of reward allocation. *Journal of Personality and Social Psychology, 29*, 435–440.

Morgan, B. S. (1976). Intimacy of disclosure topics and sex differences in self-disclosure. *Sex Roles, 2*, 161–166.

Parcel, T. L., & Cook, K. S. (1977). Status characteristics, reward allocation, and equity. *Sociometry, 40*, 311–324.

Parlee, M. B. (1981). Appropriate control groups in feminist research. *Psychology of Women Quarterly, 5*, 637–644.

Pheterson, G. I., Kiesler, S. G., & Goldberg, P. A. (1971). Evalution of the performance of women as a function of their sex, achievement, and personal history. *Journal of Personality and Social Psychology, 19*, 114–118.

Reis, H. T., & Jackson, L. A. (1981). Sex differences in reward allocation: Subjects, partners, and tasks. *Journal of Personality and Social Psychology, 40*, 465–478.

Sagan, K., Pondel, M., & Wittig, M. A. (1981). The effect of anticipated future interaction on reward allocation in same- and opposite-sex dyads. *Journal of Personality, 49*, 438–449.

Sampson, E. E. (1963). Status congruence and conitive consistency. *Sociometry, 26*, 146–162.

Sampson, E. E. (1969). Studies of status congruence. In L. Berkowitz (Ed.), *Advances in experimental social psychology* (Vol. 4). New York: Academic Press.

Sampson, E. E. (1975). On justice as equality. *Journal of Social Issues, 31*, 45–64.

Shaw, M. E., & Gilchrist, J. C. (1955). Repetitive task failure and sociometric choice. *Journal of Abnormal and Social Psychology, 50*, 29–32.

Shields, S. A. (1975). Functionalism, Darwinism, and the psychology of women: A study in social myth. *American Psychologist, 30*, 739–754.

Spence, J. T., & Helmreich, R. L. (1978). *Masculinity and femininity: Their psychological dimensions, correlates, and antecedents.* Austin, Texas: University of Texas Press.

Stein, A. H., & Bailey, M. M. (1973). The socialization of achievement motivation in females. *Psychological Bulletin, 80*, 345–366.

Stouffer, S. A., Suchman, L. A., DeVinney, L. C., Star, S. A., & Williams, R. M. (1949). *The American Soldier: Adjustment during army life* (Vol. 1). Princeton, N.J.: Princeton University Press.

Unger, R. K. (1976). Male is greater than female: The socialization of status inequality. *The Counseling Psychologist, 6*, 2–9.

Unger, R. K. (1978). The politics of gender: A review of relevant literature. In J. Sherman & F. Denmark (Eds.), *Psychology of women: Future directions of research.* New York: Psychological Dimensions, Inc.

Veroff, J. (1977). Process vs. Impact on men's and women's achievement motivitation. *Psychology of Women Quarterly, 1*, 283–293.

Vinacke, W. E. (1959). Sex roles in a three-person game. *Sociometry, 22*, 343–360.

Vinacke, W. E., Mogy, R., Powers, W., Langan, C., & Beck, R. (1974). Accommodative strategy and communication in a three-person game. *Journal of Personality and Social Psychology, 29*, 509–525.

Walster, E., Berscheid, E., & Walster, G. W. (1973). New directions in equity research. *Journal of Personality and Social Psychology. 25*, 151–176.

Walster, E., & Walster, G. W. (1975). Equity and social justice. *Journal of Social Issues, 31*, 21–43.

Walster, E., Walster, G. W., & Berscheid, E. (1978). *Equity: Theory & research.* Boston: Allyn & Bacon.

Watts, B. L., & Messe, L. A. (1982). The impact of task inputs, situational context, and sex on evaluations of rewards allocators. *Social Psychology Quarterly, 45*, 254–262.

Watts, B. L., Messe, L. A., & Vallacher, R. R. (1982). Toward understanding sex differences in pay allocation: Agency, communion, and reward distribution behavior. *Sex Roles, 8*, 1175–1187.

Whata, M. A. (1972). Preferences among alternative forms of equity. The apportionment of coalition reward in males and females. *Journal of Social Psychology, 87*, 107–115.

Wittig, M. A., Marks, G., & Jones, G. A. (1980). The effect of luck versus effort attributions on reward allocations to self and other. *Personality and Social Psychology Bulletin, 7*, 71–78.

6 The Helpful But Helpless Female: Myth or Reality?

Jane Allyn Piliavin
Department of Sociology
University of Wisconsin

Rhoda Kesler Unger
Montclair State College

It is a "well-known fact" that girls and women are kinder, less aggressive, more cooperative, more nurturant, and just all-around nicer and more helpful than are boys and men. Unfortunately, Maccoby and Jacklin (1974) and Deaux (1976), in reviews of the developmental literature and the social psychology literature respectively, find no such consistency in the research relevant to this assertion. It is also "common knowledge" that a woman in distress can expect to receive help more quickly and with more certainty—especially from a man—than can a man in similar dire straits. Again, the research literature does not provide consistent support for this assumed relationship.

Initial expectations that there would be main effects attributable to the sex of potential helpers were derived from an individual difference model. That is, men and women were expected to differ in response tendencies because of indwelling "traits" that remained operative across situations. The expectation of differences in the amount of help received by males and females in need, on the other hand, was derived from a model of social normative behavior. Researchers hypothesized the presence of strong social norms dictating that women, the weaker sex, would be generally considered in greater need of help across a wide range of settings.

We have, of course, become far more sophisticated regarding the operation of personal characteristics in interaction with the characteristics of situations. Mischel (1973) has raised serious questions regarding the existence of traits, although he has been countered by Block (1971) and many others. The typical current approach views all effects in a person X situation framework. Unger (1979) has specifically used this framework to approach the complex question of sex-related differences in behavior. This theoretical perspective suggests that

149

assumptions about one's own and others' sex-related characteristics interact with social context and situational factors to produce what are frequently termed sex-different behaviors. Given the complexities of such a model, however, main effects are hardly to be expected.

In this chapter, we explore the findings relevant to sex and gender that are found in the literature on helping behavior.[1] These findings are not clear-cut. Sex is always a relevant social variable whether we like it or not. Sex can affect any social interaction: as a characteristic of stimulus individuals, as a characteristic of focal actors, as a characteristic of "background" individuals (e.g., bystanders), interactively (i.e., cross-sex interactions may differ from same-sex interactions), and even as a characteristic of the nature of settings, independent of the actors currently on that particular social "stage."

A cautionary note about the inadequacies of both the literature and our search of it is in order. First, many studies use only one sex of person in need and/or only one sex of potential helper; in those studies, no sex by sex comparisons are, of course, possible. In other studies, both sexes of subjects are used but there is no report of the presence or absence of differences. Finally, since many studies that do find differences do not mention that fact in their titles or abstracts, our search may easily have missed them. All of these problems related to sex bias in research are, of course, seen in other areas of research as well (Grady, 1981).

The chapter is organized as follows. First, we discuss some general considerations regarding the possible effects of the sex of the potential helper and of the person in need, and regarding societal factors. Next, we present a model of the determinants of responses to a specific helping opportunity, a model we feel can help in organizing our thinking about sex and gender effects. We then address the effects of societal factors, both in perception of and response to males and females in need of help on a particular occasion. Finally, we consider the issues of the potential developmental and socialization effects of sex differences in giving and receiving help over repeated occasions, and questions of sex and power in society in relationship to the structure of helping relationships.

SOME CONSIDERATIONS REGARDING EFFECTS OF SEX OF HELPER, SEX OF "HELPEE," AND THEIR INTERACTION

When we are exploring the impact of the sex of the potential helper, we must think about the possibility of innate differences between men and women (size and strength, aggressiveness, perhaps sensitivity to others' distress cues), but more importantly about socialization effects. How does the sum total of one's

---

[1]Our definition of helping behavior is as follows: actions directed towards the assistance of another person in the absence of a priori expectations of benefit to the actor.

biological and developmental characteristics operate in interaction with the behavior setting to determine responses to helping requests or opportunities?

Since the subject's sex is frequently not the major focus of a study in the area of helping behavior, but is introduced into the analysis after the fact, there has been little systematic consideration of these variables. Therefore, it is difficult to determine whether sex of subject effects are the only so-called individual difference effects possible and/or whether they are confounded with personality variables, situational contexts, or some interaction between the two. Thus, if females and males differ in amount of or type of helping, we cannot be sure whether it is due to differential biological drives (e.g., empathic arousal), differential socialization (e.g., training of concern for others), or differential implications of the particular social environment (e.g., social expectations or social desirability effects).

When we are examining the effects of the sex of the person in need of assistance, we need to consider the impact of sex-role stereotypes. For instance, women are expected to be more dependent and also more conforming. How can we then predict responses to a nonconforming female in need of help? As another example, the factor of physical attractiveness is thought to make more difference in responses to females than to males in many social situations. Is this true for people in need of help?

These factors have been studied somewhat more systematically (as we shall see below). However, these studies are not immune to biases introduced by the implicit assumptions of the investigator. For example, certain types of emergencies are always staged with male victims, others with female victims: Subway collapses, heart attacks, and epileptic seizures have always involved males, while faints and accidents involving falling furniture have always "starred" females. The statistical rarity or novelty value of stimulus persons in terms of their situational context has not received much attention.

Finally, we must also attend to the interactive effects of the sex of both the potential helper and the recipient. Is the asymmetry due to the unequal power of males and females such that, within cross-sex interactions, effects vary depending on whether the potential helper is female and the "helpee" male, or vice versa? Furthermore, given the heterosexual orientation of the majority of people, do cross-sex situations bring subtle sexual implications to a helping response that are not present in most same-sex interactions?

SOME CONSIDERATIONS REGARDING SOCIETAL
FACTORS IN HELPING

General societal factors have also received little attention in analyses of helping behavior. Thus, Huston, Ruggiero, Conner, & Geis (1981) interviewed 32 people who had intervened during actual dangerous criminal episodes such as muggings, armed robberies, and bank holdups and compared them to a group of noninterveners matched for age, sex, education, and ethnicity. They found that interveners had considerably more exposure in terms of personal victimology than did the others. They were also taller, heavier, and had had more lifesaving, medical, and police training. These results suggest that actual crime interveners act out of a sense of capability based on their training experiences. All but one of these interveners were men.

It is difficult to manipulate changes in the normative ethos of a society within the laboratory (cf., Unger, 1981, 1983). Laboratory norms mandate a lack of relationship between subjects and a separation of the subject from his or her cultural and historical circumstances. Nevertheless, traditional cultural patterns sometimes appear when the study leaves room for them. Thus, Wiley (1973) found that when males and females interacted in a game setting in which no communication between players was permitted, no sex-related effects appeared. When, however, verbal communication between participants was permitted, traditional patterns appeared in mixed-sex interactions. Males tended to initiate a cooperative "chivalrous" strategy when playing against females compared to male opponents. The structure of the game—a matrix of numbers—presumably supported male expertise.

Because helping studies have frequently been conducted in field settings, they are probably more influenced by situational contexts than are studies in areas such as aggression or influenceability. Contextual impact is probably a strength of the area, but it does make systematic analysis much more difficult. This critical review focuses mainly upon issues raised by the context in which studies have been conducted. This should not imply, however, that personal variables are not important. A few such variables that are related to sex and gender are discussed in this review, but many others remain to be explored. In the interests of brevity, questions about what constitutes altruism, most motivational aspects of helping, and the limits of what may be labelled helping behavior are not discussed. Instead, we concentrate on the implications of the situational context for individuals who differ in sex and gender.

AN ORGANIZING MODEL OF THE DETERMINANTS OF RESPONSE TO A SPECIFIC HELPING OPPORTUNITY

Although helping behavior has been studied extensively over the past 15 years, the social psychological literature on helping has lacked an organizing framework that interrelates various forms of helping (Pearce & Amato, 1980). The lack of such a framework has made it difficult to predict when sex-related effects may be expected to occur and which aspects of helping are more sensitive to sex and gender.

What is needed is a framework that: (1) includes affective as well as cognitive responses in the potential helper to the helping occasion and (2) takes into account the processual nature of those responses. Sex and gender may enter differentially at different points in the process by which the bystander or potential helper perceives, responds emotionally, decides, and acts. A model that explicitly considers these different points in time is therefore to be desired. Similarly, the sex of the victim and of the subject, as well as the interaction between them, are likely to lead to differences in both the emotional response and in the cognitive interpretation of a situation requiring help. While most models and frameworks for helping that have been offered are processual, they deal mainly with the cognitive processing of the event. The Arousal: Cost/Reward model recently elaborated by Piliavin, Dovidio, Gaertner, and Clark (1981, 1982), however, satisfies both of these criteria.

The first step in the model involves "pre-attentive processing," a term borrowed from the perception literature (Broadbent, 1970, 1977; Neisser, 1967). During this processing a bystander or potential helper determines, often at a level below conscious awareness, whether or not an event merits attention. That is, the event is characterized as not of interest, worthy of attention, or immediately worthy of action. If it is placed in the first category, it is ignored. If the event is placed in the second category, the individual consciously attends to it in order to make a more careful assessment of the implications of action. If it is placed in the third category, immediate, often impulsive, action is taken.

Once the event has been characterized as potentially requiring some response, the second step in the model involves the arousal of an emotional state in the bystander. The model originally dealt only with the impact on helping of the kind of arousal that is best characterized as a "defense reaction" (Lynn, 1966; Sokolov, 1963). The model now includes the effects of milder forms of arousal, such as promotive tension (Hornstein, 1972; 1976); feelings of moral obligation (Schwartz & Howard, 1981); or "empathic arousal" (Batson & Coke, 1981). Sex differences in susceptibility to various kinds of arousal generated by help-requiring situations are thus a second question of interest. The motive to eliminate or reduce whatever form of arousal occurs in response to the help-requiring situation is presumed to energize the helping response, under specific combinations of the potential costs and rewards that are inherent in the situation.

Under the unusual circumstances of high situational clarity and very strong arousal, bystanders are expected to respond "impulsively," without regard to the costs involved. Typically, however, the third step in the decision process involves a more-or-less rational calculation of costs and rewards to the bystander contingent upon whether or not the victim is helped. There are two categories of such costs and rewards: costs for helping (that is, costs or rewards that the focal person will incur as a result of helping) and costs if the person in need does not receive help (that is, costs or rewards that the focal person will incur if the person in need does not receive help, whether from the focal person or others). The first set of costs and rewards includes physical danger, loss of time and effort, exposure to unpleasant or disgusting experiences, embarassment if one performs inadequately, praise, thanks, self-satisfaction, and even possibly money and fame. Neither the positive nor the negative outcomes in this category can accrue to the potential helper unless that particular person acts.

The second category of costs and rewards consists of those that result for the bystander if the person in need receives no help. All those who observe the situation of need will experience these costs in varying degrees. These include, first, empathic distress and feelings of inequity that will continue as long as the person is known or suspected to be in need. A second set of costs in this category involves feelings of shame and guilt for personal inaction as well as the perception of the rewards foregone (e.g., the praise, fame, thanks, etc., one might have received had one acted). There are myriad possible sex- and gender-related effects in the perception of costs for helping the victim and costs when the victim receives no help. A major portion of this chapter analyzes these effects.

The Piliavin et al. model (1981) is designed to help us understand the determinants of response by a potential helper in specific help-requiring situations. Thus, this model is of limited utility in our exploration of wider societal and developmental implications. These effects are contingent upon repeated sex differential experiences with needing help and the response of others to that need, as well as with giving—or being prevented from giving—help of different kinds, and the self-assessments one makes based on such experiences. The final section of this chapter deals with those effects.

GENDER EFFECTS IN PREATTENTIVE PROCESSING

Before we begin our presentation, organized by means of the steps in processing postulated in the Piliavin et al. (1981) model, we wish to quote the conclusion of the section of their book that most specifically deals with sex and gender differences:

> . . . it is important to realize that gender is an extremely complex person variable. Implicit in sex differences are physiological, anatomical, social, and developmental differences. Thus, it is particularly likely that gender can have multiple effects on helping behavior—*simultaneously* affecting costs for not helping, costs for helping and arousal. (emphasis added, p. 202)

The first step in the model involves preattentive processing of the situation. Broadbent (1970) has distinguished two types of mental sets that can affect one's preattentive processing of information: stimulus sets and response sets. In a stimulus set, an individual is expecting to encounter certain kinds of input rather than other kinds. In a response set, an individual is prepared to take a particular action. With both kinds of sets, subjects are likely to respond more quickly and more appropriately when what they are prepared for is what the situation requires.

Although we know of no research that specifically addresses gender differences in attention, we can derive some possibilities regarding sex differences in response to different kinds of help-requiring situations through an analogy to Broadbent's work. Males and females are brought up in different subcultures with different interests, abilities, and self-concepts. As a result, they may well have different stimulus and response sets. In studies of eye movements in scanning visual materials, men and women attend differentially to different subject materials. Similarly, men are more likely to have developed the skills required to change a tire, while women are more likely to have the skills needed to comfort a lost child. It is therefore possible that men don't hear a crying baby as soon as women do, and that women don't notice a motorist in distress, because those events are not relevant to their developed interests and skills.

A very fruitful area of research awaits exploration here in terms of sex, gender, and the attraction of attention. Research similar to that of McMillen, Sanders, and Solomon (1977), showing that subjects who are in a bad mood do not hear noises as readily as do those who are in a good mood, nor do they notice a person in need as quickly, could easily be repeated with male and female subjects, in relation to different types of helping opportunities.

Aside from the unconscious, preattentive processing effects just discussed, males and females may have different thresholds for defining need. Enzle and Harvey (1979) found that female subjects provided more "help" (in the form of providing mood-enhancing music or chances to participate in a drawing for a prize) to a depressed other than to a nondepressed other. Men did not. Similarly, Thalhofer (1971) found that females were more likely to volunteer to help a mentally disturbed boy than were males. It is possible that the men in these cases simply did not perceive that there was a need for help under those circumstances in which women did. Austin (1979) manipulated the amount of harm done by a thief (using the value of items stolen) and found main effects in several studies: The more harm to the victim, the more likely was a bystander to intervene. More to the point, he found sex differences in intervention such that the amount of harm had less impact on female bystanders; females and males did not differ at high levels of harm, but women were more likely to intervene at low levels than were men. Taking these three findings together, one could tentatively conclude that female bystanders become sensitive to the needs of others at a lower level of distress.

In the one study that specifically investigated the differences between males and females in perception of need, however, no differences were found. Meyer and Mulherin (1980) had subjects of both sexes rate the likelihood that they would lend money to a female or male undergraduate acquaintance in each of eight conditions in which the cause of the need was varied. They found no sex differences in reported reactions on 25 affect scales, or in estimated likelihood that the person would require assistance in the future. The difference in the results between the three other studies and this one may lie in the "as if" nature of their design. Alternatively, lending money may not be associated with gender differences in people's judgment of the appropriateness of providing help or in their ability to empathize.

In summary, the differential salience of certain types of need or categories of persons in need, the availability of particular skills, and assessments of what constitutes need may all lead to differences between male and female prospective helpers in the first step toward making a helping response.

These conclusions, however, do not tell us whether we are dealing with a main effect or some interaction between subject sex and gender in preattentive processing. Thus, if more males or more females within a study possess a particular characteristic that also influences helping, we would not be able to determine the source of the effect. Some relatively unexplored variables that may be confounded with sex are religious orientation and self-perceived sex role. Batson and Gray (1981) have found that female undergraduates who had an intrinsic orientation toward religion (as an end in itself) were as likely to offer help to a lonely female confederate when it was not wanted as when it was. Those who saw religion as a quest offered help when it was wanted, but did not do so when it was counter to the person's expressed needs. We have no way of knowing how this specific kind of religious orientation correlates with sex (although religiosity in general is more typical of females). An intriguingly similar effect has been found, however, by Sandra Bem and her associates (Bem & Lenney, 1976; Bem, Martyna, & Watson, 1976) when looking at the behavior of androgynous and sex-typed females and males. They found that androgynous males and females were extraordinarily similar in terms of their ability to play with either kittens or human infants, and in offering sympathy to a lonely same-sex transfer student. Feminine females, however, were effective only in offering sympathy, which they did to a striking degree. In these circumstances, gender appears to be a better predictor of the perception of need in others than does biological sex.

SEX AND GENDER EFFECTS IN AROUSAL

Men and boys are frequently thought to be behaviorally more "impulsive" than are women and girls, while the capacity for emotional, empathic responses— particularly to the distress of infants and children—is considered to be a feminine trait. If emotional arousal is thought to affect helping, then, as it does in the Piliavin et al. model (1981), we might have two different predictions for gender differences in helping based on these stereotypes. On the one hand, females should be more likely to respond empathically to the distress of others. On the other hand, once aroused, males should be more likely to rush to help in the face of obvious danger.

Hoffman (1977) has carefully reviewed 16 studies in which females' and males' vicarious affective responses to another's expression of affect have been compared. In all 16 cases, females received higher scores, although only a few of the differences were individually significant. This suggests a small but real difference in verbal expressions of sensitivity to others' distress. Further, Craig and Lowery (1969) have found that female subjects responded with greater physiological arousal to others' distress than did males. Kilhan and Mann (1974) have also reported that women subjects were more distressed than were men subjects by watching the "learner" suffering in a study employing the Milgram paradigm. Women also refused to continue more often and did so at a lower level of shock than did the men. Unfortunately, the "learner" and the observer-subject in this study were always of the same sex; one is not sure whether the effect was due to the subject's or to the victim's sex.

Both Simner (1971) and Sagi and Hoffman (1976), reporting a total of six studies, have found that female newborns cried more than did male newborns to tape-recorded cries of another infant. Sex differences in response to control sounds such as computer-simulated cries were not found. Of the studies known to these authors, only Coke, Batson, and McDavis (1978) found that male and female subjects did not differ in empathic arousal. In their study, the response came to a taped radio broadcast relating the plight of a female in need.

It is possible that females may be more innately sensitive to the distress of others, particularly to the distress of infants (McDougall, 1913/1908). This would have provided some evolutionary advantage. It is, however, also very clearly the case that girls are strongly socialized to be sensitive to the needs of others. As Staub concludes:

> The results with both children and adults suggest that consideration for others is a more salient and important value for females than for males . . . . It is our network of cognitions—thoughts, beliefs, and values—that guides, on the one hand, our perception of our environment and the manner in which we process those percep-tions, and on the other hand, our affective responses. . . Consideration for others' feelings and welfare is likely to lead to empathic emotional responses. (1978, pp. 257–258)

Staub later quotes Bennett and Cohen's (1959) study of 1300 people, ". . . women described themselves as 'much richer' in the qualities of warmth and empathy" (1978, p. 258).

Maccoby and Jacklin (1974) did not find differences between male and female children in helpfulness, the ability to take the role of the other, or interestingly, in "impulsiveness." Thus, there are no compelling empirical reasons to expect sex-related differences in arousal or in the impulsive response to the emergencies of others. The only finding that points conclusively to the role of differential arousal to the distress of the victim is Schwartz and Clausen's (1970) finding that lone female bystanders responded more rapidly than did lone males to an epileptic seizure emergency. Because the person in need is male, and helping may require physical strength, cost considerations should work against such a finding.

Research on sex and gender and arousal illustrates some of the problems in making generalizations in this area. These include the following: difficulties in equating self-reports of emotional distress and objective measurements of behavior reflecting that distress (females appear to be more willing to report affective responses than males); difficulties in equating arousal responses across age; and the need to use multiple measures in helping situations. For example, based on differential predictions utilizing male "impulsiveness" or female "empathy," sex-related differences might occur in terms of speed of helping, but not in the actual numbers of males and females who eventually help.

COSTS AND REWARDS FOR HELPING AND SEX AND GENDER EFFECTS[2]

As Piliavin et al. (1981) state, ". . . the effects of gender [sic] of the bystander seem most parsimoniously interpreted in terms of cost–benefit considerations" (p. 202). By the time they reach adulthood, males and females differ in a variety of important ways: sheer physical size and strength, skills and abilities, self-concept and expectations, and confidence, to name only a few. Many of the sex of bystander effects that have been found can easily be interpreted as due to the different perceived costs for helping that result from such factors.

The requirement of physical strength for performing certain helping behaviors makes them more costly for females to perform. Studies such as the subway studies in which the necessary response may involve lifting a collapsed male show strong sex effects favoring men (Piliavin & Piliavin, 1972; Piliavin, Piliavin, & Rodin, 1975; Piliavin, Rodin, & Piliavin, 1969). Many male bystanders were usually present in these studies; the women may well have assumed that they were more able to help. Schwartz and Clausen (1970) found that females were slower to go to the aid of the victim of an epileptic seizure when other bystanders (some of whom were male) were available. Similarly, in all of the studies involving auto breakdowns, males were more likely to offer help than were females (Bryan & Test, 1967; Pomazal & Clore, 1973; West, Whitney &

[2]The analysis in this section relies heavily on a portion of Emergency Intervention initially drafted by Jack Dovidio. We here gratefully acknowledge his contributions to both the literature review and the interpretation.

Schnedler, 1975). Differential expertise, as well as differential strength is involved in dealing with car problems. And the fear of attack could be another potential cost affecting the differences in all of the above studies.

Gender-role expectations can also exert a strong effect on the calculation of costs and rewards, and thus on decisions to help. In all of the above examples, the help of women might be perceived as quite inappropriate, if men are present who could do so. There are also responses that one sex or the other may simply feel uncomfortable in performing. Consistent with this suggestion, Gaertner and Bickman (1971) have found that females are less willing to call "Ralph's garage"—presumably a male milieu—at the request of a "wrong number caller," even though there is no threat in doing so and no automotive expertise is required. (A replication by Franklin in 1974, however, did not obtain a sex effect.) In several other studies in which subjects were asked to make phone calls of less sex-stereotyped kinds, no sex differences were found (Baker & Reitz, 1978; Bickman, 1974; Simon, 1971).

The relevance of the sex-role appropriateness of the requested helping act has been specifically tested in two studies. Primmer, Jaccard, Cohen, Wasserman, and Hoffing (cited in Deaux, 1976) had confederates request shoppers in a drugstore to buy either a depilatory or chewing tobacco. Dovidio, Campbell, Riguad, Yankura, Rominger, and Pine (1978) had confederates request help with either carrying or folding laundry. In both studies, males were more cooperative on male-appropriate tasks (buying tobacco, carrying laundry) while females acquiesced more readily to female-typed actions (buying depilatory, folding clothes). Subjects have also been found to be more willing to assist a female writing a cookbook than one writing a mechanics book (Deaux, 1972). There was no effect of the kind of book being written on willingness to help a male author.

Two studies have also shown that female respondents are more sensitive to a vague potential threat. In a study in which subjects were asked to reveal either their favorite color or their telephone number to a stranger, Harris and Meyer (1973) found a difference in willingness only for women. Lesk and Zippel (1975) exactly replicated these results. Again, the costs of a stranger knowing your phone number are, unfortunately, higher for women in our society.

There can also be rewards attendant upon helping another individual in need. One of the most consistent findings related to gender and helping is that cross-sex helping, at least under conditions of low cost and low threat, is greater than same-sex helping (Bickman, 1974; Dovidio, 1979; Emswiller, Deaux & Willits, 1971; Hertzog & Hertzog, 1979). It doesn't take a great deal of creative thought to come up with the interpretation that, in our predominantly heterosexual society, the reward for cross-sex helping is the opportunity for interaction with a member of the other sex. Consistent with the cross-sex helping effect is an intriguing sex of experimenter effect found by Berkowitz, Klanderman, and Harris (1964). In that study, subjects of both sexes worked harder for an unseen partner in a condition in which an experimenter of the opposite sex would see their work soon (as compared to much later). The effect did not occur when the experimenter and the subject were of the same sex.

There are several studies of the impact of manipulating the attractiveness of a female in need of help on the response of male helpers that are consistent with a reward interpretation (Gross, Wallston & Piliavin, 1975; Mims, Hartnett, & Nay, 1975; Sroufe, Chaiken, Cook, & Freeman, 1977; West & Brown, 1975). Unfortunately, there are no studies that attempt to examine the effect of the physical attractiveness of males on females' helping responses. (This is, of course, an illustration of the prevalent feeling that physical attractiveness is more important to men's responses to women than the reverse.) Pomazal and Clore (1973), in attempting to manipulate dependency by equipping hitchhikers with a knee brace and an arm sling, may have instead created an unattractiveness manipulation. They found a decrease in the helping of such a handicapped female hitchhiker, but no effect for the male.

It is interesting that the relatively consistent cross-sex helping effect, as well as the attractiveness effect, is eliminated with the introduction of rather minimal costs. The cross-sex effect was not observed when Latané and Darley (1970) and Dovidio (1979) had confederates ask for small amounts of money. Hertzog and Hertzog (1979), in a study in which donations were requested for a political cause, found that the cross-sex effect was eliminated when the requestor was accompanied by a person identified as his or her spouse. In the Gross et al. (1975) study, the effect of attractiveness was found only under low cost. That men and women may be differentially susceptible to the cost-sex effect is illustrated in two studies of thefts where threat is potentially high. Howard and Crano (1974) and Austin (1979) both found that men were more likely to help female than male victims, while women were about as likely to help males as females.

Assumptions about gender-appropriate behavior have been found to alter helping in four studies. Harris and Bays (1973) found that women were helped more when they were wearing feminine dress than when in masculine attire. Helping was related to the type of request, as well as to the kind of clothing worn. Feminine attire increased assistance with a stuck shopping cart, but did not influence acquiescence to the less sex-typed request of change for a dime. The kind of clothing worn by the confederate had a greater effect on male than on female subjects. In a similar study (Unger, Raymond & Levine, 1974), there was a three-way interaction between the sex of the subject, the sex of the requestor, and the requestor's attire. People were least likely to permit ''deviantly'' attired individuals of their own sex to go ahead in line in a supermarket or department store. Although the extent to which opening doors can be seen as helping is moot, Renne and Allen (1976) found that women were six times as likely to have a door held open when they were wearing feminine attire.

A fourth study, by Appleton and Gurwitz (1976), found that college students of both sexes volunteered to spend more time helping an applicant to that college if the applicant had expressed sex-traditional as opposed to nontraditional vocational goals. These results were not altered by the amount of effort required from the subjects. Data from these studies suggest that sex-role expectations may be more important in mediating helping under some conditions than is the nature of the person's need. That is, the potential helper may be deterred from helping a woman who is perceived, based on dress cues, either as "the wrong sort," and thus not worth helping, or as independent, and thus likely to respond unappreciatively to the proffered help.

A final point we would like to raise in regard to sex-related differences in the effects of costs for helping, involves the nature of the helping response that is typically measured. In "emergency" studies, the usual response measure is one of personal, direct intervention. This indeed is the most common type of response subjects make in such cases. It is, however, also a very masculine sex-typed response. There are only three studies we know of in which both male and female subjects were used and both a direct response and an indirect response—such as going to get the experimenter or using a telephone—were measured. In one of those studies (Schwartz & Clausen, 1970) female subjects were much more likely than were males to use the indirect response. In the other two (Schwartz & Gottlieb, 1980, Experiment 1; Shotland and Straw, 1976), there were no sex differences in utilization of direct and indirect responses. In the Shotland and Straw study, however, only four of 17 helpers used the indirect response. It is dangerous to compare studies that use different designs, but it appears that indirect responses are used more by females when such comparisons are made. Indirect responses are also more likely to be used by anyone under conditions of danger and uncertainty, and when the potential helper is anonymous and not therefore "on stage." Perhaps females are generally somewhat less certain when having to initiate action, and more sensitive to physical danger, accounting for their preference for indirect action. Moreover, males may well generally feel more "on stage" when intervention seems required, due to sex-role expectations, thus accounting for their preference for direct action.

Effects may also vary with the nature of the helping response that is measured in nonemergency studies. Pandey and Griffith (1974) found no significant sex-related differences in verbal measures of helping, liking, willingness to help, positive feelings associated with helping, or number of minutes volunteered to help a same-sex person staple and collate papers. They did find, however, significant sex-related differences in the number of minutes actually spent helping. Females helped more, in terms of both spending more time and assembling more questionnaires.

In summary, many of the differences between men and women in giving help can be interpreted as related to differences between them in their perceptions of the costs for helping. Physical responses are more costly for females, as is helping under certain kinds of threat, given women's unequal power position in society. For both sexes, sex-appropriate responses are less costly, and there is a small increment in reward contingent upon helping a member of the opposite sex. This latter effect may be limited to low-cost types of help.

SEX AND GENDER EFFECTS AND COSTS FOR THE VICTIM RECEIVING NO HELP

In the Piliavin et al. (1981) model, the bystander to a help-requiring situation cannot escape experiencing costs by inaction. There are two kinds of costs that are experienced by a potential helper when they know that the person in need has received no help. First, there are the costs of empathic distress that continue as long as one must think about the person's need. Second, there are costs related to one's self-concept (e.g., loss of self-esteem) and to the thought of rewards forgone; these costs are incurred in relationship to one's personal inaction. In general, the more severe one perceives the person's problem to be, the greater these costs will be.

Sex Effects in Receipt of Help

The literature consistently reports that females will receive more help than will males under similar conditions (e.g., Krebs, 1970). If this is indeed a general finding, it would be consistent with the notion that any problem is perceived as more severe for women, because they are seen as generally less competent. The costs for a woman receiving no help would therefore be higher for a bystander. As noted above, we do not pretend to have an exhaustive review of all of the studies that may have used males and females in need of help. However, we present all of those that we have found in Table 6.1.

The conclusions to be drawn from this table are not all that clear, although the weight of evidence does point in the expected direction. In studies involving automobile mishaps—flat tires, stranded motorists, hitchhikers in trouble— females are uniformly helped more often than males. Similarly, in two studies involving travel directions, in two studies involving the theft of possessions, and in the Latané and Dabbs (1975) "pencil dropping" study, females are helped more often than males. In the other studies, cross-sex effects, no effects, or interactions with other variables are found. Some of these interactions involve sex-related stereotypes (e.g., appropriate dress or dependency). It appears, then, that females are consistently helped more than males in situations in which females can be assumed to be helpless by virtue of their socialization. This finding is still quite consistent with the idea that it is the perceived costs for the victim receiving no help that produce the sex effect. In less sex-typed situations, such as stapling questionnaires or lending money, costs for a female receiving no help would not be seen as greater than costs for a male.

Gender Effects on Perceived Costs for the Victim
Receiving No Help

We mentioned above that, in general, the greater the severity problem of the person in need, the greater will be the perceived costs to the observer for the person receiving no help. One can make more specific predictions if one knows something about the observers' self-concepts and the expectations they have for their own behavior, as well as any other attitudes and personality characteristics they possess.

We can propose how these variables might produce gender effects. For example, we have mentioned that women generally describe themselves as empathic and nurturant, or at least hold these qualities as ego-ideals. Refusing to help a dependent other should, then, be more costly for the average woman than for the average man. In studies proven consistent with this reasoning, Schopler and his colleagues (Schopler, 1967; Schopler & Bateson, 1965; Schopler & Matthews, 1965) found sex differences in helping related to the dependency of the potential recipient. As the dependency of the recipient increased, females helped more and males helped less. Females were also more sensitive than were males to the visual ability of a caller (blind vs. sighted) who requested that a message be relayed from a purported "wrong number call" (Baker & Reitz, 1978). They were also more responsive than males to the dependency of the male victim. Enzle and Harvey (1979) found a positive correlation between the perceived need of another and helping among females, and a negative relationship among males, when the need involved emotional support for a depressed person. (Note that males were also less likely to consider this true "need.") On the other hand, Barnes, Ickes, & Kidd (1979) failed to find any sex-related effects in a study that manipulated both dependency and intentionality of the dependency (i.e., lack of ability vs. lack of effort). Males and females were equally willing to lend notes when dependency was high and perceived as unintentional.

Gender effects also appear not to occur when manipulations of dependency lead to decreased attractiveness of the person in need. Thus, Bickman (1971) found that stimulus persons supposedly most in need (i.e., they dressed less well) were less likely to be given back a dime that they had left in a phone booth. However, no sex of subject effects (or main effects of stimulus person, or interactions) were found in this study.

Males and females also react to the needs of handicapped individuals in a similar manner. The apparent dependency of these individuals does not greatly increase the tendency of others to assist them (Pomazal & Clore, 1973; Ungar, 1979). The unwillingness to help handicapped individuals appears to be more related to their lack of attractiveness than to their dependency. Samarotte and Harris (1976) found that both males and females were more willing to assist a male confederate in picking up dropped envelopes when he wore a bandage than when they saw him with an eyepatch and facial scar. Similarly, Thayer (1973)

TABLE 6.1

A Summary of Studies in Which Sex of Victim/Requestor of Help Was Varied

Author/Date	Situation Used	Results
Ahmed (1979)	Stranded motorist (on highway)	Female victim helped more (marginally)
Penner, Dertke, & Achenbach (1973)	Stranded motorist (on highway)	Female victim helped more (effect strongest with white victim)
Pomazal & Clore (1973)	Stranded motorist (two studies, both on highway)	Female victim helped more: 1) standing by flat tire, 2) hitching ride by disabled vehicle
West, Whitney, & Schnedler (1975)	Stranded motorist (two studies, both on the road)	Female victims helped more in both studies; effect holds across race, and across neighborhoods defined by race
Simon (1971)	Stranded motorist (wrong number call)	Female caller helped more; significant cross-sex effect with male subjects
Clark (1974)	Stranded motorist (wrong number call)	Female caller helped more (very strong)
Franklin (1974)	Stranded motorist (wrong number call, rural south)	No sex effects
Snyder, Gretner, & Keller (1974)	Hitchhiker (stares at motorist or does not)	Single female helped more than single male or mixed dyad, but only in "stare" condition
Piliavin, Piliavin, & Broll (1976)	Person falls down stairs	Faster response to help female victim
Austin (1979)	Theft	Female victim helped more
Howard & Crano (1974)	Theft	Female victim helped more
Latané & Dabbs (1975)	Dropped pencils in elevators (three different cities)	Female victim helped more; sex effect greatest in deep south
Renne & Allen (1976)	Encumbered (or not) individual approaches door	Females more likely to have doors held open; interaction with attire and encumbrance
Lerner & Frank (1974)	Dropped groceries in market	Cross-sex helping effect; males helped slightly more overall
Valentine & Ehrlichman (1979)	Dropped change; victim wearing sling	Male victims overall helped more; interactions with sex of helper, eye contact manipulation
Ungar (1979)	Victim given wrong directions on subway platform (Canada)	Significant cross-sex effect
Pearce (1980)	Request for travel directions in bus terminal	Females helped more when natives (American), not when foreigners (Australian)

Borofsky, Stollak, & Messé (1971)	Role-played physical attack	Female attacked by a male helped *least* among the four combinations of sex of attacker and victim; male bystanders
Karabenick, Lerner, & Breecher (1973)	Campaign worker drops political literature	No sex effect. Victim similar in political persuasion to helper helped more
Takooshian, Haber & Lucido (1976)	Lost child	No effect of sex of child; no cross-sex or sex of helper effects
Bihm, Gaudet, & Sale (1979)	Lost letter technique (on car)	Females helped other females more
Benson, Karabenick, & Lerner (1976)	Lost-letter technique (grad. school application)	No effect of sex of victim (effects of race and attractiveness)
Barnes, Ickes, & Kidd (1979)	Request to lend class notes	No sex effects
Bickman (1974)	Request to participate in an experiment	Three studies on phone get cross-sex effects; one face-to-face gets no effect
Hertzog & Hertzog (1979)	Request to participate in an experiment	Cross-sex effect when alone; no effect when requestor is with purported spouse
Gruder & Cook (1971)	Written request to staple questionnaires	Interaction of sex of requestor and dependency of requestor
Dovido (1979)	Two studies with simple requests	Low threat request gets cross-sex effect; request for 30¢ gets no cross-sex effect
Harris & Baudin (1973)	Request for a change for a dime	No sex effects. Well dressed requestor helped more
Emswiller, Deaux & Willits (1971)	Request for 10¢ for a phone call	Cross-sex effect
Latané & Darley (1970)	Request for 20¢	No cross-sex effect
Thayer (1973)	Request to make phone call for deaf person	Cross-sex effect
Harris & Meyer (1973)	Request to sign petition (high or low threat)	No sex effects. Females signed less under high threat conditions
McGovern & Holmes (1976)	Petition-signing	"Neatly dressed" Ss (presumably conservatives) sign less for females
Primmer, Jaccard, Cohen, Wasserman, & Hoffing (1974)	Buy product for other shopper in a hurry	No effect of sex of requestor. Effect of sex of bystander X appropriateness of product (chewing tobacco vs. depilatory)
Unger, Raymond, & Levine (1974)	Request to get ahead in line at supermarket	Significant cross-sex effect; males help females more; deviantly dressed victims helped least by subjects of own sex
Brigham & Richardson (1979)	Attempt to purchase item for slightly less than it cost	Females helped more, especially if well dressed
Appleton & Gurwitz (1976)	Request to spend time with college applicants	No sex of victim effect or interaction; significant effect of sex-appropriateness of career aspirations; females volunteer more overall

found that supposedly deaf confederates were assisted less in making a phone call when they wore an ungainly hearing device than when they wore a more unobtrusive aid. Pancer, McMullen, Kabatoff, Johnson, and Pond (1979) found that college students of both sexes maintained a greater distance from a table set up for charitable donations when a handicapped person sat there than when an apparently unimpaired person did so. None of these studies found significant sex of subject differences in behavior toward handicapped and nonhandicapped people.

Finally, gender-related effects may appear when the situation involves socially normative expectations about the behavior of females and males. Thus, Gruder and Cook (1971) have found that the perception of need or dependency influences the degree to which women but not men in need are assisted. Dependency appears to be seen as more appropriate for females than for males (Broverman, Vogel, Broverman, Clarkson, & Rosenkrantz, 1972). Any review of sex role stereotypes in the communications media (cf. O'Leary, 1977; Unger, 1979b) indicates that males are portrayed as more competent, independent, and active than females. A discussion of some possible sources and effects of this difference in the perception of the dependency of males and females in need is addressed in more detail in the final section of this chapter. Moreover, males in our culture, more than females, probably think that they are expected to take responsibility in dangerous emergencies. In such situations, then, the costs to them for inaction should be higher than for females, leading them to intervene more frequently. Unfortunately, the tendency of investigators to use only male subjects in truly dangerous emergencies hampers our ability to pursue the answer to this question.

Sex Differences in the "Diffusion of Responsibility" Effect

The best known generalization in the helping and altruism literature is probably the "diffusion of responsibility" effect, first discovered by Darley and Latané (1968). This finding—also called the "bystander effect"—is that any individual bystander will be less likely to help as the number of other bystanders known by him or her to be present and able to help increases.

Unfortunately, there has been too little precision in discussions of this concept. Actually, there are three potential processes that can be operating in situations in which multiple bystanders are present: diffusion of responsibility, informational social influence, and normative social influence. Diffusion of responsibility, or the experiencing of a decreased sense of obligation to act (in our terms, lowered costs for not helping) can occur whether one is in the physical presence of the other bystanders or whether one is merely aware of their existence. Informational and normative social influence generally can have an effect only when one is in the presence of others, face-to-face.

There appear to be no sex differences in the operation of informational and normative social influence. Under face-to-face conditions, the "bystander effect" occurs as much for males as it does for females (see Latané & Nida, 1981). The influence of the sex of other bystanders under these conditions, however, has received no systematic attention. Thus we can draw few conclusions about gender-related experiences in informational and normative social influences. In their review of the literature on bystander intervention, Latané and Nida (1981) note that various studies have found inhibition of helping by males in the presence of other males, by males in the presence of females, and by females in the presence of other females. They claim that the combination of females in the presence of males has not been investigated.

Teger and Henderson (1971), however, speculate that males may be less likely to use females as a valid source of information about what behavior is appropriate in a given emergency. When males have observed another male fail to help a person in apparent pain behind a locked door of a closet, less helping has occurred than when no confederate is present. After seeing a female offer no assistance, on the other hand, males have helped as much as if they had witnessed the emergency alone. This effect may be explained in terms of the similarity of the subject to the bystanders. Smith, Smythe, and Lien (1972) have found that males are much less likely to react to the apparent distress of a victim when a bystander similar to themselves has failed to react than when the nonreactive bystander is dissimilar. Similarly, adult males respond more rapidly in the presence of a nonresponding child than when another adult is present (Ross, 1971). Rather than serving as a cue for adults' own behavior, the presence of children may focus responsibility on them. Sex, like age, may serve as a socially normative cue. More research is needed to determine whether these effects are due to the stimulus effects of status or to perceived similarity between the actor and other bystanders.

Under those circumstances in which only the "pure diffusion" effect can be operating—that is, when bystanders are physically separated from one another— the diffusion of responsibility effect occurs almost exclusively among female bystanders. An examination of the only two studies that have employed both sexes of subjects in all experimental conditions of a "pure diffusion" design is particularly informative. Schwartz and Clausen (1970) and Schwartz and Gottlieb (1980, Experiment 2) both have found statistically significant diffusion effects for females but not for males. This consistent pattern of sex differences may be attributable to the higher personal costs for not helping perceived by men, and undoubtedly associated with cultural expectations. As noted previously, for many emergency situations males may also perceive their costs for helping to be lower than do women. Supportive of this notion, to the extent that assistance requires physical strength (e.g., moving a large bookcase), the costs for intervening may be relatively higher for females than for males. Thus, perceived high costs for helping may also be an important facilitator of the diffusion effect. Bystanders caught in a high cost for helping–high cost for not helping situation frequently resolve their dilemma by reinterpreting the necessity of their involvement. Believing that someone else will help, or has already helped, is one such device. Supportive of this notion, in violent theft emergencies involving particularly high costs for helping (Schwartz & Gottlieb, 1980, Experiment 1; Schwartz & Gottlieb, 1976), "pure" diffusion effects occured for both male and female bystanders.

The level of arousal may also influence the diffusion of responsibility, and it may also provide a partial explanation for the sex difference that is often found in "pure diffusion." In one study (Piliavin, Piliavin, & Trudell, 1974), male subjects who were pre-aroused by seeing violent or sexually explicit films showed a diffusion effect, while subjects who were not pre-aroused did not. Data from a study by Gaertner and Dovidio (1977, Study 1) clearly demonstrate (1) that solitary subjects (all women) are more aroused than those who believe others to be present and (2) that this arousal mediates response time. These analyses suggest not only that changes in psychophysiological arousal accompany the process of diffusion, but also that arousal has a central mediating effect on helping behavior. As we have mentioned, women are likely to experience more arousal upon exposure to another's distress than are men. From these data, it would appear that, by getting males more emotionally aroused, the same diffusion effect can be obtained among men as among women. The process by which the diffusion effect is related to emotional arousal, however, remains obscure.

COSTS FOR HELPING AND COSTS FOR NOT HELPING AND VIOLENCE AGAINST WOMEN[3]

Due to the current increased concern over the high rates of rape and wife abuse, we must examine three studies involving physical assaults. Borofsky, Stollak, and Messé (1971), in a role-playing study that was, however, apparently compelling, exposed subjects to a psychodrama involving a fight that appeared to "get out of hand." The fight was between same- or opposite-sex individuals; in the male–female fight, sometimes the male was the aggressor, sometimes the female. The rate of intervention was uniformly high, except by male subjects in the fights in which a man was attacking a woman, where it was quite low.

Shotland and Straw (1976) followed this initial finding with a series of five experiments. The first study involved a highly believable staged fight in which a man attacked a woman in an elevator, which opened on the floor where subjects bad been left alone to finish an experiment. The major independent variable was whether the couple were presented as strangers ("Get away from me, I don't know you."), or as married ("I don't know why I ever married you."). Only 4

---

[3]The following four paragraphs are quoted almost verbatim from Piliavin, et al., 1981, by permission of the authors and the publisher.

of 21 subjects intervened in the "married" fight, while 13 of 20 took action with the "strangers"—a highly significant difference. Male and female subjects were equally likely to intervene, and direct intervention was the most likely response.

The remaining four studies reported in the Shotland and Straw article involved showing videotapes of the fights to other groups of subjects. Some suggestive findings include the following: (1) The possibility of injury to the woman was perceived as greater in the "stranger" fight (higher costs for not helping); (2) Both men and women expect that intervention will result in the potential helper being attacked more often in the "married" fight (higher costs for helping); (3) Subjects of both sexes feel more responsibility to intervene and think the victim wants their help more in the "stranger" fight (higher costs for not helping). (4) When videotapes are shown in which any reference to the nature of the relationship between the combatants has been edited out, 67 percent of subjects spontaneously suggest that the couple has some relationship. In this connection, a third study should be mentioned briefly. Anderson (1974) found 100 percent intervention by both individuals and groups of subjects in a simulated rape that was clearly an attack by a stranger.

The results of these three pieces of research are clear. In cases of physical assault by a man on a woman, costs of intervention are perceived as high. Bystanders tend to assume that there is a relationship between the people, unless it is clear that there is not. When the people are seen as related the bystander perceives even higher costs of intervention, which justify noninterference in an intimate relationship. The Shotland and Straw (1976) results do not show a difference between males and females in this regard; the original Borofsky et al. (1971) study does. In either case, the implications for public attitudes concerning the rights of married women are disturbing (see Gelles, 1972; Martin, 1977).

Thus, the Piliavin et al. (1981) model can help us to systematize the findings about gender differences in helping behavior at the level of the individual bystander. There are socialization factors, social interaction factors, and possibly biological differences that lead to differences in how men and women perceive and are aroused by the problems of others, and how they assess the costs of acting or refraining from action. In the final section of this chapter, we turn to an analysis of the developmental and societal impacts of these different patterns of helping and being helped among men and women.

SOCIETAL FACTORS IN PERCEPTION OF AND RESPONSE TO MALES AND FEMALES IN NEED OF HELP

Social norms about the necessity of being particularly helpful to females, and the more specific norm—sometimes known as chivalry—that men must be especially responsive to women's needs, have not yet disappeared from our society. Adherence to these norms appears to be stronger in the South than in other regions, as illustrated by the results of Latané and Dabbs (1975). They found a larger effect of the sex of the person who dropped small objects in elevators upon the rate of helping among male subjects in the South than in other parts of the country. One effect of the norm of chilvalry could be that women will be offered "help" when they neither perceive a need for it nor want it, while women who offer similar "help" to men may meet with outrage (e.g., Walum's study on opening doors, 1974). By the same token, men who really need help in such stereotyped circumstances (e.g., when approaching a door while burdened down by heavy packages) often go unaided. A second example is provided by a laboratory investigation that has left room for subject interpretations regarding what strategies are appropriate in playing a game (Wiley, 1973). Males have been found to offer "chivalrous" cooperative strategies when playing against females, but to use more competitive strategies when playing against other men.

We have discussed the effects of the sex of the person in need on the likelihood of receiving help. A main effect of sex is found in many, although by no means all, of these situations, and there is some consistency to the situations in which it is found. Generally, women are helped more in situations that are stereotyped as ones in which women are less competent than men to cope with the problem: car troubles, traveling alone, and thefts. Situations involving vehicles of any sort appear to be more strongly associated with assumptions concerning female helplessness. As somewhat of an aside here, we note that socialization factors undoubtedly account in large part for these differences. Studies of sex-role stereotypes in children's media indicate that women are far more likely to be portrayed as the passengers than as the drivers of cars (Women on Words and Images, 1972). Also consistent with this finding, girls are far less likely to receive vehicles as toys than are boys (Rheingold & Cook, 1975). Children are well known to incorporate these social messages into their play at an early age. As one example of this, Mathews (1977) has found that nursery school boys, as compared to girls, include a much larger number of distant and nondomestic locales (presumably reached by vehicle) in their fantasy play.

FACTORS AFFECTING THE ACTIVATION OF SEX-ROLE NORMS REGARDING HELPING

What other aspects of the situation or of the individual in need of help might we expect to elicit these social norms or make them more salient? Physical attractiveness appears to enhance the amount of help a female receives (Mims, Hartnett, & May, 1975; Sroufe, Chaikin, Cook, & Freeman, 1977; West & Brown, 1975). None of these studies, unfortunately, attempts to examine the effect of physical attractiveness in males.

Recent evidence suggests that physical attractiveness is important in the perception not only of females but also of males (Heilman & Saruwatari, 1979; Wallston & O'Leary, 1981). Unger, Hildebrand, and Madar (1982) have found that physical attractiveness in both females and males is associated with perceptions about involvement in socially deviant activities. Less attractive individuals are perceived to be more likely to be politically radical or homosexual. Less attractive males are seen as more likely to be aspiring to a stereotypically feminine occupation than are more attractive males. Physical attractiveness also appears to be associated with perceptions about physical stigmas ranging from major (e.g., epilepsy; Hannson & Duffield, 1976) to minor problems (e.g., the common cold; Unger, Brown, & Larsen, 1983).

More relevant to our concern in this chapter, attractiveness appears to mediate assumptions about gender-appropriate characteristics. Attractive males are seen as masculine and attractive females are seen as feminine (Lemay & Unger, 1982). As we know from the stereotyping literature, masculinity and femininity are associated with perceptions about independence and dependence, assertiveness and passivity, initiative and helplessness. Thus, physical attractiveness may produce a "double bind" for women. Women are encouraged to be as attractive as possible. "Being" rather than "doing" appears to be a central aspect of the portrayal of the female sex by the mass media (cf. Foreit et al., 1980, for an interesting example). This study examines the content of newspaper articles featuring males and females. Moreover, attractive girls may be penalized more for their cognitive competence than are less attractive girls or comparably attractive boys (Dion, 1974). Heilman and Saruwatari (1979) have found that attractiveness enhances the perception of a male's qualifications for a managerial position while it detracts from the perception of a female with equivalent credentials. More attractive females, in contrast, are considered more qualified for accessory positions such as secretary or receptionist. In sum, there is evidence that attractiveness is associated with perceptions about appropriate gender roles, and that roles and situations interact to influence both between- and within-sex helping behavior. One reason why attractive females may be helped more, then, may be that they are considered more likely to possess the gender appropriate characteristics of incompetence and helplessness.

Judgments about the perceived social desirability and appropriateness of role-related behavior are, of course, not restricted to sex-related effects. Katz, Cohen, and Glass (1975) have found that white males have been more willing to answer phone questions about a consumer product when the callers introduce themselves as "Negro" than when they introduce themselves as "black" or offer no racial label. Compliance also declines with increasing assertiveness of the caller and has done so especially for identifiably minority callers. Similarly, females in need of help—using the "wrong number technique"—have been helped less when they are associated with a less reputable organization, NOW, as compared to a more traditional one, the American Red Cross (Shaffer & Graziano, 1980).

SEX-ROLE IDEOLOGY AND RESPONSES TO PEOPLE
IN NEED

Gender-related expectations are typically implicit rather than explicit. These expectations are often recognized neither by the researchers nor by the subject; thus, such expectations are difficult to manipulate or control. Measurement of the sex-role ideology of subjects may demonstrate that many so-called sex differences are actually due to differences in gender-related expectations, if these expectations are differentially distributed in males and females. For example, Fink et al. (1975) have found that males respond to a campus blood drive appeal based on equity more than to one based on the dependency of others, while females do not. This sex difference, however, has been found only among those subjects who hold to a traditional orientation. Wallston (1976) has also found behavioral differences in help-seeking among men who differ in sex-role ideology. Traditional males seek less help from others on a masculine task and more help on a feminine task. Males with a nontraditional ideology—feminists—do not alter their help-seeking according to the sex-typing of the task.

Because deviance is largely in the eye of the beholder, the sex-role ideology of the perceiver may also determine reactions to out-of-role behavior in males and females. One study (McGovern & Holmes, 1976) has found traditionally or conservatively attired subjects less willing to sign a petition when requested by a female than when requested by a male.[4] Differences relating to ideology have been found in one study examining the effects of pro- and anti-liberation attitudes of males on their responses to the provocation of aggression by females. Pro-liberation males were more likely to respond intensely to blows with a pillow-bat than were more traditional anti-liberation males (Young, Beier, Beier & Barton, 1975). The tendency of traditional male to reciprocate less intensely during a physical bout with a woman is consistent with an ideology of chivalrous behavior. Interestingly, a recent study by Touhey (1979) has found that traditional males (based on scores on a "macho" scale) make more extreme judgments in their evaluations of the photographs of women who are varied in physical attractiveness than do nontraditional males. This study, then, links another aspect of gender with the personal ideology of the beholder.

PERCEPTIONS OF THE RECIPIENTS OF HELP

While helping is generally seen as a problematic act for the potential benefactor, most people regard helping as having positive outcomes for the recipient. An

---

[4]The attire of subjects does appear to predict the values they hold (Unger & Raymond, 1974), but direct examinations of this area are generally lacking. (However, see Lind, 1974 for a study in which social and political attitudes of college students were shown to be related to their manner of dress. In an experimental portion of the study, students also made judgments about the attitudes of others based on their clothing and grooming.)

increasing amount of literature, however, has reexamined the meaning of helping for the recipient. Helping can no longer be regarded as having only a positive value for the recipient. Moreover, this literature has uncovered issues relevant to our consideration of how the helping situation may differ for males and females.

Lerner and Lichtman (1968) found that female subjects devalued their female partner when she asked for help. They saw her as less attractive, especially if she was perceived to have asked out of fear of electric shock. Wispé and Kiecolt (1980) recently investigated the perceptions of males and females viewing a videotape of a female who was either helped or not helped following an accident with a broken grocery bag. The victims were devalued both when they were ignored by a male and when they were helped by a female, relative to the other two possible conditions. Inferences about the victim, then, were influenced primarily by the behavior of others toward her—not by her own behavior.

McGovern, Ditzian, and Taylor (1975a) placed male subjects in a situation in which they could help confederates of either sex by volunteering to divert electric shocks meant for the confederate to themselves. Males volunteered to take the shocks significantly more often for the females than for the males. At the same time, they rated the females as significantly weaker and more dependent. Females were seen as smaller, although the confederates were all approximately the same height and build. Subjects paired with a female confederate were also more anxious. Her perceived dependency appears to have caused a conflict in the subjects, who were afraid of taking the shocks but felt an obligation to volunteer to take them.

A subsequent study by the same group (McGovern, Ditzian, & Taylor, 1975b) indicated that the males' behavior was maintained, at least in part, by gender-related social demands. They stopped volunteering for shocks when the female confederate did not thank them. They also showed negative reactions to such a nonreinforcing female. They rated her as significantly more unfair, unpredictable, cowardly, ugly, bad, and ill-humored than did those subjects who were thanked by the confederate.

Female subjects appear to be aware of the potentially negative effects of being helped on the image others may have of them. They are less reluctant to seek help from an attractive female confederate when she has been designated as a fellow subject than when she is labelled an experimenter (Stokes & Bickman, 1974). In contrast, they are more likely to request help from a female designated as an experimenter when she is less, rather than more, attractive. In other words, females appear to be unwilling to seek assistance from other females whom they perceive to be of a status higher than their own. (Either professional designation or physical attractiveness may serve to create a salient status asymmetry.) Females are particularly unwilling to ask for help from an attractive female when a future meeting is expected (Nadler, 1980). Expectations of a face-to-face confrontation may increase evaluation apprehension. Even when no interaction is expected, physical attractiveness appears to enhance the social power of women with both women and men (Dabbs & Stokes, 1975).

Unfortunately, none of these studies has varied both the sex of the recipient and the sex of the helper. Nonetheless, it is interesting, in view of both the belief and the reality that females are offered help more frequently than are males, that female recipients of help appear to be devalued by their helpers and that they seem to be aware of this relationship.

THE IMPACT OF HELP ON THE RECIPIENT

What do we know about the impact of receiving help on the recipient? A number of studies suggest that being helped by others is viewed as a threat to self-esteem by females as well as by males (Fisher, Nadler & Whitcher-Alagna, 1982). In one study, females who asked for help on a laboratory task were more likely to have lower self-esteem and achievement motivation than were those who continued to work on their own (Tessler & Schwartz, 1972). In that study, help was also sought more frequently if the causes of having difficulty could reasonably be attributed externally rather than to the self. In another study, receiving aid from a similar other had a negative-effect on male recipients' situational self-esteem and self-confidence, whereas receiving aid from a dissimilar other produced positive effects (Fisher & Nadler, 1974). In another study (Fisher & Nadler, 1976), male subjects' most negative reactions were produced by the unsolicited aid of an individual with much greater resources than their own. It is noteworthy that, in one study, males accepted help more readily from similar others only when an opportunity to repay was anticipated (Clark, Gotay & Mills, 1974). In fact, males from a number of cultures indicated that they preferred donors who obliged them to return resources more than those who asked for nothing in return (Gergen, Ellsworth, Maslach & Seipel, 1975). No comparable data are available for women. Given the purported sex differences in perceptions of equity (see Kahn & Gaeddert, this volume), we might expect to find a sex difference.

Broll, Gross, and Piliavin (1974) found female subjects less reluctant to accept help when it was offered than when they had to ask for it. Subjects also liked the helper more when the help was offered than when they had to ask for it. A large-scale replication of this study in a metropolitan welfare department found very similar results. Recipients in a condition in which they had to call the worker for services requested fewer new services than did those in a condition in which the worker called them periodically to offer aid. Recipients preferred the latter arrangement and liked their workers better (Piliavin & Gross, 1977). Asking for help apparently involves an embarrassing public admission of inadequacy or inability to cope. Helpers who require this admission are therefore liked less.

Level of self-esteem has also been found to influence whether or not assistance is requested and the degree of assistance asked for. Morris and Rosen (1973) found that males who were made to feel adequate on a task (simulating work done by handicapped individuals) subsequently asked for more assistance from a male confederate than did those who were told they had performed badly at the task. Being helped also appears to have different effects on males who enter the situation with high as compared to low self-esteem. Only high self-esteem individuals appear to be threatened by receiving aid from similar others (Nadler, Fisher & Streufert, 1976). Although parallel studies have not been done with female subjects, comparable studies suggest that few sex differences may be expected. For example, Tessler and Schwartz (1972) found that only women with high self-esteem were more reluctant to seek help when the task was central to the self than when it was perceived as peripheral. A recent study by DePaulo, Brown, Ishii, and Fisher (1981) found that only women with higher dispositional self-esteem performed better on a task either after receiving no help or after receiving help from a partner who provided this assistance in a threatening manner.

Reactions to being helped appear to be similar among males and females. When being helped highlights the recipient's inferiority and need it appears to be harmful to individuals of both sexes. Both women and men appear to be aware of the potentially negative consequences of being helped. Because comparable studies using both males and females as subjects have not yet been done, it is difficult to determine whether gender-related assumptions affect when and from whom help will be sought.

SOCIALIZATION TO HELPLESSNESS

Individuals who are exposed to a series of insoluble problems, or to inescapable punishment are less likely to solve a subsequent series of problems that do have a solution (Hiroto & Seligman, 1975). Exposure to such conditions appears to engender the belief that responding does not produce reinforcement. These conditions produce a state of learned helplessness. Responses to learned helplessness conditions include the disruption of performance, decreased persistence, and the avoidance of tasks in which failure has been experienced. The social norms that dictate higher levels of helping for females than for males may, in a similar way, lead to the development of a generalized sense of helplessness in women. In many situations, female behavior appears similar to the behavior manifested in the "classic" learned helplessness paradigm (Dweck & Licht, 1980).

Carol Dweck has conducted an important series of studies of the developmental aspects of learned helplessness and its effects upon achievement. She has shown that children who stress those factors that imply that success is attainable through continued effort tend to maintain or improve their performance when failure occurs—regardless of their prior performance on the task (Dweck, 1975; Dweck & Repucci, 1973). Such studies indicate that the amount of exposure to success or failure experiences alone is not sufficient to explain children's achievement behavior. The cognitive links children make between such experiences and their perceived causes appear to be much more important.

DIFFERENCES IN ATTRIBUTIONS AMONG MALES
AND FEMALES

Dweck has also demonstrated that females make different assumptions about the sources of their successes and failures than do males. In particular, girls are more likely to blame their failures on a lack of ability, while boys are more likely to cite motivational or external factors, such as lack of effort or the prejudice of the agent of evaluation (Dweck & Bush, 1976; Nicholls, 1975). These differential attributions produce sex-related differential expectations in novel situations. Thus, it has been found, in individuals ranging from grade school (Crandall, 1969) through college (Vaughter, Gubernick, Matossion & Haslett, 1974), that males predict higher performance in school than their previous performance would warrant, whereas females tend to predict that their performance will be poorer than previous evidence would suggest. This pattern occurs despite the fact that, on the average, females receive better grades than males throughout the school years.

These sex-related differences in attributional patterns are associated with differential reactions on the part of boys and girls to new situations. Following failure on an achievement task, grade school boys show recovery of success expectancies following any change in the evaluation situation, whereas girls show as much recovery as boys only when the ability area being evaluated changes (Dweck, Goetz & Strauss, 1980). Moreover, the expectancy level of girls returns to the initial expectancy level to a lesser extent than the expectancy level of boys. Dweck and her associates suggest that the differential socialization of females and males has led to girls' greater tendency to attribute failure to a generalized lack of ability. Boys' attributions for failure, in contrast, appear to be more task- and situation-specific.

SEX-DIFFERENT SOCIALIZATION FOR HELPLESSNESS

Differential socialization patterns in this area have begun to be explored. Teachers seem to criticize boys more than girls, but the kind of negative feedback that boys receive appears to be relatively uninformative about their abilities (Dweck, Davidson, Nelson & Enna, 1978). Indeed, the negative feedback boys receive seems to be readily attributable to the negative attitude of the teacher, transgressions of a nonintellectual nature (conduct or neatness), or a lack of motivation. In contrast, failure feedback for girls appears to be given in a way that leads them to view failure as highly indicative of their lack of ability. Praise appears to be given in an opposite pattern—as a more valid indicator of the ability of boys than of girls.

There are also indications of differential socialization patterns more closely related to the area of receiving help. Teachers appear to reinforce the dependent behaviors of girls more than that of boys (Serbin, O'Leary, Kent & Tornick, 1973). Different patterns of reinforcement or extinction, using adult attention as the reward, can readily alter the dependent and independent play behaviors of young children (Serbin, Connor & Citron, 1978). Although direct parental reinforcement of dependent behaviors in girls has not been demonstrated, mothers appear to respond to requests for assistance from their daughters differently than they respond to similar requests from their sons. Rothbart and Rothbart (1976) found that mothers more often reinforced girls' help-seeking by giving active help and encouragement. Help-seeking by boys was more likely to be ignored or denied.

GENDER-RELATED EXPECTATIONS AND SEX DIFFERENCES IN SOCIALIZATION

Males may receive not only more contingent feedback about the outcome of their behaviors (Deaux & Taynor, 1973), but also more rewards for their successes. A recent study by Olejnik (1980) found that college students rewarded children as much on such stimulus characteristics as sex and age as on their actual achievements. In general, boys received more rewards for a comparable success than did girls.

Gender-related expectations may underlie this sex-different reward pattern. It is illuminating in terms of our previous discussion of attractiveness that, while attractive boys were penalized for failure less than unattractive boys, attractive girls were penalized more than unattractive ones in an achievement setting (Dion, 1974). Attractiveness appears to be associated with gender-related expectations: Attractive females are expected to be competent in social rather than in cognitive arenas. There is some evidence that more attractive women may, indeed, be more socially responsive (Goldman & Lewis, 1977) and that such behaviors may be reinforced in them by the behaviors of those with whom they interact (Snyder, Tanke & Berscheid, 1977).

There is, of course, no evidence that social responsiveness and cognitive competence are necessarily incompatible skills. There is, however, evidence suggesting that people who perceive themselves as relatively helpless may respond differentially to others' needs depending on the kind of help required. This relationship may underlie the rather puzzling finding that women who define themselves as feminine are not any more competent in actively playing with animals or babies than other individuals, but are extraordinarily supportive in passively listening to another woman in need of a sympathetic ear (Bem, Martyna & Watson, 1976). Both emotional empathy and passivity are clearly prescribed gender correlates of being female. Gender rather than sex differences may also underlie such phenomena as females choosing objectively easier tasks than males, but perceiving them as more difficult (Foersterling, 1980). This analysis indicates that we must focus upon the subjective reality people bring with them to the helping situation, as well as on its objective reality.

Females' sense of powerlessness and helplessness appears to be fostered by everyday customs mandating their greater need for help. Two empirical studies by Langer and Benevento (1978) indicate that individuals can erroneously infer incompetence from situational factors, in spite of previous success on the assigned task and the random nature of the labels used. Langer and Benevento have found that being assigned an explicit label (assistant) that connotes inferiority relative to another person, engaging in a consensually defined task, no longer engaging in a previously performed task now engaged in by another, or allowing someone else to do something for one may render the individual subjectively helpless.

Females are more likely, both in their occupational and in their family roles, to be placed in such situations. Females may also be more willing to select helpless power strategies in order to get their way (Johnson, 1974). When the individual acquires help by means of such strategies, he or she appears to lose self-esteem. In contrast, when the individual solicits help by means of strategies connoting competence or self-confidence, she or he gains self-esteem. As noted above, individuals with high self-esteem appear to seek less help from others than do those with low self-esteem. Sex-related differences, then, may both lead to and derive from circular processes involving differential attributions and expectations about the need for help, and "real" differences in willingness to ask for help and in the response to requests for assistance. These, then, both lead to and produce sex-related differences in self-appraisal, which lead to further differences in help-seeking behavior, thereby fulfilling initial social expectations.

SEX AND POWER: SOCIETAL FACTS IN THE STRUCTURE OF HELPING RELATIONSHIPS

Because sex and gender-role phenomena are embedded in a matrix of unarticulated cultural values that are not easily accessible to our usual empirical methodology (Unger, 1981b), social psychologists have failed to pay adequate attention to them. There are, however, considerable data that show high correlations between sex, social status, and personal power in our society, from early childhood through adulthood (Unger, 1976; 1978). The effects of these relationships on individual males and females, however, are obscured by the existence of societal rules regulating the behavior of males and females as classes. Individuals can avoid a sense of personal responsibility for either a gain or loss of power because of the integration of power relations within the social structure. Indeed, most people are probably largely unaware of the operation of power in their everyday lives.

Power relationships are maintained, in part, through their invisibility. Therefore, individuals may be particularly resistant to changes in the relevant social mores. Spence and Helmreich (1978) have noted that there is greater disagreement between the sexes in the United States on questions relating to ''normative'' social interactions (including when and how women should be helped by men) than there is on questions relating to purely economic issues. Areas in which there are intense reactions to the violation of expectations may signal the existence of important implicit social norms. For example, Walum (1974) postulated the existence of such norms as explaining confrontational encounters when the ritual of who opens the door for whom was violated. One cannot locate such sensitive areas in the laboratory. Thus, social psychology may be well advised to look to both sociology and anthropology for further answers. For example, one may explore the role of protective legislation in maintaining women's sense of impotence when dealing with the physical environment and with their failure to choose as broad a range of vocational goals as do men. Anthropological studies suggest that concepts about chivalry appear to be most important in cultures in which women have a relatively low degree of social status (Sanday, 1974).

The observable patterns of who helps and who is helped are neither socially arbitrary nor meaningless. Giving help appears to enhance an individual's sense of personal power, whereas being helped detracts from it. Classes of individuals who typically choose masculine styles of power to obtain assistance from others appear to be quite unwilling to solicit that assistance by claiming to be helpless (Johnson, 1974). An examination of socialization pressures related to helping suggests that many behaviors generally viewed as reflecting intrapsychic differences may instead be related to the stimulus functions of sex pervasive in the social environment. Some of these effects may be seen as self-fulfilling prophecies; that is, individuals may react to helping situations in terms of both their own and others' expectations. Status differences in helping transactions may both reflect and produce power differences. Some of the sex-related effects in helping may therefore actually reflect confounds of status and/or power differences with the effect of sex (Unger, 1978).

SUMMARY AND CONCLUSIONS

This survey of the literature on sex, gender, and helping behavior shows that research on these issues still has a long way to go. Simple analyses of sex-related differences—using sex as either a subject or a stimulus variable—are not sufficient to explicate the complex interactions among sex, gender, situational contexts, and personality variables. A few conclusions, however, appear to be warranted.

1. Sex-related effects may impinge at every step of the process involved in the determination of whether or not help will be offered: during perceptual processing, arousal of feelings and emotions, calculations of costs for helping or not helping, and in the choice of the response to be made. Many suggestive relationships have been presented and explored. However, due to the relative dearth of studies that have explicitly manipulated either sex or gender in relationship to this process, we can reach few firm conclusions regarding when and where sex and gender intrude.

2. Gender as a social norm or an expectation enters into the helping situation as either an interactive or a confounding variable. Assumptions about both appropriate and deviant sex-role behaviors, and about the probability that a particular sex will be found in a particular context or situation both influence helping. Unfortunately, these factors also interact with the personality and other individual characteristics of individuals. Little effort has yet been made to separate general societal attributions and expectations from those that might be characterized as intrapsychic individual differences.

3. The nature of the relationship between important stimulus characteristics of persons (such as status or physical attractiveness) that influence helping, and that may be confounded with sex, remains to be explicated.

4. More studies using multiple measures and multiple characteristics of helping as dependent variables would be particularly helpful. We need to distinguish between self-perceptions of empathy, judgments of one's helpfulness, intent to help, actual helping, speed of helping, and type of helping. Contradictory predictions based on sex and gender might be reconciled by a comparison of such measures.

5. Situational analyses appear to offer particularly fertile ground for study. It is necessary to determine a priori what conditions are most likely to produce sex-stereotypic patterns of helping—men helping more and women being helped more. Models that are linked to developmental and socialization phenomena may also be very useful.

6. The effect of being helped on self-appraisal is clearly in need of further work. From the standpoint of the sociology of knowledge it is interesting that the assumption that being helped is good for the recipient has only recently been challenged. The relative number of studies of decisions to help versus recipient reactions to help is evidence of an active interventionist bias in American psychology (see Brickman, Rabinowitz, Karuza, Coates, Cohn, & Kidder, 1982). This bias may also account for the relative omission of females as subjects and definers of problem areas in traditional social psychology.

7. A further question involves the determinants of the decision to request help. How is this decision made? What stimulus characteristics of the potential benefactor and of the situation are important, in relationship to the sex and gender of the person in need?

8. Differences in orientation toward helping also require a more intensive analysis. Helping is a prosocial activity. Some kinds of help may be offered to others at the cost of one's own ability to help oneself. Thus, what kind of help is offered to whom may have important implications. For example, does women's purported greater sensitivity to the needs of others interfere with their ability to deal with their own needs? Further analyses of altruistic "other" orientations would clearly be valuable.

This analysis concludes with the assertion that a comprehensive treatment of the role of sex and gender in issues relating to helping requires that we attend to the interface between individual behaviors and social systems. The study of sex and gender is so intertwined with the nature of the social relationship between humans and their societies that it can not be totally explicated through laboratory research. The helping literature has ventured further outside this narrow frame-work than most other content areas of social psychology because most of the work has been done in field settings (on which the realities of social structure impinge). However, no serious attention has yet been paid to the dynamics of the role of sex and gender in the helping relationship. Further study of the intersec-tion of these two areas of study can only enrich our understanding both about the nature of and implications of helping in our society, and of the impact of sex and gender in human relationships.

ACKNOWLEDGMENTS

Some of the research reported in this chapter and much of the thinking was supported by National Science Foundation Grants GS-1901, GS-27053, and GS-32335 to Jane Allyn Piliavin and Irving M. Piliavin. The writing of Emergency Intervention, from which much of this analysis was taken, was facilitated by the University of Wisconsin Graduate School, which provided the first author with salary support during the spring semester of 1977. Preparation of this chapter was greatly facilitated by our having access to the text editing facilities of the Center for Demography and Ecology at the University of Wisconsin, and the gracious help of Ann Cooper. Our thanks also go to Sally Zollner for manuscript typing, particularly for typing the bibliography. Judy Howard's comments on the manuscript have been invaluable, although she is in no way responsible for the flaws that remain. The order of authorship was decided on the basis of who wrote the first draft. Contributions to the final product were equal.

REFERENCES

Ahmed, S. M. S. (1979). Helping behavior as predicted by diffusion of responsibility, exchange theory, and traditional sex norm. *Journal of Social Psychology, 109,* 153–154.

Anderson, J. (1974, May). *Bystander intervention in an assault.* Southeastern Psychological Association Meetings, Hollywood, Florida.

Appleton, H. L. & Gurwitz, S. B. (1976). Willingness to help as determined by the sex-role appropriateness of the helpseeker's career goals. *Sex Roles, 2,* 321–330.

Austin, W. (1979). Sex differences in bystander intervention in a theft. *Journal of Personality and Social Psychology, 37,* 2110–2130.

Baker, L. D. & Reitz, J. (1978). Altruism toward the blind: Effects of sex of helper and dependency of victim. *Journal of Social Psychology, 104,* 19–28.

Barnes, R. D., Ickes, W., & Kidd, R. F. (1979). Effects of the perceived intentionality of another's dependency on helping behavior. *Personality and Social Psychology Bulletin, 5,* 367–372.

Batson, C. D. & Coke, J. S. (1981). Empathy: A source of altruistic motivation for helping? In J. P. Rushton and R. M. Sorrentino (Eds.), *Altruism and Helping Behavior,* Hillsdale, N.J.: Lawrence Erlbaum Associates.

Batson, C. D. & Gray, R. A. (1981). Religious orientation and helping behavior: Responding to one's own or to the victim's needs. *Journal of Personality and Social Psychology, 40,* 511–520.

Bem, S. L., & Lenney, E. (1976). Sex-typing and the avoidance of cross-sex behavior. *Journal of Personality and Social Psychology, 33,* 48–54.

Bem, S. L., Martyna, W., & Watson, C. (1976). Sex-typing and androgyny: Further explorations of the expressive domain. *Journal of Personality and Social Psychology, 34,* 1016–1023.

Bennett, F. M., & Cohen, L. R. (1959). Men and women: Personality patterns and contrasts. *Genetic Psychology Monographs, 59,* 101–155.

Benson, P. L., Karabenick, S. A., & Lerner, R. M. (1976). Pretty pleases: The effects of physical attractiveness, race, and sex on receiving help. *Journal of Experimental Social Psychology, 12,* 409–415.

Berkowitz, L., Klanderman, S. B., & Harris, R. (1964). Effects of experimenter awareness and sex of subject and experimenter on reactions to dependency relationships. *Sociometry, 27,* 327–337.

Bickman, L. (1971). The effects of social status on the honesty of others. *Journal of Personality and Social Psychology, 85,* 87–92.

Bickman, L. (1974). Sex and helping behavior. *Journal of Social Psychology, 93,* 43–53.

Bihm, C., Gaudet, I., & Sale, O. (1979). Altruistic responses under conditions of anonymity. *Journal of Social Psychology, 109,* 25–30.

Block, J. (1971) *Lives Through Time.* Berkeley, Calif: Bancroft Books.

Borofsky, G., Stollak, G., & Messé, L. (1971). Bystander reactions to physical assault: Sex differences in socially responsible behavior. *Journal of Experimental Social Psychology, 7,* 313–318.

Brickman, P., Rabinowitz, V., Karuza, J., Coates, D., Cohn, E., & Kidder, L. (1982). Models of helping and coping. *American Psychologist, 37,* 368–384.

Brigham, J. C., & Richardson, C. B. (1979). Race, sex, and helping in the marketplace *Journal of Applied Social Psychology, 9,* 314–322.

Broadbent, D. E. (1977). The hidden preattentive processes. *American Psychologist, 32,* 109–119.

Broadbent, D. E. (1970). Stimulus set and response set: Two kinds of selective attention. In Mostofsy, D. I. (Ed.), *Attention: Contemporary theories and analysis.* New York: Appleton-Century-Crofts.

Broll, L., Gross, A. E., & Piliavin, I. (1974). Effects of offered and requested help on help seeking and reactions to being helped. *Journal of Applied Social Psychology, 4,* 244–258.

Broverman, I. K., Vogel, S. R., Broverman, D. M., Clarkson, F. E., & Rosenkrantz, P. S. (1972). Sex-role stereotypes: A current reappraisal. *Journal of Social Issues, 28,* 59–78.

Bryan, J. H., & Test, M. J. (1967). Models and helping: Naturalistic studies in aiding behavior. *Journal of Personality and Social Psychology, 6,* 400–407.

Clark, R. D., III (1974). Effects of sex and race on helping behavior in a nonreactive setting.

Representative Research in Social Psychology, 5, 1–6.

Clark, M. S., Gotay, C. C. & Mills, J. (1974). Acceptance of help as a function of similarity of the potential helper and opportunity to repay. *Journal of Applied Social Psychology, 4*, 224–229.

Coke, J. S., Batson, C. D., & McDavis, K. (1978). Empathic mediation of helping: A two-state model. *Journal of Personality and Social Psychology, 36*, 752–766.

Craig, K. D., & Lowery, H. G. (1969). Heart-rate components of conditioned vicarious autonomic responses. *Journal of Personality and Social Psychology, 11*, 381–387.

Crandall, V. C. (1969). Sex differences in expectancy of intellectual and academic reinforcement. In C. P. Smith (Ed.). *Achievement-related motives*. New York: Russell Sage.

Dabbs, J. M., Jr., & Stokes, N. A., III. (1975). Beauty is power: The use of space on the sidewalk. *Sociometry, 38*, 551–557.

Darley, J. M. & Latané, B. (1968). Bystander intervention in emergencies: Diffusion of responsibility. *Journal of Personality and Social Psychology, 8*, 377–383.

Deaux, K. (1972). *Sex and helping: Expectations and attributions*. Paper presented at the meetings of the American Psychological Association, Honolulu, Hawaii, September.

Deaux, K. (1976). *The behavior of men and women*. Monterey, Calif.: Brooks/Cole.

Deaux, K. & Taynor, J. (1973). Evaluation of male and female ability; Bias works both ways. *Psychological Reports, 32*, 261–262.

DePaulo, B. M., Brown, P. L., Ishii, S., & Fisher, J. D. (1981). Help that works: The effects of aid on subsequent task performance. *Journal of Personality and Social Psychology, 41*, 478–487.

Dion, K. K. (1974). Children's physical attractiveness and sex determinants of adult punitiveness. *Developmental Psychology, 10*, 722–778.

Dovidio, J. F. (1979). *Costs, anticipated costs, and sex differences in helping*. Unpublished manuscript, Colgate University.

Dovidio, J. F., Campbell, J. C., Rigaud, S., Yankura, J., Rominger, L., & Pine, R. (1978). *Androgyny, sex-roles, and helping*. Unpublished manuscript, Colgate University.

Dweck, C. S. (1975). The role of expectations and attributions in the alleviation of learned helplessness. *Journal of Personality and Social Psychology, 31*, 674–685.

Dweck, C. S., & Bush, E. S. (1976). Sex differences in learned helplessness: I. Differential debilitation with peer and adult evaluators. *Developmental Psychology, 12*, 147–156.

Dweck, C. S., Davidson, W., Nelson, S., & Enna, B. (1978). Sex differences in learned helplessness: II. The contingencies of evaluative feedback in the classroom and III. An experimental analysis. *Developmental Psychology, 14*, 268–276.

Dweck, C. S., Goetz, T. E., & Strauss, N. L. (1980). Sex differences in learned helplessness: IV. An experimental and naturalistic study of failure generalization and its mediators. *Journal of Personality and Social Psychology, 38*, 441–452.

Dweck, C. S., & Licht, B. G. (1980). Learned helplessness and intellectual achievement. In M. E. P. Seligman & J. Garber (Eds.), *Human helplessness: Theory and application*. New York: Academic Press.

Dweck, C. S., & Reppucci, N. D. (1973). Learned helplessness and reinforcement responsibility in children. *Journal of Personality and Social Psychology, 25*, 109–116.

Emswiller, T., Deaux, K., & Willits, J. E. (1971). Similarity, sex, and requests for small favors. *Journal of Applied Social Psychology, 1*, 284–291.

Enzle, M. E., & Harvey, M. D. (1979). Recipient mood states and helping behavior. *Journal of Experimental Social Psychology, 15*, 170–182.

Fink, E. L., Rey, L. D., Johnson, K. W., Spenner, K. I., Morton, D. R., & Flores, E. T. (1975). The effects of family occupational type, sex, and appeal style on helping behavior. *Journal of Experimental Social Psychology, 11*, 43–52.

Fisher, J. D., & Nadler, A. (1974). The effect of similarity between donor and recipient on recipient's reactions to aid. *Journal of Applied Social Psychology, 4*, 230–243.

Fisher, J. D., & Nadler, A. (1976). Effect of donor resources on recipient self-esteem and self-help. *Journal of Experimental Social Psychology, 12,* 139–150.

Fisher, J. D., Nadler, A., & Whitcher-Alagna, S. J. (1982). Recipient reactions to aid. *Psychological Bulletin, 91,* 27–54.

Foreit, K. G., Agor, T., Byers, J., Larue, J., Lokey, H., Palazzini, M., Patterson, M., & Smith, L. (1980). Sex bias in the newspaper treatment of male-centered and female-centered news stories. *Sex Roles, 6,* 475–480.

Foersterling, F. (1980). Sex differences in risk-taking: Effects of subjective and objective probability of success. *Personality and Social Psychology Bulletin, 6,* 149–152.

Franklin, B. J. (1974). Victim characteristics and helping behavior in a rural Southern setting. *Journal of Social Psychology, 93,* 93–100.

Gaertner, S. L., & Bickman, L. (1971). Effects of race on the elicitation of helping behavior: The wrong number technique. *Journal of Personality and Social Psychology, 20,* 218–222.

Gaertner, S. L. & Dovidio, J. F. (1977). The subtlety of white racism, arousal, and helping behavior. *Journal of Personality and Social Psychology, 35,* 691–707.

Gelles, R. J. (1972). *The violent home: A study of physical aggression between husbands and wives.* Beverly Hills, Calif.: Sage.

Gergen, K. J., Ellsworth, P., Maslach, C., & Seipel, M. (1975). Obligation, donor resources, and reactions to aid in three cultures. *Journal of Personality and Social Psychology, 31,* 390–400.

Goldman, W., & Lewis, P. (1977). Beautiful is good: Evidence that the physically attractive are more socially skilled. *Journal of Experimental Social Psychology, 13,* 125–130.

Grady, K. E. (1981). Sex bias in research design. *Psychology of Women Quarterly, 5,* 628–636.

Gross, A. E., Wallston, B. S., & Piliavin, I. M. (1975). Beneficiary attractiveness and cost as determinants of responses to routine requests for help. *Sociometry, 38,* 131–140.

Gruder, C. L., & Cook, T. D. (1971). Sex, dependency, and helping. *Journal of Personality and Social Psychology, 19,* 290–294.

Hannson, R. C., & Duffield, B. J. (1976). Physical attractiveness and the attribution of epilepsy. *Journal of Social Psychology, 99,* 233–240.

Harris, M. B., & Baudin, H. (1973). The language of altruism: The effects of language, dress, and ethnic group. *Journal of Social Psychology, 91,* 37–41.

Harris, M. B., & Bays, G. (1973). Altruism and sex roles. *Psychological Reports, 32,* 1002.

Harris, M. B., & Meyer, F. (1973). Dependency, threat, and helping. *Journal of Social Psychology, 90,* 239–242.

Heilman, M. E., & Saruwatari, L. R. (1979). When beauty is beastly: The effect of appearance and sex on evaluations of job applicants for managerial and nonmanagerial jobs. *Organizational Behavior and Human Performance, 23,* 360–372.

Hertzog, R. L., & Hertzog, D. J. (1979). Ingratiation as a mediating factor in intersex helping behavior. *Journal of Social Psychology, 108,* 281–282.

Hiroto, D. S., & Seligman, L. R. (1975). Generality of learned helplessness in man. *Journal of Personality and Social Psychology, 31,* 311–327.

Hoffman, M. L. (1977). Sex differences in empathy and related behaviors. *Psychological Bulletin, 84,* 712–720.

Hornstein, H. A. (1976). *Cruelty and kindness: A new look at aggression and altruism.* Englewood Cliffs, N.J.: Prentice-Hall.

Hornstein, H. A. (1972). Promotive tension: The basis of prosocial behavior from a Lewinian perspective. *Journal of Social Issues, 28,* 191–218.

Howard, W., & Crano, W. D. (1974). Effects of sex, conversation, location, and size of observer group on bystander intervention in a high risk situation. *Sociometry, 37*(4), 491–507.

Huston, T. L., Ruggiero, M., Conner, R., & Geis, G. (1981). Bystander intervention into crime: A study based on naturally occurring episodes. *Social Psychology Quarterly, 44,* 14–23.

Johnson, P. (1974, May). *Social power and sex-role stereotypes.* Paper presented at the meeting of the Western Psychological Association, San Francisco.

Karabenick, S. A., Lerner, R. M., & Breecher, M. D. (1973). Relation of political affiliation to helping behavior on election day, November 7, 1972. *Journal of Social Psychology, 91,* 223–227.

Katz, I., Cohen, S., & Glass, D. (1975). Some determinants of cross-racial helping behavior. *Journal of Personality and Social Psychology, 32,* 964–970.

Kilhan, W., & Mann, L. (1974). Level of destructive obedience as a function of transmitter and executant roles in the Milgram obedience paradigm. *Journal of Personality and Social Psychology, 29,* 696–702.

Krebs, D. L. (1970). Altruism—an examination of the concept and a review of the literature. *Psychological Bulletin, 73,* 258–302.

Langer, E. J., & Benevento, A. (1978). Self-induced dependence. *Journal of Personality and Social Psychology, 36,* 886–893.

Latané, B., & Dabbs, J. M. (1975). Sex, group size, and helping in three cities. *Sociometry, 38,* 180–194.

Latané, B. & Darley, J. M. (1970). *The unresponsive bystander: Why doesn't he help?* New York: Appleton-Century-Crofts.

Latané, B., & Nida, S. (1981). Ten years of research on group size and helping. *Psychological Bulletin, 89,* 308–324.

Lemay, M., & Unger, R. K. (1982, April). *The relationship between physical attractiveness and gender-appropriate characteristics: Two methods of measurement.* Paper presented at the meetings of the Eastern Psychological Association.

Lerner, M. J., & Lichtman, R. R. (1968). Effects of perceived norms on attitudes and altruistic behavior toward a dependent other. *Journal of Personality and Social Psychology, 9,* 226–232.

Lerner, R. M., & Frank, P. (1974). Relation of race and sex to supermarket helping behavior. *Journal of Social Psychology, 94,* 201–203.

Lesk, S., & Zippel, B. (1975). Dependency, threat, and helping in a large city. *Journal of Social Psychology, 95,* 185–186.

Lind, C. (1974). *Social-political attitudes and appearance of college students.* Unpublished doctoral dissertation, University of Wisconsin.

Lynn, R. (1966). *Attention, arousal, and the orientation reaction.* Oxford: Pergamon.

Maccoby, E. E., & Jacklin, C. (1974). *The psychology of sex differences.* Stanford, Calif.: Stanford University Press.

Martin, D. (1977). *Battered wives.* New York: Pocket Books.

Mathews, W. S. (1977). Sex-role perception, portrayal, and preference in the fantasy play of young children. *Resources in Education,* August, Document No. ED 136949.

McDougall, W. (1913). *An introduction to social psychology (5th Ed.).* Boston: John W. Luce & Co. (Originally published 1908).

McGovern, J. L., & Holmes, D. S. (1976). Influence of sex and dress on cooperation: An instance of "person" chauvinism. *Journal of Applied Social Psychology, 6,* 206–210.

McGovern, L. P., Ditzian, J. L., & Taylor, S. P. (1975a). Sex and perception of dependency in a helping situation. *Bulletin of the Psychonomic Society, 5,* 336–338.

McGovern, L. P., Ditzian, J. L., & Taylor, S. P. (1975b). The effect of one positive reinforcement on helping with cost. *Bulletin of the Psychonomic Society, 5,* 421–423.

McMillen, D. L., Sanders, D. Y., & Solomon, G. S. (1977). Self-esteem, attentiveness, and helping behavior. *Personality and Social Psychology Bulletin, 3,* 257–261.

Meyer, J. P. & Mulherin, A. (1980). From attribution to helping: An analysis of the mediating effect of affect and expectancy. *Journal of Personality and Social Psychology, 39,* 201–210.

Mims, P., Hartnett, J. & Nay, W. (1975). Interpersonal attractiveness and help-volunteering as a function of physical attractiveness. *Journal of Psychology, 89,* 125–131.

Mischel, W. (1973). Toward a cognitive social learning reconceptualization of personality. *Psychological Review, 80,* 252–283.

Morris, S. C., III, & Rosen, S. (1973). Effects of felt adequacy and opportunity to reciprocate on help seeking. *Journal of Experimental Social Psychology, 9,* 265–276.

Nadler, A. (1980). "Good looks do not help": Effects of helper's physical attractiveness and expectations for future interaction on help-seeking behavior. *Personality and Social Psychology Bulletin, 6,* 378–383.

Nadler, A., Fisher, J. D., & Streufert, S. (1976). When helping hurts: Effects of donor–recipient similarity and recipient self-esteem on reactions to aid. *Journal of Personality, 44,* 392–409.

Neisser, U. (1967) *Cognitive psychology.* New York: Appleton-Century-Crofts.

Nicholls, J. (1975). Causal attributions and other achievement related cognitions: Effects of task, outcome, attainment value, and sex. *Journal of Personality and Social Psychology, 31,* 379–389.

O'Leary, V. E. (1977). *Toward understanding women.* Monterey, Cal.: Brooks/Cole.

Olejnik, A. B. (1980). Socialization of achievement: Effects of children's sex and age on achievement evaluations by adults. *Personality and Social Psychology Bulletin, 6,* 68–73.

Pancer, S. M., McMullen, L. M., Kabatoff, R. A., Johnson, K. G., & Pond, C. A. (1979). Conflict and avoidance in the helping situation. *Journal of Personality and Social Psychology, 37,* 1406–1411.

Pandey, J. & Griffith, W. (1974). Attraction and helping. *Bulletin of the Psychonomic Society, 3,* 123–124.

Pearce, P. L. (1980). Strangers, travelers, and Greyhound terminals: A study of smallscale helping behaviors. *Journal of Personality and Social Psychology, 38,* 935–940.

Pearce, P. L. & Amato, P. R. (1980). A taxonomy of helping: A multidimensional scaling analysis. *Social Psychology Quarterly, 43,* 363–371.

Penner, L. A., Dertke, M. C., & Achenback, C. J. (1973). The 'flash' system: A field study of altruism. *Journal of Applied Social Psychology, 3,* 362–370.

Piliavin, I. M. & Gross, A. (1977). The effects of separation of services and income maintenance on AFDC recipients. *Social Service Review, 51*(3).

Piliavin, I. M., Piliavin, J. A., & Rodin, S. (1975). Costs, diffusion, and the stigmatized victim. *Journal of Personality and Social Psychology, 32,* 429–438.

Piliavin, I. M., Rodin, J., & Piliavin, J. A. (1969). Good samaritanism: An underground phenomenon? *Journal of Personality and Social Psychology, 13,* 289–299.

Piliavin, J. A., Dovidio, J. F., Gaertner, S. L., & Clark, R. D., III. (1981). *Emergency intervention.* New York: Academic Press.

Piliavin, J. A., Dovidio, J. F., Gaertner, S. L., & Clark, R. D., III. (1982). Responsive bystanders: The process of intervention. In Derlega, V. and Grzelak J., *Cooperation and helping behavior: Theories and research.* New York: Academic Press.

Piliavin, J. A., & Piliavin, I. M. (1972). The effects of blood on reactions to a victim. *Journal of Personality and Social Psychology, 23,* 253–261.

Piliavin, J. A., Piliavin, I. M., & Broll, L. (1976). Time of arrival at an emergency and likelihood of helping. *Personality and Social Psychology Bulletin, 2,* 273–276.

Piliavin, J. A., Piliavin, I. M., & Trudell, B. (1974). *Incidental arousal, helping, and diffusion of responsibility.* Unpublished data, University of Wisconsin.

Pomazal, R. J., & Clore, G. L. (1973). Helping on the highway: The effects of dependency and sex. *Journal of Applied Social Psychology, 3,* 150–164.

Primmer, C., Jaccard, J., Cohen, J. L., Wasserman, J., & Hoffing, A. (1974). *The influence of the sex-appropriateness of a task on helping behavior in the laboratory and the field.* Unpublished manuscript, University of Illinois.

Renne, K. S., & Allen, P. C. (1976). Gender and the ritual of the door. *Sex Roles, 2,* 167–174.

Rheingold, H. L., & Cook, K. V. (1975). The contents of boys' and girls' rooms as an index of parents' behavior. *Child Development, 46,* 459–463.

Ross, A. S. (1971). Effect of increased responsibility on bystander intervention: The presence of children. *Journal of Personality and Social Psychology, 19,* 306–310.

Rothbart, M. K., & Rothbart, M. (1976). Birth order, sex of child, and maternal help-giving. *Sex Roles, 2* 39–46.

Sagi, A., & Hoffman, M. (1976). Empathic distress in the newborn. *Developmental Psychology, 12,* 175–176.

Samarotte, G. C., & Harris, M. B. (1976). Some factors influencing helping: The effects of an handicap, responsibility, and requesting help. *Journal of Social Psychology, 98,* 39–45.

Sanday, P. R. (1974). Female status in the public domain. In M. Z. Rosaldo & L. Lamphere (Eds.). *Women, culture, and society.* Stanford, Calif.: Stanford University Press.

Schopler, J. (1967). An investigation of sex differences on the influence of dependence, *Sociometry, 30,* 50–63.

Schopler, J. & Bateson, N. (1965). The power of dependence. *Journal of Personality and Social Psychology, 2,* 247–254.

Schopler, J., & Matthews, M. (1965). The influence of perceived causal locus of dependence on the use of interpersonal power. *Journal of Personality and Social Psychology, 2,* 609–612.

Schwartz, S. H., & Clausen, G. T. (1970). Responsibility, norms, and helping in an emergency. *Journal of Personality and Social Psychology, 16,* 299–310.

Schwartz, S. H. & Gottlieb, A. (1980). Bystander anonymity and reactions to emergencies. *Journal of Personality and Social Psychology, 39,* 418–430.

Schwartz, S. H., & Gottlieb, A. (1976). Bystander reactions to a violent theft: Crime in Jerusalem. *Journal of Personality and Social Psychology, 34,* 1188–1199.

Schwartz, S. H., & Howard, J. A. (1981). A normative decision-making model of altruism. In J. P. Rushton & R. M. Sorrentino (Eds.), *Altruism and helping behavior.* Hillsdale, N.J.: Lawrence Erlbaum Associates.

Serbin, L. A., Connor, J. M., & Citron, C. C. (1978). Environmental control of independent and dependent behaviors in preschool girls and boys: A model for early independence training. *Sex Roles, 4,* 867–875.

Serbin, L. A., O'Leary, K. D., Kent, R. N., & Tonick, I. J. (1973). A comparison of teacher response to the preacademic and problem behavior of boys and girls. *Child Development, 44,* 796–804.

Shaffer, D. R., & Graziano, W. G. (1980). Effects of victims' race and organizational affiliation on receiving help from blacks and whites. *Personality and Social Psychology Bulletin, 6,* 366–372.

Shotland, R. L., & Straw, M. K. (1976). Bystander response to an assault: When a man attacks a woman. *Journal of Personality and Social Psychology, 34,* 990–999.

Simner, M. (1971). Newborn's response to the cry of another infant. *Developmental Psychology, 5,* 136–150.

Simon, W. E. (1971). Helping behavior in the absence of visual contact as a function of sex of person asking for help and sex of person being asked for help. *Psychological Reports, 28,* 609–610.

Smith, R., Smythe, L., & Lien, D. (1972). Inhibition of helping behavior by a similar or dissimilar nonreactive fellow bystander. *Journal of Personality and Social Psychology, 23,* 414–419.

Snyder, M., Grether, J., & Keller, K. (1974). Staring and compliance: A field study on hitchhiking. *Journal of Applied Social Psychology, 4,* 165–170.

Snyder, M., Tanke, K. D., & Berscheid, E. (1977) Social perception and interpersonal behavior: On the self-fulfilling nature of social stereotypes. *Journal of Personality and Social Psychology, 35,* 656–666.

Sokolov, E. N. (1963). *Perception and the conditioned reflex.* Oxford: Pergamon Press.

Spence, J. T., & Helmreich, R. (1978). *Masculinity and feminity.* Austin: University of Texas Press.

Sroufe, R., Chaikin, A., Cook, R., & Freeman, V. (1977). The effects of physical attractiveness on honesty: A socially desirable response. *Personality and Social Psychology Bulletin, 3*, 59–62.

Staub, E. (1978) *Positive social behavior and morality, Vol. 1: Social and personal influences.* New York: Academic Press.

Stokes, S. J., & Bickman, L. (1974). The effect of the physical attractiveness and role of the helper on seeking. *Journal of Applied Social Psychology, 4*, 286–294.

Takooshian, H., Haber, S., & Lucido, D. J. (1976). *Helping responses to a lost child in city and town.* Paper presented at American Psychological Association meetings, Washington, D.C.

Teger, A. I., & Henderson, J. E. (1971, April). *An examination of the social influence hypothesis of bystander intervention in emergencies.* Paper presented at the meeting of the Eastern Psychological Association, New York City.

Tessler, R. C., & Schwartz, S. H. (1972). Help seeking, self-esteem, and achievement motivation: An attributional analysis. *Journal of Personality and Social Psychology, 21*, 318–326.

Thalhofer, N. N. (1971). Responsibility, reparation, and self-protection as reasons for three types of helping. *Journal of Personality and Social Psychology, 19*, 144–151.

Thayer, S. (1973). Lend me your ears: Racial and sexual factors in helping the deaf. *Journal of Personality and Social Psychology, 28*(1), 8–11.

Touhey, J. C. (1979). Sex-role stereotyping and individual differences in liking for the physically attractive. *Social Psychology Quarterly, 42*, 285–289.

Ungar, S. (1979). The effect of effort and stigma on helping. *Journal of Social Psychology, 107*, 23–28.

Unger, R. K. (1979). *Female and male: Psychological perspectives.* New York: Harper & Row.

Unger, R. K. (1976). Male is greater than female: The socialization of status inequality. *The Counseling Psychologist, 6*, 2–9.

Unger, R. K. (1978). The politics of gender: A review of relevant literature. In J. Sherman & F. Denmark (Eds.), *The psychology of women: Future directions of research.* New York: Psychological Dimensions.

Unger, R. K. (1981). Sex as a social reality: Field and laboratory research. *Psychology of Women Quarterly, 5*, 645–653.

Unger, R. K. (1983). Through the looking glass: No Wonderland yet! *Psychology of Women Quarterly, 8*, 9–32.

Unger, R. K., Brown, V. H., & Larsen, M. V. (1983). Physical attractiveness and physical stigma: Menstruation and the common cold. In S. Golub (Ed.). *Menarche: An interdisciplinary view.* Lexington, Mass.: D. C. Heath.

Unger, R. K., Hildebrand, M., & Madar, T. (1982). Physical attractiveness and assumptions about social deviance: Some sex by sex comparisons. *Personality and Social Psychology Bulletin, 8*, 293–301.

Unger, R. K., & Raymond, B. J. (1974). External criteria as predictors of values: The importance of race and attire. *Journal of Social Psychology, 93*, 295–296.

Unger, R. K., Raymond, B. J., & Levine, S. (1974). Are women discriminated against? Sometimes! *International Journal of Group Tensions, 4*, 71–81.

Valentine, M. E., & Erhlichman, H. (1979). Interpersonal gaze and helping behavior. *Journal of Social Psychology, 107*, 193–198.

Vaughter, R. M., Gubernick, D., Matossian, J., & Haslet, B. (1974, August). *Sex differences in academic expectations and achievement.* Paper presented at the meeting of the American Psychological Association, New Orleans.

Wallston, B. S. (1976). The effects of sex-role ideology, self-esteem, and expected future interactions with an audience on male help seeking. *Sex Roles, 2*, 353–365.

Wallston, B. S., & O'Leary, V. E. (1981). Sex and gender make a difference: The differential perceptions of women and men. In L. Wheeler (Ed.). *Review of personality and social psychology, Vol. 2.* Beverly Hills, Cal.: Sage.

Walum, L. R. (1974). The changing door ceremony: Notes on the operation of sex-roles in everyday life. *Urban Life and Culture, 2,* 506–515.

West, S. G., & Brown, T. J. (1975). Physical attractiveness, the severity of the emergency, and helping: A field experiment and interpersonal simulation. *Journal of Experimental Social Psychology, 11,* 531–538.

West, S. G., Whitney, G., & Schnedler, R. (1975). Helping a motorist in distress: The effects of sex, race, and neighborhood. *Journal of Personality and Social Psychology, 31,* 691–698.

Wiley, M. G. (1973). Sex roles in games. *Sociometry, 36,* 526–541.

Wispé, L. and Kiecolt, J. (1980). Victim attractiveness as a function of helping and nonhelping. *Journal of Social Psychology, 112,* 67–73.

Women on Words and Images. (1972). *Dick and Jane as victims.* Princeton, N.J.

Young, D. M., Beier, E. G., Beier, P., & Barton, C. (1975). Is chivalry dead? *Journal of Communications, 25,* 57–64.

7 Adding Gender to Aggression Research: Incremental or Revolutionary Change?

J. Macaulay
Madison, Wisconsin

> *Scientific development depends in part on a process of nonincremental or revolutionary change. Some revolutions are large, like those associated with the names of Copernicus, Newton, or Darwin, but most are much smaller, like the discovery of oxygen or the planet Uranus. The usual prelude to changes of this sort is, I believed, the awareness of anomaly, of an occurrence or set of occurrences that does not fit existing ways of ordering phenomena.*
> —Thomas S. Kuhn, *The Essential Tension*, 1977, p. xvii.

INTRODUCTION

This paper has its origins in a review of studies on "sex differences in aggression" by Frodi, Macaulay, and Thome (1977). These three reviewers were all trained in experimental social psychology, and were all, at that time, at a major research institution. Two other details are also relevant: All three authors are women, and we were writing during the time when our profession had just begun to discover that women's social behavior is not merely men's social behavior with more error variance.

Our training dictated that we turn to the experimental social psychology and personality journals for our review. We did not review work on aggression done by researchers in other disciplines, and we decided to limit our review to studies of adults. We took our definition of aggression to be the behavior so labeled studied by social psychologists, mainly in laboratory experiments. We found that studies of adults of *both* sexes comprised only a small portion of the literature on adult aggression. However, that literature was so large that even a small segment amounted to enough to make a review worthwhile.

We expected to find some theoretically relevant surprises, but did not (at least on my part) expect to question our understanding of what the study of aggression was all about and how one should go about studying women's aggression. What happened, first, was that we found women to be as aggressive as men in over half of the studies in which "sex differences"[1] were analyzed—seldom more aggressive, but often equally so. There were far too many studies with no gender differences to support any theory that strong biological factors, deeply ingrained personality traits, or well-learned gender roles make even a majority of women reliably or consistently very much less aggressive than men. This had not been recognized in any previous major discussions or reviews of aggression research, presumably because of the overwhelming influence of the belief that women are innately nonaggressive. Few researchers who failed to find the expected gender differences did more than express surprise, if that, or occasionally fashion explanations based on their version of gender stereotypes. (For example, see Baron, 1977, pp. 220–221: Baron believes that no-difference findings are relatively recent and so reflect changes in women's roles; however, the studies cited by Frodi et al. [1977] do not show increasing female aggressiveness over time.) We found serious consideration of the possibility that females could or would be aggressive if they felt free to do so in only a few studies of children's behavior.

In the course of our effort to figure out what factors led to gender differences in these experimental studies, we began to reassess our topic. For example, we talked about "provocation" and how anger is expressed because, when we looked at women's aggressive behavior, we found that we had to consider the impetus to aggression and its mode of expression as major variables. We found that the standard concepts underlying the manipulated (independent) variables

---

[1]Social psychologists studying "sex differences" have generally been talking about differences in behavior among "subjects" with different stimulus values for the researcher (Grady, 1979). Many researchers—particularly those studying aggression—have assumed that observed behavior differences, as well as observed physical differences, parallel biological differences. This assumption is usually a matter of faith, not evidence. For example, changes in an aggression research laboratory script can create or wipe out "sex differences," suggesting that they are culturally and not biologically determined (see, for example, Mallick & McCandless, 1966; Richardson, Bernstein & Taylor, 1979). Given the assumption that "sex difference" probably equals "biological difference," we then have a serious terminology problem. After studying a variety of proposed solutions to this problem, I have settled on the following usage: "Sex" refers to clearly biological differences (in physical appearance, in "sexual" behavior such as intercourse, etc.). "Gender" refers to socially acknowledged differences, such as "masculinity" and "femininity," and to social behavior differences that tend to parallel observable physical differences. When the biological basis of a difference among people with different stimulus values (e.g., among men and women) is unclear, "gender" is used. A "gender difference" may or may not be biologically determined or influenced; a sex difference definitely is. (See Gould & Kern-Daniels, 1977; McConaghy, 1979; Unger, 1979.)

were not relevant to the factors we felt we needed to examine. The standard laboratory situation in our set of studies usually involved a procedure designed to anger people as a way of setting the stage for studying their expected aggressive behavior. This procedure varied *between* experiments, but was almost never varied *within* experiments. We came to believe that many of the elements taken for granted in this procedure (for example, uniform sex of experimenter) would turn out to be major explanatory variables for findings of gender differences or no gender differences. Women's behavior in these situations was not only an anomaly (given the belief that women were not, by nature, aggressive), the laboratory situation itself turned out to be much more mysterious than anyone trained in and loyal to the experimental method would have expected. There was a host of unknown main and interactive effects that made these situations unfathomably opaque.

Empirically unanswerable questions were a major product of this review; sturdy generalizations were not. These unanswerable questions amounted to something more than a mere catalogue of needed improvements in experimental "control" or additions to the standard set of dimensions and variables for viewing aggression. For my part, when I began contemplating the research necessary to answer them, I realized I had to consider the experience of anger, reactions to provocation other than overt aggression as usually defined, gender norms and situational expectations, and other topics not often considered in the social psychological literature on aggression. I also realized that it would be valuable to know what researchers in clinical psychology, sociology, social work, and political science knew about aggression—even if I still limited my search for knowledge to empirical research on individual aggression.

A sample of the kinds of questions I was left with—and still cannot answer with much clarity—will illustrate the wider focus toward which consideration of women's aggression must lead:

1. If many women are less aggressive than the average man, then how do these women respond to provocation? How do they express their anger when they do express it?

2. Are women made angry by different things than men? More generally, what kinds of individual differences are there in what makes people angry?

3. What are the major variations in people's preferred and avoided modes of expressing or dealing with anger? Do various kinds of aggression have different meanings for different people, and are there actions not usually labeled "aggression" that serve as such for some people? For example, can ignoring one's tormentor serve as retaliatory *action*?

4. What effects do different social expectations for women's and men's behavior have in anger-provoking situations, and how do these expectations vary across situations? Can we know the meaning of *any* results of experimental studies on aggression without knowing how the experimenter's instructions al-

tered the usual, unspoken expectations for public behavior by angered individuals?

5. Are some children (mostly girls) actively socialized into peaceableness as an alternative to aggressiveness? If so, how is this done? Are girls taught to cope with anger, or are they just taught to repress or deny anger? If the latter, does this tend to make them sick, as many clinicians suggest, or does it make them into hapless victims, as Burgess (1962) suggested it would for men? More generally, is mere control (muting, diversion, and repression) of some innately aggressive bent among humans the best we can hope for, or is it rational to work for a truly peaceful society?

This paper concerns the reorganization of thinking and research on aggression that these questions seem to demand. They reflect the "awareness of anomaly" that Kuhn refers to in the quotation that introduces this paper; that is, women have been an anomaly for aggression researchers, and a dawning awareness of this leads to questions that will then lead to radically different aggression research. I don't think that the publication of the Frodi et al. review shook "the established ways of ordering phenomena." Rather, I think that we stumbled on the source of some serious doubts as to the theoretical and pragmatic usefulness of traditional aggression research—doubts that cannot be ignored and that will eventually lead to a paradigmatic shift in psychologists' understanding of aggression.[2] As described below, we have been in the midst of a "crisis" in social psychology (as have our siblings in other social science fields) for a full decade, but even apparently devastating critiques seem to have done little to change the practice of academic social psychology.[3] What will change it, and is perhaps beginning to change it, is not the accumulation of critiques of method and theory, but the inability of normal (i.e., traditional) social psychology to deal with

[2]The term "paradigm" is used here as Kuhn originally intended, to denote that which is accepted by a community of scholars as its "disciplinary matrix" (Kuhn's now preferred term). Ritzer (quoted by Gove, 1979, p. 800) defined "paradigm" as follows:

A paradigm is a fundamental image of the subject matter within a science. It serves to define what should be studied, what questions should be asked, and what rules should be followed in interpreting the answers obtained. [It] subsumes, defines, and interrelates the exemplars, theories and methods, and instruments that exist within it.

The exemplars (problem-solving explanations and models) are readily found in textbooks. The basic theories can be found in theoretical writings, or they can be read out of the symbolic generalizations that all researchers understand, although consensus as to significance may be lacking. (For example, take the term "catharsis.") For an elaboration of what Kuhn intended to describe, as opposed to uses by those who have embraced his theory, see the index entries for "paradigm" in Kuhn's 1977 book.

[3]This paper is largely concerned with social psychology as it is practiced by psychologists, not that practiced by sociologists, which has a different orientation and different (though parallel) problems. (See Boutilier, Roed & Svendsen, 1980, for a comparison of these siblings' crises.)

questions such as the above using normal methods—this is, I think, what Kuhn's historical analysis tells us.[4]

To put the problem another way, we suffer from what Koch (1981) calls a "pathology of knowledge." One of the disease syndromes he describes, Number 14, fits the area of aggression research particularly well: a "tendency to buy into stable or fashionable profession-centered myths with a minimum of prior critical examination, to accept congealed group suppressions concerning bypassed problems or data; or alternate theoretical possibilities; or intrinsic (and sometimes patent) limits on the scope, analytic or predictive specificity, and so on, attainable in the field in question" (p. 259). The cure will be sought only when the disease becomes seriously bothersome. It is only when laboratory-generated data prove insufficient as answers to important questions; when our store of "findings" do not allow us to explain, much less predict or change, behavior such as child abuse, sexual violence, mugging for fun and profit, chronic victimization, and so on; when normal science blocks, stunts, or distorts research directly addressed to such matters; that the scholar-patient takes the plunge into curative reshaping of paradigms.

The rest of this paper describes what normal science in the area of aggression has been like, what the results have been for research and theory, how conven-

---

[4]Kuhn's writings concern the "mature" sciences, such as physics and the life. Social psychology does not qualify as mature (Kuhn, 1977, p. 42), and certain details of Kuhn's model do not fit social research. For example, our major lines of research do not concern the solution of "puzzles"; rather, we test hypotheses that we expect to be confirmed. Most importantly, social psychology's areas do not "possess a body of consistent theory capable of producing refined predictions"   the mark of a "developed scientific field" (Kuhn, 1977, pp. 118–119). Furthermore, some of what social scientists have enthusiastically embraced in Kuhn's writings turns out to be of problematic status, in the opinion of some of Kuhn's philosophy of science colleagues. (See Siegel, 1980, for a review of much of this criticism.)

In spite of these problems of fit, social scientists have seen Kuhn's model of change in scientific ideas as a source of insight into the development of their own fields. Without borrowing the complete historical model—and any of its attendant problems—they have found it particularly useful to apply the concept of "paradigmatic shift" (which Kuhn originally borrowed from psychology) to their own observations of change. This borrowing has not been without additional critics (Harvey, 1982). Peterson (1981) argues that the use of Kuhn's ideas in social psychology "curbs discussion of fundamental issues." However, he presents a less than telling indictment, and seems to have in mind the adoption of Kuhn's complete model. In the present paper, at least, it is hard to see how my limited borrowing could constitute the avoidance of debate on any issues, or an obscuring of history. I have applied Kuhn's ideas more by analogy than directly.

I found that Kuhn's model of the development of a science provides a good fit to the social history of the social psychology of aggression (Kuhn, 1970; 1977, see especially pp. 118–119; see also Baumgardner, 1976). I have also found, along with others, that Kuhn's model of how established paradigms limit change yields substantial insights into the cause of what appear to be major shortcomings in social psychology. Finally, I believe that Kuhn's writings help bring some fundamental issues out of hiding, indirectly enlarging, not narrowing, the scope of theoretical inquiry into human aggression.

tion has been maintained, and how the addition of the study of women's behavior may have begun to affect convention in this area. First, however, some definitions are needed.

Some Definitions

The usage of standard terms in the aggression area tends to reflect theoretical decisions, and so it varies as a function of a writer's theoretical orientation. Given this variability, it is necessary for clarity in a paper such as this to give at least a few definitions. In doing so, I am necessarily suggesting what the conceptual building blocks of a broadened and reshaped study of aggression might be. *Aggression* is used here as a label for behavior that includes more than physical violence. There are many forms of aggression. At one extreme, the category includes physical battering, intentionally inflicted severe deprivation, vitriolic verbal abuse, and psychological torture—e.g., *violence*. At the other extreme are such things as unwelcome touching, the delivery of electric shocks in psychologists' laboratories, insult, and minor deprivations.

The delivery of painful physical stimulation to a target person is not necessarily the most severe form of aggression. Rather than measuring the severity of aggression by looking to the character of the behavior, it is better to look to the damage done, and that damage need not be physical. Some damage is easy to measure: For example, the neglect of a child can result in a variety of maladies ranging from slow growth to death. Other kinds of damage, such as the effect of psychological torture or secondary effects such as the destruction of social relations, are probably impossible to place with exactitude on an ordinal scale.

Implicit in the examples given above is the assumption that aggression involves the intent to harm another. Intent is defined from the actor's point of view and so may be only uncertainly inferred from an actor's words, deeds, and the severity of the damage done. Thus, to take a difficult case, the neglect of a child may or may not constitute aggression. If the caretaker's intent is to deprive the child, the caretaker is an aggressor. If the caretaker is merely stupid or confused, his or her behavior is not aggression, but merely inappropriate, incompetent, or mistaken. *Indirect aggression* is that accomplished through a third person or an institution. An example of indirect aggression is getting one's enemy fired by giving him or her unfair, negative evaluations. The term "indirect" is not used here, as it has been in some writings, to mean only verbal aggression, or to mean aggression through exclusion or deprivation. These usages seem to be predicated on the assumption that verbal aggression or negative psychological sanctions are mere substitutes for physical aggression that the actor is prevented from using, i.e., that a nonphysical aggressor would really prefer to beat up his or her victim. I do not know of any evidence that supports this assumption, and it is disavowed here.

Anger is the emotion (or state of emotional arousal) preceding some but not all aggression. Anger may be contemporary, historical (remembered, and possibly revived through symbolic activity), or chronic—e.g., *hostility*. Anger may be labeled "annoyance" or "hurt" by the actor, and the labels given to arousal by the actor undoubtedly shape the outcome, which may or may not be aggressive behavior.

Anger results from *provocation*, which may be another's deliberate, hurtful act or intentional thwarting, from deprivation or impersonal "frustration," of goal-directed behavior, or from disappointed expectations or amorphous dissatisfaction. (Many writers use the word "stimulus" for what is called "provocation" here; however, "stimulus" is also often used to mean "cue"—the immediate stimulus or signal for action. "Provocation" is, I hope, a less confusing term.)

Provocation leading to anger can have several results. If it leads to agression, the action may be directed at the source of provocation or at someone or something else. That is, aggression can be *displaced*. Conflict can also be coped with without aggression, and anger can be expressed or abated without resort to direct, indirect, or displaced retaliation. Coping without retaliation may be satisfying for a victim, or it may result in contemporary anger becoming chronic hostility.

Furthermore, some aggression may not be preceded by provocation and may be unaccompanied by present anger. Such aggression is usually termed *instrumental* in order to distinguish it from "hostile" or "angry" aggression. Instrumental aggression represents a method of goal achievement involving the use of power of one sort or another over others who stand in the way or whose injury benefits the aggressor. Goals achieved through aggression may be material (for example, armed robbery yields cash) or relational (for example, beating a spouse establishes dominance). However, as the spouse-beating example suggests, aggression may be both instrumental and hostile, and the distinction is hard to maintain (cf. Zillman, 1979). "Instrumental" and "hostile" probably should be replaced by labels that more clearly suggest the mixes of motives likely to prompt aggression.

There is a continuum from goal-oriented "assertion" (which is not aggressive) to instrumental aggression. This continuum is hard to describe because we lack common labels for intermediate points where motives and effects might be mixed, and because our cultural norms and terminology are inexact and confusing, as common usage shows. For example, the admirable (in our culture) "aggressive" salesman is probably seldom aggressive, but assertive and persuasive, while the sometimes admirable "physical" hockey player or "aggressive" football player may be both assertive and aggressive to varying degrees and for both hostile and instrumental reasons.

It has been suggested that the "aggression" studied by psychologists may be a reification of a category that includes many kinds of behavior involving many kinds of motives and emotions (Carolyn Sherif, personal communication). Aggression theorists are usually implicitly talking about some kind of antinormative use of force or power, but as researchers they most often work with situations in which their subjects are goaded to "aggression" that can be viewed by actors and observers alike as normatively justified; evidence of guilt, in fact, would ruin the planned interpretation of some experiments. At the same time, these theorists are not avowed pacifists. If pushed, many would admit to a belief that some behavior they call aggression is not antinormative according to their values. Also note that the illustrations of "aggression" used above did not cover war, overtly aggressive athletic encounters such as boxing matches, spanking the hand of a child reaching for a hot stove, childish wrestling, or being excessively assertive ("pushy")—all of which are often included in the category of aggression. In other words, aggression is a sloppy category, in both scholarly and common usage. Professor Sherif suggested that a paradigmatic shift might begin with (or be signaled by) the reconceptualization and renaming of the behavioral phenomena now subsumed under "aggression." Perhaps our recent struggles to sort out our usages by distinguishing types of aggression is such a signal. (See, e.g., Zillman, 1979, in addition to the effort made above.)

FORCES THAT SHAPED FOUR DECADES OF RESEARCH ON AGGRESSION

Origins

The scientific study of the psychology of aggression seems to have begun with the publication of *Frustration and Aggression* by Dollard, Doob, Miller, Mowrer, and Sears in 1939; at any rate, one seldom sees citations in this area dated earlier than this. The ideas in *Frustrations and Aggression* have several roots. First, there were the social needs and values peculiar to socially conscious scholars in the middle of the Depression. The economic frustrations and bouts of political and racial violence by deprived groups were social problems that demanded explanation by those whose business was explanation. Second, these ideas were rooted in "common sense"—e.g., the dominant cultural beliefs concerning aggression, by that time thoroughly laced with Freudian views of human nature. And third, these ideas were rooted in the dominant scholarly themes of the era, Freudianism and behaviorism. The latter was imbued with positivism, which, as a practical matter, meant that the experimental method and "laboratory science" came to dominate the research paradigms in social psychology.

At the time Frodi et al. undertook their review, the social psychology of aggression had had about 35 years of development. By that time there was a consensus among social psychologists on the best ways of generating data, on standards for analysis and reporting, on the first-, second- and third-best journals to report in, and on the vocabulary in which the major arguments were to be phrased. In other words, a dominant paradigm had developed (see footnote 2). As described below, this paradigm, for a variety of social and cultural reasons, produced models of men's behavior, with women's behavior covered only as an afterthought.

Cultural Beliefs about Women and Aggression

Research and explanation of results in social psychology have been heavily influenced by the psychological theories that are popular in Western culture, their theoretical pretensions notwithstanding. This is particularly true when it comes to women and aggression. Of course, popular psychology itself owes much to "scientific psychology," particularly Freud's, as any survey of fiction in the twentieth century will show. Those who don't take introductory psychology in college can get a course from the popular press. In other words, popular and "scientific" psychology run an exchange of theories of human behavior.

Some cultural beliefs may be empirically verifiable and even if they are not, they may be useful as explanations of behavior. On the whole, however, it has been easier to find disconfirming evidence for the validity of cultural beliefs than to find supporting evidence when it comes to women and aggression. (For example, see Frodi et al., 1977.) Nonetheless, these beliefs are persistent, even in the face of manifest inconsistencies among the beliefs themselves.

The following list of beliefs is derived from the literature on aggression (especially the discussion sections of research articles), from conversations with psychologists and nonpsychologists on gender differences in aggression, and from fiction, women's magazines, the Sunday papers, etc.

1. Women are innately nonaggressive. (See just about any pre-1980 general discussion of aggression that mentions women in passing.)

2. Women express their anger in "sneaky" ways. Their aggressive behavior is "indirect" and verbal, meaning that women aggress without using physical violence or that women cover up their aggression with prosocial explanations (cf. Feshbach, 1969).

3. Women are unable to express anger because they have been trained to repress anger, or because they are innately passive, or both (cf. Kaplan, 1977).

4. Women are prone to sudden, unexpected bursts of "fury"—with fury defined as near-violence or actual violence (cf. Fox, 1977). These bursts are sometimes viewed as irrational overreactions to minor slights, teasing, etc. There is a hydraulic analogy being made here, possibly related to the belief that women are trained to "repress anger" (cf. Kaplow, 1973).

5. Angry women are sick and in need of psychological treatment, especially if "passive aggressive" (a clinician's epithet for a style of aggression involving mild verbal aggression and deprivation that can sometimes amount to psychological torture). This follows from both (1) and (3): Angry women are having

identity problems, are rejecting their proper sex role, are being poisoned by bottled-up anger, or are being destroyed by aggression turned inward—or all of these things at once. (Caplan and Nelson's 1973 analysis of "blaming the victim" may be illuminating here.)

6. Women are fiercely aggressive in defense of their children (cf. Moyer, 1974). This is a biological trait. A woman who could condone sexual or physical abuse of her child, then, is barely human.

7. Jealousy is a common source of women's aggression because women are very possessive of the men that they are attached to. This, too, may be a biological trait, related to women's biological role as child-bearer and child-nurturer.

Beliefs and Values in Academic Social Psychology

There is another set of beliefs and values more generally characteristic of academic psychology that has shaped both the theoretical paradigms that determine what questions to ask and the research paradigms that tell us how to ask questions and the proper way to determine their answers. Recognition of the fact that beliefs and values inevitably play a part in our research, no matter how "scientific" we try to be, began to appear regularly in the late 1960s, along with a host of criticisms of how social psychology was done. (These writings were not entirely novel; some diligent critics picked up references to strong criticism of social psychology's drift that went back to the 1930s.) By the mid-1970s the stream of critical self-analysis among academics had reached such proportions that we began to talk about the "crisis in social psychology," not sure perhaps what the crisis was, but recognizing that something might be shaky in the foundations of our discipline (cf. Elms, 1975).

There are far too many of these critiques to review here. Instead, I will describe some major themes that are particularly relevant to the area of aggression research.[5] I should note, first, that for every generalization below, some studies can be found that contradict it. These are exceptions, however; the generalizations follow easily when we look at dominant research trends—dominant not only in terms of proportions of studies, but also in terms of the status of the journals that publish major work, as well as in terms of the work of the most productive and eminent researchers.

---

[5] A list of a few significant and relevant writings, including some whose ideas have probably been absorbed into the present paper but have not been cited, is as follows: Boutilier et al., 1980; Buss, 1975; Caplan, 1975; Cronbach, 1975; Elms, 1975; Epstein, Suedfeld & Silverstein, 1973; Gergen, 1978; Gergen & Morawski, 1980; Jahoda, 1979; Knutson, 1978; Lubek, 1979; McGuire, 1973; Pepitone, 1976; Ring, 1967; Sampson, 1977, 1978, 1981; Schuck & Pisor, 1974; Schultz, 1969; Sherif, 1978, 1979; Silverman, 1977; Tedeschi, 1980; Tiefer, 1978; Toch, 1980; Veroff, 1978. See also Gaebelein, 1981, and Manicas & Secord, 1983, for significant critiques published after this paper was written.

Male Centrism.   In social psychology men have been the measure of human-kind and questions about men's behavior have been considered intrinsically important. (There are many reviews of the state of social psychology that come to this conclusion. See Weisstein, 1970, for an early version and *SASP Newsletter*, 1978, *4(4)* and 1979, *5(3)* for later versions.) Aggression is viewed as a serious social problem and it is thought to be a peculiarly male trait, and so the study of *male* aggression and control of men's normal urges is particularly important. Conversely, the study of females' responses to provocation, of females' use of aggression to achieve their goals, and of gender differences generally is given low priority.

The dominance of men's studies is seen particularly clearly when one counts the number of males and females in research reports in the social psychology literature, at least up until the mid-1970s. This dominance is seen in the area of aggression as well as in other areas. (See Carlson, 1971; Carlson & Carlson, 1961; Dipboye & Flanagan, 1979; Frodi et al., 1977; Holmes & Jorgensen, 1971; Kurstin-Young, Sparks, & Watson, in press; McCormack, 1978; McKenna & Kessler, 1977; Reardon & Prescott, 1977; Schultz, 1969; Schwabacher, 1972; Signorella, Vegega, & Mitchell, 1981; and Smart, 1966.) The Carlson 1971 counts, for example, show that the ratio in two leading journals even then was two male subjects to every female subject. When both sexes were used, gender differences were very often not analyzed or not reported (Levenson, Gray, & Ingram, 1976).

There are a number of factors that explain this imbalance. One is a simple researcher's rule of thumb that one gets "better results"—that is, more publishable—by studying men (McGuire, 1968; Prescott, 1978), but major explanatory factors can also be found in more scientifically respectable values. Sampson (1977, 1978) suggests that "self-contained individualism" is one of these. This is both a dominant value in the capitalist system and one that directs the course of psychological research. Psychologists seem to particularly value what Sampson calls "individual self-sufficiency." What they study is the individual ego, self-contained, divorced from any systems broader than the self or any context larger than the laboratory. "Subjects" are dealt with as isolated human atoms who will react in lawful ways to bombardment by "stimuli" controlled by the scientist-researcher. Sampson also suggests that the scientific enterprise is not only a primarily male activity but also part of the male subculture. The dominant paradigm is one "glorifying one set of values (the masculine) while denigrating another (the feminine) for all matters that have become important (i.e., scientific) for the culture" (Sampson, 1970, p. 1338).

The research on aggression, at least up until about 1980, provides an apt illustration of Sampson's points. This is not to say that aggressiveness is a value being promoted, but that the topic is important because aggressiveness is believed to be a central *male* characteristic, with direct retaliatory aggression as the prototypical self-contained individualistic response. Most simply, male researchers are interested in what men do and, naturally enough, they have focused on what men were thought to be peculiarly capable of, which includes physical violence. Thus, as Frodi et al. (1977) found, the alternatives to aggression that might occur in laboratory situations in which aggression is expected from men were not allowed, or were not observed if they were allowed. The experimental paradigm only allowed recording "no response" or "low aggression." Attention to alternatives such as retreat, conciliation, negotiation, help-seeking, containment, or nonviolent correction would have meant turning away from concentration on what was defined as the most important aspect of the subjects' behavior—their aggressiveness. The individualist solution does not encompass initiation of social processes involving more than the individual subject, such as negotiation or help-seeking. Attention to an *interaction* between a "subject" and a provoker would be inconsistent with the positivist view of "subjects" as individuals emitting responses in a "controlled" situation. It might also have meant allowing male subjects to behave in unmasculine ways—to retreat, for example, the choice of the culturally despised "sissy." Furthermore, broadening the subjects' behavioral options could have meant allowing them to control and change social circumstances, and that might challenge the experimenter's power to define reality in the laboratory. (See Sampson, 1981.)[6]

Manipulation and Control in the Preferred Mode of Inquiry.   Another value scheme that permeates the dominant research paradigm is what Carlson (1972) calls the "agentic (masculine) mode of inquiry involving manipulation, quantification and control." Carlson borrowed the agency-communion concept from Bakan and applied it to researcher behavior seen in the 1958 and 1968 personality literature (Carlson, 1971; Carlson & Carlson, 1961). She not only found "agentic" research to be dominant but also felt that it was stifling development in her field. The solution she advocated was a turn to "naturalistic, qualitative and open" research, shaped by an orientation toward "communion" rather than agency. "The issue," she said, "is *not* that of scientific versus humanistic approaches, but rather one of liberation from constraints of research paradigms which are simply incapable of meeting genuine scientific requirements for personological study" (1972, p. 21).

Carlson's conceptual diagnosis of the limitations of normal research in her field also applies to aggression research. The latter has been largely "experimental" and narrowly focused on easily quantifiable bits of behavior emitted by "subjects" who are "run" in a uniform "laboratory" situation, said to be

[6]Sampson believes that "By failing to probe beyond the prevailing empirical reality into the underlying structure by which that reality has been generated, . . . the positivist–empiricist tradition treats the temporary and the historical as though it were eternal and natural" (1981, *6*, p. 34). See also Boulding, 1979.

"controlled." The jargon is that of an agentic approach. Control in the classic scientific sense is the elimination of variance other than that under study; it is the sine qua non for "the development of precise theories" (Berkowitz, 1970, p. 307). For psychologists, this passport to respectability mainly involves the manipulation of people in the name of "science." Usually some of these people are designated "control subjects" and others "experimental subjects," but all are controlled as closely as possible during the course of the "experiment." The manipulation is accomplished by constricting stimulation and limiting normal interaction. The laboratory is usually a bare windowless cell, furnished only with the desired "experimental" stimuli and perhaps a stock of experimental equipment. Interaction is usually strictly scripted, with perhaps no face-to-face contact with other "subjects." Of the scores of tangible and intangible factors that define any situation for participants, a selected few are varied in such a way as to produce measurable variations in the elements of behavior designated as "dependent variables."

That the result of this manipulation and control is, from the subjects' point of view, not only novel but probably often bizarre is not considered relevant within this research paradigm. Atmosphere, oddity, environmental barrenness, and a variety of norms for behavior with authoritative strangers may affect behavior but they are assumed to affect all subjects similarly, and if they don't they merely contribute to "error variance."

These uniform factors may, however, influence subjects' behavior as strongly as the "independent variables" that the experimenter attends to, and they may also determine the effect of the latter. For example, Berkowitz and others have produced evidence of a "weapons effect" in the laboratory (Turner, Simons, Berkowitz, and Frodi, 1977). That is, if the experimenter leaves a gun on the work table, subjects' reactions to the situation tend to be affected. The gun in these experiments is, of course, a recognized independent variable. But we can hypothesize a whole series of "guns" at work in the standard laboratory situation that have not been studied and are not recognized for the influence they have on subjects' behavior. These are "guns" that are introduced as part of the "control" thought to be necessary for scientific validity. For example, common control practices are to match the subject's sex to the target or instigator's sex, and to employ a single and so constant-sex experimenter. The end result is a complex but unmonitored evocation of norms for male and female behavior in the presence of strangers of the same or opposite sex (cf. Frodi et al., 1977, p. 642). A major limitation in laboratory research has has been, in fact, experimenters' general neglect of norms as determinants of behavior (Pepitone, 1976).

Another major problem resulting from the manipulation and control inherent in the standard laboratory situation is that we induce our subjects not only to be "aggressive," but also to actively attempt to understand the situation and to monitor their own behavior. Langer has contrasted this set with the "mindlessness" of much behavior in familiar settings and has concluded that the generalization from mindful to mindless behavior may not be valid (Langer & Newman, 1979). Her point seems particularly well-taken for aggression research when one contrasts, say, a person angered by a coworker's petty insults during the course of a normal workday with a person angered by a stranger in an awe-inspiring "psychological laboratory" providing an elaborate device to sup-posedly teach rote memorization by means of shocks to a learner's fingers as a means of interacting with the insulter. (For those who are unfamiliar with aggres-sion research, that machine is part of one of the most common laboratory scripts.)

Faith in the Generalizability of Results.   The problem all this creates for aggression research is similar to the problem that Carlson saw for personality research: The data produced may well be something other than the data we need for a broad understanding of aggression as a human phenomenon. Much social psychological research is introduced in terms of a social problem ("television and aggression," for example) and concluded in terms of relevance of the find-ings for that problem. Social psychologists have not been shy about generalizing freely from the people (and other animals) they study to "mankind" (a term usually assumed to designate women as well as men; see, e.g., Dan & Beekman, 1972).

In fact, there are a number of serious limitations on the generalizability of much laboratory research. First are the limitations of samples. The American social psychology of aggression has been based in large part on young,[7] white, male, middle-class students who take an introductory course at a major research university (Higbie, Millard, & Folkman, 1982; Schultz, 1969). Generalization to mankind is very seldom empirically justified; instead, it is commonly justified by unsupported assumptions and fingers-crossed faith. Despite the many critics of research practice and a journal referee system that maintains high standards in research design and analysis, blowing the whistle on unwarranted generalization is rare (cf. Jahoda, 1979).

As with the matter of who is studied, the narrow range of stimuli, situations, and responses that have been studied sets limits on the generalizability of much aggression research, and here, too, the problem is seldom squarely faced. (See, e.g., Maher's complaints, 1978.) For example, the type of aggressive response elicited in the laboratory has not been considered to be of theoretical importance, other than to distinguish verbal and physical aggression. But researchers' design choices show that they know type of response is important—they do not have

---

[7]These students are implicitly assumed to be adults; this is not a branch of adolescent psychology. However, our habit of calling subjects "males and females" perhaps stems not only from a desire to appear as scientific as those who study nonhuman animals, but also to avoid the discomfort of deciding whether our not-quite-adult subjects are boys and girls or men and women.

subjects rap their insulters' knuckles, but shock their fingers in a non-face-to-face encounter. Both actions may be equally aggressive in some respects, but we know from our general stock of social knowledge that there is a difference. Published work on aggression does not reflect such knowledge.

More generally, aggression researchers have not looked into the meaning of the responses they study—for both doers and receivers—yet they draw broad significance from their findings. Their study seldom begins with examination of provocation, anger, goals and response selection; rather, it focuses on the outcome, "aggression," with a few "manipulation checks" to justify drawing the desired conclusions. Most experimenters have tended to brush the difficult matter of intent into the black box of unexamined error variance (cf. Knutson, 1973, 1978). Furthermore a number of critics have suggested that responses in aggression studies are often mislabeled (Baron & Eggleston, 1972; Hynan, 1979; Tedeschi, Gaes, & Rivera, 1977)[8], and subjects' freedom of choice (cf. Baron, 1977, p. 75) misperceived. For example, a lack of response in a situation designed to elicit aggression would be recorded as nonaggression but might instead represent inaction due to constricted choice or even be defined by the subject as an aggressive turning of one's back to situational demands. I am not arguing that the behavior in "aggression" experiments is never seen by subjects as aggressive by their own definition (it may or may not be), but rather that the meaning of the behavior is a variable seldom examined by experimenters. (See Berkowitz & Donnerstein, 1982, for the argument that this must be examined if laboratory research is to be of value.)

Finally, one of the major limitations to generalizability for aggression research is, of course, that only the mildest forms of aggression can be studied in the laboratory, and the experimental script makes the elicited behavior almost always appear justifiable in form at least, if not in intensity. Even if the researcher is observing what the subjects themselves would call aggression, it is not the kind of aggression seen most often in daily life, such as petty insults directed at friends and relatives in an ongoing relationship; violence to defenseless people in the unpoliced, private confines of the family home; "criminal" violence by strangers who want what we have and don't mind hurting us in the process of getting it; and so on.

Of course we cannot, for ethical and safety reasons, study much hurtful and unjustified aggression in the laboratory, or even in field experiments. However, blind faith in the experimental method has led social psychology to ignore what

---

[8]Tedeschi and his colleagues have been critical of the assumption that behavior is justifiably labeled aggressive because the *researcher* sees it as aggressive (see Tedeschi et al., 1977). However, rather than working toward a taxonomy of behaviors or exploring their social definition fully, Tedeschi and his colleagues have moved in the direction of reconceptualizing the area in terms of "coercive power" (Tedeschi, Smith, & Brown, 1974). This seems to me to sidestep the problem uncovered.

seems obvious to outsiders: our habits of generalization are sometimes absurd. The problem is particularly acute when we move from the consideration of individual male aggression—the traditional area of study—to problems such as violence within the family, or rape, or some of the other phenomena that events of recent decades have caused to be newly labeled as social problems. Rather than letting the question dictate the method, researchers have tended to move from the social problem to a statement of a hypothesis that would be testable in the laboratory; with "findings" in hand, they go on to claim social significance for the research. Toch (1980, p. 659) calls this last step a "disjuncture" amounting to "schizoscience." For example, he says, "in considering television's impact on violent crime, we invoke laboratory studies that show the effects of suggestive film clips on modeled doll abuse and we gather views about hypothetical violence from heavy television viewers. Direct links between television impact and real-life violence [by adults] remain unexplored. . . ." In another context Toch (1978) had acknowledged that some aggression researchers escape this trap; see his appreciative comments on a study of violent criminals by Berkowitz (1978a). This study, however, is not typical, and Toch's statements hold true for a great proportion of the aggression research done by social psychologists. (See, for example, another study by Berkowitz—supposedly significant for understanding the dynamics of child abuse—involving female college students' recommendations for discipline of misbehaving children shown on videotape in the laboratory; Berkowitz & Frodi, 1979.)

Defense of the Experimental Method.   The defenders of the experimental method have responded to criticism of laboratory research by arguing that it is the only way to discover regularities in human behavior and, with such discoveries, to move from period- and culture-bound descriptive theory to formal theory with law-like statements (cf. Berkowitz & Donnerstein, 1982; Henshel, 1980; Martin, 1979; West & Gunn, 1978). The basic positivist assumption is that psychology is a science, like physics, which uncovers "laws" that "enable one to predict and control phenomena as they occur under natural circumstances" (Bandura, 1973, p. 63). There is no room within this assumption for gender differences, much less for individual differences, as many critics have complained. A separate psychology of aggression for women and men would be even more philosophically unacceptable than a separate psychology for human and nonhuman aggression has been to many theorists (cf. Berkowitz, 1978a, p. 698). Rather, the problem of individual differences that the theory cannot handle tends to be dismissed as referring to mere epiphenomena.

   The logic of such defenses of experimental or "scientific" psychology has some merit, but the defenders go too far. In practice, the cult of the experiment has straitjacketed scientific investigation. There is more to science than "controlled" experiments. As Koch (1981) puts it, one of the "pathologies of knowledge" in psychology is that "tendency to select—usually on extraneous bases like amenability to 'control'. . . .a 'simple case' and then to assume it will be merely a matter of time and energy until the 'complex' case can be handled by application of easy composition rules" (p. 258). In fact, laboratory research cannot tell us all we need to know in order to understand aggression. The "simple cases" of instigation to aggression that we can study in the laboratory are not simple building blocks that together make up the kind of aggression we find, say, in a prison group. The studies of something like weapons-presence as a stimulus to aggression may well contribute valuable insights, but the prison situation as a whole is a complex of many *interacting* elements, and the *interaction* cannot safely or ethically be duplicated in the laboratory.

It is not just the physical situation and situational details that cannot be duplicated; it is the "psychological attributes" of complex violence that fail to match the "psychological attributes" of laboratory research. Berkowitz and Donnerstein (1982) argue that proper attention to these attributes will allow us to generalize from the laboratory to general human behavior. They are probably right, but they don't go far enough. Proper attention to the psychological attributes of research situations will also reveal the witlessness of much of the generalization that psychologists have relied on to justify the significance of their research in the past, as well as the severe limitations of the laboratory method.

The remedy for problems with laboratory research is neither abandonment nor simply cleaning up its practice. Laboratory research alone is not enough. It should be regarded as one method among many, to be adopted as part of a multimethod strategy when a case can be made for its appropriateness (cf. Gergen, 1978; McGuire, 1973). Laboratory research is not necessarily more limited than "representative design" or "field research" (cf. Dipboye & Flanagan, 1980), and there is no cure-all to be found in the systematic observation of the real world (e.g., "correlational" research, which has its own limitations). But as long as use of ecological, demographic, archival, self-report, and field observation data are shunned, social psychologists will never be able to lay claim to being authorities on human aggression (or on the regularities of human behavior in general).

The Dominant Theoretical Paradigm in the Study of Aggression

I have been arguing that psychology's beliefs and values have strongly influenced the course of research, as well as defining the questions to be asked. Taken as a whole, they can be said to have shaped the dominant theoretical paradigm that produces researchable hypotheses. There are, of course, competing theories and models of aggressive behavior, but they are covered by an overarching paradigm that defines the controversies involved and points out the battleground and the language in which these arguments are waged. Examples of this commonality are to be found in the following questions:

1. Is frustration a necessary and sufficient antecedent to aggression? The hypothesis that frustration normally leads to aggression, at least among men, can be countered with a hypothesis that aggression is a learned response to frustration and so cannot be said to be the normal (inevitable or biologically determined) reaction to frustration. Both sides understand the concepts of "frustration" and "aggression" and, aside from the problem of loose usage, no definitions are needed in discourse among disputants. They share the assumption that "frustration leads to aggression" is an empirically verifiable or falsifiable proposition. (See, e.g., Berkowitz, 1978b.)

Questions from outside this paradigm might turn to variations in the antecedents of apparently similar acts. For example, is a spouse killing impulsive (done without thought to the consequences) or instrumental, defensive or offensive, the result of contemporary emotion recognized as anger or fear or the result of cold hatred, and what alternative behaviors were possible? Whatever the answers, some "frustration" and consequent aversive stimulation can easily be adduced as a cause of the killing. What would be critical to research that advances understanding, however, is not the fact of the actor's experience of aversive stimulation but the qualitative variations and consequences of this experience.

2. Can angry people cathart their aggressive urges? Again, whether one belongs to the school that denies the validity of the hydraulic anology or to the school that says anger must be vented to avoid explosion, there are common concepts involved. Both schools can test their apparently irreconcilable views with a teacher–learner shock machine set-up and possibly even use the same cover story with only a few details varied. Questions from outside this paradigm might ask: "Is there a difference between denying anger and voluntarily or involuntarily foregoing expression of anger?" and then, "What are the possible consequences (plural possibilities)?"

The outlines of the dominant paradigm for human aggression employed by American social psychologists can be drawn from the usual research questions asked and from the manner in which their answers are sought—i.e., from published research. If one reads such writers as Lorenz (1966), Tiger (1969), and Ardrey (1967), or Western fiction generally, it is apparent that the model is standard in Western thought. More than that, it is part of our social reality, generated and sustained by social structure (Sampson, 1981). The basic views are as follows.

Whether shaped by biology or learning, or both, man's natural, normal, and usual reaction to frustration or provocation is to lash out, physically, against the perceived cause or a convenient substitute target. This hypothesis can be conditioned in several ways: Perhaps only "arbitrary" frustration leads to aggression because only arbitrary frustration is provoking, or perhaps arousal must be labeled anger if aggression is to result, or perhaps the frustration must be capable of being perceived as a "personal attack" or an "ego threat" (Baron, 1977;

Wills, 1981); or perhaps aggression results only when pain is involved (Berkowitz, 1978b). These conditions do not alter the underlying paradigm. (See, e.g., Berkowitz, 1978b, pp. 697–702. A succinct statement of this model was given by Miller, 1941, quoted by Berkowitz, p. 696.)

The paradigm specifies various external and internal variables that shape aggression. They may deflect it, mute it, determine the specific behavior, and even cause flight or passivity rather than fighting, but they are still seen as variables acting on an expected, reliable response. The preferred explanation for aggressive behavior is individual, as I have argued. There is no place in this model for an interactive person-norms-situation process whereby the hypothesized response to frustration or provocation could be selected out of an array of possible aggressive *and nonaggressive* responses. The model comprehends control of aggression but not nonaggressive action as a full-fledged normal or usual response.

After writing a draft of this paper, I went back over a number of important writings on aggression by social psychologists. I found that what I have described as the dominant theoretical paradigm for the study of aggression fits the empirical work these writers rely on but not all of their discussion. Bandura, for example, in his 1973 book, *Aggression: A Social Learning Analysis*, argued that "In social learning theories, rather than frustration generating an aggressive drive, aversive treatment produces a general state of emotional arousal that can facilitate a variety of behaviors, depending on the type of responses the person has learned for coping with stress and their relative effectiveness" (p. 53). On the following page Bandura presented a detailed model that should have generated research that would answer many of the questions listed at the beginning of this paper. However, it did not do so. Bandura's theory generated much research, but almost all of it was within the dominant paradigm. The problem is that even when the design and analysis of research seems to be situation-centered (as it sometimes is in social learning studies or in the context of a theory seeing aggression as, say, "stimulus-bound"), the dominant paradigm creates blinders to the possibility that something other than "inhibition" causes response variance in aggression level. For example, Bandura says at one point that certain studies show that "low aggressive modeling by females reflects differential inhibition rather than differential learning of aggression." He does not notice that the girls' behavior in these studies may have included responses other than the aggression or no aggression to which the experimenter attended. And yet he later says, "Aggression can . . . best be reduced . . . by developing more effective means of coping with interpersonal problems." He sought clinical data to support the idea of alternative responses, but he did not see that he had disallowed them while working within the confines of the experimental research paradigm.

Another serious limitation of the major theoretical models is that they are models of men's behavior, with women assumed to be generally nonaggressive.

In Dollard et al's (1939) original frustration–aggression theory, and in Miller's later version (1941), there was an implicitly normal connection between frustration (or a state of arousal that must be "anger") and aggression. If women are very seldom aggressive, it follows that it must be hard to frustrate or anger them to begin with, therefore no research time need be spent studying women. But of course women do experience anger and do respond to frustration one way or another. Thus, there is some absurdity in the origins of the basic paradigm. More pragmatically, the inclusion of women in an experiment was known to be asking for trouble because common sense and experience showed that one was likely to encounter gender differences that were hard to explain. For example, as a novice researcher I learned the hard way not to use "female subjects" when a mixed-sex sample yielded some striking gender differences. In terms of the model, the results for the women were aberrant. They could be explained, but not within the model. The end result was that half the time and grant money spent was wasted gathering "unusable" data; they were not reported.

Of course decisions like this must hamper theory development, but such absurdity is not noticed as long as the focus of research on male behavior is only implicit. In practice, this has meant that researchers have sometimes studied both men and women and have not looked at gender differences or even reported on the sex of the subject at all. (See Kurstin-Young et al., in press.) This may indicate a lack of scholarly socialization on the part of these researchers because, in terms of the model and for practical reasons, it would seem to be a mistake to study both sexes. Frodi et al. (1977) found that many researchers overcame this handicap by various means without changing the male orientation of the model (although they tended to be unable to get their work published in the top journals, as the Frodi et al. reference list shows). On one hand, as long as the expectation of differences was not articulated, the lack of gender differences did not require comment. On the other hand, finding gender differences was no surprise and also called for little comment unless the researcher wanted to declare the "obvious" fact that women are not aggressive. Of course gender differences are only actuarial findings, and since women's mean aggression scores are never at the bottom of the scale, this means that some women are aggressive. This has not been enough to draw attention to anomalous findings because the traditional analyses used by social psychologists have not caused researchers to notice the information contained in variance statistics. (See Tresemer, 1975 and Sohn, 1980, for discussions of this common problem.) Perhaps the hardest findings to deal with were those that showed an interaction between gender and the major variable of interest. Here, too, researchers have had little trouble maintaining the integrity of the model. One can always drop the data for women, as I did once. Or, one can ignore the finding. (Carlson, 1971, describes a study where sex differences of greater magnitude than differences in other variables were simply not mentioned.) And if all else fails, stereotypy, with its inherent contradictions, can be mined for an explanation. For example, one can say that women are more patient than men or more mercurial than men depending on whether one has found women slower or faster than men in reacting to insult.

Having presented the aggression paradigm as very much male-oriented, I have to back-track and point out some side assumptions in the study of aggression plus some research habits that bring data on women into the picture, if not women themselves. First, there is a research corollary, unspoken but clearly visible in choice of subjects for study of these side issues (McKenna & Kessler, 1977). This corollary says that variable type should be matched to gender in order to maximize the production of usable (interpretable and so reportable) data. Second, within the aggression paradigm there are a few variables that seem more feminine than masculine—for example guilt, because it is believed that women experience more guilt than men after aggressing. Therefore it follows that one should use female subjects when studying aggression guilt. The decision to do so is supported by pragmatic considerations. Women are more available in the subject pool usually used. This results from the fact that somewhat more women than men usually take introductory psychology and from the predeliction for studying men rather than women, which means that the men in the pool are used more quickly.

Of course the decision to use women in something like the study of aggression guilt involves the belief that women can be induced to behave aggressively in the laboratory. This poses no problem, even though women are assumed to be generally nonaggressive. Because the assumption is unstated, inconsistency with practice is not perceived and, in fact, women can be induced to aggress in the justified aggression situation that experimenters usually set up (Frodi et al., 1977).

The end result is that findings for a sideline variable such as guilt, based on data mainly from women, are incorporated into theory supported by findings for mainline variables based on data mainly from men. (For example see Storck and Sigall, 1979; they offer a gender-neutral discussion of findings for women's reactions to attractiveness and victimization, variables that often produce gender differences.) This habit must surely have warped theorizing and model development. It is here, too, that the neglect of norms generally—and of gender norms in particular—is particularly debilitating for theory and understanding of aggression because we end up knowing nothing about the usual operation of norms in sex-integrated settings (cf. Unger, 1983).

The Social Structure of Academic Psychology

The internal social structure of academia is a major contributor to the stability of psychology's dominant paradigms. In spite of many strong criticisms (many more than those recited here), it looked for a long time as if practice would remain untouched. There are a number of nonideological reasons for this.

To begin with, most established social psychology researchers were well socialized into respect for and practice within the dominant paradigms during graduate school. What they learned got them a doctorate, publications, grants, and eventually job security. Their faith in the importance of "testing hypotheses" in "controlled experiments" has been well reinforced. The crisis-in-social-psychology literature made them aware of problems with what they knew as normal science, but they saw the solution as improvement in their research paradigms—better control, etc.—not as radical change in method or hypothesis generation. (For example, see Pepitone, 1976; Schlenker, 1974; West & Gunn, 1978.)

It would, of course, be very difficult if not foolhardy for established researchers to react otherwise. They have invested in the trappings of laboratory research and would be reluctant to trade their machines and research space for the possibly unreliable trappings of other methods. They know how to do laboratory research and how to get it published, and as a look at the major journals still shows their culture continues to accord high status to the dominant paradigms (Weissberg, 1976). Publish or perish is still the basic career rule for academics who want research careers at research-oriented institutions (Lowe, 1976; M. Sherif, 1977).

Another social structure factor that maintains the established paradigms is the isolation of social psychologists who study aggression from others interested in aggression. Social psychologists in psychology departments tend to have little contact with social psychologists in sociology (Blank, 1978; Wilson & Shafer, 1978). Comparative psychologists study animal aggression and their work is often positively referred to by social and developmental psychologists, but a meaningful exchange of ideas is rare. There is very little interchange between clinicians who study aggressiveness as pathology and social psychologists who study aggression as a normal response to provocation. There is more cross reference between social and developmental psychologists, but a check of division membership suggests that it is the latter who maintain the ties; prominent aggression researchers who are identified as social psychologists don't belong to the developmentalists' division, but developmentalists interested in aggression belong to the social psychology division. Some psychologists study "conflict resolution," but this is done in the context of laboratory games and although their variables include such things as "hostility," there seems to be no exchange of ideas with those who study aggressive resolution of experimentally induced hostility.

Beyond these subfields of psychology, there are other disciplines that study aggression. Some sociologists, anthropologists and political scientists study mass and political violence while others study conflict and dispute resolution. Anthropologists have amassed data on socialization for and away from aggressive response to provocation, but social psychologists know only the rare studies published in psychology journals. Until recently, child abuse was the province of social workers and "marriage and family" sociologists; and only the latter studied other aspects of domestic violence. Their research was not generally recognized as the study of aggression by social psychologists (Knutson, 1978). Sociologists and criminologists studied homicide, but psychologists did not, although one would think that this was the apex of individual aggression. Finally, criminologists studied rape, which was not defined as violence and was not studied by psychologists until recently.

The separation between these fields was not absolute. One might find a convention program featuring a panel of experts from several disciplines, and major writers on aggression tend to refer to major findings in other fields—either in support of their own theories or in reference to the implications of their theories for understanding phenomena they themselves have not studied directly. There is, however, a clear conceptual separation that can be seen in the index to *Psychological Abstracts*. If one is interested in all aspects of aggression, one has to check out almost a dozen terms; the only terms showing regular cross-listing are "aggression" and "aggressiveness." For example, an article on rape is cited only under "violence" while an article on the relationship between sexual arousal and aggression is cited only under "aggression."

An illuminating explanation for the conceptual isolation of related fields is to be found in Campbell's (1969) "fish scale model." He conceives of scholarly topics as overlapping scales, patterned as are the scales of a fish. Conventional "disciplines" are areas that have been defined over time as subsets of scales. Some subsets of scales fall in the center of a discipline and, for various political and cognitive reasons, come to be seen as its core. Other subsets (for example, psychology and law or reproductive behavior) fall at the periphery of a discipline area and may include scales that belong to another discipline or to no discipline at all. Furthermore, scholars from different disciplines working in the same area are in different departments that are geographically separated. As a result of all this, when it comes to the satisfaction of collegial needs (to discuss one's ideas with others, especially) and when it comes to career needs (to publish and get tenure), even the marginal members stick to the people, paradigms, and journals within their own discipline.

Truly interdisciplinary work is much admired by some but participants have tended to accumulate professional disadvantages (Campbell, 1969; Macaulay, 1976). Generally, the aspiring academic in a research-oriented institution probably still does best by sticking to the study of scales within his or her discipline— and the closer to the core the better. A social psychologist interested in women and aggression—say, child abuse—should study not child abusers but young female college students' recommendations for disciplining various misbehaving children as shown on videotape in a laboratory set-up. The control of stimuli is important when it comes to publication; the problem of the generalizability of results is not. Although theory development might dictate studying actual child abuse in order to be able to construct relevant analogs for laboratory research and to generalize with confidence from laboratory results, the time and effort involved in doing this is unlikely to pay off in career security. This is not to say that there is no support for doing more than this; nonlaboratory studies are now appearing more often in the best journals. Still, journal reviewers tend to be those whose success was forged within the dominant paradigms and, as Lindsey (1978) has shown, they tend to like that which confirms their own views.

RECENT HISTORY: HAS ANYTHING CHANGED?

The study of individual aggression has changed in several respects within the last five to ten years. How radical is this change and what brought it about? It is clear that at least some of the changes are likely to have a major impact on research and theory and that some of them stem from the study of the psychology of women's behavior, as such, and of women's behavior in comparison with men's behavior. At the same time, there are signs that the view of women's behavior as anomalous in the context of normal psychological science is not yet widespread.

The answers to these questions about change were initially sought by a reading of abstracts of articles, papers, and book chapters collected from late 1975 to early 1982. These were clipped from *Psychological Abstracts* and gathered through regular perusal of social psychology, developmental psychology, psychology of women, and sociology journals. The index terms used when searching *Psychological Abstracts* were aggression, aggressiveness, anger, attack, catharsis, child abuse, homicide, hostility, and violence. Other work was found by skimming the most relevant sections of *Psychological Abstracts*. In addition, the collection includes papers obtained at professional meetings and through correspondence. From 1982 until the final revision of this paper, the collection was augmented somewhat unsystematically but nonetheless grew impressively.

The first observation is that male centrism may no longer be a central characteristic of aggression research. Over this period there was a growing number of articles concerned not only with gender differences but also with questions specifically related to women, anger, and aggression. Much of this, of course, was found in journals specializing in the study of women and women's concerns, but some was also found in the mainline, established journals.

The second observation has two angles to it. On one hand, a substantial portion of the research with mixed-sex samples and even of women-only samples still follows the traditional research paradigm, with the teacher-shocking-student script still very popular. Self-contained individualism still seems to be a dominant value, and modes of inquiry involving manipulation, quantification, and control still describe the dominant research paradigm. Generalization to both sexes from one sex and from laboratory to social problems is still common. Citation patterns still show most researchers looking inward to their own subfields and seldom outward to other disciplines. There is little sign that popular beliefs about women and aggression are being widely questioned by academics—several miscitations of the review by Frodi et al. were found. (See, e.g., Geen & Donnerstein, 1983.)

On the other hand, one can now find a substantial amount of research published, about to be published, or planned that deviates from what has been normal science in the area of aggression. This kind of work first appeared in 1978. In looking for work that would begin to answer the questions posed in the introduction to this paper, counting only that which did not fit the standard paradigms in some major respect, I found I had only one or two pieces a year up to 1977. But in 1978 there were four; in 1979, eleven; 1980, seven; and from 1981 on more than a dozen a year. Some examples are:

—A study of mood-induction techniques used in laboratory studies (Polivy, 1981). Perhaps this portends more attention to the meaning of the laboratory manipulations for subjects.

—A series of surveys on everyday experiences of provocation and anger (Averill, 1983). Averill studied nonstudents as well as students, women as well as men, and looked at the whole array of responses and nonresponses, positive and negative, aggressive and nonaggressive. His findings are startlingly unpredictable by normal aggression theory.

—An abstract of a paper that reflects a new concern with differentiating aggressive and assertive behaviors, "Mapping the domains of assertive and aggressive behavior classes" (Mauger, Hook, Adkinson, & Hernandez, 1979), and a book exploring measurement of human aggression and its relation to theoretical debates on aggression (Edmunds & Kendrick, 1980).

—A paper by Straus (1979) concerning the variety of responses to intrafamily conflict, including both aggressive and nonaggressive behavior and clarifying the conceptual labels usually used in describing such conflict. Straus and his colleagues have done much to breach the isolation between psychologists and sociologists interested in aggression. Little of their work has been published in psychology journals, but there is some evidence that his group's broad, comprehensive concepts are beginning to influence psychologists' views. (See Straus, Gelles & Steinmetz, 1980.)

—A study of boys' and girls' evaluations of aggressive, assertive, and passive behaviors by male and female story characters and of how these evaluations change with age (Connor, Serbin, & Ender, 1978). I hope this signals the beginning of attention to peer expectations, development of gender norms, and responses to others' aggression where "others" are more than a genderless, undifferentiated, interactionless group or the experimenters' programmed stooges.

—A discussion of the significance of findings of gender differences in aggression, with the suggestion that there is something more to girls' socialization than training in the inhibition of aggression (Eron, 1980). The author feels that girls are encouraged to develop qualities that are antithetical to aggressive behavior and that we might do well to socialize our sons in the same way as we socialize our daughters.

—A study of "naturally occurring aggressive behavior in a realistic setting," using only male college students and a contrived set-up, but also multiple measures and attention to the character of the situation. The report concludes with a plea for studies that "employ more ecologically valid settings and measures of aggressive behavior" (Kulik & Brown, 1979).

As some of these examples show, I found that concern with women's behavior seems to have stimulated some paradigmatic innovation in research; as other examples suggest, this is not the only apparent spur to change in the area of aggression research. Presumably the great outpouring of crisis-in-social-psychology literature prompted some change. However, this crisis was recognized as early as the early 1970s; thus, its influence would seem to be somewhat slow-acting. Furthermore, the crisis literature has tended to pose rather general problems, with only passing reference to problems of theory in specific content areas. My survey suggests that the posing of questions outside of standard paradigms and the awareness of anomalies that the dominant theories cannot handle—specifically, the awareness of women's behavior as anomalous—spurred more innovative research than the general problems raised in the crisis literature.

Such assertions are difficult to prove. Change in social science does not ride in on lightning bolts. One might readily grasp the significance of, say, the discovery of a new subatomic particle, but not of a finding that women are sometimes very aggressive when they are not expected to be so. Furthermore, indisputably clear trends are hard to spot in the great and varied stream of social research, and my effort to spot trends is undoubtedly subject to idiosyncratic bias.

Whatever we might finally conclude as to the extent, character, and causes of change, it is clear, however, that there has been a change in focus on the part of many researchers from male behavior to male *and* female behavior. The attention to women's behavior and to gender and sex differences in itself constitutes a major change in research habits. Beyond this, the introduction of women brings up questions that go to other aspects of the conventional paradigm, as I have tried to show throughout this paper, and at least some researchers are attending to these questions in significant ways. For example, the question of how norms for women's behavior affect laboratory results is new, and once introduced should make it difficult to go back to the assumption that as long as the situation is "controlled" we can ignore the specifics of what it means to participants, male as well as female.

In addition, there are some less obvious effects of the new concern for women's behavior. Take, for example, the current interest in "assertiveness." My collection of references shows that the early research in this area stemmed from a feminist concern to overcome women's training in submissiveness. But gender is not only one of many variables of interest, and one of the problems currently being debated in the "assertiveness" literature concerns the meaning of the concepts of "assertiveness" and "aggressiveness." This, in turn, calls into question the arbitrary labeling of the dependent variable by researchers, bringing such questions as the matter of intent into the open. In other words, the introduction of a novel population (women) and concern for a previously neglected behavior (assertiveness) that came to be seen as somehow related to aggression has prompted a much-needed reexamination of concepts and terminology. Once forced to this rethinking, it should be hard to continue to view the results of experiments in the traditional paradigm (teacher-learner shock experiments, for example) as generalizable to all kinds of "aggression."

And finally, as evidence that the new view of women as worthy of study has profoundly influenced the nature of aggression research, we can point to the topics that were of little interest to researchers before the rise of feminism in the 1970s (cf. the analysis by Rose, 1977). These topics include rape, domestic violence, the relationship between sexual arousal and violence, and the effects of violent pornography. Some of these topics have merely been shaped so to fit the conventional aggression research paradigms, but even here they have been redefined as serious social problems rather than mere titillating curiosities. Other topics have been developed in isolated pieces; some social psychologists study sexual arousal and "violence" in the laboratory and others study rape in the field, with little cross-citation as yet. However, there is some research in these areas that involves multimethod approaches, thoughtful laboratory research, and a willingness to let the research interest shape the selection of research method rather than the reverse. (For example, see research by Frieze and her colleagues on spouse abuse that combines insights from laboratory studies of attribution processes, data on how society views battered women, and the results of a survey of battered and not-battered wives (Frieze, Knoble, Washburn, & Zomnir, 1980).

WHAT NEXT?

The innovations described in the examples above are minor when taken alone. Some may merely be responses to narrow questions and simple methodological impasses rather than revolutionary steps following the perception of broad theoretical or methodological problems. But I think that they may at least presage a paradigmatic revolution. Larger changes are on the way, not yet observable in print but discernable in work now in the prepublication communication network and in research proposals. For evidence here I have to rely on what I have seen by way of papers refereed for journals, preliminary reports of work-in-progress, research proposals reviewed for granting agencies, and conversations in convention hallways, as follows:

—I reviewed two research projects that seemed to respond to the various calls for nonlaboratory ecological studies of social phenomena (e.g., Bronfenbrenner, 1977; Cronbach, 1975; Elms, 1975; Gibbs, 1979; Glaser & Strauss, 1967; McGuire, 1973). Both proposals called for systematic observations of situations, cues and response, and both planned complex and apparently creative analyses of the data collected. Neither researchers cited any of the writings in the list above. Perhaps they were unaware of them, or perhaps the impetus to such radical departures from normal research paradigms is simply in the air.

—A social psychological study of murderers and their acts, perhaps building on Berkowitz's unique study of violent men in English prisons (1978a), or perhaps answering Toch's plea to "debrief" the doers of the behavior that aggression researchers profess to be interested in.

—Studies showing a shift from "sex" as an independent variable that yields only more-than and less-than differences, to gender as a variable with qualitatively different effects. In this new conception there is no single "role" for each sex; rather, the focus is on situation-specific norms that tend to be gender-related.

—Studies and discussions on the relationship between television and violence with indications that media researchers and laboratory researchers are beginning to exchange ideas.

There is still more that I would expect to see, given the ideas that are in the air. These ideas demand the use of archival data, social statistics, and self-reports, as well as traditional laboratory and field observation. We will need to use more sophisticated and varied data analyses and to demote analysis of variance from king to group member. We have become aware that the aggression we observe is influenced by the net effect of salient norms, and that these depend on the sex of observers, provokers, and victims. As the number of variables we must attend to increases, and as we move from simple dichotomies to qualitative analyses of behavior, our designs must increase in sophistication.

As researchers work on the puzzles of women's responses to provocation, and as we realize that they are anomalous in terms of the accepted paradigms and that even among angry men, nonaggression is not deviant, we will be forced to reconstruct our theory of aggression. (For a beginning, see Averill, 1983.) It is not only scholarly questions that will prompt this reworking. The social movement that we have called "women's liberation" has led to the questioning of women's place in society and of the structure of relations between women and men. Whatever the political fortunes of the women's liberation movement, we are not going to return to the status quo of the 1950s. Rather, the restructuring of relations and the recasting of women's roles will continue along its rocky path. This cannot help but affect social psychological research because it involves the kind of questioning that is at the heart of social psychology's subject matter. (See, e.g., Deaux, 1984.) As social forces shaped the original research on aggression, casting it in terms of the frustration–aggression model, so present social forces will influence future theory. Psychology's views of human behavior have drifted away from the visions of Freudian and behaviorist theory, and some of what was once our cultural "common sense" is now considered racist and sexist. Inevitably methods and research questions will also change, perhaps so slowly as to be nearly invisible to active researchers, but radically nonetheless.

Apart from the influence of feminist concerns on the direction of research, there is discontent in the air over the practice of social psychology. There is pressure from several directions to broaden our perspectives. In the area of aggression, it is time to study the full range of behavior following provocation (and a good place to start is with women's responses). It is time to open up communication with researchers in areas such as conflict resolution, criminal violence, political violence, etc., as well as to consider the cross-cultural differences and similarities of aggression.

Much of what I have said about social psychology's potential has been summarized by Carolyn Sherif (1978) in this way:

> If the social-psychological study of women is to have long-range value for women as well as for social psychology, it has to be historical, comparative, related to the social structure and social values indigenous in every social situation, developmental, focused upon interactions among women and with men, and to employ experimentation as a final step in analysis of a problem, rather than as a routine housekeeping tool like the vacuum cleaner or as a substitute for reality.

If we realize this potential in aggression theory, we will then be working from a paradigm that includes the processes leading to aggression as well as aggression itself, and that views destructive aggression as one of several possible consequences of provocation and not as simply a normal, innate, male response. We would then have seen a paradigmatic revolution.

REFERENCES

Ardrey, R. (1967). *The territorial imperative*. New York: Atheneum.

Averill, J. R. (1982). *Anger and aggression: An essay on emotion*. New York: Springer-Verlag.

Averill, J. R. (1982). Studies on anger and aggression: Implications for theories of emotion. *American Psychologist, 38*(11), 1145–1160.

Bandura, A. (1973). *Aggression: A social learning analysis*. Englewood Cliffs, N.J.: Prentice-Hall.

Baron, R. A. (1977). *Human aggression*. New York: Plenum.

Baron, R. A., & Eggleston, R. J. (1972). Performance on the "aggression machine": Motivation to help or harm? *Psychonomic Science, 26*(6), 321–322.

Baumgardner, S. R. (1976). Critical history and social psychology's "crisis." *Personality and Social Psychology Bulletin, 2*, 460–465.

Berkowitz, L. (1970). Theoretical and research approaches in experimental social psychology. In A. R. Gilgen (Ed.), *Contemporary scientific psychology*. New York: Academic Press.

Berkowitz, L. (1974). Some determinants of impulsive aggression: The role of mediated associations with reinforcements for aggression. *Psychological Review, 81*, 165–170.

Berkowitz, L. (1978a). Is criminal violence normative behavior? Hostile and instrumental aggression in violent incidents. *Journal of Research in Crime & Delinquency, 15*, 148–161.

Berkowitz, L. (1978b). Whatever happened to the frustration–aggression hypothesis? *American Behavioral Scientist, 21*(5), 691–708.

Berkowitz, L., & Donnerstein, E. (1982). External validity is more than skin deep: Some answers to criticisms of laboratory research. *American Psychologist, 37*(3), 245–257.

Berkowitz, L., & Frodi, A. (1979). Reactions to a child's mistakes as affected by her/his looks and speech. *Social Psychology Quarterly, 42*(4), 420–425.

Blank, T. O. (1978). Two social psychologies: Is segregation inevitable or acceptable? *Personality and Social Psychology Bulletin, 4*(4), 553–556.

Boulding, E. (1979). Deep structure and sociological analyses: Some reflections. *The American Sociologist, 14*(2), 70–75.

Boutilier, R. G., Roed, J. C., & Svendsen, A. C. (1980). Crises in the two social psychologies: A critical comparison. *Social Psychology Quarterly, 43*(1), 5–17.

Bronfenbrenner, U. (1977). Lewinian space and ecological substance. *Journal of Social Issues, 33*(4), 199–212.

Burgess, A. (1962). *A clockwork orange.* New York: Penguin.

Buss, A. R. (1979). The emerging field of the sociology of psychological knowledge. *American Psychologist, 30*, 988–1002.

Campbell, D. T. (1969). Ethnocentrism of disciplines and the fish-scale model of omniscience. In M. Sherif & C. Sherif (Eds.), *Interdisciplinary relationships in the social sciences.* Chicago: Aldine.

Caplan, N., & Nelson, S. D. (1973). On being useful: The nature and consequences of psychological research on social problems. *American Psychologist, 28*(3), 199–211.

Caplan, P. J. (1975). Sex differences in antisocial behavior: Does research methodology produce or abolish them? *Human Development, 18*, 444–460.

Carlson, E. R., & Carlson, R. (1961). Male and female subjects in personality research. *Journal of Abnormal and Social Psychology, 61*, 482–483.

Carlson, R. (1971). Where is the person in personality research? *Psychological Bulletin, 75*, 203–219.

Carlson, R. (1972). Understanding women: Implications for personality theory and research. *Journal of Social Issues, 28*(2), 17–32.

Connor, J. M., Serbin, L. A., & Ender, R. A. (1978). Responses of boys and girls to aggressive, assertive, and passive behaviors of male and female characters. *Journal of Genetic Psychology, 133*(1), 59–69.

Cronbach, L. J. (1975). Beyond the two disciplines of scientific psychology. *American Psychologist, 30*, 116–127.

Dan, A., & Beekman, S. (1972). Male versus female representation in psychological research. *American Psychologist, 27*, 1078.

Deaux, K. (1984). From individual differences to social categories. *American Psychologist, 39*(2), 105–116.

Dipboye, R. L., & Flanagan, M. F. (1979). Research settings in industrial and organizational psychology: Are findings in the field more generalizable than in the laboratory? *American Psychologist, 34*(2), 141–150.

Dollard, J., Doob, L., Miller, N., Mowrer, O., & Sears, R. (1939). *Frustration and aggression.* New Haven: Yale University Press.

Edmunds, G., & Kendrick, D. C. (1980). *The measurement of human aggression.* Chichester, England: Horwood.

Elms, A. C. (1975). The crisis of confidence in social psychology. *American Psychologist, 30*, 967–976.

Epstein, Y. M., Suedfeld, P., & Silverstein, S. J. (1973). The experimental contract: Subjects' expectations of and reactions to some behaviors of experimenters. *American Psychologist, 28*(3), 212–221.

Eron, L. D. (1980). Prescription for reduction of aggression. *American Psychologist, 35*(3), 244–252.

Feshbach, N. D. (1969). Sex differences in children's modes of aggressive responses toward outsiders. *Merrill-Palmer Quarterly, 15*(3), 249–258.

Fox, R. (1977). The inherent rules of violence. In P. Collett (Ed.), *Social rules and social behavior.* Totowa, N.J.: Roman & Littlefield.

Frieze, I. H., Knoble, J., Washburn, C., & Zomnir, G. (1980). Characteristics of battered women and their marriages. Unpublished paper, University of Pittsburgh.

Frodi, A., Macaulay, J., & Thome, P. R. (1977). Are women always less aggressive than men? A review of the experimental literature. *Psychological Bulletin, 84*(4), 634–660.

Gaebelein, J. W. (1981). Naturalistic versus experimental approaches to aggression: Theoretical and methodological issues. *Aggressive Behavior, 7*(4), 325–339.

Geen, R. G., & Donnerstein, E. I. (1983). *Aggression: Theoretical and empirical reviews* (Volumes 1 and 2). New York: Academic Press.

Gergen, K. J. (1978). Experimentation in social psychology. A reappraisal. *European Journal of Social Psychology, 8,* 507–527.

Gergen, K. J., & Morawski, J. (1980). An alternative metatheory for social psychology. In L. Wheeler (Ed.), *Review of personality and social psychology* (Vol. 1). Beverly Hills, Calif.: Sage.

Gibbs, J. C. (1979). The meaning of ecologically oriented inquiry in contemporary psychology. *American Psychologist, 34,* 127–140.

Glaser, B. G., & Strauss, A. L. (1967). *The discovery of grounded theory.* Chicago: Aldine.

Gould, M., & Kern-Daniels, M. (1977). Toward a sociological theory of gender and sex. *American Sociologist, 12,* 182–189.

Gove, W. (1979). Review of G. Ritzer, *Sociology: A Multiple Paradigm Science,* 1975. *Contemporary Sociology, 8*(6), 799–800.

Grady, K. E. (1979). Androgyny reconsidered. In J. H. Williams (Ed.), *Psychology of women: Selected readings.* New York: W. W. Norton.

Harvey, L. (1982). The use and abuse of Kuhnian paradigms in the sociology of knowledge. *Sociology, 16*(1), 85–101.

Henshel, R. L. (1980). The purposes of laboratory experimentation and the virtues of deliberate artificiality. *Journal of Experimental Social Psychology, 16,* 466–478.

Higbie, K. L., Millard, R. J. & Folkman, J. R. (1982). Social psychology research during the 1970s: Predominance of experimentation and college students. *Personality and Social Psychology Bulletin, 8*(1), 180–183.

Holmes, D. S. & Jorgensen, B. W. (1971). Do personality and social psychologists study men more than women? *Representative Research in Social Psychology, 2,* 71–76.

Hynan, M. T. (1979). Shock delivery in human aggression experiments: Aggression or button-pushing? *Aggression Research, 5,* 186–187. (Abstract)

Jahoda, G. (1979). A cross-cultural perspective on experimental social psychology. *Personality and Social Psychology Bulletin, 5*(2), 142–148.

Kaplan, A. G. (1977, September). *Women and anger in the therapeutic relationship: Introduction.* Paper presented at the meeting of the American Psychological Association, San Francisco.

Kaplow, S. (1973). Getting angry. In A. Koedt, E. Levine, & A. Rapone (Eds.), *Radical feminism.* New York: Quadrangle Books.

Knutson, J. F. (1973). Aggression as manipulable behavior. In J. F. Knutson (Ed.), *Control of aggression: Implications for basic research.* Chicago: Aldine-Atherton.

Knutson, J. F. (1978). Child abuse as an area of aggression research. *Journal of Pediatric Psychology, 3*(1), 20–27.

Koch, S. (1981). The nature and limits of psychological knowledge: Lessons of a century qua "science." *American Psychologist, 36*(3), 257–269.

Kuhn, T. S. (1970). *The structure of scientific revolutions* (2nd ed.). Chicago: University of Chicago Press.

Kuhn, T. S. (1977). *The essential tension: Selected studies in scientific tradition and change.* Chicago: University of Chicago Press.

Kulik, J. A., & Brown, R. (1979). Frustration, attribution of blame, and aggression. *Journal of Experimental Social Psychology, 15*(2), 183–194.

Kurstin-Young, C., Sparks, W. M., & Watson, G. W. (in press). Have we really come a long way? Sexism in research. *Psychology of Women Quarterly,* in press.

Langer, E. J., & Newman, H. M. (1979). The role of mindlessness in a typical social psychological experiment. *Personality and Social Psychology Bulletin, 5*(3), 295–298.

Levenson, H., Gray, M. J., & Ingram, A. (1976). Research methods in personality five years after Carlson's survey. *Personality and Social Psychology Bulletin, 2*(2), 158–161.

Lindsey, D. (1978). *The scientific publication system in social science.* San Francisco: Jossey-Bass.

Lorenz, K. (1966). *On aggression.* New York: Harcourt, Brace, & World.

Lowe, R. H. (1976). A survey of social psychological methods, techniques, and design: A response to Helmreich. *Personality and Social Psychology Bulletin, 2,* 116–118.

Lubek, I. (1979). A brief social psychological analysis of research on aggression in social psychology. In A. R. Buss (Ed.), *Psychology in social context.* New York: Irvington.

Macaulay. J. (1976). Some notes on interdisciplinary endeavors. In J. Macaulay (Ed.), *Understanding the potential and limits of effective legal action* (Report to the National Science Foundation). Unpublished manuscript, University of Wisconsin-Madison.

Maher, B. A. (1978). Stimulus sampling in clinical research: Representative design reviewed. *Journal of Consulting and Clinical Psychology, 46*(4), 643–647.

Mallick, S. K. & McCandless, B. R. (1966). A study of catharsis of aggression. *Journal of Personality and Social Psychology, 4*(6), 591–596.

Manicas, P. T., & Secord, P. F. (1983). Implications for psychology of the new philosophy of science. *American Psychologist, 38*(4), 399–413.

Martin, M. W. (1979). The role of the experiment in the social sciences. *The Sociological Quarterly, 20,* 581–590.

Mauger, P. A., Hook, J. D., Adkinson, D., & Hernandez, S. K. (1979). Mapping the domains of assertive and aggressive behavior classes. *Personality and Social Psychology Bulletin, 5*(3), 269. (Abstract)

McConaghy, M. J. (1979). "Gender" versus "sex": Comment on Gould and Kern-Daniels. *The American Sociologist, 14*(2), 120.

McCormack, T. (1978). Machismo in media research: A critical review of research in violence and pornography. *Social Problems, 25*(5), 544–555.

McGuire, W. (1968). Personality and susceptibility to social influence. In E. Borgatta and W. W. Lambert (Eds.), *Handbook of personality theory and research.* Chicago: Rand McNally.

McGuire, W. (1973). The yin and yang of progress in social psychology. *Journal of Personality and Social Psychology, 26,* 446–456.

McKenna, W., & Kessler, S. J. (1977). Experimental design as a source of sex bias in social psychology. *Sex Roles, 3*(2), 117–128.

Miller, N. E. (1941). The frustration–aggression hypothesis. *Psychological Review, 48,* 337–342.

Moyer, K. E. (1974). Sex differences in aggression. In R. C. Freedman, R. M. Richart, R. L. Vanderwiele, & L. O. Stern (Eds.), *Sex differences in behavior.* New York: Wiley.

Pepitone, A. (1976). Toward a normative and comparative biocultural social psychology. *Journal of Personality and Social Psychology, 34*(4), 641–653.

Peterson, G. L. (1981). Historical self-understanding in the social sciences: The use of Thomas Kuhn in Psychology. *Journal for the Theory of Social Behaviour, 11*(1), 1–30.

Polivy, J. (1981). On the induction of emotion in the laboratory: Discrete moods or multiple affect states? *Journal of Personality and Social Psychology, 41*(4), 803–817.

Prescott, S. (1978). Why researchers don't study women: The responses of 62 researchers. *Sex Roles, 4*(6), 899–905.

Reardon, P., & Prescott, S. (1977). Sex as reported in a recent sample of psychological research. *Psychology of Women Quarterly, 2*(2), 157–161.

Richardson, D. C., Bernstein, S., & Taylor, S. P. (1979). The effect of situational contingencies on female retaliative behavior. *Journal of Personality and Social Psychology, 37*(11), 2044–2048.

Ring, K. B. (1967). Experimental social psychology: Some sober questions about some frivolous values. *Journal of Experimental Social Psychology, 3,* 113–123.

Rose, V. M. (1977). Rape as a social problem: A byproduct of the feminist movement. *Social Problems, 25*(1), 75–89.

Sampson, E. E. (1977). Psychology and the American Idea. *Journal of Personality and Social Psychology, 35*(1), 767–782.

Sampson, E. E. (1978). Scientific paradigms and social values: Wanted—a scientific revolution. *Journal of Personality and Social Psychology, 36*(11), 1332–1343.

Sampson, E. E. (1981). Psychology as a social problem. *SASP Newsletter, 7*(5), 27–28; *7*(6), 34–35.

Schlenker, B. R. (1974). Social psychology and science. *Journal of Personality and Social Psychology, 29,* 1–15.

Schuck, J., & Pisor, K. (1974). Evaluating an aggression experiment by the use of simulating subjects. *Journal of Personality and Social Psychology, 29*(2), 181–186.

Schultz, D. P. (1969). The human subject in psychological research. *Psychological Bulletin, 72,* 214–228.

Schwabacher, S. (1972). Male versus female representation in psychological research: An examination of the *Journal of Personality and Social Psychology,* 1970, 1971. *JSAS Catalog of Selected Documents, 2,* 20–21 (Ms. No. 82).

Sherif, C. W. (1978). Social psychological study of women: Why so long becoming? *SASP Newsletter (The Society for the Advancement of Social Psychology), 4*(4), 2, 12.

Sherif, C. W. (1979). Bias in psychology. In J. A. Sherman & E. T. Beck (Eds.), *The prism of sex: Essays in the sociology of knowledge.* Madison, Wis.: University of Wisconsin Press.

Sherif, M. (1977). Crisis in psychology: Some remarks toward breaking through the crisis. *Personality and Social Psychology Bulletin, 3* 368–382.

Siegel, H. (1980). Objectivity, rationality, incommensurability and more. *British Journal of the Philosophy of Science, 31,* 359–384.

Signorella, M. L., Vegega, M. E., & Mitchell, M. E. (1981). Subject selection and analyses for sex-related differences: 1968–1970 and 1975–1977. *American Psychologist, 36*(9), 988–990.

Silverman, I. (1977). Why social psychology fails. *Canadian Psychological Review 18,* 353–358.

Smart, R. B. (1966). Subject selection bias in psychological research. *Canadian Psychologist, 7a,* 115–121.

Sohn, D. (1980). Critique of Cooper's meta-analytic assessment of the findings on sex differences in conformity behavior. *Journal of Personality and Social Psychology, 39*(6), 1215–1221.

Storck, J. T., & Sigall, H. (1979). Effect of a harm-doer's attractiveness and the victim's history of prior victimization on punishment of the harm-doer. *Personality and Social Psychology Bulletin, 5*(3), 344–347.

Storr, A. (1968). *Human aggression.* New York: Atheneum.

Straus, M. A. (1979). Measuring intrafamily conflict and violence: The Conflict Tactics (CT) scales. *Journal of Marriage and the Family, 41*(1), 75–88.

Straus, M. A., Gelles, R. J., & Steinmetz, S. K. (1980). *Behind closed doors: Violence in the American family.* Garden City, N. Y.: Anchor/Doubleday.

Tedeschi, J. T. (1980). Toward integration of the two social psychologies. *SASP Newsletter 6*(4), 4–5.

Tedeschi, J. T., Gaes, G. G., & Rivera, A. N. (1977). Aggression and the use of coercive power. *Journal of Social Issues, 33*(1), 101–125.

Tedeschi, J. T., Smith, R. B., & Brown, R. C. (1974). A reinterpretation of research on aggression. *Psychological Bulletin, 81*(9), 540–562.

Tiefer, L. (1978). The context and consequences of contemporary sex research: A feminist perspective. In W. McGill, D. Dewsbury, & B. Sachs (Eds.), *Sex and behavior: Status and prospectus.* New York: Plenum Press.

Tiger, L. (1969). *Men in groups.* New York: Random House.

Toch, H. (1978). Normatively hostile, purposefully hostile, or disinhibitedly bloody angry? *Journal of Research in Crime and Delinquency, 15,* 162–165.

Toch, H. (1980). Evolving a "science of violence." *American Behavioral Scientist, 23*(5), 653–665.

Tresemer, D. (1975). Measuring "sex differences." *Sociological Inquiry, 45*(4), 29–32.

Turner, C. W., Simons, L. S., Berkowitz, L. & Frodi, A. (1977). The stimulating effect of weapons on aggressive behavior. *Aggressive Behavior, 3*(4), 355–378.

Unger, R. K. (1979). Toward a redefinition of sex and gender. *American Psychologist, 34*(11), 1085–1094.

Unger, R. K. (1983). Through the looking glass: No wonderland yet! *Psychology of Women Quarterly, 8*(1), 9–32.

Veroff, J. (1978). Discovering dimensions of achievement motivation by studying women's achievement strivings. *SASP Newsletter, 4*(4), 7–8.

Weissberg, N. C. (1976). Methodology or substance? A response to Helmreich. *Personality and Social Psychology Bulletin, 2,* 119–121.

Weisstein, N. (1970). "Kinder, kuche, kirche" as scientific law: Psychology constructs the female. In R. Morgan (Ed.), *Sisterhood is powerful.* New York: Vintage.

West, S. G., & Gunn, S. P. (1978). Some issues of ethics and social psychology. *American Psychologist, 33*(1), 30–35.

Wills, T. A. (1981). Downward comparison principles in social psychology. *Psychological Bulletin, 90*(2), 245–271.

Wilson, D. W., & Schafer, R. B. (1978). Is social psychology interdisciplinary? *Personality and Social Psychology Bulletin, 4*(4), 548–552.

Zillman, D. (1979). *Hostility and aggression.* Hillsdale, N.J.: Lawrence Erlbaum Associates.

8 Gender and Influenceability: Stereotype Versus Behavior

Alice H. Eagly
Purdue University

Wendy Wood
University of Wisconsin—Milwaukee

In our society, there is widespread belief in sex differences in how easily people accept and exert influence. Women are perceived to be relatively easy to influence and as having little influence over others. Various stereotype studies have found that women, when compared with men, are perceived to be more easily influenced, more dependent, less agressive, less dominant, and less able to act as leaders (Broverman, Vogel, Broverman, Clarkson, & Rosenkrantz, 1972; Spence, Helmreich, & Stapp, 1974; Taylor, Fiske, Etcoff, & Ruderman, 1978; Williams & Bennett, 1975). According to social stereotypes about gender, then, women are relatively conforming, persuasible, and easily led; furthermore, they lack the ability to lead, influence, or dominate others. In this chapter, we examine the origins of such beliefs and attempt to assess their accuracy as a description of actual sex differences.

The beliefs that people commonly have about gender's effects on social influence reflect the reciprocal nature of the influence process: When one person successfully exerts influence, another person is influenced. The two parties of such an encounter can be referred to as the *agent* and the *recipient* of influence. Sex differences in the behavior and effectiveness of agents of influence are discussed in the literature on leadership (S. M. Brown, 1979) and social power (Johnson, 1976). The present chapter focuses instead on whether male and female recipients respond similarly to influence attempts. Specifically, we explore the sex differences in influenceability that have been established by laboratory research, and contrast these behavioral differences with stereotypic beliefs about women's and men's influenceability.

225

RECENT REVIEWS OF RESEARCH ON
INFLUENCEABILITY SEX DIFFERENCES

Several recent reviews of the social influence literature have addressed the question of whether experimental research has found women to be more easily influenced than men. Maccoby and Jacklin's (1974) review, as well as Eagly's (1978) more extensive review both employ the "voting method" of analysis, which tallies the number of studies reporting statistically significant sex differences (in each direction) as well as the number reporting no difference. The major finding of both analyses was that the majority of studies reported no significant sex differences. Among the minority that reported significant differences, however, almost all differences were in the direction of greater female than male influenceability.

Before the advent of statistical methods for integrating research findings, the fact that most studies failed to find significant sex differences would have led to the conclusion that there is no overall difference. However, statistical methods of research integration, often termed *meta-analysis* (Glass, McGaw, & Smith, 1981), may lead to slightly different conclusions concerning the sex difference (Cooper & Rosenthal, 1980). A meta-analysis aggregates the results of independent studies testing the same hypothesis, thereby providing a quantitative assessment of an effect over an entire body of research. Because many individual studies may have lacked adequate power to detect small differences, it is reasonable to base conclusions about the size and statistical significance of an effect on the evidence provided by an entire group of relevant studies.

Applying meta-analytic procedures to the social influence studies in Maccoby and Jacklin's (1974) sample, Cooper (1979) found that men were significantly less influenceable than women only for *group pressure conformity* studies, an experimental paradigm typified by the well-known Asch (1956) and Sherif (1935, 1936) research. In conformity studies, subjects are usually informed that other people hold a particular belief or attitude, which is discrepant from the subjects' own positions. In conformity studies involving group pressure, the influencing agents are other group members. These other members have surveillance over the subjects' responses to their influence induction; that is, these other members know (or appear to know) whether the subjects have conformed to their views.

Additional evidence for a sex difference in group pressure conformity studies was obtained by Eagly and Carli's (1981) meta-analysis, which was based on the considerably larger Eagly (1978) sample of studies. Yet, because of the larger sample, Eagly and Carli found that the sex difference was also significant for (a) conformity experiments not involving group pressure and (b) persuasion experiments, in which a communicator presented arguments supporting a position on an issue. However, in a meta-analytic framework, the statistical significance of an effect should not be given a great deal of emphasis, as even a very small difference may attain significance when based on a large sample of studies.

To evaluate the importance and practical significance of the sex difference, Eagly and Carli (1981) examined its magnitude. Magnitude was assessed in terms of its *effect size*, a standardized score defined as the difference between the means of male and female groups divided by the within-group standard deviation assumed to be common to the two populations (Cohen, 1977). Eagly and Carli reported an effect size of between .16 and .26, based on the total 148 experiments included in their sample. According to the rough guideline that .20 represents a small effect size and .50 represents an effect of moderate magnitude (Cohen, 1977), the sex difference in influenceability obtained in the reviewed research is fairly small. The small magnitude of this sex difference is also evident from the similarity in the responses of male and female subjects: The percentage of the male and female response distributions that was nonoverlapping was estimated to be between 12% and 19%. In terms of correlational statistics, this sex difference corresponds to a point-biserial correlation between sex and influenceability that is between .08 and .13. In other words, sex accounts for only about 1% of the variability in how easily people are influenced. Becker's (in press) reanalysis of Eagly and Carli's (1981) data has further confirmed the small size of the sex difference.

All reviewers of sex differences in influenceability have suggested that this difference is larger for group pressure conformity experiments than for other types of social influence experiments. Eagly and Carli's (1981) meta-analysis found an effect of between .23 and .32 for the group pressure experiments. Although relatively small, this effect was significantly larger than that obtained for persuasion studies and nonsignificantly larger than that obtained for other conformity experiments, which did not involve group pressure or surveillance by an influencing agent.[1]

Social influence laboratory paradigms other than persuasion and conformity have not been thoroughly examined for sex differences. Yet it should be noted that Eagly (1978) found little evidence of female influenceability in a variety of these paradigms (e.g., suggestibility, obedience, social learning and conditioning). In general, then, evidence that women are more influenceable is clearest for one social setting—that of group pressure conformity experiments (see also Becker, in press). Even in this context, the sex difference is quite small. In view of the small size of this difference and the fact that the majority of social influence studies have not obtained significant differences, it is striking that psychologists have commonly believed that the sex difference in influenceability is large. Psychologists (e.g., Krech, Crutchfield, & Ballachey, 1962; Nord, 1969) typically have described the sex difference in influenceability as ''large, strong, clear,'' and ''well established'' and have claimed that it is ''general'' and ''consistent.'' For example, Freedman, Carlsmith, and Sears stated in their 1970 social psychology textbook that ''The most consistent and strongest factor

[1]Comparisons involving the other conformity studies must be interpreted cautiously because relatively few of these studies were available for the meta-analysis and, as a consequence, the effect size estimate was less reliable for studies of this type.

that differentiates people in the amount they conform is their sex. Women conform more than men . . . This difference between men and women has been
found in virtually every study in which both sexes participated'' (p. 239). These
statements about sex differences are typical of those included in textbooks and
reviews of social influence research that were published prior to the recent
review articles on sex differences in influenceability.

If Freedman, Carlsmith, and Sears meant that this "difference" was statistically significant, their statement about "virtually every study" is grossly in
error: Eagly and Carli (1981) found that only 24% of the studies in their sample
obtained a statistically significant difference in the female direction. Further, a
mean effect of between .16 and .26 cannot be described as a strong factor
differentiating men and women. It seems, then, that psychologists have exaggerated the size and consistency of the sex difference shown by these laboratory
findings.

EXPLANATIONS FOR SEX DIFFERENCES IN INFLUENCEABILITY

The possible origins of the sex difference in influenceability have been explored
from several perspectives. We review the explanations typically offered by psychologists, which have generally been tested in laboratory settings. Whether
such research can be generalized to the full range of social settings, is, however,
an open question. Laboratory experimental findings, though informative, may be
valid only in the social context that researchers have provided in their laboratories. A comprehensive explanation of the sex difference in influenceability
would reflect the variety of settings in which men and women commonly interact
(see Eagly, in press). Therefore, we also consider a causal factor, the relative
status of men and women, which is especially important in natural settings,
where male and female roles often differ in status.

One major limitation of many explanations is that they have difficulty accounting for the variation in the magnitude of the sex difference according to the
type of laboratory setting. The explanations psychologists have favored have
been tailored to explain a difference that they presumed to be consistent across
social influence settings. Until recently, group pressure conformity experiments
were not identified as an especially likely site for the sex difference. Therefore,
most explanations have not been specifically examined for their relevance to this
setting.

Submissiveness of the Female Role and Related Explanations

Traditionally, the sex difference in influenceability was attributed to the "submissiveness of the female role." According to this explanation, women's gender
role prescribes that females should yield to social influence. Females were

thought to learn this definition of their role as a product of socialization pressures that apply differentially to boys and girls. Middlebrook's (1974) social psychology textbook provided a typical statement of this line of reasoning: "The feminine role in our society has traditionally emphasized passivity and yielding so that when little girls are socialized into their roles, they may be trained to yield" (p. 190).

The female submissiveness idea can be viewed as one of several possible explanations based on attributes that are thought to be linked to gender. Depending on one's theoretical orientation, such attributes are either aspects of gender roles or aspects of sex-typed personality traits. These interpretations are popularly conceptualized in terms of a two-dimensional model emphasizing agentic and communal qualities. Following Bakan's (1966) discussion of this distinction, agentic qualities are manifested by self-assertion, self-expansion, and the urge to master, whereas communal qualities are manifested by selflessness, concern with others, and a desire to be at one with others. Accordingly, men are assumed to be oriented toward agentic (also called task-oriented or instrumental) concerns, and women toward communal (also called social-emotional or expressive) concerns (e.g., Bakan, 1966; Block, 1973; Ruble & Ruble, 1982). This agentic vs. communal distinction is an important aspect of the measures of gender-differentiating traits that contrast a femininity dimension—which represents mainly qualities of nurturance, warmth, and expressiveness—with a masculinity dimension—which represents mainly qualities of dominance, mastery, and task competence (Bem, 1974; Spence & Helmreich, 1978).

In studies of sex stereotypes (e.g., Broverman et al., 1972) and sex-typed vs. androgynous personalities (e.g., Bem, 1975; Spence & Helmreich, 1978), those attributes that are most directly related to social influence (e.g., aggressive, independent, dominant) are components of the agentic, or "masculine," dimension of gender. Such research suggests that resistance to influence, as well as the ability to lead, are important aspects of agency. From this viewpoint, then, the claim that female submissiveness accounts for the sex difference in influenceability implies that women are deficient in self-assertion and the urge to master.

In contrast to this traditional view of social influence's close link to agentic concerns, Eagly (1978) has recently suggested that female influenceability, because it is strongest in group pressure settings, may be a product of women's communal concerns—their commitment to preserving social harmony and enhancing positive feelings among group members. Agreeing with other group members can be a way of demonstrating social support and expressing concern with the well-being of others, as suggested by the fact that agreement is classified as a positive social–emotional act in Bales's (1950) system for content-analyzing small group interaction. This explanation links women's receptivity to influence to their expressive specialization and superior interpersonal competence.

The female submissiveness explanation, then, focuses on only one aspect of the way in which gender may affect social influence. It locates the causal factor

in the female gender role and personality and neglects the male role and personality. Explanations focusing on the male gender role and personality (e.g., on
males' agentic qualities, or on their possible deficiency in interpersonal or expressive skills) have received little attention. Further, the female submissiveness
idea is more closely allied with the agentic aspects of gender specialization than
with the communal aspects. As Hansson, Allen, and Jones (1980) have argued,
both agency and communion may be relevant to interpreting sex differences
obtained in conformity studies, and Buss (1981) has shown that dominance
behaviors can express both agentic and communal concerns. A more balanced
analysis would thus consider how both of these aspects of gender specialization
are related to the sex difference.

Sex as a Status Variable

According to another type of explanation for the influenceability sex difference,
sex functions as a status variable (see Eagly, 1983). Women's greater influenceability is thought to stem from their lower status relative to men. Of course,
women's roles have changed somewhat over the last decade, as indicated by
women's increased participation in the labor force. Yet such changes have not
counteracted status differences between men and women in occupational settings
(L. K. Brown, 1979), and it is doubtful that status differences have been overcome in other natural settings.

    Agreeing with other people is linked with status because higher status people
are generally perceived as having the right to make demands of those of lower
status, and they are more effective in inducing compliance (Schopler, 1965).
Women, as persons of lower status, may thus be more conforming and persuasible than men.

    A more subtle version of the status argument suggests that the status dif-
ference that exists between men and women in our society may engender behavioral sex differences in influenceability even in settings in which men and women
occupy exactly the same social roles. As Unger (1976, 1978) has argued, many
behavioral differences between men and women may be a function of the general
association between maleness and high status in our society. From a sociological
perspective, these behavioral sex differences arise from the tendency for sex to
function as a status cue (Berger, Rosenholtz, & Zelditch, 1980). Status cues lead
people to have expectations about each other's behavior so that people who have
characteristics ordinarily associated with higher status in our society (e.g., maleness) are assumed to be more competent and authoritative (Driskell & Webster,
in press; Zeller & Warnecke, 1973). Because of the impact that these expectations have on social interaction, people who have characteristics that are not
highly evaluated in the society then tend to comply with those who have characteristics associated with higher status.

Female Superiority in Verbal Ability

A few psychologists (e.g., McGuire, 1969) have suggested that the tendency for women to yield more readily to influence may be a product of their superior verbal ability. Sex differences in verbal ability have been established, especially in the teenage and early college-age populations heavily represented as subjects in psychological experiments. Given that attitude change ordinarily increases with accurate comprehension of the content of persuasive messages (e.g., Eagly, 1974; Eagly & Warren, 1976), it seems plausible that verbal ability, which increases comprehension, may lead to heightened opinion change.

Individual differences in verbal ability, however, are only relevant for accepting influence inductions that are relatively difficult to comprehend. In persuasion research, communications often do contain complex argumentation, but in conformity studies, the positions taken by communicators are simply conveyed and are not supported by argumentation. Therefore, the comprehension explanation of the sex difference in influenceability predicts larger sex differences in the female direction for persuasion research than conformity research. The tendency for the sex difference to be smaller in persuasion than in group pressure conformity experiments, then, argues against verbal ability as a mediator of the influenceability sex difference. In addition, direct tests of this link between males' and females' comprehension of persuasive messages and the resulting opinion change (e.g., Eagly, 1974) have failed to substantiate this interpretation of the influenceability sex difference.

Biased Selection of Stimulus Materials for Experiments

In the late 1970's when many psychologists began to question traditional assumptions about men and women, a number of writers suggested that the sex difference demonstrated by conformity and persuasion experiments might be an artifact of biased stimulus materials. This explanation has appeared in several social psychology textbooks (e.g., Baron & Byrne, 1977; Jones, Hendrick, & Epstein, 1979). According to this argument, researchers have tended to choose influence inductions more compatible with men's expertise and interests than with women's. Persuasion and conformity research have repeatedly demonstrated that individuals are more readily influenced to the extent that they lack information about a topic or regard it as trivial and unimportant (e.g., Allen, 1965; Endler, Wiesenthal, Coward, Edwards, & Geller, 1975; McGuire & Papageorgis, 1961; Miller, 1965; Rhine & Severance, 1970). Women subjects supposedly lack information and interest concerning the topics used in experiments and are therefore easily influenced.

The popularity of explanations based on biased content is largely due to Sistrunk and McDavid's (1971) conformity research. They presented subjects with questionnaire items pretested to be masculine, feminine, or neutral, according to whether men, women, or neither were judged more interested and expert. When subjects received normative opinions deviating from their own opinions, women were, in general, more conforming than men on masculine items, and men were more conforming than women on feminine items; on neutral items there was no sex difference. These findings, as well as subsequent replications (e.g., Goldberg, 1974, 1975), suggest that the content of influence inductions can strongly affect the magnitude and direction of sex differences in influenceability.

The relation between content and influence obtained in these studies does not establish that a bias in favor of masculine content underlies sex difference findings in the literature. In influenceability research, masculine content may have been no more common than feminine content and may not have been overrepresented, compared with natural settings. Even if masculine content has been overrepresented, the variations between studies in content sex-typing may not have been nearly so large as the experimental manipulations devised by Sistrunk and McDavid and, moreover, they may not have been strong enough to have a discernible effect on the outcome of the studies.

In their meta-analysis of sex differences reported in social influence experiments, Eagly and Carli (1981) directly tested the hypothesis that content of influence inductions has been biased in the masculine direction. For each of the topics employed in the persuasion experiments in their sample, Eagly and Carli obtained the subjects' judgments of how interested and how knowledgeable they considered themselves.[2] These judgments provided no evidence that masculine stimulus materials were more common than feminine. In fact, females claimed to be significantly more interested in the topics of the persuasion studies than were males, although the mean difference in males' and females' ratings was very small. No sex difference was obtained on the ratings of knowledge. Thus, the idea that researchers have selected a larger proportion of male-oriented topics than is characteristic of the natural environment was not supported.[3]

Eagly and Carli's (1981) findings on self-reported interest and knowledge, of course, must be interpreted cautiously in view of the possible conservatism of their test of biased topic selection. No doubt their subjects' ratings differed from

[2]Content of influence inductions was examined solely for persuasion studies because they generally included a statement describing the topic of each message employed. In contrast, conformity studies typically utilized a large number of items, and investigators generally reported only a few sample items. Therefore, for the conformity literature, it was not possible to determine whether the overall content of influence inductions was sex-typed.

[3]Yet on a correlational basis, there was a tendency for masculine topics to be associated with greater female persuasibility. Thus, consistent with Sistrunk and McDavid's (1971) findings, biased content of influence inductions may be a source of artifact in particular experiments; for example, the choice of a masculine topic such as military service or football would increase the chances of obtaining female influenceability. Yet the absence of evidence for an overall masculine content bias argues against biased content as the explanation for greater influenceability among women in the research literature as a whole.

ratings that might have been obtained from the subjects who served in the original persuasion experiments. Nevertheless, the lack of support for a masculine bias in stimulus materials is sobering in view of the ease with which psychologists have accepted the idea in recent years.

Bias in Favor of Sex Differences Flattering to Researchers' Own Sex

Another artifactual cause for the influenceability sex difference was suggested by Eagly and Carli (1981). They argued that researchers might be biased in favor of obtaining or reporting sex differences that were flattering or enhancing to persons of the researcher's own sex. In support of this idea, Eagly and Carli found that 79% of the authors in their sample were male, and male authors obtained larger sex differences in the female direction. For studies authored by women, there was no sex difference. That these results may reveal a tendency to obtain or report flattering sex difference findings was further substantiated by Eagly and Carli's reanalysis of the findings of a meta-analytic review of sex differences in decoding nonverbal cues (Hall, 1978). Hall's review had established that women are more accurate at decoding nonverbal cues than are men. The reanalysis showed that female authorship was associated with larger sex differences, meaning poorer performance by men. In view of findings showing that not being easily influenced and sensitivity to others are both favorably evaluated (Anderson, 1968; Broverman et al., 1972), it appears that, at least for social behavior of these two types, researchers portray their own sex more favorably than the opposite sex.

The relations that have been obtained between the sex of researchers and the sex difference outcomes of their experiments raise questions about the mechanisms by which researchers' gender may affect their experiments. It is possible that male and female researchers behave differently in designing experiments, implementing experimental designs, or reporting sex difference findings. Eagly and Carli (1981) favored the idea that females, when compared with males, may have more often reported a finding of no difference in influenceability to counter a popular negative stereotype about women. To guard against such selectivity, we recommend that researchers report all sex difference findings they obtain— regardless of whether these findings are statistically significant or seem interesting, and, above all, regardless of whether these findings are congenial to the researchers' beliefs about sex differences.

It should also be noted that the association between the sex of researchers and their findings does not provide a complete explanation for the sex difference that has been obtained in influenceability experiments. Eagly and Carli (1981) estimated that, had men and women been equally represented as social influence researchers, the overall influenceability sex difference would have been between .11 and .18 in effect size terms. A sex difference of this magnitude is indeed small, but it would likely prove significant when aggregated across a relatively large sample of experiments.

Summary of Explanations for the Sex Difference

There are five types of explanations that have been offered for the influenceability sex difference. These explanations are based on (a) the conceptualization of gender in terms of differences in agentic or communal orientation; (b) the assumption that sex functions as a status variable; (c) the idea that women have superior verbal ability; (d) the assumption that the stimulus materials utilized in the research have been biased toward masculine interests; and (e) the assumption that researchers, the majority of whom are male, have tended to portray their own sex more favorably than the opposite sex. Research findings have not favored either the verbal ability explanation or the one based on biased stimulus materials. The remaining explanations provide plausible accounts of the sex difference, and further research is needed to test their validity.

RECENT RESEARCH ON SEX DIFFERENCES IN GROUP PRESSURE CONFORMITY EXPERIMENTS

As discussed earlier, one gender-based explanation for the sex difference that highlights women's communal orientation is that women are more concerned than men about the quality of interpersonal relations in the groups in which they participate (Eagly, 1978). Presumably, conformity serves the social function of fostering group cohesiveness and enhancing amicability among group members. We believe that research testing this interpersonal interpretation is worthwhile because past research has suggested that sex differences were larger in group pressure settings. We have, then, endeavored to find out if women conform more than men in group settings because they take greater responsibility for establishing and maintaining positive interpersonal bonds.

As noted above, concern for other people has been identified as an aspect of femininity, both in psychologists' theories about gender and in stereotypic beliefs about how the sexes differ. Theorists have suggested that a feminine orientation emphasizes communal qualities implying concern for the welfare of other people. In addition, studies of sex stereotypes have shown that perceivers believe that women are nurturant, warm, and sensitive to others (e.g., Broverman et al., 1972; Williams & Bennett, 1975).

Empirical support for the idea that women manifest interpersonal concern can be found in several domains. For example, Hoffman's (1977) review of sex differences in empathy suggested that females are more empathic than males, and Hall's (1978, 1980) meta-analyses found females more skilled at both sending and receiving nonverbal messages.

Group process studies examining the content of interaction have generally classified a higher proportion of the acts performed by females than those performed by males as social-emotional behaviors (Anderson & Blanchard, 1982; Piliavin & Martin, 1978; Strodtbeck & Mann, 1956). Also, both women's coalition behavior (Bond & Vinacke, 1961; Senn, 1967; Uesugi & Vinacke, 1963; Vinacke, 1959) and their reward-allocation behavior in equity experiments (Kahn, Lamm, Krulewitz, & O'Leary, 1980; Leventhal & Lane, 1970) have been described as more oriented toward the maintenance of harmonious interactions than have men's behaviors. Finally, female bargaining behavior has been regarded as more oriented to the social attributes of other players than is male behavior (Bedell & Sistrunk, 1973; Kahn, Hottes, & Davis, 1971; Rubin & Brown, 1975).

Eagly, Wood, and Fishbaugh (1981) Conformity Experiment

This experiment explored the interpersonal concern explanation of the sex difference commonly obtained in group pressure experiments. If this explanation is correct, then women's greater conformity should be limited to circumstances in which group members believe that their opinions are under the surveillance of other members. Only with surveillance could conformity have its presumed positive impact on interpersonal relations.

In this experiment, some subjects believed that their opinions were under other members' surveillance, and other subjects believed that they were not under surveillance. Eliminating surveillance was expected to eliminate any sex difference. Further, the assumption that women are concerned about interpersonal relations implied that a sex difference obtained with surveillance was due to women's increased conformity. If men were not particularly concerned about the impact of their behavior on the quality of social relations, they should be little affected by other members' surveillance over their opinions. It was thus predicted that surveillance would increase females' conformity but have no impact on males' conformity.

Evidence partially consistent with this prediction was reported in a conformity experiment by Newton and Schulman (1977), which incorporated a surveillance manipulation. In their experiment, for one of two types of stimulus materials, greater conformity by females than males was obtained only when subjects' opinions were under surveillance. This sex difference was accounted for largely by females' greater conformity with surveillance than without it, although it was also a product of males' lesser conformity when under surveillance. Yet these findings were weakened by the elimination of 40% of the subjects for suspicion of deception and other difficulties.

In the Eagly, Wood, and Fishbaugh (1981) experiment, an initial measure of subjects' opinions on various campus issues was obtained. Subjects then reported in groups of two males and two females to a study that was ostensibly concerned with impression formation in groups. Subjects first participated in a short group discussion, which was designed to build a feeling of identification with their group. If the sex difference is based on women's interpersonal orientation, it should be manifested primarily in circumstances such as these, which engage concern about successful group process.

Subsequent interaction took place with the subjects seated in individual cubicles. For each of four issues, subjects (a) read the opinions supposedly indicated by the other three group members; (b) gave their impressions of these other group members by rating the other members' knowledgeability and involvement; and (c) indicated their own opinions on the issue. The opinions attributed to the other group members were constructed to disagree with subjects' initial opinions on three out of the four issues.

To convince subjects in the surveillance condition that the other group members would know how they had responded, subjects' names appeared on the forms on which they indicated their opinions, and these forms were (ostensibly) distributed to the rest of the group. In the no-surveillance condition, subjects were led to believe that other members would not know how they responded. In this condition, subjects' opinion forms were not labeled with their names, and the completed forms were not distributed to other group members.

The results of the experiment were consistent with the hypothesis that women would conform more than men only if members' opinions were under each other's surveillance, but the effect of surveillance on the responses of each sex was not as predicted. As shown in Table 8.1, women conformed more than men when subjects believed that their opinions were under the surveillance of other

TABLE 8.1
Mean Opinion Conformity of Males
and Females during Group Interaction
(Eagly, Wood & Fishbaugh, 1981)

Surveillance of Opinions	Sex of Group Members	
	Male	Female
Surveillance	6.92_a	8.51_b
No surveillance	8.12_b	8.55_b

Note. Cell ns = 35–38. Means are adjusted postopinion scores on a 15-point scale on which higher numbers indicate greater agreement with the other group members. Subscripts represent the results of a Newman-Keuls analysis. Means without at least one common subscript differ from each other at the .05 level of significance.

group members, $F(1, 141) = 9.21, p < .01$, and there was no sex difference in the no-surveillance condition $(F < 1)$. The Sex X Surveillance interaction approached significance, $F(1, 141) = 3.31, p = .07$.

The surprising aspect of these findings is that the amount women conformed was unaffected by whether the other members of the group had access to subjects' opinions. As shown by the Newman-Keuls analysis in Table 8.1, the effect of surveillance was to lessen men's conformity rather than to increase women's conformity. Men's conformity with surveillance was significantly less than women's conformity with surveillance, and significantly less than men's or women's conformity without surveillance.[4]

These conformity sex differences are not readily interpreted in terms of women's attention to the quality of interpersonal relations. Because men decreased their conformity under surveillance and women did not manifest the expected increase in conformity, the findings suggest that a nonconforming tendency on the part of males might sometimes underlie sex differences in conformity. The basis for such an effect may be norms governing the male gender role that specify that men should remain independent and not agree very closely with other members. Certainly the inclusion of attributes such as *independent* and *not easily influenced* in the cluster of agentic traits stereotypically attributed to men (Broverman et al., 1972) suggests that deviation from others' opinions may be normatively prescribed for men in our society.[5]

That the origin of male nonconformity may be social norms about how men ought to behave in groups is suggested by the sensitivity of males' opinions to the surveillance manipulation. The finding that men were nonconforming only under surveillance shows that men's greater nonconformity depended on having an audience (in this case, other group members). This finding is not adequately explained by the assumption that independence functions as a masculine personality trait, because a general trait should be manifested even without an audience. The fact that individual differences in masculinity or femininity (Spence & Helmreich, 1978) did not correlate significantly with conformity for men or

---

[4]This study also explored whether the opinions males and females expressed during the group interaction reflected their genuine beliefs. To examine this issue, all subjects gave their opinions twice after receiving the other members' opinions: Once (with or without surveillance) as a part of the exchange of opinions between group members and again after this interaction had been terminated. Although conformity was less after the interaction than during it, males and females were similar in the extent to which they maintained their changed opinions after the interaction.

[5]Although the surveillance manipulation only affected men's behavior in this experiment, Eagly and Chrvala (in press) subsequently found that older (19 years and up) female subjects conformed more with surveillance than without it, whereas surveillance did not significantly affect males' conformity or the conformity of younger (under 19 years) subjects. Following a status interpretation of these findings, surveillance would be expected to affect the behavior of men and other high status individuals only under circumstances in which nonconformity is perceived to result in effective leadership. Under circumstances that accentuate the positive consequences of conformity for low status individuals, surveillance would be expected to affect the behavior of women.

women is also unfavorable to a personality interpretation. A social role interpretation suggests that males' independence was limited to the surveillance condition because only with surveillance could nonconformity be perceived to win social approval for compliance with the normative pressure to be independent. To understand this aspect of male behavior more fully, it is helpful to explore in more detail the social pressures that may guide and shape such a public self-presentation. We begin by analyzing the social functions of nonconformity in small groups.

The extensive research literature on conformity suggests that a key feature of nonconforming behavior is that it attracts attention (Ridgeway, 1978, 1981). As shown, for example, by Schachter's (1951) research on opinion deviation, more communication is directed to a nonconforming group member than to other members. The consequences of being the center of attention because of one's deviant opinions can be favorable or unfavorable. The possible negative outcomes, illustrated by Schachter's research, include being rejected and labeled a person whose views are unworthy of being given serious consideration. The potential gains, illustrated by Moscovici's (1976, 1980) research, include exerting effective leadership by convincing the other group members that one's own view is superior to theirs.

The fact that men who gave their opinions under surveillance were especially likely to deviate from the group consensus may reflect that, for men, successful influence is a more probable outcome of nonconformity than is rejection by the other group members. Empirical research provides some support for such sex differences in the consequences of nonconformity. Research stemming from the work of Hollander (1960, 1964) has demonstrated that, in general, male nonconformity is more likely to result in effective influence than female nonconformity and less likely to result in rejection, especially in the context of a male group (Ridgeway & Jacobson, 1977). Hollander's notion of "idiosyncrasy credit," which suggests that successful influence must be preceded by initial conformity to the norms of the group, seems to apply to females who violate group norms in an otherwise all-male group but not to members of groups with other sex compositions (Ridgeway, 1981; Ridgeway & Jacobson, 1977; Wahrman & Pugh, 1972, 1974).

A promising interpretation of these sex differences in the consequences of nonconformity flows from the assumption, introduced earlier in this chapter, that sex functions as a status cue in newly formed groups (Berger, Fisek, Norman, & Zelditch, 1977; Berger, Rosenholtz, & Zelditch, 1980; Lockheed & Hall, 1976; Meeker & Weitzel-O'Neill, 1977). According to the status argument, people typically do not enter groups on an equal footing but enter identified to each other in terms of visible attributes that convey information about social status. Sex informs group members about status because, in general, men in our society have been accorded higher status than women.

When individuals enter a group, their interaction is affected by perceived status because status cues lead people to have expectations about each other's performance. In particular, higher status people are expected to contribute more effectively to the group's task and consequently are given—and take—more opportunities to participate. Because they are assumed to be competent, their comments are taken seriously. Therefore, they have more latitude for nonconformity without facing rejection by the other group members. Lower status people who deviate from the group consensus face greater risk of rejection because they are not assumed to be competent.

This argument suggests that it is due to men's higher status that their nonconformity results in successful influence. Lacking status, women must proceed more cautiously and are not as free as men to move quickly away from a group consensus.

This interpretation, then, emphasizes contemporaneous social pressures stemming from status-based expectancies. Such an approach is useful for analyzing men's and women's interactions in natural settings because status and gender are closely related in most organizations (see Eagly, 1983). The relation between gender and status in natural settings should have a strong impact on people's beliefs about sex differences in social influence, and, as we have already argued, these beliefs then affect social interaction. In the next section, we describe research that examines whether perceivers' beliefs about such sex differences reflect the distribution of men and women into social roles varying in status.

STEREOTYPES ABOUT SEX DIFFERENCES IN INFLUENCEABILITY

The research we describe in this section examines how gender and status affect perceptions of how easily people are influenced. The link between gender and status in natural settings may explain why sex differences are perceived in a number of traits closely related to social influence (Broverman et al., 1972; Williams & Bennett, 1975), even though psychological research has suggested that the influenceability sex difference is quite small.

This explanation for the sex difference implies that perceived differences in men's and women's influence may contain a "kernel of truth," as women are most commonly observed in low status roles that give them little authority. In contrast, previous explanations for the establishment and maintenance of beliefs about sex differences have focused on factors other than those that contribute to the validity of stereotypic beliefs. For example, according to psychodynamic analyses, stereotypic beliefs serve the psychic needs of the perceiver. Stereotypes that derive from unconscious needs and drives are unlikely to accurately portray the stereotyped group. One example of this kind of defensively motivated perception may be a belief in a just world, in which the relatively disadvantaged are perceived to deserve their plight (Lerner, Miller, & Holmes, 1976).

Other analyses suggest that stereotypes are not defensively oriented, but are a consequence of normal cognitive functioning (Hamilton, 1979). Stereotyping, or categorizing people into social groups, is thought to be little more than a way of simplifying the person perception process. In order to reduce the complexity of social information, perceivers group people into categories according to similarities in important features (e.g., sex, race, personality type). If the resulting categories are best described in terms of knowledge structures such as implicit personality theories (Ashmore & Del Boca, 1979), schemata (Hamilton, 1979), and prototypes (Cantor & Mischel, 1979), it is likely that stereotypes have specific effects on the future processing of information concerning the stereotyped group. For example, stereotypes appear to affect the encoding, interpretation, retention, and retrieval of information in ways that maintain the original beliefs (Hamilton, 1979).

The cognitive processes by which stereotypes are initially established have received less attention. Hamilton and Gifford (1976) provide suggestive evidence that perceived relations between members of particular groups and personality dispositions may not be based on any true association between the two. Rather, minority group members are perceived to have characteristics with low probability of occurence merely because the group members and characteristic are both rare. To the extent such an "illusory correlation" provides the foundation for differential perceptions of social groups, stereotypes can develop and flourish in the face of no real evidence for group differences.

However, the idea that people's beliefs about gender do not correspond to reality is unlikely to be correct. Perceivers are not likely to be profoundly wrong because everyday life offers them so many opportunities to obtain information about sex differences. Of course, inaccurate information concerning men and women may be derived from a variety of sources, such as the mass media (Tuchman, Daniels, & Benét, 1978) and other socializing agents. For example, bias on the part of parents and teachers is suggested by the finding that they describe boys and girls as differing in a wide variety of social behaviors, whereas observations of children at play have provided evidence for sex differences in only a small subset of these behaviors (Lott, 1978). Yet perceivers have ample opportunity to correct biased information about gender through information gleaned from their direct encounters with men and women, and from their own past histories as men or women. In fact, research has suggested that stereotypes are more accurate to the extent that people are in frequent contact with members of the stereotyped group (Triandis & Vasilliou, 1967). From this perspective, it is implausible that beliefs about gender fail to represent the main contours of women's and men's actual characteristics.

One explanation for gender stereotypes about social influence that assumes that they are based on reality is, as we have already noted, that men are more likely than women to have high status roles. Given the association between status and influence, women (and lower status persons more generally) may be constrained to accept the advice of others, whereas men (and higher status persons) may be freer to accept or reject influence attempts.

This analysis of gender stereotypes about social influence is one form of the more general idea that the stereotypes of social groups are products of the perceived distribution of group members into roles (see also Eagly & Steffen, 1984). Although our analysis focuses only on the status of men's and women's roles, other aspects of these roles may account for perceived sex differences in social behaviors other than influence. For example, Kiesler (1975) has argued that people tend to evaluate an individual woman's achievements less favorably than an individual man's, even when their products are objectively equal, because men outnumber women as successful achievers in many occupations. Stereotypes about social attributes such as race, ethnicity, and age may also be affected by perceived group differences in the distribution of people into roles. In particular, it has been argued that beliefs about racial differences stem from an inferred difference in social class, as blacks are relatively more concentrated in lower socio-economic groups than are whites in our society (Feldman, 1972; Smedley & Bayton, 1978; Triandis, 1977).

Eagly and Wood's (1982) Stereotype Research

To test our distributional theory of gender stereotypes, we carried out three studies exploring whether sex differences in status underlie perceptions of sex differences in social influence. In these studies, each subject was presented with a written scenario of two people interacting at work. In the scenarios, one employee (the communicator) attempted to influence another employee (the recipient) on an isue of company policy. The communicator was described as feeling strongly about the issue and explaining his or her reasons to a recipient who did not favor this type of policy. Subjects judged the success of the influence attempt. In order to provide an internal replication of the design, half of the scenarios were set in a bank and half in a supermarket.

In the first experiment, some subjects were given information about the sex of the employees (conveyed through appropriate sex-typed names), without any more specific information about status. It was expected that (a) a male communicator trying to persuade a female recipient would be perceived as a communicator with higher status than the recipient; and (b) a female communicator trying to persuade a male recipient would be perceived as a communicator with lower status than the recipient. These inferences about relative status were expected to lead these subjects to conclude that a male communicator would be more successful in influencing a female recipient than a female communicator would be in influencing a male recipient.

Other subjects in this study were given highly valid information about status, conveyed by the job titles of the communicator and recipient, in addition to the information about sex (see the design in Table 8.2). High status jobs were designated by bank vice president or supermarket manager and low status jobs by bank teller or supermarket cashier. With the addition of job titles, subjects were not expected to infer status from gender, nor were gender cues expected to affect their judgments about the success of the influence attempts. Instead, subjects were expected to consider successful influence a more likely outcome the higher was the status of the communicator's job and the lower was the status of the recipient's job.

Each scenario concluded by having the communicator ask the recipient whether he or she "goes along with" the policy recommended by the communicator. Subjects predicted the recipient's response. Subjects' predictions were thought to depend on whether the recipient's response to influence was public or private. Perceptions of two public responses were examined—behavioral compliance with the communicator's recommendation and oral agreement in the communicator's presence. It seemed likely that status differences in a communicator's favor would legitimize demands for subordinates to show public yielding to influence. Perception of recipients' private agreement with the communicator was expected to be less strongly affected by status, because the private change of recipients' opinions is not accessible to communicators. For these reasons, the hypotheses concerning gender and status were predicted to hold for behavioral compliance and oral agreement, but not for private agreement.

Eagly and Wood's (1982) results were generally consistent with the assumption that perceivers believe in gender differences in social influence because they believe that men and women differ in status. Subjects' inferences about sex

TABLE 8.2
Mean Likelihood of Recipient's Behavioral Compliance
(Eagly & Wood, 1982)

| | | Scenarios Including Job Titles | | | |
| | | Low-Status Communicator | | High-Status Communicator | |
Sex of Dyad Members	Scenarios Omitting Job Titles	Low-Status Recipient	High-Status Recipient	Low-Status Recipient	High-Status Recipient
Male communicator addressing female recipient	9.02	7.61	6.51	10.60	8.23
Female communicator addressing male recipient	7.44	7.51	5.64	11.08	7.76

Note. Higher numbers indicate greater compliance.

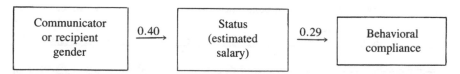

FIG. 8.1.   Results of structural analysis for conditions that omitted job titles in
Eagly and Wood's (1982) Experiment 1. (Path coefficients appended to the arrows
are significant beyond the .05 level.)

differences in status were documented by having them estimate the communicator's or recipient's salary. For the scenarios that omitted job titles, subjects
also gave their "best guess" concerning the communicator's or recipient's job
title. As anticipated, according to both of these measures, subjects inferred that
the men in the scenarios held higher status jobs than the women when job titles
were omitted.

The behavioral compliance findings for the scenarios omitting job titles are
presented in Table 8.2. Compliance was considered more likely when the communicator was male and the recipient was female than when the communicator
was female and the recipient was male, $F(1, 387) = 4.88, p < .05$. A structural
analysis was performed to explore further whether perceived compliance was
mediated by inferred status differences. This analysis examined the relations
between behavioral compliance and its hypothesized determinants, inferred status (estimated salary) and the gender of the communicator and the recipient.[6] As
shown in Figure 8.1, the significant prediction of behavioral compliance from
estimated salary indicated that higher communicator status was associated with
greater compliance to the communicator's demands and higher recipient status
was associated with less compliance. The significant path between estimated
salary and gender of the communicator or recipient indicated that males were
perceived to have higher status than females. A chi-square goodness-of-fit test
(Specht, 1975) indicated that the proposed causal model adequately represented
the relations in the obtained data, $\chi^2(1) = 1.23, p > .25$. These results are
consistent with the assumption that subjects inferred status on the basis of gender
and then predicted behavioral compliance on the basis of inferred status.

In contrast, for subjects who were given job titles as well as gender for the
communicator and recipient, job title status was employed in preference to

---

[6]The structural analysis employed partial correlations, calculated to remove the effects of the
manipulated variables. The analysis estimated the parameters of the causal model separately for the
status omitted and comparison conditions by first constructing multiple regression equations in which
behavioral compliance was predicted from salary estimates and the gender of the communicator or
recipient. Any predictor that failed to show at least a marginally significant ($p < .10$) relationship to
compliance was deleted from the equation. Each regression was recomputed with only its remaining
predictor, and the resulting beta weight was interpreted as a path coefficient (Kerlinger & Pedhazur,
1973).

gender as a basis for predicting behavioral compliance. As shown in Table 8.2, compliance was thought to be more likely when the communicator had high rather than low status, $F(1, 387) = 53.14$, $p < .001$, and when the recipient had low rather than high status, $F(1, 387) = 35.01$, $p < .001$.[7] In the structural analysis, gender was not a significant predictor of estimated salary or of compliance. In short, when both job title and gender cues were available, subjects relied on status in preference to gender when predicting behavior compliance.[8]

This experiment, then, reveals the perceived relations between gender, status, and social influence. The results are consistent with the interpretation that subjects' inferences about men's and women's status form the basis of their predictions about sex differences in behavioral compliance. Yet an ambiguity remains in these findings: The design, which confounded communicator gender and recipient gender, did not test whether gender of the communicator or gender of the recipient or both are critical in determining the amount the recipient is perceived to be influenced by the communicator.

To clarify this point, Eagly and Wood conducted a second experiment, in which the sex of the communicator and the sex of the recipient were varied orthogonally (with the result that same-sex as well as opposite-sex scenarios were utilized). This second experiment again found that, without job titles, a male communicator was perceived to induce significantly more behavioral compliance in a female recipient than a female communicator did in a male recipient. The experiment further revealed that the gender of both the communicator and recipient contributed (about equally) to this difference.

To further clarify the nature of the power the male communicator was perceived to have over the female recipient, a third experiment varied whether the communicator and recipient were employed by the same organization. A communicator whose authority is based on hierarchical status should induce behavioral compliance only in subordinates employed by the same organization, since the sanctions and resources controlled by the communicator should ordinarily have impact only within the same organizational hierarchy. In contrast, the influence of a communicator whose power derives from an attribute such as competence would not depend on having the recipient employed by the same

---

[7]Several additional significant effects were obtained on perceived compliance in the scenarios that included job titles: A Communicator Status X Recipient Status interaction reflected that the difference between the low and high status recipients was stronger when the communicator had high rather than low status. In addition, compliance was thought more likely in the supermarket than the bank, but, consistent with a Setting X Communicator Status interaction, this setting difference was significant with a low status communicator and nonsignificant with a higher status communicator.

[8]It is interesting to note, however, that research suggests that subjects' actual compliance is a function of the influencing agent's general status characteristics, such as sex and race, as well as their task-specific attributes, such as position in the organization (Webster & Driskell, 1978).

organization, and private agreement would be affected at least as strongly as behavioral compliance.

This experiment utilized scenarios with opposite-sex employees whose job titles were not indicated. Again, men were perceived to induce more behavioral compliance in women than women induce in men, and this effect was confined to those conditions in which the communicator and the recipient were employed by the same organization. Private agreement with the communicator's recommendation was not perceived to be affected by the sex of the people in the scenarios.

Perceptions of the recipient's oral agreement in the communicator's presence were not affected by gender or status in these experiments. It was predicted that effects on oral agreement would parallel the effects on behavioral compliance because both responses were public and subject to sanction by superiors. Indeed, subsidiary measures administered in the first experiment showed that subjects did believe that subordinates agreed with superiors because they feared negative consequences. However, our initial ideas failed to take account of subjects' apparent belief that status and kindness are linked. Thus, this more subtle theory of oral agreement, as revealed by our subsidiary measures, included the belief that people agree with lower status communicators in order to avoid hurting their feelings. The coexistence of this belief with the subjects' belief that sanctions control oral agreement evidently obscured any status-mediated effects of the gender of the communicator and recipient.

Implications for Understanding Gender Stereotypes

Two aspects of these findings deserve exploration in relation to the gender stereotype about influenceability: (a) the stereotypic sex difference was obtained on perceived behavioral compliance but not on other responses to influence, and (b) this perceived sex difference in behavioral compliance appeared to be mediated by status inferences. These findings suggest that stereotypic beliefs about behavioral compliance stem from an inferred sex difference in status. Yet it should be recognized that the scenarios were constructed so that the higher status person possessed a form of authority intrinsically linked to behavioral compliance. This high status person has formal authority and access to resources or, in Kelman's (1961) terms, had means control vis-á-vis the lower status person. Kelman has suggested that power of this type results in compliance rather than internalized opinion change, and our respondents evidently agreed. Yet gender may be perceived as linked to bases of power in addition to means control, and these other bases may have quite different implications for social influence.

If perceivers infer stereotypic gender differences in credibility or competence (Deaux & Emswiller, 1974; Miller & McReynolds, 1973), male communicators would be likely to be perceived as effective in eliciting female recipients' private agreement, in addition to their behavioral compliance. Inferences concerning gender differences in competence may be especially likely when people's high status provides them with access to information and training unavailable to those of lower status. Subjects were unlikely to make such an inference in the present research because the influence inductions we used concerned topics for which superiors and subordinates can be expected to have similar levels of expertise. Our research, then, provides a partial, yet informative view of the status inferences that underlie perceived sex differences in social influence.

The general idea that sex stereotypes derive from differences in the perceived distribution of males and females into social roles that vary in a number of features (including status), could provide an explanation of the content of stereotypes in domains other than influence as well. In particular, Eagly and Steffen (1984) recently demonstrated that the beliefs that women are communal and men are agentic stem from perceivers' observations that women are more likely than men to be homemakers and less likely to be employed in the paid work force.

Our social structural explanation of gender stereotyping, emphasizing the inference perceivers make from sex cues, is in harmony with certain other efforts to understand stereotyping as ordinary cognitive processing. In particular, it is compatible with an analysis of sex stereotypes as prior probabilities in a Bayesian analysis (Locksley, Borgida, Brekke, & Hepburn, 1980; Locksley, Hepburn, & Ortiz, 1982). Locksley and her colleagues found perceived sex differences in a target person's assertiveness only when the subjects did not have other information about the target's prior levels of assertiveness. In Bayesian terms, the prior probabilities of the behavior of men and women were revised on the basis of diagnostic information about assertiveness. In our research, information about job status functioned in this way as diagnostic information that caused the subjects to revise their estimates of behavioral compliance.

CONCLUSION

The research we have reviewed suggests that an adequate answer to the question of whether women are more readily influenced than men must encompass several considerations in addition to sex difference findings from laboratory experiments on conformity and persuasion. In fact, the first hint that our story would have such complexity was the contradiction that we encountered between the clear-cut stereotype that women are easily influenced and laboratory findings showing that the behavioral sex difference is quite small.

To account for the apparent paradox between stereotypic perceptions and behavior in laboratory settings, it is helpful to compare the social settings that have been represented in experimental research with the settings in which men and women interact in daily life. In most research, men and women are assigned exactly the same social role, that of subject in an experiment, yet within most organizations men and women are differently distributed into social roles. Men are relatively more concentrated in higher status positions whereas women are concentrated in lower status positions. These status differences result in behavioral sex differences in influence and influenceability.

People who are lower in a hierarchy go along with those who are higher in the hierarchy because, within defined limits, higher status people are perceived to have the right to make demands. The extent to which people who possess legitimate authority in fact obtain ready compliance from subordinates has been demonstrated in many contexts. When a status hierarchy is clear-cut, subordinates often agree to a wide range of requests, even when the requested behavior is potentially damaging to oneself (Orne & Evans, 1965), or to other people—as in Milgram's (1965, 1974) obedience research. Because men, on the average, hold higher status positions than do women, within most organizations men are more likely to possess the legitimate authority that results in power over others and resistance to demands by other persons.

Perceivers observe sex differences in the distribution of individuals into social roles varying in status, and, as a consequence, utilize sex as a general status cue in a variety of situations. Therefore, when superior and subordinate roles are not defined, inferred sex differences in status form the basis for perceivers' beliefs about sex differences in exerting and accepting influence. Perceivers infer a modest relation between sex and status, and on this basis conclude that women are somewhat more influenced by men than men are by women.

As noted above, the idea that sex functions as a status cue is congruent with the theory of status characteristics (Berger, Fisek et al., 1977; Berger, Rosenholtz et al., 1980). Within this tradition, it is maintained that sex functions as a *diffuse status characteristic*—an attribute that provides a basis for general evaluative reactions. Diffuse status characteristics (e.g., sex, age, race) carry information about one's general competence and value. Those at one level or "state" of such a characteristic are highly valued (e.g., males are evaluated favorably), whereas those at another level or "state" are less highly valued (e.g., females are less favorably evaluated).

Inferences made on the basis of diffuse status characteristics do not stem from information about people's current role relationships. Rather, they have their origin in individuals' past experiences in society. According to this theory, then, the inferences that people make on the basis of gender in any one context are a product of the meaning that gender actually has in the larger society.

Status characteristics such as sex affect social interaction in new situations. According to the Berger viewpoint, these effects on interaction occur because participants have expectations about their own and others' behavior, based on status characteristics. Individuals who have a favorable standing in terms of diffuse status characteristics are both given and take more opportunity to state their views and to exert leadership, are evaluated as performing better, are more often rewarded for their performances, and have more influence. People who have less favorable standing on the basis of diffuse status characteristics are not assumed to be especially competent and are given and take less opportunity to state their views and to lead. In this way, behavioral sex differences in influence-ability are created.

The impact of perceivers' expectations on actual social influence can be regarded as one particular version of the *self-fulfilling prophecy effect* (Jones, 1977; Rosenthal & Rubin, 1978). Darley and Fazio (1980) have argued that such expectancy confirmations arise out of a sequence of interpersonal events. Expec-tations about the appropriate behavior of men and women are generally shared by all participants in an interaction, and affect expectancies for one's own and others' behavior. Confirmation may thus arise out of a sequence of interactions in which participants (a) form expectancies based on their general experience with men and women; (b) interact with each other in a manner that is consistent with the perception of greater competence and authority in men than in women; and (c) consequently lead male and female participants to behave in a manner that maintains their original beliefs. Thus, behavior is elicited that objectively confirms perceivers' expectancies. Empirical demonstrations of the sequence of events by which self-fulfilling prophecy effects occur have focused on behavioral confirmation of stereotypes about sex (Skrypnek & Snyder, 1982; Zanna & Pack, 1975), physical attractiveness (Anderson & Bem, 1981; Snyder, Tanke, & Berscheid, 1977), and other attributes (Snyder & Swann, 1978).

The idea that expectancies about gender affect social interaction is consistent with the findings of laboratory group pressure experiments, in which males' and females' conformity is observed while group members are under each others' surveillance. In this context, men and women are assigned exactly the same social role—that of subject in an experiment. Men do not have higher status in terms of a formal role structure in these laboratory groups. Yet women are often found to be more conforming. Sex may function as a diffuse status characteristic in such groups because the sex-status correlation in our society establishes expec-tancies about one's own authority and competence relative to that of other group members. These expectancies then operate via the mechanisms suggested in the literature on expectancy confirmation to create behavioral sex differences in instrumental behaviors such as leadership and influenceability. Because a se-quence of interactions is evidently needed to induce behavioral confirmations, it is not surprising that the sex difference is obtained only with surveillance by other group members. Surveillance induces the perception of interdependence because subjects believe that the other group members are monitoring their reactions.

As Eagly (1983) recently argued, the sequence of interactions stemming from the perceived link between gender and status may be most likely to characterize interaction between members of newly formed groups, such as laboratory groups. The impact of sex as a diffuse status characteristic may not be strong enough to affect people's expectations in the presence of the more specific status characteristics often salient in other contexts, as job title and years of work experience are salient in organizational settings. Consistent with this reasoning, in Eagly and Wood's (1982) perceived influence experiments male and female behavior was thought to differ in the scenarios omitting job titles, because men were believed to have higher status, yet in the conditions in which men and women were assigned comparable job titles, they were believed to display the same amount of compliance.

According to our analysis, the "kernel of truth" underlying perceivers' beliefs that women are easily influenced is that in our society men tend to hold higher status positions than women and therefore possess more legitimate authority. This gender stereotype may then become a self-fulfilling prophecy that produces conforming behavior in situations not involving formal status differences between women and men. Further, the perceived relations between gender, status, and influenceability may be exaggerated, as stereotypes lead perceivers to process information in a way that confirms the original beliefs. Perceivers who believe that women are easier to influence than men may maintain this reality in part through biased processing of the information they glean from social interaction.

Perceivers may manifest, in addition, the fundamental attribution error (Ross, 1977) and thus incorrectly attribute to internal attributes—such as gender-based personality attributes—behaviors that are actually due to situational constraints. In particular, perceivers fail to make appropriate adjustments for the effects of the social roles that people play (Ross, Amabile, & Steinmetz, 1977). For example, women who hold jobs in which they assist others or perform services for others may be perceived as compliant because they are women or possess "feminine" personality traits.

Perceivers' focus on internal causes of behavior is compatible with the conventional psychological perspective that the main result of socialization is a set of personal dispositions or personality traits. From such a perspective, girls and boys are exposed to different socialization pressures (e.g., Barry, Bacon, & Child, 1957; Rosenkrantz, Vogel, Bee, Broverman, & Broverman, 1968) and learn to behave in ways that are consistent with the definition of gender in their society. Men and women, according to such an analysis, emerge as adults with different personalities—men with personalities in which agentic qualities are dominant, and women with personalities in which communal qualities are dominant. The behavioral differences between adult men and adult women are held to be a product of these differing personal characteristics. Further, adults are thought to choose roles that are consistent with these sex-typed personalities. Men, because of their agentic qualities, become primary family providers and choose careers demanding self-assertion and mastery. Women, because of their communal qualities, become primary nurturers of children and choose occupatoins that are oriented toward helping or serving others.

In contrast to these analyses of gender differences as a product of personality, the account we have offered of the origin of influenceability sex differences stresses social roles. Role theorists (e.g., Brim, 1960) have long maintained that socialization instills knowledge of a wide variety of behavioral modes. Socialization also imparts knowledge of what behaviors are appropriate in what settings; indeed, individuals continue to gain knowledge of this type every time they enter a new organizational setting. People regulate their actions on the basis of the perceived appropriateness of behaviors.

Our analysis of gender-relevant behavior suggests, however, that a theory based solely on perceived behavioral appropriateness is insufficient. As we have already argued, expectancies based on individuals' total experience in groups and organizations carry over to new settings and thereby tend to establish in these new settings the general pattern of behavioral differences that already exists in the society. A social psychological analysis of such self-fulfilling prophecy effects, then, augments the sociological analysis that is based on the differing distributions of men and women into hierarchical roles.

In recent years, other psychologists (e.g., C. W. Sherif, 1980; Spence & Helmreich, 1980) have also begun to question the view that behavioral sex differences arise primarily from personality or temperament differences between the sexes. Some reservations stem from the difficulties psychologists have encountered in obtaining consistent findings when predicting behavior on the basis of gender-differentiating personality traits, as assessed by scales of masculinity and femininity. Yet such difficulties are in part methodological, as studies usually attempt to predict relatively specific behaviors on the basis of extremely general personality traits. As Epstein (1980) has argued, endeavors of this sort may fail to produce consistent findings because of the absence of a reliable measure of behavior, one that aggregates behaviors across occasions or settings.

Also contributing to the difficulties encountered in predicting behavior from gender-based measures of personality is the simplicity of any perspective that predicts sex-role behaviors from masculine and feminine traits. As this chapter demonstrates, in our own research we have moved away from an initial interest in gender-linked personality traits (e.g., female submissiveness, female interpersonal concern, male independence) as explanations for the influenceability sex difference, and have increasingly focused our attention on roles, norms, and expectancies. Other researchers also seem to be gaining an increasing appreciation for these social psychological determinants of gender-relevant behavior. As Spence and Helmreich suggested, "In accounting for sex-role behaviors, many other variables, such as abilities, interests, attitudes, values, and external pressures must be taken into account" (1980, p. 161). Indeed it is just these other variables that are the focus of our analysis of sex differences in influenceability. Primary among these other variables are the perceived demands inherent in social roles and the impact that status-based expectancies have on behavior.

ACKNOWLEDGEMENTS

Research reported in this chapter was supported by National Science Foundation Grants BNS77-11671, BNS79-24471, and BNS80-23311 to the senior author. The authors thank Hank Bates, Linda Carli, and Shelly Chaiken for their comments on a draft of this chapter.

REFERENCES

Allen, V. L. (1965). Situational factors in conformity. In L. Berkowitz (Ed.), *Advances in experimental social psychology* (Vol. 2). New York: Academic Press.

Anderson, L. R., & Blanchard, P. N. (1982). Sex differences in task and social emotional behavior. *Basic and Applied Social Psychology, 3,* 109–139.

Anderson, N. H. (1968). Likeableness ratings of 555 personality-trait words. *Journal of Personality and Social Psychology, 9,* 272–279.

Anderson, S. M., & Bem, S. L. (1981). Sex typing and androgyny in dyadic interaction: Individual differences in responsiveness to physical attractiveness. *Journal of Personality and Social Psychology, 41,* 74–86.

Asch, S. E. (1956). Studies of independence and conformity: I. A minority of one against a unanimous majority. *Psychological Monographs, 70* (9, Whole No. 416).

Ashmore, R. D., & Del Boca, F. K. (1979). Sex stereotypes and implicit personality theory: Toward a cognitive–social psychological conceptualization. *Sex Roles, 5,* 219–248.

Bakan, D. (1966). *The duality of human existence.* Chicago: Rand McNally.

Bales, R. F. (1950). *Interaction process analysis.* Cambridge, Mass.: Addison-Wesley.

Baron, R. A., & Byrne, D. (1977). *Social psychology: Understanding human interaction* (2nd ed.) Boston: Allyn & Bacon.

Barry, H., Bacon, M. K., & Child, E. L. (1957). A cross-cultural survey of some sex differences in socialization. *Journal of Abnormal and Social Psychology, 55,* 327–332.

Becker, B. J. (in press). Influence again: Another look at studies of gender differences in social influence. In J. S. Hyde & M. Linn (Eds.), *The psychology of gender: Advances through meta-analysis.* Baltimore: Johns Hopkins University Press.

Bedell, J., & Sistrunk, F. (1973). Power, opportunity costs, and sex in a mixed-motive game. *Journal of Personality and Social Psychology, 25,* 219–266.

Bem, S. L. (1974). The measurement of psychological androgyny. *Journal of Consulting and Clinical Psychology, 42,* 155–162.

Bem, S. L. (1975). Sex role adaptability: One consequence of psychological androgyny. *Journal of Personality and Social Psychology, 31,* 634–643.

Berger, J., Fisek, M. H., Norman, R. Z., & Zelditch, M., Jr. (1977). *Status characteristics and social interaction: An expectation states approach.* New York: American Elsevier.

Berger, J., Rosenholtz, S. J., & Zelditch, M., Jr. (1980). Status organizing processes. In A. Inkeles, N. J. Smelser, & R. H. Turner (Eds.), *Annual Review of Sociology* (Vol. 6). Palo Alto, Calif.: Annual Reviews.

Block, J. H. (1973). Conceptions of sex roles: Some cross-cultural and longitudinal perspectives. *American Psychologist, 28,* 512–526.

Bond, J. R. & Vinacke, W. E. (1961). Coalitions in mixed-sex triads. *Sociometry, 24,* 61–75.

Brim, O. G., Jr. (1960). Personality development as role-learning. In I. Iscoe & H. Stevenson (Eds.), *Personality development in children.* Austin: University of Texas Press.

Broverman, I. K., Vogel, S. R., Broverman, D. M., Clarkson, F. E., & Rosenkrantz, P. S. (1972). Sex-role stereotypes: A current appraisal. *Journal of Social Issues, 28,* 59–78.

Brown, L. K. (1979). Women and business management. *Signs: Journal of Women in Culture and Society, 5,* 266–288.

Brown, S. M. (1979). Male versus female leaders: A comparison of empirical studies. *Sex Roles, 5,* 595–611.

Buss, D. M. (1981). Sex differences in the evaluation and performance of dominant acts. *Journal of Personality and Social Psychology, 40,* 147–154.

Cantor, N., & Mischel, W. (1979). Prototypes in person perception. In L. Berkowitz (Ed.), *Advances in experimental social psychology* (Vol. 12). New York: Academic Press.

Cohen, J. (1977). *Statistical power analysis for the behavioral sciences* (2nd ed.). New York: Academic Press.

Cooper, H. M. (1979). Statistically combining independent studies: A meta-analysis of sex differences in conformity research. *Journal of Personality and Social Psychology, 37*, 131–146.

Cooper, H. M., & Rosenthal, R. (1980). Statistical versus traditional procedures for summarizing research findings. *Psychological Bulletin, 87*, 422–449.

Darley, J. M., & Fazio, R. H. (1980). Expectancy confirmation processes arising in the social interaction sequence. *American Psychologist, 35*, 867–881.

Deaux, K., & Emswiller, T. (1974). Explanations of successful performance on sex-linked tasks: What is skill for the male is luck for the female. *Journal of Personality and Social Psychology, 29*, 80–85.

Driskell, J. E., Jr., & Webster, M. Jr. (in press). Status generalization: New data. In J. Berger & M. Zelditch, Jr. (Ed.), *Status, attribution, and rewards*. San Francisco: Jossey-Bass.

Eagly, A. H. (1974). Comprehensibility of persuasive arguments as a determinant of opinion change. *Journal of Personality and Social Psychology, 29*, 758–783.

Eagly, A. H. (1978). Sex differences in influenceability. *Psychological Bulletin, 85*, 85–116.

Eagly, A. H. (1983). Gender and social influence: A social psychological analysis. *American Psychologist, 38*, 971–981.

Eagly, A. H. (in press). Some meta-analytic approaches to examining the validity of gender-difference research. In J. Hyde & M. Linn (Eds.), *The psychology of gender: Advances through meta-analysis*. Baltimore: Johns Hopkins University Press.

Eagly, A. H., & Carli, L. L. (1981). Sex of researchers and sex-typed communications as determinants of sex differences in influenceability: A meta-analysis of social influence studies. *Psychological Bulletin, 90*, 1–20.

Eagly, A. H., & Chrvala, C. (in press). *Sex differences in conformity: Status and gender-role interpretations. Psychology of Women Quarterly*.

Eagly, A. H., & Steffen, V. J. (1984). Gender stereotypes stem from the distribution of women and men into social roles. *Journal of Personality and Social Psychology, 46*, 735–754.

Eagly, A. H., & Warren, R. (1976). Intelligence, comprehension, and opinion change. *Journal of Personality, 44*, 226–242.

Eagly, A. H., & Wood. W. (1982). Inferred sex differences in status as a determinant of gender stereotypes about social influence. *Journal of Personality and Social Psychology, 43*, 915–928.

Eagly, A. H., Wood, W., & Fishbaugh, L. (1981). Sex differences in conformity: Surveillance by the group as a determinant of male nonconformity. *Journal of Personality and Social Psychology, 40*, 384–394.

Endler, N. S., Wiesenthal, D. L., Coward, T., Edwards, J., & Geller, S. H. (1975). Generalization of relative competence mediating conformity across different tasks. *European Journal of Social Psychology, 5*, 281–287.

Epstein, S. (1980). The stability of behavior: II. Implications for psychological research. *American Psychologist, 35*, 790–806.

Feldman, J. M. (1972). Stimulus characteristics and subject prejudice as determinants of stereotype attribution. *Journal of Personality and Social Psychology, 21*, 333–340.

Freedman, J. L., Carlsmith, J. M., & Sears, D. O. (1970). *Social psychology*. Englewood Cliffs, N.J.: Prentice-Hall.

Glass, G. V., McGaw, B., & Smith, M. L. (1981). *Meta-analysis in social research*. Beverly Hills, Calif.: Sage.

Goldberg, C. (1974). Sex roles, task competence, and conformity. *Journal of Psychology, 86*, 157–164.

Goldberg, C. (1975). Conformity to majority type as a function of task and acceptance of sex-related stereotypes. *Journal of Psychology, 89*, 25–37.

Hall, J. A. (1978). Gender effects in decoding nonverbal cues. *Psychological Bulletin, 75,* 845–857.

Hall, J. A. (1980). Gender differences in nonverbal communication skills. *New Directions for Methodology of Social and Behavioral Science,* No. 5, 63–77.

Hamilton, D. L. (1979). A cognitive-attributional analysis of stereotyping. In L. Berkowitz (Ed.), *Advances in experimental social psychology* (Vol. 12). New York: Academic Press.

Hamilton, D. L., & Gifford, R. K. (1976). Illusory correlation in interpersonal perception: A cognitive basis of stereotypic judgments. *Journal of Experimental Social Psychology, 12,* 392–407.

Hansson, R. O., Allen, M. M., & Jones, W. H. (1980). Sex differences in conformity: Instrumental or communal response? *Sex Roles, 2,* 207–212.

Hoffman, M. L. (1977). Sex differences in empathy and related behaviors. *Psychological Bulletin, 84,* 712–722.

Hollander, E. P. (1960). Competence and conformity in the acceptance of influence. *Journal of Abnormal and Social Psychology, 61,* 365–369.

Hollander, E. P. (1964). *Leaders, groups, and influence.* New York: Oxford University Press.

Johnson, P. (1976). Women and power: Toward a theory of effectiveness. *Journal of Social Issues, 32,* 99–110.

Jones, R. A. (1977). *Self-fulfilling prophecies: Social, psychological, and physiological effects of expectancies.* Hillsdale, N.J.: Lawrence Erlbaum Associates.

Jones, R. A., Hendrick, C., & Epstein, Y. M. (1979). *Introduction to social psychology.* Sunderland, Mass.: Sinauer Associates.

Kahn, A., Hottes, J., & Davis, W. L. (1971). Cooperation and optimal responding in the Prisoner's Dilemma game: Effects of sex and physical attractiveness. *Journal of Personality and Social Psychology, 17,* 267–279.

Kahn, A., Lamm, H., Krulewitz, J. E., & O'Leary, V. E. (1980). Equity and equality: Male and female means to a just end. *Basic and Applied Social Psychology, 1,* 173–197.

Kelman, H. C. (1961). Processes of opinion change. *Public Opinion Quarterly, 25,* 57–78.

Kerlinger, F. N., & Pedhazur, E. J. (1973). *Multiple regression in behavioral research.* New York: Holt, Rinehart, & Winston.

Kiesler, S. B. (1975). Actuarial prejudice toward women and its implications. *Journal of Applied Social Psychology, 5,* 201–216.

Krech, D., Crutchfield, R. S., & Ballachey, E. L. (1962). *Individual in society: A textbook of social psychology.* New York: McGraw-Hill.

Lerner, M. J., Miller, D. T., & Holmes, J. G. (1976). Deserving and the emergence of forms of justice. In L. Berkowitz (Ed.), *Advances in experimental social psychology* (Vol. 9). New York: Academic Press.

Leventhal, G. S., & Lane, D. W. (1970). Sex, age, and equity behavior. *Journal of Personality and Social Psychology, 15,* 312–316.

Lockheed, M. E., & Hall, K. P. (1976). Conceptualizing sex as a status characteristic: Applications to leadership training strategies. *Journal of Social Issues, 32,* 111–124.

Locksley, A., Borgida, E., Brekke, N., & Hepburn, C. (1980). Sex stereotypes and social judgment. *Journal of Personality and Social Psychology, 39,* 821–831.

Locksley, A., Hepburn, C., & Ortiz, V. (1982). Social stereotypes and judgments of individuals: An instance of the base-rate fallacy. *Journal of Experimental Social Psychology, 18,* 23–42.

Lott, B. (1978). Behavioral concordance with sex-role ideology related to play areas, creativity, and parental sex typing of children. *Journal of Personality and Social Psychology, 36,* 1087–1100.

Maccoby, E. E., & Jacklin, C. N. (1974). *The psychology of sex differences.* Stanford, Calif.: Stanford University Press.

McGuire, W. J. (1969). The nature of attitudes and attitude change. In G. Lindzey & E. Aronson (Eds.), *Handbook of social psychology* (2nd ed., Vol. 3). Reading, Mass.: Addison-Wesley.

McGuire, W. J., & Papageorgis, D. (1961). The relative efficacy of various types of prior belief-defense in producing immunity against persuasion. *Journal of Abnormal and Social Psychology, 62,* 327–337.

Meeker, B. F., & Weitzel-O'Neill, P. A. (1977). Sex roles and interpersonal behavior in task-oriented groups. *American Sociological Review, 42,* 92–105.

Middlebrook, P. N. (1974). *Social psychology and modern life.* New York: Knopf.

Milgram, S. (1965). Some conditions of obedience and disobedience to authority. *Human Relations, 18,* 57–76.

Milgram, S. (1974). *Obedience to authority: An experimental view.* New York: Harper & Row.

Miller, G. R., & McReynolds, W. (1973). Male chauvinism and source competence: A research note. *Speech Monographs, 40,* 154–155.

Miller, N. (1965). Involvement and dogmatism as inhibitors of attitude change. *Journal of Experimental Social Psychology, 1,* 121–132.

Moscovici, S. (1976). *Social influence and social change.* New York: Academic Press.

Moscovici, S. (1980). Toward a theory of conversion behavior. In L. Berkowitz (Ed.), *Advances in experimental social psychology* (Vol. 13). New York: Academic Press.

Nemeth, C., Endicott, J., & Wachtler, J. (1976). From the '50s to the '70s: Women in jury deliberations. *Sociometry, 39,* 293–304.

Newton, R. R., & Schulman, G. I. (1977). Sex and conformity: A new view. *Sex Roles, 3,* 511–521.

Nord, W. R. (1969). Social exchange theory: An integrative approach to social conformity. *Psychological Bulletin, 71,* 174–208.

Orne, M. T., & Evans, F. J. (1965). Social control in the psychological experiment: Antisocial behavior and hypnosis. *Journal of Personality and Social Psychology, 1,* 189–200.

Piliavin, J., & Martin, R. R. (1978). The effects of the sex composition of groups on style of social interaction. *Sex Roles, 4,* 281–296.

Rhine, R. J., & Severance, L. J. (1970). Ego-involvement, discrepancy, source credibility, and attitude change. *Journal of Personality and Social Psychology, 16,* 175–190.

Ridgeway, C. L. (1978). Conformity, group-oriented motivation, and status attainment in small groups. *Social Psychology, 41,* 175–188.

Ridgeway, C. L. (1981). Nonconformity, competence, and influence in groups: A test of two theories. *American Sociological Review, 46,* 333–347.

Ridgeway, C. L., & Jacobson, C. K. (1977). Sources of status and influence in all-female and mixed-sex groups. *Sociological Quarterly, 18,* 413–425.

Rosenkrantz, P., Vogel, S., Bee, H., Broverman, I., & Broverman, D. M. (1968). Sex-role stereotypes and self-concepts in college students. *Journal of Consulting and Clinical Psychology, 32,* 287–295.

Rosenthal, R., & Rubin, D. B. (1978). Interpersonal expectancy effects: The first 345 studies. *Behavioral and Brain Sciences, 3,* 377–415.

Ross, L. D. (1977). The intuitive psychologist and his shortcomings: Distortions in the attribution process. In L. Berkowitz (Ed.), *Advances in experimental social psychology* (Vol. 10). New York: Academic Press.

Ross, L. D., Amabile, T. M., & Steinmetz, J. L. (1977). Social roles, social control, and biases in social-personality processes. *Journal of Personality and Social Psychology, 35,* 485–494.

Rubin, J. Z., & Brown, B. R. (1975). *The social psychology of bargaining and negotiation.* New York: Academic Press.

Ruble, D. N., & Ruble, T. L. (1982). Sex stereotypes. In A. G. Miller (Ed.), *In the eye of the beholder: Contemporary issues in stereotyping.* New York: Praeger.

Schachter, S. (1951). Deviation, rejection, and communication. *Journal of Abnormal and Social Psychology, 46,* 190–207.

Schopler, J. (1965). Social power. In L. Berkowitz (Ed.), *Advances in experimental social psychology* (Vol. 2). New York: Academic Press.

Senn, D. J. (1967). Dyadic attraction and coalition formation (Doctoral dissertation, University of Massachusetts, 1967). *Dissertation Abstracts International, 28*, 1529A–1530A. (University Microfilms No. 67-12, 543).

Sherif, C. W. (1980). *Needed concepts in the study of gender identity*. Presidential address (Division 35) presented at the meeting of the American Psychological Association, Montreal.

Sherif, M. (1935). A study of some social factors in perception. *Archives of Psychology, 27*, No. 187, 1–60.

Sherif, M. (1936). *The psychology of social norms*. New York: Harper.

Sistrunk, F., & McDavid, J. W. (1971). Sex variable in conformity behavior. *Journal of Personality and Social Psychology, 17*, 200–207.

Skrypnek, B. J., & Snyder, M. (1982). On the self-perpetuating nature of stereotypes about women and men. *Journal of Experimental Social Psychology, 18*, 277–291.

Smedley, J. W., & Bayton, J. A. (1978). Evaluative race-class stereotypes by race and perceived class of subjects. *Journal of Personality and Social Psychology, 36*, 530–535.

Snyder, M. L., & Swann, W. B. (1978). Behavioral confirmation in social interaction: From social perception to social reality. *Journal of Experimental Social Psychology, 14*, 148–162.

Snyder, M. L., Tanke, E. D., & Berscheid, E. (1977). Social perception and interpersonal behavior: On the self-fulfilling nature of social stereotypes. *Journal of Personality and Social Psychology, 35*, 656–666.

Specht, D. A. (1975). On the evaluation of causal models. *Social Science Research, 4*, 113–133.

Spence, J. T., & Helmreich, R. L. (1978). *Masculinity & femininity: Their psychological dimensions, correlates, & antecedents*. Austin: University of Texas Press.

Spence, J. T., & Helmreich, R. L. (1980). Masculine instrumentality and feminine expressiveness: Their relationships with sex role attitudes and behaviors. *Psychology of Women Quarterly, 5*, 147–163.

Spence, J. T., Helmreich, R., & Stapp, J. (1974). The Personal Attributes Questionnaire: A measure of sex-role stereotypes and masculinity–femininity. *JSAS Catalog of Selected Documents in Psychology, 4*, 43. (Ms. No. 617)

Strodtbeck, F. L., & Mann, R. D. (1956). Sex role differentiation in jury deliberations. *Sociometry, 19*, 3–11.

Taylor, S. E., Fiske, S. T., Etcoff, N. L., & Ruderman, A. J. (1978). Categorical and contextual bases of person memory and stereotyping. *Journal of Personality and Social Psychology, 36*, 778–793.

Triandis, H. C. (1977). *Interpersonal behavior*. Monterey, Calif.: Brooks/Cole.

Triandis, H. C., & Vassiliou, V. (1967). Frequency of contact and stereotyping. *Journal of Personality and Social Psychology, 7*, 316–328.

Tuchman, G., Daniels, A. K., & Benét, J. (1978). *Hearth and home: Images of women in the mass media*. New York: Oxford University Press.

Uesugi, T. K., & Vinacke, W. E. (1963). Strategy in a feminine game. *Sociometry, 26*, 75–88.

Unger, R. K. (1976). Male is greater than female: The socialization of status inequality. *The Counseling Psychologist, 6*, 2–9.

Unger, R. K. (1978). The politics of gender: A review of relevant literature. In J. Sherman & F. Denmark (Eds.), *Psychology of women: Future directions of research*. New York: Psychological Dimensions.

Vinacke, W. E. (1959). Sex roles in a three-person game. *Sociometry, 22*, 343–360.

Wahrman, R., & Pugh, M. D. (1972). Competence and conformity: Another look at Hollander's study. *Sociometry, 35*, 376–386.

Wahrman, R., & Pugh, M. D. (1974). Sex, conformity and influence. *Sociometry, 37*, 137–147.

Webster, M., & Driskell, J. E. (1978). Status generalization: A review and some new data. *American Sociological Review, 43,* 220–236.

Williams, J. E., & Bennett, S. M. (1975). The definition of sex stereotypes via the Adjective Check List. *Sex Roles, 1,* 327–337.

Zanna, M. P., & Pack, S. J. (1975). On the self-fulfilling nature of apparent sex differences in behavior. *Journal of Experimental Social Psychology, 11,* 583–591.

Zeller, R. A., & Warnecke, R. (1973). The utility of constructs as intervening variables in the interpretation of experimental results. *Sociological Methods and Research, 2,* 85–110.

9

Women and Men in Love: Gender Differences in Close Heterosexual Relationships

Letitia Anne Peplau
University of California, Los Angeles

Steven L. Gordon
California State University, Los Angeles

Studies of heterosexual couples are a relatively new focus in social psychology. Early work on interpersonal attraction (e.g., Festinger, Schachter & Back, 1950; Newcomb, 1961) concerned the development of friendship in naturalistic settings. In the later 1960s, however, research on interpersonal attraction moved into the laboratory; for the next decade, studies of first encounters between strangers were predominant (Byrne & Griffitt, 1973). Social psychologists have only recently turned their attention from first impressions to the development of enduring male–female relationships.

Rubin's (1973) *Liking and loving: An invitation to social psychology* was one of the first attempts to integrate social psychological findings about love relationships. In the late 1970s, reviews of work on interpersonal attraction (e.g., Berscheid & Walster, 1978; Huston & Levinger, 1978) broadened to include discussions of love and close relationships. As the 1980s approached, several books on the psychology of close relationships appeared (e.g., Burgess & Huston, 1979; Cook & Wilson, 1979; Hinde, 1979; Kelley, 1979; Levinger & Raush, 1977; Murstein, 1976). Today, the emphasis within social psychology has clearly shifted from initial attraction among strangers to the dynamics of enduring close relationships (e.g., Kelley et al., 1983). The series of volumes on *Personal relationships* edited by Duck & Gilmour (e.g., 1981) and the new *Journal of Social and Personal Relationships* begun in 1984 are indicative of the interest in this field. The empirical study of women and men in love, once the province of sociologists and marital therapists, is now being claimed by social psychologists as well.

The origins of this change in social psychology are diverse. As researchers have become less obsessed with laboratory techniques, it has become more

257

acceptable to study relationship processes that do not fit experimental paradigms. Advances in research design and statistical methods have also contributed. Social changes, most notably the increased divorce rate, have challenged traditional views of love and commitment. "The unproblematic remains unquestioned and uninvestigated" (Levinger & Raush, 1977, vii). Love relationships and their dissolution have now taken their place alongside prejudice, violence, and international conflict as a "social problem" worthy of investigation.

The changing roles of women in American society and the emergence of feminist psychology have also contributed to an interest in close, heterosexual relationships. Common assumptions about relationships—that the man should be the "head" of the family, that highly differentiated male–female roles enhance relationships, that marriage is more important to women than to men—are being challenged. Familiar interpretations of the relations between the sexes are also being questioned. For example, do women sometimes use crying and pouting as influence techniques because of socialization for emotional expressiveness, or because of their lesser status and power in heterosexual relationships? An awareness that gender per se may not adequately account for observed male-female differences has led researchers to begin studies of the impact of sex-role attitudes and sex-role self-concept on behavior in relationships. It is becoming clear that sex differences provide an important window into close relationships, shedding light on basic interpersonal processes.

This chapter takes stock of research findings about gender differences in heterosexual love relationships. Much of the existing research has been descriptive, aimed at documenting male-female differences. Explanations about the causes of these sex-linked patterns have often been offered *post hoc*. Where possible, we have speculated about the origins of observed sex differences. Our belief is that future research should move beyond mere description and focus explicitly on explaining sex differences in close relationships.

Our review is organized around six major issues. We begin by asking what men and women want and value in love relationships. Next, we consider sex differences in falling in love, and examine whether one sex is more romantic than the other. Three sections investigate key facets of interaction in relationships— communication, the division of labor, and power. A sixth section concerns the psychological consequences of relationships, and provides evidence that marriage may be more beneficial to the psychological well-being of men than of women. In a concluding section, we discuss directions for future research.

WHAT WOMEN AND MEN WANT IN RELATIONSHIPS

The experiences of women and men in close relationships are shaped by their attitudes and values. Most Americans value love relationships highly. Although stereotypes depict men as more resistant to marriage and "settling down" than women, actual gender differences in expectations about marriage are very small. For example, a study of college students (Hill, Rubin & Peplau, 1976; Rubin, Peplau & Hill, unpublished data) asked men and women about the likelihood that they would eventually get married. Among students currently in a steady dating relationship, only 3% of the men and 1% of the women said they would "definitely" never marry. Among students not currently "going with" one partner, 5% of the men and none of the women said they would definitely never marry. Intimacy and its institutionalized expression in marriage are major goals for most heterosexual women and men.

Men have somewhat more traditional attitudes about relations between the sexes than do women. When asked about such matters as whether the husband should be the primary wage earner for the family and whether the wife should have major responsibility for homemaking and childcare, men consistently endorse more traditional male-female role differentiation (e.g., Osmond & Martin, 1975; Parelman, 1983; Peplau, 1976; Scanzoni & Fox, 1980; Spence & Helmreich, 1978; Tomeh, 1978). For example, one survey (Astin, King & Richardson, 1980) asked students entering college in the fall of 1980 whether "women's activities should be confined to the home." About 35% of the men agreed with this statement, compared to only 19% of the women. In any particular dating or marital relationship, partners tend to be relatively similar in their sex-role attitudes. For example, in a sample of college dating couples, Peplau (1976) reported a significant correlation of .48 between partners' scores on a 10-item sex-role attitude scale. Traditionalists are usually matched with traditionalists and feminists with feminists. Nonetheless, there is also likely to be a small but consistent difference in the relative traditionalism of partners, with women being more pro-feminist than their male partners.

Relationship values are also reflected in people's goals for dating or for marriage. Much commonality has been found in men's a d women's relationship priorities. For example, one study of dating couples (Rubin, Peplau & Hill, unpublished data) asked college students to rate the importance of six goals as a reason for entering their current dating relationship. Both sexes gave the greatest importance to a desire "to have a good time with someone" and "to have a friend of the opposite sex." Men and women both gave the lowest priority to the desire "to find a marriage partner" or "to have a guaranteed date," and intermediate importance to the desire "for sexual activity" and "to fall in love." However, whereas men rated sex more important than love, women rated love more important than sex.

Several studies have asked husbands and wives to rank the importance of various marriage goals. Levinger (1964) found that the overall ranking of nine goals was, in the order of their importance: affection, companionship, happy children, personal development, religion, economic security, attractive home, wise financial planning, and a place in the community. Levinger found few sex differences: Both sexes emphasized affection and companionship and gave low priority to task-oriented goals about the standard of living. There is also some evidence that the ranking of such goals is affected by social class (Farber, 1957). Across all social classes, women rank affection high, but men vary. Levinger has suggested that "The more a couple is assured of economic security and occupational stability, the more likely it is that the husband will share the wife's concern with socio-emotional matters" (1964, p. 442). Working-class men, on the other hand, may put less emphasis on companionship than do their wives (e.g., Rubin, 1976).

More recent studies have attempted to go beyond the ranking of fairly global goals in order to identify more precisely those specific features of relationships that are most important to women and to men. Cochran and Peplau (in press) asked college students to rate the importance of 22 features of love relationships, such as partners having similar attitudes, sharing many activities, sexual exclusivity, and disclosing intimate feelings. A factor analysis of responses indicated that values clustered around two themes. "Dyadic attachment" values concerned a desire for a close and relatively secure love relationship, and were reflected in an emphasis on seeking permanence in a relationship, wanting to reveal personal feelings, sharing many activities with the partner, and valuing sexual exclusivity. "Egalitarian autonomy" values indicated a concern with maintaining one's independence. This theme was reflected in wanting to have separate interests and friends apart from the dating relationship, and wanting to preserve one's independence within the relationship by dividing decision-making and finances in an egalitarian manner. Men and women did not differ significantly in their ratings of dyadic attachment issues; both sexes were equally likely to value—or to devalue—these more traditional features of close relationships. Students' attachment values were unrelated to their general sex-role attitudes. In contrast, the sexes did differ in their ratings of personal autonomy values. Women were more likely than men to emphasize the importance of independence and equality. In addition, students with pro-feminist attitudes gave greater value to maintaining separate interests outside the relationship and to equality within the relationship. (When the effects of sex-role attitudes were controlled, women continued to score higher on autonomy values.) It should be emphasized, however, that although significant sex differences in autonomy were found, their magnitude was small. There was much overlap in the expressed values of both sexes. Indeed, the relative ranking of specific values was highly similar for both women and men.

Also pertinent are findings from a study of young married couples by Parelman (1983). She examined spouses' ideals of marital closeness—what each considered to be the important ingredients of an ideal marriage. Women gave greater importance to feeling emotionally involved with the spouse and to verbal self-disclosure. Women also gave greater importance to partners' being independent and self-reliant. Men gave greater emphasis to themes of "sacrifice and dependency"—feeling responsible for the partner's well-being, spending time with the spouse, putting the spouse's needs first. Parelman concluded that "in this sample, women were more concerned with maintaining their separate activities and interests and with accommodating less to their spouse." Parelman noted, however, that the similarities between men and women were much greater than the differences. Further, she found that gender was not as good a predictor of relationship values as were measures of sex-role attitudes. For both sexes, pro-feminist attitudes were associated with wanting less sacrifice and dependency, greater independence, less similarity, fewer traditional role divisions, and greater verbal expressiveness.

People's preferences about relationships can also be seen in the traits they seek in a partner. Not surprisingly, there is much commonality in the qualities desired by men and women. Both sexes seek a partner who is affectionate, understanding, and has the right "personality" (e.g., Laner, 1977; Pietropinto & Simenauer, 1981; Wakil, 1973). Nonetheless, small but consistent gender differences do emerge. American culture encourages sex-linked asymmetries in the characteristics of dating and marriage partners (Bernard, 1972; Peplau, 1976). Women are traditionally taught to seek a man who is taller, older, more "worldly," more occupationally successful—someone to be a protector and provider. Men are traditionally taught to desire a woman who is an attractive companion and will be a good mother and homemaker. Empirical evidence (Burchinal, 1964; Hudson & Henze, 1969) indicates that people's personal preferences often reflect these cultural norms.

Several studies reveal that men put greater importance on a partner's physical attractiveness and sex appeal than do women (Hudson & Henze, 1969; Huston & Levinger, 1978; Pietropinto & Simenauer, 1981). In one study (Laner, 1977), 48% of heterosexual college men rated "good looks" as very important in a "permanent partner," compared to only 16% of college women. Women often give greater emphasis to a partner's intelligence and occupational attainment (e.g., Burchinal, 1964; Hudson & Henze, 1969; Langhorne & Secord, 1955). In Laner's (1977) study, 70% of the women ranked being "intelligent" as very important, compared with 53% of the men. The comments of a husband and wife interviewed by Pietropinto and Simenauer (1981) illustrate these common gender differences:

Husband: She was attractive, vivacious, and interesting. I thought she would prove to be a loving companion, a wonderful wife and mother.
Wife: We were in love. . . . He went out of his way to make me happy. I felt he could be a good provider and give me financial security (p. 43).

Studies of actual mate selection suggest that these sex-linked preferences are not always translated into action. In general, dating partners and spouses tend to be reasonably similar in social characteristics (Leslie, 1976). For instance, Hill et al. (1976) found that college dating couples were significantly matched in age, height, physical attractiveness (as rated from photos by a panel of judges), educational aspirations, and SAT scores. When asymmetries do occur, however, it is more often the boyfriend or husband who is older, has more education, and is higher in occupational attainment (Bernard, 1972; Leslie, 1976; Rubin, 1968). This phenomenon, called the "marriage gradient," has led sociologists to speculate that the pool of "eligible" partners may be smallest for high-status, occupationally successful women and for low-status, occupationally less successful men.

Taken together, the available studies of what men and women want in close relationships lead to several general conclusions. First, there is much overall consensus between men's and women's relationship values. In actual relationships, male-female agreement is usually futher enhanced by the selection of a partner who shares compatible attitudes and is similar in background. Second, whereas most American women strongly value affection and companionship in relationships, men are more variable on this theme. In middle-class and college samples, men and women generally give equal importance to companionship. In working class samples, some men de-emphasize companionship. Women of all social classes appear to view verbal self-disclosure as a more important component of intimacy than do men. Third, among college educated younger adults, the importance of personal independence may be more salient for women than it is for men. Our speculation is that women cannot take personal autonomy for granted to the same extent that men can. For men, love relationships have never precluded outside activities or careers. For women, these have often been seen as incompatible (e.g., Horner, 1970). Family historians (e.g., Degler, 1980) suggest that this century is witnessing women's struggle for autonomy outside the home. For younger, educated women this may lead to a greater concern with maintaining separate interests and friends in addition to having a primary love relationship. Fourth, women are generally more likely to endorse change in the traditional marital roles of women and men. Finally, there is some evidence that men and women prize somewhat different qualities in their love partners. Men often seek partners who are youthful and sexually attractive; women more often value men's experience and occupational achievements. It may be that these asymmetrical partner preferences are most pronounced among conservative individuals who seek relationships with clearcut male–female role differentiation. Whether feminists show a similar pattern is unknown at present.

Our understanding of sex roles in close heterosexual relationships benefits from these examinations of what men and women want in relationships. But existing research leaves many unanswered questions. We do not know how well most people are able to articulate their personal values and goals. Such issues may not be very salient for some people, whose answers to researchers may be heavily influenced by stereotypes and social desirability pressures. We do not know whether the sexes interpret values such as "affection" and "companionship" in similar ways. It is possible that when men think of companionship they imagine joint activities such as hiking or going to a movie, whereas women think of intimate conversations (Caldwell & Peplau, 1982). We know little about how relationship values affect people's actual selection of partners and behavior in relationships. An especially important question may be whether sex differences in values lead to conflict and problems in heterosexual relationships. Finally, we can profitably ask how young people's relationship values are affected by the changing roles of men and women in American society.

FALLING IN LOVE

Is one sex more "romantic," or prone to falling in love more easily? The answer depends a good deal on terminology (Gordon, 1981). We find it useful to distinguish people's ideology or beliefs about the nature of love from their subjective experiences in a close relationship.

Love Ideologies

A distinction has frequently been made between romantic versus pragmatic beliefs about love (e.g., Hobart, 1958; Knox & Sporakowski, 1968). The romantic person believes that true love lasts forever, comes but once, is strange and incomprehensible, and conquers barriers of custom or social class. The pragmatist rejects these ideals, knowing that we can each love many people, that economic security is more important than passion, and that some disillusionment surely accompanies marriage.

By these criteria, men are apparently more romantic than women. Several studies (e.g., Fengler, 1974; Hobart, 1958; Knox & Sporakowski, 1968; Rubin, 1970; Rubin, Peplau, & Hill, 1981) have found small but consistent sex differences on various romanticism scales. Further evidence comes from responses to questions about the importance of love as a basis for marriage. For example, Kephart (1967) asked students, "If a boy (girl) had all the other qualities you desired, would you marry this person if you were not in love with him/her?" Most of the men (65%) said no, compared to only 24% of the women. Finally, recent research developing a typology of six styles or orientations to love (e.g., Hatkoff & Lasswell, 1979; Lasswell & Lobsenz, 1980; Lee, 1977) further corroborates this picture. Hatkoff and Lasswell (1979) found that women were more likely than men to adopt "logical" or "best friends" approaches to love. Men were more likely to be "romantics" who believed in love at first sight, or "game players" who enjoyed flirtation.

Intrigued by these findings, social scientists have freely speculated about the reasons for men's greater romanticism. The most common explanation concerns the social and economic context of mate selection. As Waller (1938) explained, "A man, when he marries, chooses a companion and perhaps a helpmate, but a woman chooses a companion and at the same time a standard of living. It is necessary for a woman to be mercenary'' (p. 243). Men, it seems, can afford to be more frivolous in love. Other explanations (see Rubin et al., 1981) have emphasized women's presumed lesser emotional dependence on men, or have cited the greater stigma of spinsterhood as a reason for women's willingness to marry regardless of love (Knox & Sporakowski, 1968). Whether social changes increasing women's financial independence and making singlehood more acceptable will alter these sex differences remains to be seen.

The Experience of Love

Another research tradition has investigated sex differences in the intensity of a person's feelings toward his or her partner. Rubin (1970, 1973) argued that love and liking are qualitatively distinct attitudes toward another person, and he developed separate scales to assess each. The 9-item Liking Scale measures feelings of respect and affection toward another. The 9-item Love Scale assesses feelings of attachment, caring, and intimacy. Rubin found that, on the average, boyfriends and girlfriends love each other equally yet girlfriends reported greater liking for their dating partner. Rubin interpreted this in terms of a possible masculine bias in items on the Liking Scale (e.g., questions about recommending the partner for a responsible job). Rubin also reported that the correlation between a person's liking and love for their partner was higher among men (.56) than among women (.36). He speculated that women may make finer discriminations between these two attitudes than do men. Finally, Rubin's research demonstrated the utility of distinguishing a romantic love ideology from one's feelings of love for a specific partner. Rubin found that love scores were significantly correlated with progress toward permanence in the relationship during the school year, but only for romantics. For students who rejected romanticism and espoused a more pragmatic ideology of love, progress in the relationship was unrelated to love for the partner. (For more recent data, see Hill et al., 1976.)

The Symptoms of Romantic Love.   Although the sexes may not differ in global assessments of their love for each other, other aspects of the love experience do distinguish men and women. In dating relationships, women are more likely than men to report various emotional symptoms of love. In one study (Kanin, Davidson & Scheck, 1970), women were more likely to report that they were ''floating on a cloud,'' ''wanted to run, jump or scream,'' had ''trouble concentrating,'' ''felt giddy and carefree,'' and had a general sense of wellbeing. Dion and Dion (1973, 1975) also found greater feelings of euphoria among women. Whether these results represent actual sex differences in the experience of love, or simply women's greater willingness to disclose intimate feelings is unclear.

Speed of Falling in Love. Rubin, Peplau, and Hill (1981) have reviewed evidence that men tend to fall in love more readily than women. For example, men report that they recognize feelings of love earlier in the development of a relationship than do women (Burgess & Wallin, 1953; Cate & Huston, 1980; Kanin et al., 1970). In a computer dating study (Coombs & Kenkel, 1966), men reported greater "romantic attraction" to their randomly assigned partner than did women. In another study (Kephart, 1967), twice as many men as women said they were "very easily attracted" to opposite-sex partners. And, among college dating couples, Rubin (1970) found that in short-term relationships, men scored higher on his Love Scale than did their girlfriends; no sex differences were found among longer-term couples. These differences may be tied to men's greater romanticism, but they may also result from men's greater emphasis on physical attractiveness in a partner—a characteristic that is easily ascertained. The man's role as initiator in dating relationships may also contribute to his higher level of initial attraction.

Which sex is more romantic? Discussions of this matter will benefit from greater precision in terminology. Among young adults, men are stronger proponents of a romantic love ideology than are women, and men report falling in love earlier in the development of a relationship. But women report more emotional and euphoric symptoms of love. The origins of these sex differences, like the romantic's conception of love, remains mysterious.

COMMUNICATION

Are women the expressive or socio-emotional leaders in close relationships? The discussion of this issue has often suffered from vagueness in defining the central concept. We focus specifically on research about gender differences in self-disclosure and interactional style.

Self-Disclosure

The sharing of intimate feelings is often considered the hallmark of a close relationship (Jourard, 1959). Yet folk wisdom suggests that men are often less expressive than women. A working class couple interviewed by Lillian Rubin illustrates this pattern:

Wife: He doesn't ever think there's anything to talk about. I'm the one who has to nag him to talk always, and then I get disgusted.
Husband: I'm pretty tight-lipped about most things most of the time, especially personal things. I don't express what I think or feel. She keeps trying to get me to, but, you know, it's hard (cited in L. B. Rubin, 1976, p. 124).

Just how common are the sex differences in disclosure found in this couple? The clearest evidence of sex differences comes from studies of same-sex friendship. Throughout adult life, women often disclose more personal information to friends than do men (Cozby, 1973), and are more likely to say that they have an intimate, same-sex confidant (Booth, 1972; Booth & Hess, 1974; Lowenthal & Haven, 1968). Women are also more likely to enjoy "just talking" with their same-sex friends, and to say that talking helped form the basis of their relationship (Caldwell & Peplau, 1982).

Studies of heterosexual couples present a more complex picture. In general, people disclose more to their spouse than to anyone else (Jourard & Lasakow, 1958; Rosenfeld, Civikly, & Heron, 1979). A norm of reciprocity in self-disclosure generally encourages similar levels of disclosure between partners. Nonetheless, wives sometimes disclose more than their husbands do (Burke, Weir & Harrison, 1976; Hendrick, 1981; Jourard, 1971; Komarovsky, 1967; Levinger & Senn, 1967). This sex difference has been observed in both working-class and middle-class couples. For example, in *Blue Collar Marriage* (1967), Komarovsky reported diverse patterns of self-disclosure: 35% of the couples interviewed had equal and full disclosure by both spouses, 10% had equal and moderate disclosure, and 24% had equal but meager disclosure. In 21% of the couples, the wife disclosed more; in 10% the husband disclosed more. Education and social class often have dramatic effects on the general level of self-disclosure by both husbands and wives. Komarovsky found that only 35% of men with less than a high school education disclosed fully to their wives, compared with 61% of those men who had completed high school. In Komarovsky's view, the less educated working-class man is the prototype of the inexpressive male.

Komarovsky argues that when there is low disclosure in a marriage, it is typically the husband who blocks communication. This would be consistent with the notion that men generally prefer lower levels of verbal communication. Burke and Weir (1977) examined how spouses react to stress. They found that wives were more willing to tell their husbands when they were feeling tense and to try to explain their feelings. In general, women may be more likely than men to seek emotional support from other people when they are feeling stressed or depressed (e.g., DeBurger, 1967; Funkabiki, Bologna, Pepping & Fitzgerald, 1980; Pearlin & Schooler, 1978).

Some studies of college students (e.g., Komarovsky, 1976; Rubin, Hill, Peplau & Dunkel-Schetter, 1980) suggest that younger, more educated couples may be moving away from the traditional pattern of silent men and talkative women toward a pattern of more equal and intimate disclosure by both sexes. For example, a study of college dating couples (Rubin et al., 1980) found that high proportions of both men and women reported having disclosed their thoughts and feelings "fully" to their partners in almost all domains. Disclosure was higher among men and women who had egalitarian sex-role attitudes than among more traditional couples. A few small sex differences were found. When students perceived unequal disclosure in their relationships, it was more often the man who was considered less revealing. Men revealed less than women on specific topics, such as their greatest fears. Overall, however, disclosure tended to be quite symmetrical. Taken together, self-disclosure research shows that women are sometimes—but not always—more verbally expressive than men. The extent to which this pattern is influenced by social class, education, and changing cultural values is an important topic for future research.

Several researchers (e.g., Blood & Wolfe, 1960; Komarovsky, 1967) have suggested that low self-disclosure in marriage is linked to broader patterns of sex-role differentiation in which the husband's life centers around work and the wife's around children and homemaking. This is illustrated in the comments of a working-class husband: "I can't find anything to talk [to my wife] about. The kinds of things she wants to talk about are kidstuff and trivial . . . I can talk to the fellows at work about the things I like to talk about—cars, sports, work" (Cited in Komarovsky, 1967, p. 150). Sex differences in the interests and experience of husbands and wives may inhibit cross-sex verbal expressiveness.

A closer examination of the content of conversations between the sexes appears warranted. Derlega et al. (1981) found that in mixed-sex dyads, women, when compared with men, disclosed more on "feminine" topics and less on "masculine" topics. Hacker (1981) found that in mixed-sex friendships, a third of the women revealed their weaknesses but concealed their strengths (compared with none of the men) and a third of men revealed their strengths but concealed their weaknesses (compared with none of the women.) Komarovsky (1967) found that working-class wives preferred to talk about themselves, their homes, and their relationships with family and friends; their husbands preferred to talk about cars, sports, work, and politics. An intensive study of a single married couple who wore radio transmitters throughout a day (Soskin & John, 1963) similarly found that the wife talked more about her feelings and experiences, while the husband gave more information and directions.

Interactional Style

Sex differences in communication may be evident not only in what the sexes reveal to each other, but, perhaps more importantly, in how they interact. An early study by Leik (1963) used a modification of the Bales coding scheme to assess interaction in families who were asked to discuss issues about family values and goals. In groups comprising a mother, father, and daughter, Leik found no significant gender differences in behaviors classified as expressive, nor in task-oriented actions. In contrast, triads composed of a husband, wife, and daughter who were unrelated to each other did show sex differences. In such groups, the men engaged in significantly less expressive behavior and greater task behavior than did the women. Leik proposed that sex-role differentiation in expressive leadership is less likely in families where individuals interact frequently and privately, than in groups of strangers.

Other research (e.g., Henley, 1977; Lakoff, 1975) has found sex differences in several aspects of male–female communication, such as the use of language and nonverbal behavior. Unfortunately, few of these studies have explicitly investigated close, heterosexual relationships. One exception is a study by Fishman (1978), who analyzed tape-recordings of spontaneous conversations by heterosexual couples, and found clear sex differences in the form of verbal interaction. For example, women asked questions three times more often than did their male partners. Women appeared to be more supportive of male speakers than vice versa; they were also more skilled at using "mm's" and "oh's" to indicate interest and attention. Fishman concluded that there is a "division of labor" in conversation, with women doing the greater share of the work. These interesting findings need to be confirmed by more extensive research.

Although the available research is limited, it hints that women may function as facilitators of communication in heterosexual couples. One interpretation is that this pattern attests to women's greater communication skills and expressive leadership. Another interpretation (see Fishman, 1978) is that it reflects women's lower status in male–female relations: Men can afford to neglect communication because women can be counted on to do the work.

THE DIVISION OF LABOR

Close relationships entail not only the communication of personal information and feelings, but also the accomplishment of specific tasks. For a dating couple, this may mean planning a picnic or organizing a party. For married couples, it typically includes providing for the welfare of the family, maintaining a joint household, and often rearing children. There is abundant evidence that men and women contribute differently to their close relationships. For example, Wenz (cited in Kidder, Fagan & Cohn, 1981) asked people what they gave and received in their close relationship with a person of the opposite sex. Men reported contributing more than women in instrumental areas: providing money and being an intelligent and informed person. Women reported contributing more in socioemotional and homemaking areas: showing affection, remembering special occasions, and doing housework.

Most of the available research on distinctions between "men's work" and "women's work" has investigated married couples. Here, we focus on sex differences in paid employment and the performance of family tasks.

Paid Employment

In an influential analysis of the American family, Parsons (1955) argued that the husband's instrumental leadership in the family is fundamentally tied to his nearly exclusive role as breadwinner. According to Parsons, the husband's economic contribution to the family is complemented by the wife's contribution as mother and homemaker. Recent research, however, demonstrates that the actual economic contribution of women to the family is typically more substantial than has been assumed. A cross-cultural study (Aronoff & Crano, 1975) found that in nonindustrial societies, women contribute an average of 44% of subsistence production through such activities as gathering, hunting, fishing and agriculture—and they do this in addition to their domestic responsibilities. In American society, a majority of married women currently work outside the home for pay, and this proportion increases annually. The presumed "typical" American family with a working husband, nonemployed wife and two children is increasingly becoming uncommon (Pifer, 1978). Has women's increased participation in the occupational sphere led to an increase in men's participation in domestic activities?

Family Work

There is clear evidence that husbands and wives perform different types and amounts of what Pleck (1981a) has called "family work"—housework and childcare. For example, Levinger (1964) found sex differences in which spouse performed such activities as repairing things around the house, doing the dishes, keeping in touch with relatives, and taking out the trash. As further evidence that these behaviors are sex-typed, Levinger found a negative correlation between how frequently the husband and wife performed each activity; the more often one spouse performed a task, the less frequently it was performed by the partner.

The most accurate and detailed information about family work patterns comes from time budget studies (e.g., Berk, 1980; Pleck & Rustad, 1980; Robinson, 1977; Walker, 1970; Walker & Woods, 1976) in which individuals keep careful accounts of how they spend their time. Such data support two major conclusions: First, wives do the bulk of household work and childcare. Second, this pattern is not significantly altered if the wife also has fulltime paid employment outside the home.

In an illustrative study, Robinson (1977) found that the husband's total family work averaged about 11.2 hours per week. In contrast, wives who were fulltime homemakers spent about 53.2 hours per week. More important, wives employed fulltime spent 28.1 hours on family work. Thus, employed wives spent roughly three times as many hours on family work as did their employed husbands. The amount of time the husband spent on family activities was *not* related to whether his wife worked outside the home. The consequence is that employed wives have significantly less free time than do either fulltime homemakers or employed husbands. Another study (Robinson et al., 1977) found that in a family with an employed wife and a preschool child, the husband had roughly 339 minutes of "free time" per day compared to only about 221 minutes for the wife—a difference of two hours each day. Women perform most homemaking and child-care activities, regardless of whether or not they have a job outside the home.

There is some evidence that these sex differences in family work may be decreasing. In a review of relevant studies, Pleck (1981a) has argued that in the 1970s, women's contribution to family work decreased and men's increased—with estimates of the amount of change ranging from about 5% to 20% for each sex. Pleck suggests that this trend signals an increased convergence in the patterns of work and family roles for both sexes, and that it has reduced the role overload previously experienced by married women who worked fulltime for pay. Whether Pleck's optimistic view of recent trends will be corroborated by future studies is an important, unanswered question.

Why does a traditional division of labor in marriage persist, even when wives are employed fulltime for pay? Several explanations have been proposed. First, we should note that common explanations for women's traditional family role do not adequately account for current patterns. The belief that childbearing and nursing make it sensible for women to engage in domestic activities might explain why people resist paid employment for women. But given that a large proportion of wives *are* employed outside the home, biological explanations alone cannot account for the lack of change in the husband's role. Similarly, the "availability hypothesis" (Blood & Wolfe, 1960)—that household work is allocated on the basis of the partners' time and skills—does not explain why employed wives spend many more hours on family work than their husbands do. Two more plausible explanations will be briefly considered.

Several analyses point to the influence of *economic conditions* on the division of labor in the family (see Farkas, 1976; Lloyd, 1975; Perrucci, Potter, & Rhoads, 1978). One hypothesis is that spouses allocate their time between family work and paid employment so as to maximize their economic efficiency. Thus, men do less homemaking than women because men can better contribute to the family by their paid labor. Given the current sex stratification of occupations and the discrimination against women in employment, this fairly rational and pragmatic hypothesis seems, at first glance, to be quite reasonable. However, evidence linking the relative wages of husbands and wives to household work arrangements has been inconsistent (see review in Farkas, 1976; Lloyd, 1975; Perrucci et al., 1978). Thus, this does not appear to be an adequate explanation.

A more interactional view of how economic factors can influence marital roles is suggested by Berk and Berk (1979). They found that the work schedule of an employed wife was important to the division of labor at home. If the wife worked during the day, her husband did not help with the dinner dishes. In families where the wife worked an evening shift, however, necessity led many husbands to do after-dinner chores. "In other words, an important part of husbands' contributions to household work may rest on two conditions: the existence of certain household needs after dinner and an employed wife who leaves for work just about that time" (p. 231). Analyses at this more proximal, interactive level seem a fruitful direction for research.

Another explanation points to the important effects of the *attitudes and shared norms* held by spouses about childcare and housework. Although Americans' sex-role attitudes have become more egalitarian in the past two decades (Mason, Czajka, & Arber, 1976), many people continue to believe that family work should be women's work, even when wives have paid jobs outside the home (Yankelovich, 1974). Two studies (Beckman & Houser, 1979; Perrucci et al., 1978) have directly examined the impact of spouses' sex-role attitudes on the division of family work. In both cases, people with more traditional attitudes reported lower levels of husband participation in housework and childcare. One study of working wives (Robinson et al., 1977) found that the desire for husbands to provide "more help with household chores" was greater among younger wives and wives with pro-feminist attitudes.

Social scientists have speculated about the specific attitudes supporting men's lower participation in family work. For some people, the belief that traditional marital roles are essential to the psychological development of children may bolster a traditional division of labor (Mason et al., 1976). Some may consider it demeaning or psychologically harmful for men to engage in traditionally feminine tasks (Pleck, 1975). People may also believe that women's family work simply counts for less than paid employment (Kidder et al., 1981).

Americans generally report being satisfied with the husband's current level of participation in family tasks (Harris, 1971). Studies of working women (e.g., Bryson et al., 1976; Robinson et al., 1977) have found that over two-thirds of employed wives are satisfied with the division of labor in their marriage. A common theme emerging from studies of dual-worker families is the belief that the employed wife's major responsibility should still be as homemaker, and the husband's major responsibility should still be as breadwinner. Even when a wife works fulltime for pay, her job is often interpreted as less important than her husband's job or than her own family obligations. The comments of a successful woman professor illustrate this view: "Even though my career is clearly secondary, I don't feel cheated in any way because I want it this way. If I didn't want it this way, I think the marriage institution as we know it . . . would be disrupted and that my marriage wouldn't be a successful one" (Cited in Paloma & Garland, 1971, p. 534). Adherence to a "norm of male superiority" in intellectual and occupational achievement continues to be widespread, even among college students who support the idea of women working for pay (Komarovsky, 1976; Peplau & Rook, 1978).

POWER AND DECISION-MAKING

Power is a basic element in all relationships, yet it has proved frustratingly difficult for researchers to investigate in close relationships. Research on power in dating and marital relationships has encountered knotty conceptual and methodological problems (see Cromwell & Olson, 1975; Huston, 1983; Safilios-

Rothschild, 1970). We consider three aspects of power: sex-typing in domains of decision-making, the balance of power in a relationship, and power tactics.

Decision Making: His and Hers

Although most American couples say that many of their decisions are "mutual," partners usually do have sex-typed areas of influence. Boyfriends may have greater say about recreational activities, making decisions about how a couple spends their leisure time together; girlfriends may have more say about progress toward sexual intimacy in the relationship (Peplau, 1984). In marriage, husbands typically make decisions about their own job, the family car, and insurance. Wives typically decide about meals, home decorating, and the family doctor (c.f., Blood & Wolfe, 1960; Centers, Raven & Rodrigues, 1971). The division of labor between the sexes includes not only who does which tasks, but also who makes various decisions.

The Balance of Power

Is the general power structure of American heterosexual relationships male-dominant or egalitarian? Unfortunately, research provides no definitive answer to this deceptively simple question.

A common approach to assessing marital power (e.g., Blood & Wolfe, 1960; Centers et al., 1971) is to ask one spouse to indicate which partner typically makes each of several types of decisions (e.g., about insurance and home decorating). These are summed to arrive at an overall index indicating whether one spouse makes more decisions than the other. Studies using this method have often concluded that American marriages are usually egalitarian. For example, Centers et al. (1971) reported that only about 10% of marriages were husband-dominant, 4% were wife-dominant, and the rest were relatively egalitarian (i.e., decisions were either shared or divided equally). The interpretation of these and similar findings is, however, controversial (see discussion by Safilios-Rothschild, 1970).

In these decision-making studies, researchers decide a priori which family decisions are important and determine how to combine these decisions into an overall index of family power. In a widely cited study, Blood and Wolfe (1960) deliberately included four "masculine" areas and four "feminine" areas, weighted each type of decision equally, and then concluded that most couples are egalitarian. The assumptions implicit in this research strategy are questionable: Whether the husband's decision to move the family to a new city in order to advance his career is equivalent to the wife's decision to serve the family pot roast is open to debate. Of equal concern is that participants in a relationship may perceive and evaluate power differently than observers (Olson, 1977). The wife who appears to outsiders to make most of the family's decisions may actually cater scrupulously to her husband's wishes and see herself as implementing his ideas. In addition, partners may differ from each other in their views about the balance of power in their relationship (Hill, Peplau & Rubin, 1981; Peplau, 1984).

One alternative approach has been to ask individuals about their perceptions of power in the relationship. For example, one study (Peplau, 1984) asked members of college dating couples, "Who do you think has more of a say about what you and your partner do together—your partner or you?" Only about 45% of the young adults thought that their relationship was "exactly equal" in power. When the relationship was unequal, students said it was usually the man who had more say (40%) rather than the woman (15%). The high proportion of students reporting greater male power is all the more striking given that most students rejected a patriarchal model for relationships. When asked which partner should ideally have more say, 95% of women and 87% of men said that both partners should ideally have exactly equal say.

The analysis of factors that tip the balance of power in favor of one partner rather than the other has been a topic of sustained research interest (e.g., Cromwell & Olson, 1975; Peplau, 1984; Rollins & Bahr, 1976). Three factors seem important. First, social convention has long given men greater status and authority in male–female relations (cf., Bernard, 1972). The belief that the husband should be the "head" of the family, or that the boyfriend has the right to be "leader" can give men a power advantage in heterosexual relationships. Second, consistent with social exchange theory (Blau, 1964; Thibaut & Kelley, 1959), the balance of power is influenced by the relative resources of the partners, such as education or income. For example, in Peplau's (1984) study of college couples, the woman's educational and career goals were an important predictor of power. If the girlfriend aspired to less than a bachelor's degree, 87% of the students reported that the man had greater power; if the girlfriend planned to pursue an advanced degree, only 30% reported that the man had greater power. There is also evidence (e.g., Heer, 1958) that paid employment increases wives' relative power in marriage. Kidder et al. (1981) have suggested that the prospects for an egalitarian relationship are further enhanced when both partners contribute and receive similar rewards from a relationship. A third factor influencing power is the relative involvement or dependency of the two partners. As social exchange theory predicts, when there is an imbalance of involvement in a relationship, the partner who is less involved often has greater influence. Dependency on a relationship can be based on many factors, including both attraction to the partner, and the lack of alternative opportunities. Traditional marital roles have put wives at a power disadvantage, as Bernard (1972) colorfully notes:

Take a young woman who has been trained for feminine dependencies, who wants to "look up" to the man she marries. Put her at a disadvantage in the labor market. Then marry her to a man who has a slight initial advantage over her in age, income, and education, shored up by an ideology with a male bias. . . . Then expect an egalitarian relationship? (p. 146)

The effects of contemporary changes in sex roles on power in male–female relationships are an important topic for future research.

Power Strategies

Another facet of power in close relationships concerns the tactics that individuals use to try to influence one another. Only a few studies of power strategies have explicitly focused on dating and marital relationships (Falbo & Peplau, 1980; Frieze, 1979; Kaplan, 1975; McCormick & Jesser, 1983; Raven, Centers, & Rodrigues, 1975; Raush, Barry, Hertel, & Swain, 1974; Raven, Centers, & Rodrigues, 1975). Although it is too early to draw firm conclusions about sex differences in power tactics, the available data are provocative.

In one study (Raven et al., 1975), wives were more likely to attribute "expert" power to their husbands than vice versa. Husbands indicated that their wives more often used "referent" power, appealing to the fact that they were all part of the same family and should see eye to eye. In a study of interaction in dating couples, Kaplan (1975) found that boyfriends offered information more often than their girlfriends did. Girlfriends were more likely to disagree with an idea or contradict information given by their boyfriend. Kaplan suggested that whereas men take an assertive stance, women derive power from resisting male initiatives. Kaplan viewed this as consistent with a traditional pattern in which the man "proposes" and the woman "opposes."

In another study of college dating relationships, Falbo and Peplau (1980) found that men were more likely to report using direct and mutual power strategies, such as bargaining or logical arguments, than were women. In contrast, women were more likely to report using indirect and unilateral strategies, such as becoming silent and withdrawn, or pouting. Women's strategies were similar to those of individuals (regardless of sex) who perceived themselves as relatively less powerful than their partner.

Somewhat similar results were found in Raush et al.'s (1974) study of newlyweds. In role-playing conflictual interactions, husbands more often attempted to resolve the conflict and restore harmony; wives more often were cold and rejecting, or used appeals to fairness or guilt induction. The researchers suggested that "women, as a low power group, may learn a diplomacy of psychological pressure to influence male partners' behavior" (p. 153). In a more recent study, Gottman (1979) examined the behavior of spouses in structured situations varying in degrees of conflict. In low conflict situations, the husband responded to the wife's negative behavior in a positive way more often. In the high conflict situations, however, it was the wife who was agreeable and expressed positive affect in response to the husband's complaints. Gottman concluded that "in our culture, it appears to be the wife's responsibility to keep negative affect from escalating in high conflict situations'' (p. 210).

Another perspective on the complex matter of how men and women respond in conflict situations is provided by Kelley and his associates (1978). They investigated what young couples say and do during naturally occurring conflicts. Both sexes expected the woman to cry and sulk, and to criticize the boyfriend for his insensitivity to her feelings. The man was expected (again, by both sexes) to show anger, to reject the woman's tears, to call for a logical and less emotional approach to the problem, and to give reasons for delaying the discussion. Partners in actual dating relationships reported that their conflict interactions were consistent with these stereotypes. Kelley et al. interpreted this pattern as reflecting gender differences in people's general orientation to conflict. The man is a conflict-avoidant person who finds the display of emotions uncomfortable or upsetting. The woman is a conflict-confronting person, who is frustrated by avoidance and asks that the problem be discussed and that feelings be considered. Kelley et al. further suggested that the placating behavior seen in the husbands studied by Rausch et al. (1974) reveals how a conflict-avoidant person behaves when he or she cannot escape dealing with an issue. Kelley et al. proposed that these sex differences in the approach to conflict stem from the socialization of women as socioemotional specialists, and the socialization of men as task specialists. It seems equally plausible to us that different orientations to conflict reflect the current power structure of a relationship. If men have greater power in a relationship, they may have nothing to gain by discussing problems with their partner and may benefit from avoidance. If women have lesser power, they may see confrontation as the only way to protect or to enhance their own position.

Finally, although Americans like to think of close relationships in sentimental terms, it is important to recognize that physical coercion can and does occur. In survey studies of marital power tactics (e.g., Raven et al., 1975), few spouses reported the use of coercion of any kind. But, as Frieze (1979) has pointed out, these data may be affected by social desirability biases. In a study using in-depth interviews, Frieze (1979) found higher rates of reported coercive tactics. It is likely that physical force is most often used as a last resort when other influence strategies appear ineffective. Nonetheless, researchers (e.g., Steinmetz, 1978) estimate that about 3.3 million American wives and over a quarter million husbands have experienced severe beatings from their spouses. Although we do not have precise information on how frequently physical coercion is used as an influence strategy, it appears that this tactic is predominantly used by men against women.

In summary, research suggests that men and women do use somewhat different power tactics to influence one another. These differences may reflect three interrelated factors. First, as a result of sex-role socialization, men and women may learn somewhat different influence strategies or approaches to interpersonal conflict. It is difficult, for example, to imagine a traditional American husband using tears as a power tactic. Second, men and women may have characteristically different goals in interpersonal interactions. Kelley et al. (1978) linked conflict behavior to preferences for avoiding versus confronting conflict. In another context, McCormick (1979) demonstrated that sex differences in influence tactics used in sexual encounters are closely tied to men's goal of persuading a partner to have sex, and women's desire to resist sexual advances. Third, both power tactics and interpersonal goals may reflect, in some measure, the general power structure of heterosexual relationships. To the extent that partners have different resources in terms of skills, physical strength, expertise, money, and the like, they may be disposed to use different power strategies.

SATISFACTION AND WELL-BEING

Cultural stereotypes often depict marriage as a crowning achievement for women, who "finally trap a man," and something of a defeat for men, who are forced to abandon the "carefree" life of a bachelor. These images might lead us to believe that women are more satisfied with their love relationships than are men. Yet research examining subjective satisfaction with relationships, and the impact of relationships on psychological well-being find few sex differences. If anything, marriage may be more beneficial to men than to women (Bernard, 1972).

Satisfaction

Much research has examined partners' evaluations of their satisfaction or happiness in a relationship, especially marriage. Despite both methodological and conceptual problems with this literature (discussed by Aldous, Osmond, & Hick, 1979; Laws, 1971; Lewis & Spanier, 1979; McNamara & Bahr, 1980), several general trends can be identified.

No consistent sex differences have been found in global ratings of personal satisfaction with dating relationships or marriage. In dating relationships, boyfriends and girlfriends usually report equal and high levels of satisfaction and closeness (e.g., Cochran & Peplau, in press; Risman, Hill, Rubin, & Peplau, 1981). Presumably, most dating relationships that are not mutually gratifying are short-lived.

Studies of marital satisfaction are more numerous and complex (see reviews by Aldous et al., 1979; Hicks & Platt, 1970; Lewis & Spanier, 1979). In general, most husbands and wives report that their marriage is satisfying, and spouses' happiness ratings are positively correlated. Differences between the sexes, when they do emerge, are small. The results from three large surveys investigating the quality of life in many domains are illustrative. Gurin, Veroff, and Feld (1960) asked Americans to rate the quality of their marriage. Similar proportions of men and women rated their marriage as "very happy" (45% of the women and 48% of the men), and as "not at all happy" (3% of the women, 2% of the men). In another large scale study (Bradburn, 1969), about 60% of wives and husbands rated their marriage as "very happy." The exception to this pattern occurred among those in the lower socio-economic group, where only 49% of wives compared to 59% of husbands rated their marriage as "very happy." In a more recent survey by Campbell, Converse, and Rodgers (1976), 56% of wives and 60% of husbands indicated that they were "completely" satisfied with their marriage. Asked if they had ever wished they had married someone else, 70% of the women and 72% of the men said they had "never" wished for a different spouse.

The marriage and family literature contains many smaller-scale investigations of marital satisfaction that have produced inconsistent sex differences. Several studies have found that husbands report higher marital satisfaction than wives (e.g., Burr, 1970; Komarovsky, 1967; Renne, 1970). A few studies (e.g., Spanier, Lewis & Cole, 1975) have found that at certain times in the life cycle, women report greater marital satisfaction. Other studies have found no sex differences (e.g., Gilford & Bengtson, 1979; Rollins & Cannon, 1974). We conclude that there are probably no appreciable differences in the reported marital satisfaction of most American husbands and wives, although small sex differences may occur in specific subpopulations.

Although global assessments of marital satisfaction are quite similar for men and women, it is useful to examine the ways in which gender and sex roles may influence marital quality for both spouses. We turn now to a consideration of sex differences in the correlates of marital satisfaction, and to an examination of the impact of role differentiation, role consensus, paid employment, and the balance of power on satisfaction.

Gender Differences in the Correlates of Satisfaction.   Global assessments of marital satisfaction may have somewhat different determinants for women and for men. For example, Levinger (1964) found that global marital satisfaction was related to expressions of affection and supportiveness for both sexes (see also Hendrick, 1981). However, sexual satisfaction was more strongly related to overall marital satisfaction for husbands than for wives, and communication was of greater importance to wives than to husbands. A more recent study (Wills, Weiss & Patterson, 1974) found that for husbands (but not wives), marital satisfaction was related to the frequency of pleasurable instrumental activities in the relationship. For wives (but not for husbands), marital satisfaction was associated with the frequency of pleasurable affectional activities. An examination of the factors that contribute to marital satisfaction for both sexes is an important direction for future research.

Role Differentiation.   Is marital satisfaction linked to the overall degree of sex-role differentiation—whether husband and wife have rigidly distinct versus shared roles? Two different views on this matter can be identified (Aldous et al., 1979). Some (e.g., Parsons, 1955) have argued that the existence of clear-cut and complementary roles is beneficial to marriage and to the spouses' happiness. In contrast, others such as Komarovsky (1967) have proposed that the "separate worlds of the sexes" in traditional marriage set the stage for marital discontent.

Empirical evidence about the impact of role differentiation on marital happiness is mixed. In a study of British couples, Bott (1971) found no relationship between marital satisfaction and the degree of role segregation. Similar results were obtained in a study of middle-class American families (Rainwater, 1965). But some evidence has been found linking role-sharing in marriage to greater enjoyment of couple activities (Rapoport, Rapoport & Thiessen, 1974), and to reporting fewer serious problems in marriage (Rainwater, 1965). In a study of blue collar marriages, Komarovsky (1967) found that the divergent interests of the sexes contributed to dissatisfaction with marital communication. One reason for these mixed findings may be that people's global assessments of marital satisfaction are based not only on their actual experiences, but also on their aspirations (Komarovsky, 1967). Couples with rigid differentiation of husband–wife roles may expect little interaction or sharing between spouses, and judge their marriage on that basis. More generally, traditional and nontraditional couples may use different yardsticks in assessing marital success.

Role Consensus.   The specific pattern of interaction that a couple adopts is probably less important to satisfaction than whether the partners agree about the pattern. Several studies (reviewed in Hicks & Platt, 1970; Lewis & Spanier, 1979) document the importance of "role fit" or consensus between the marital role expectations and behavior of spouses (e.g., Chadwick, Albrecht & Kunz, 1976). It seems almost a truism that an ardent feminist who desires shared roles in marriage will be happier with a partner who supports these views than with a staunch traditionalist (cf. Bahr & Day, 1978). Disagreement between spouses about marital roles is a major source of potential conflict and dissatisfaction.

Several older studies (reviewed in Hicks & Platt, 1970; Laws, 1971) found that marital satisfaction was significantly linked to the wife's ability to perceive her husband as he perceives himself, and to conform to his expectations—but not vice versa. Laws (1971) referred to this as the norm of wife-accommodation, and explained that "an accommodative (or empathic, or considerate) spouse contributes to *anyone's* marital satisfaction, . . . and the social norms decree that it shall be the wife's role" (p. 501). This pattern may occur because husbands and wives share a stereotype of masculinity and perceive the husband as enacting it. The opposite pattern has not been found; marital satisfaction is not related to the husband's ability to perceive the wife as she sees herself. New research on this issue would be useful.

Paid Employment.   Many studies have found that the greater the husband's occupational success and income, the greater the marital satisfaction of both spouses (Lewis & Spanier, 1979). Recently, Aldous et al. (1979) suggested that this relationship may actually be curvilinear, with extremely low and high occupational success by the husband detracting from the enjoyment of marriage. The impact of the wife's employment status on marital satisfaction is more controversial.

Some family theorists such as Parsons (1955) have viewed role differentiation as essential to marital success and so emphasized the hazards of wives' venturing into the occupational domain. Early studies (reviewed in Hicks & Platt, 1970) seemed to show that marriages were often less happy when wives were employed fulltime, rather than being fulltime homemakers or working for pay only part-time. More recent studies (e.g., Booth, 1979; Staines, Pleck, Shepard, & O'Connor, 1978) cast doubt on this conclusion, however, and suggest that the impact of wives' employment on marital satisfaction is complex. Research is beginning to identify factors that influence the impact of wives' employment on marital satisfaction—such as social class, the woman's choice of employment, and the husband's attitudes about his wife's employment. In thinking about this issue, it seems essential to distinguish wives who enjoy paid employment and have supportive husbands from wives who prefer to stay home, or whose husbands object to their employment.

Several studies show that paid employment can have beneficial effects for wives. For example, Burke and Weir (1976) found that employed wives were happier and had higher self-esteem than did fulltime homemakers. The impact of the wife's employment on her husband's marital satisfaction has been a recent topic for inquiry. Burke and Weir reported that husbands were more satisfied with their marriage and were healthier when their wives did not work fulltime for pay. But studies with larger samples and better controls (e.g., Booth, 1979; Staines et al., 1978) have not replicated this pattern. Rather, no relationship has been found between the wife's employment status and her husband's marital happiness, experience of stress, or personal health. We agree with Lewis and Spanier (1979) that overall marital satisfaction is probably highest when both partners are satisfied with the wife's employment status.

The Balance of Power.   Satisfaction in heterosexual relationships is significantly associated with the balance of power or decision-making. One study (Peplau, 1984) examined the balance of power in college-age dating couples. No differences were found between equal-power and male-dominant couples on measures of satisfaction, closeness, or staying together versus breaking up over a two-year period. In contrast, however, both boyfriends and girlfriends reported less satisfaction in relationships where the woman had greater say. Studies of married couples (e.g., Blood & Wolfe, 1960; Centers et al., 1971; Lu, 1952; Rainwater, 1965) have generally found high levels of satisfaction among both egalitarian and male-dominant marriages, and lesser satisfaction among female-dominant marriages. Illustrative findings come from a study by Centers et al. (1971). Over 70% of individuals in husband-dominant and egalitarian marriages reported being "very satisfied," compared to only 20% of those in wife-dominant relationships. Minor variations have been found across studies in whether greater satisfaction is found among egalitarian or male-dominant couples; no clear conclusion emerges on this point. It is usually more comfortable, however, to adhere to traditional patterns of male dominance or newer patterns of egalitarianism than to experience female dominance.

Psychological Well-Being

Although husbands and wives typically report roughly equal satisfaction—or dissatisfaction—with their marriage, evidence suggests that marriage provides greater health benefits to men than to women. In general, married individuals enjoy better mental and physical health, report greater happiness and psychological well-being, and experience fewer symptoms of psychological distress than do the single, divorced, or widowed. But evidence also indicates that the positive effects of marital status are greater for men than for women (Bernard, 1972; Dohrenwend & Dohrenwend, 1976; Gove, 1972; Knupfer, Clark & Room, 1966; Lynch, 1977; Pearlin & Johnson, 1977). Gove (1979) concluded that "marriage is more beneficial to men than women, whereas being single is if anything more stressful for men than for women" (p. 57). A common pattern is for married men to score highest on measures of psychological well-being, married and single women to score moderately, and single men to receive the lowest scores. For example, Perlman, Gerson and Spinner (1978) found that widowed men were significantly lonelier than married men; among women, no significant difference was found in loneliness between those who were married and those who were widowed. Although some contradictory evidence has been reported (e.g., Warheit, Holzer, Bell, & Arey, 1976), the bulk of existing research suggests that husbands often enjoy better mental health than wives.

The reasons for the differential effects of marriage for women and men are not well understood, but several possible explanations have been offered (e.g., Bernard, 1972; Peplau, Bikson, Rook, & Goodchilds, 1982). Although response biases and differential selection into marriage for women and men may contribute to this pattern (Bernard, 1972), they do not offer a complete explanation (Gove, 1979). Several researchers have suggested that the traditional homemaker's role is less rewarding than the breadwinner's role. Housework is seen as unstructured, frustrating, and low in prestige (Gove, 1979). For employed wives, there may also be problems of role overload, since husbands do not typically share fully in homemaking and childcare (e.g., Robinson et al., 1977). Power differences favoring husbands may also contribute in some cases. In short, it has been proposed that asymmetries in the roles of husbands and wives, and inequities in the family division of labor may put women at a disadvantage.

Others have suggested that men benefit from marriage in part because wives serve as important social and emotional resources for their husbands. For example, it is often wives who initiate and maintain relations with friends and relatives. Knupfer, Clark, and Room (1966) speculated that the "man's lesser ability to form and maintain personal relationships creates a need for a wife, as the expressive expert, to perform this function for him" (p. 848). As a result, unmarried men experience an "expressive hardship." The caring functions of the wife may extend into nursing the husband when he is ill and encouraging him to take care of his own health (Troll & Turner, 1979).

At present, the reasons why marriage contributes more to the psychological health of husbands than of wives remain an intriguing puzzle. Speculations abound, but are typically post hoc and unsubstantiated by solid research. Equally puzzling is the discrepancy between findings for marital happiness and psychological well-being. Even though wives exhibit more psychological distress than husbands, both groups report roughly equal marital satisfaction. A better understanding of the social and psychological factors that determine satisfaction with relationships is needed. We know little about the psychological algebra that people use in arriving at overall assessments of their relationships, and whether such processes differ by gender or sex role.

DISCUSSION

Our review of the research on gender differences in heterosexual relationships has found both similarities among the goals and experiences of women and men—and some consistent differences. Space limitations have forced us to omit other areas in which sex differences have also been observed, such as sexuality (e.g., Allgeier & McCormick, 1983; Symons, 1979) and reactions to breakups (e.g., Rubin et al., 1981).

We have said little about the important methodological problems that arise in studying couples (see Harvey, Christensen, & McClintock, 1983; Hill, 1981) and the ways in which these problems may distort research findings about sex differences in relationships. For example, social psychological research on relationships has often relied on college students and other "convenience" samples; we do not know how representative the sex differences we have described are of couples throughout the life-cycle or from various racial and socioeconomic groups. In addition, the effects of volunteer bias on relationship studies are not well understood. Hill, Rubin, Peplau, and Willard (1979) have argued that volunteer samples may under-represent couples with the most traditional sex-role behaviors. Finally, Hill (1981) has recently suggested that the use of inappropriate statistical analyses is common in couples research and can lead to inflated estimates of partner similarity and agreement, perhaps masking the extent of actual sex differences. There is reason for caution in interpreting the results of existing studies of sex differences in close relationships.

Descriptive Typologies

An adequate description of women and men in love must go beyond a simple list of differences to understand the patterning and internal organization of sex roles. How, for example, are various components of a relationship—power, self-disclosure, the division of labor, and personal satisfaction—interrelated? One approach to this question has been to develop typologies of male–female relationships.

Burgess and Locke (1960) contrasted an institutional orientation, where the family is an economic production unit headed by a strong patriarch, and a companionship orientation, where the family is based on mutual love and affection, and is run by democratic consensus. Scanzoni and Scanzoni (1976) identified four patterns in which the relations between husband and wife are that of owner and property, head to complement, senior partner and junior partner, and equal partners. In an extension of ideas developed by Pleck (1976), Peplau (1983) has distinguished three relationship patterns. In traditional marriage, the husband is accorded greater authority, the wife does not work for pay, and clearcut male–female role differentiation is maintained. In modern marriage, greater emphasis is given to companionship. Paid employment for the wife is accepted, so long as it does not interfere with her traditional homemaker responsibilities or jeopardize the husband's role as breadwinner. Egalitarian marriage, more an ideal than a common reality in American life, is founded on a rejection of male dominance and role differentiation based on sex. The characterization of relationships along dimensions of power, role differentiation, and companionship is common to all typologies. Whether through typologies or some other analytic strategy, effort is needed to provide an integrated description of gender-linked patterns in relationships.

Explaining Gender Differences

One crucial direction for future research is to study directly the factors that create and maintain sex-linked patterns, rather than relying on post hoc explanations. Such analyses could potentially encompass a wide array of causal factors, ranging from proximal, immediate causes to more distal and historical ones. Analyses might profitably examine the effects of the characteristics of *individual* partners (e.g., personal attitudes, self-concept, habits, biological predispositions), features of the *dyad* (e.g., similarities and asymmetries in involvement or personal resources; shared norms) and features of the *social context*. We have seen that social class can have a significant impact on the patterning of interaction in relationships. Other features of the social environment, such as cultural norms and values, social networks, patterns of paid employment, and access to birth control information also deserve study.

Building Successful Relationships

A concern with relationships (and their dissolution) raises questions about how to create gratifying relationships. Feminist psychologists have challenged traditional psychological prescriptions. At the level of personality, it was once believed that healthy adults had to have a clearcut and secure sense of their "masculinity" or "femininity" (see Pleck, 1981b). Today, psychologists are suggesting that greater sex-role flexibility, whether it is called androgyny or sex-role transcendence (e.g., Garnets & Pleck, 1979) is beneficial to individual functioning. At the dyadic level, a similar shift is occurring. Family sociologists (e.g., Parsons, 1955) used to emphasize the benefits of highly differentiated male–female roles in marriage. Such patterns were believed to increase efficiency, decrease competition and conflict, foster mutual dependency, and encourage marital stability. Today, all of these assumptions have been questioned (see Peplau, 1983). It is argued instead that traditional male–female roles often prevent partners from being the kind of companion each wants (e.g., Friedland, 1982). There is a growing belief that role sharing and flexibility may be more beneficial to heterosexual relationships.

It should be emphasized, of course, that research demonstrating the benefits of egalitarian relationships is very limited. Nonetheless, examples of the inhibiting effects of traditional sex differences are readily found. Rubin (1976) has described one marriage:

> When they try to talk, she relies on the only tools she has. . . . She becomes progressively more emotional and expressive. He falls back on the only tools he has; he gets progressively more rational—determinedly reasonable. She cries for him to attend to her feelings. . . . He tells her it's silly to feel that way. . . [His] clenchteeth reasonableness invalidates her feelings (p. 117).

Clinical discussions emphasize similar problems. For instance, Napier (1978) has described a "rejection–intrusion" pattern in distressed couples. One partner, typically the woman, seeks closeness and reassurance while the other, typically the man, desires greater separateness and independence. When the woman's bids for affection are rebuffed, she feels hurt, rejected and misunderstood. As a result of the wife's attempts at closeness, the husband feels intruded upon and engulfed. Whether socialization for sex-role similarity and the building of relationships based on equality would reduce such problems is an intriguing question.

A Social Psychology of Close Relationships

Social psychology has been criticized from time to time (e.g., Pepitone, 1981) for an overemphasis on individual processes such as impression formation or social cognition, and for a neglect of interpersonal processes in dyads and groups. The renewed interest of recent years in close relationships promises to move research on couples more squarely into the mainstream of American social psychology (Kelley et al., 1983). We welcome this change in the field.

As social psychologists seek to broaden their understanding of social relationships, the impact of gender and culturally-based sex roles cannot be ignored. Symons (1979) has argued that "the comparison of males and females is perhaps the most powerful available means of ordering the bewildering diversity of data on human sexuality" (p. 4). This argument can be extended to many aspects of social interactions; gender differences are a common feature of heterosexual relationships in comtemporary society. Bernard's (1972) notion that in every marriage (and we would add in every heterosexual relationship) there are really two relationships—his and hers—which are experienced differently and which have distinct personal consequences for each sex is compelling. No examination of close relationships can be wholly complete or wholly accurate unless it recognizes differences in the experiences and behaviors of women and men. The careful description and causal analysis of gender differences in relationships is a major avenue for understanding basic processes of interaction in close relationships.

ACKNOWLEDGMENT

This chapter was written in 1982. We gratefully acknowledge the helpful comments we received from Bram Buunk, Valerian Derlega, Irene H. Frieze, Susan S. Hendrick, Charles T. Hill, Robert Hinde, Carol Kendrick, Louise Kidder, Daniel Perlman, Joseph Pleck and Barbara S. Wallston. Correspondence may be addressed to L. A. Peplau, Department of Psychology, UCLA, Los Angeles, CA 90024 or to S. L. Gordon, Department of Sociology, California State University, Los Angeles, CA 90032.

REFERENCES

Aldous, J., Osmond, M. W., & Hicks, M. W. (1979). Men's work and men's families. In W. R. Burr, R. Hill, F. I. Nye & I. L. Reiss (Eds.), *Contemporary theories about the family* (Vol. 1). New York: Free Press.

Allgeier, E. R., & McCormick, N. B. (Eds.) (1983). *Changing boundaries: Gender roles and sexual behavior*. Palo Alto, Calif.: Mayfield.

Aronoff, J., & Crano, W. D. (1975). A re-examination of the cross-cultural principles of task segregation and sex role differentiation in the family. *American Sociological Review, 40*, 12–20.

Astin, A. W., King, M., & Richardson, G. T. (1980). *The American freshman: National norms for fall 1980.* Los Angeles: American Council on Education.

Bahr, S. J., & Day, R. D. (1978). Sex role attitudes, female employment, and marital satisfaction. *Journal of Comparative Family Studies, 9,* 55–65.

Beckman, L. J., & Houser, B. B. (1979). The more you have, the more you do: The relationships between wife's employment, sex-role attitudes and household behavior. *Psychology of Women Quarterly, 4*(2), 160–174.

Berk, R. A., & Berk, S. F. (1979). *Labor and leisure at home: Content and organization of the household day.* Beverly Hills, Calif.: Sage.

Berk, S. F. (Ed.) (1980). *Women and household labor.* Beverly Hills, Calif.: Sage.

Bernard, J. (1972). *The future of marriage.* New York: Bantam Books.

Berscheid, E., & Walster, E. H. (1978). *Interpersonal attraction* (2nd ed.). Menlo Park, Calif: Addison-Wesley.

Blau, P. M. (1964). *Exchange and power in social life.* New York: Wiley.

Blood, R. O., & Wolfe, D. M. (1960). *Husbands and wives: The dynamics of married living.* New York: Free Press.

Booth, A. (1972). Sex and social participation. *American Sociological Review, 37,* 183–193.

Booth, A. (1979). Does wives' employment cause stress for husbands? *The Family Coordinator, 28*(4), 445–449.

Booth, A., & Hess, E. (1974). Cross-sex friendship. *Journal of Marriage and the Family, 36,* 38–47.

Bott, E. (1971). *Family and social network* (2nd ed.). New York: Free Press.

Bradburn, N. (1969). *The structure of psychological well-being.* Chicago: Aldine.

Bryson, R. B., Bryson, J. B., Licht, M. H., & Licht, B. G. (1976). The professional pair: Husband and wife psychologists. *American Psychologist, 31*(1), 10–16.

Burchinal, L. G. (1964). The premarital dyad and love involvement. In H. T. Christensen (Ed.), *Handbook of marriage and the family.* Chicago: Rand McNally.

Burgess, E. W., & Locke, H. J. (1960). *The family: From institution to companionship* (2nd ed.). New York: American.

Burgess, E. W., & Wallin, P. (1953). *Engagement and marriage.* Philadelphia: Lippincott.

Burgess, R. L., & Huston, T. L. (Eds.) (1979). *Social exchange in developing relationships.* New York: Academic Press.

Burke, R. J., & Weir, T. (1976). Relationship of wives' employment status to husband, wife and pair satisfaction and performance. *Journal of Marriage and the Family, 38,* 279–287.

Burke, R. J., & Weir, T. (1977). Husband–wife helping relationships: The "mental hygiene" function in marriage. *Psychological Reports, 40,* 911–925.

Burke, R. J., Weir, T., & Harrison, D. (1976). Disclosure of problems and tensions experienced by marital partners. *Psychological Reports, 38,* 531–542.

Burr, W. R. (1970). Satisfaction with various aspects of marriage over the life cycle. *Journal of Marriage and the Family, 32,* 29–37.

Byrne, D., & Griffitt, W. (1973). Interpersonal attraction. In P. H. Mussen & M. R. Rosenzweig (Eds.), *Annual review of psychology.* Palo Alto, Calif.: Annual Review.

Caldwell, M. A., & Peplau, L. A. (1982). Sex differences in same-sex friendship. *Sex Roles, 8*(7), 721–732.

Campbell, A., Converse, P. E., & Rodgers, W. L. (1976). *The quality of American life.* New York: Russell Sage Foundation.

Cate, R. M., & Huston, T. L. (1980). *The growth of premarital relationships: Toward a typology of pathways to marriage.* Unpublished manuscript, Oregon State University.

Centers, R., Raven, B. H., & Rodrigues, A. (1971). Conjugal power structure: A re-examination. *American Sociological Review, 36,* 264–278.

Chadwick, B. A., Albrecht, S. L., & Kunz, P. R. (1976). Marital and family role satisfaction. *Journal of Marriage and the Family, 38*(3), 431–450.

Cochran, S. D., & Peplau, L. A. (in press). Value orientations in heterosexual relationships. *Psychology of Women Quarterly.*

Cook, M., & Wilson, G. (Eds.) (1979). *Love and attraction.* Oxford, England: Pergamon.

Coombs, R. H., & Kenkel, W. F. (1966). Sex differences in dating aspirations and satisfaction with computer-selected partners. *Journal of Marriage and the Family, 28*, 62–66.

Cozby, P. C. (1973). Self-disclosure: A literature review. *Psychological Bulletin, 79*, 73–91.

Cromwell, R. E., & Olson, D. H. (Eds.) (1975). *Power in families.* New York: Wiley.

DeBurger, J. E. (1967). Marital problems, help-seeking, and emotional orientation as revealed in help-request letters. *Journal of Marriage and the Family, 29*, 712–721.

Degler, C. N. (1980). *At odds: Women and the family in America from the revolution to the present.* New York: Oxford University Press.

Derlega, V. J., Durham, B., Gockel, B., & Sholis, D. (1981). Sex differences in self-disclosure: Effects of topic content, friendship and partner's sex. *Sex Roles, 7*(4), 433–447.

Dion, K. K., & Dion, K. L. (1975). Self-esteem and romantic love. *Journal of Personality, 43*, 39–57.

Dion, K. L., & Dion, K. K. (1973). Correlates of romantic love. *Journal of Consulting and Clinical Psychology, 41*, 51–56.

Dohrenwend, B. P., & Dohrenwend, B. S. (1976). Sex differences in psychiatric disorders. *American Journal of Sociology, 81*, 1447–1454.

Duck, S., & Gilmour, R. (1981). *Personal relationships 1: Studying personal relationships.* London: Academic Press.

Falbo, T., & Peplau, L. A. (1980). Power strategies in intimate relationships. *Journal of Personality and Social Psychology, 38*(4), 618–628.

Farber, B. (1957). An index of marital integration. *Sociometry, 20*, 117–118.

Farkas, G. (1976). Education, wage rates, and the division of labor between husband and wife. *Journal of Marriage and the Family, 38*(3), 473–483.

Fengler, A. P. (1974). Romantic love in courtships: Divergent paths of male and female students. *Journal of Comparative Family Studies, 5*(1), 134–139.

Festinger, L., Schachter, S., & Back, K. (1950). *Social pressures in informal groups: A study of human factors in housing.* Stanford, Calif.: Stanford University Press.

Fishman, P. M. (1978). Interaction: The work women do. *Social Problems, 25*(4), 397–406.

Friedland, R. F. (1982). *Men's and women's satisfying and frustrating experiences in close relationship interactions.* Unpublished doctoral dissertation, University of California, Los Angeles.

Frieze, I. H. (1979, April). *Power and influence in violent and nonviolent marriages.* Paper presented at the annual meeting of the Eastern Psychological Association, Philadelphia.

Funabiki, D., Bologna, N. C., Pepping, M., & Fitzgerald, K. C. (1980). Revisiting sex differences in the expression of depression. *Journal of Abnormal Psychology, 89*, 194–202.

Garnets, L., & Pleck, J. H. (1979). Sex-role identity, androgyny, and sex-role transcendence: A sex-role strain analysis. *Psychology of Women Quarterly, 3*(3), 270–283.

Gilford, R., & Bengtson, V. (1979). Measuring marital satisfaction in three generations: Positive and negative dimensions. *Journal of Marriage and the Family, 41*(2), 387–398.

Gordon, S. L. (1981). The sociology of sentiments and emotion. In M. Rosenberg & R. H. Turner (Eds.), *Social psychology: Sociological perspectives.* New York: Basic Books.

Gottman, J. M. (1979). *Marital interaction: Experimental investigations.* New York: Academic Press.

Gove, W. (1972). The relationships between sex roles, mental illness, and marital status. *Social Forces, 51*, 34–44.

Gove, W. (1979). Sex differences in the epidemiology of mental disorder: Evidence and explanations. In E. S. Gomberg & V. Franks (Eds.), *Gender and disordered behavior.* New York: Bruner-Mazel.

Gurin, G., Veroff, J., & Feld, S. (1960). *Americans view their mental health.* New York: Basic Books.

Hacker, H. M. (1961). Blabbermouths and clams: Sex differences in self-disclosure in same-sex and cross-sex friendship dyads. *Psychology of Women Quarterly, 5*(3), 385–401.

Harris, L., & Associates. (1971). *The Harris survey yearbook of public opinion 1970.* New York: Louis Harris.

Harvey, J., Christensen, A., & McClintock, E. (1983). Research methods in studying close relationships. In H. H. Kelley et al., *Close relationships.* New York: Freeman.

Hatkoff, T. S., & Lasswell, T. E. (1979). Male/female similarities and differences in conceptualizing love. In M. Cook & G. Wilson (Eds.), *Love and attraction.* London: Pergamon.

Heer, D. M. (1958). Dominance and the working wife. *Social Forces, 35,* 341–347.

Hendrick, S. S. (1981). Self-disclosure and marital satisfaction. *Journal of Personality and Social Psychology, 40*(6), 1150–1159.

Henley, N. M. (1977). *Body politics: Power, sex and nonverbal communication.* Englewood Cliffs, N.J.: Prentice Hall.

Hicks, M. W., & Platt, M. (1970). Marital happiness and stability: A review of the research in the sixties. *Journal of Marriage and the Family, 32,* 553–574.

Hill, C. T. (1981, September). *Statistical analysis of dyadic data: Similarity, agreement, and reciprocity.* Unpublished manuscript, University of Washington.

Hill, C. T., Peplau, L. A., & Rubin, Z. (1981). Differing perceptions in dating couples: Sex roles vs. alternative explanations. *Psychology of Women Quarterly, 5*(3), 418–434.

Hill, C. T., Rubin, Z., & Peplau, L. A. (1976). Breakups before marriage: The end of 13 affairs. *Journal of Social Issues, 32*(1), 147–168.

Hill, C. T., Rubin, Z., Peplau, L. A., & Willard, S. G. (1979). The volunteer couple: Sex differences, couple commitment, and participation in research on interpersonal relationships. *Social Psychology Quarterly, 4,* 415–420.

Hinde, R. A. (1979). *Towards understanding relationships.* London: Academic Press.

Hobart, C. W. (1958). The incidence of romanticism during courtship. *Social Forces, 36,* 362–367.

Horner, M. S. (1970). Femininity and successful achievement: A basic inconsistency. In J. M. Bardwick, E. Douvan, M. S. Horner, & D. Guttmann (Eds.), *Feminine personality and conflict.* Belmont, Calif.: Brooks-Cole, 1970.

Hudson, J. W., & Henze, L. F. (1969). Campus values and mate selection: A replication. *Journal of Marriage and the Family, 31,* 772–775.

Huston, T. L. (1983). Power. In H. H. Kelley, et al., *Close relationships.* New York: Freeman.

Huston, T. L., & Levinger, G. (1978). Interpersonal attraction and relationships. *Annual Review of Psychology, 29,* 115–156.

Jourard, S. M. (1959). *The transparent self.* New York: Van Nostrand.

Jourard, S. M. (1971). *Self-disclosure: An experimental analysis of the transparent self.* New York: Wiley-Interscience.

Jourard, S. M., & Lasakow, P. (1958). Some factors in self-disclosure. *Journal of Abnormal and Social Psychology, 56,* 91–98.

Kanin, E. J., Davidson, K. R., & Scheck, S. R. (1970). A research note on male-female differentials in the experience of heterosexual love. *Journal of Sex Research, 6*(1), 64–72.

Kaplan, S. L. (1975). *The exercise of power in dating couples.* Unpublished doctoral dissertation, Harvard University.

Kelley, H. H. (1979). *Personal relationships: Their structures and processes.* Hillsdale, N.J.: Lawrence Erlbaum Associates.

Kelley, H. H., Berscheid, E., Christensen, A., Harvey, J. H., Huston, T. L., Levinger, G.,

McClintock, E., Peplau, L. A., & Peterson, D. R. (1983). *Close relationships*. New York: Freeman.

Kelley, H. H., Cunningham, J. D., Grisham, J. A., Lefebvre, L. M., Sink, C. R., & Yablon, G. (1978). Sex differences in comments made during conflict within close heterosexual pairs. *Sex Roles, 4*(4), 473–491.

Kephart, W. M. (1967). Some correlates of romantic love. *Journal of Marriage and the Family, 29*, 470–474.

Kidder, L. H., Fagan, M. A., & Cohn, E. S. (1981). Giving and receiving: Social justice in close relationships. In M. J. Lerner & S. C. Lerner (Eds.), *The justice motive in social behavior*. New York: Plenum.

Knox, D. H., & Sporakowski, M. J. (1968). Attitudes of college students toward love. *Journal of Marriage and the Family, 30*, 638–642.

Knupfer, G., Clark, W., & Room, R. (1966). The mental health of the unmarried. *American Journal of Psychiatry, 122*, 841–851.

Komarovsky, M. (1967). *Blue-collar marriage*. New York: Random House.

Komarovsky, M. (1976). *Dilemmas of masculinity*. New York: Norton.

Lakoff, R. (1975). *Language and woman's place*. New York: Harper & Row.

Laner, M. R. (1977). Permanent partner priorities: Gay and straight. *Journal of Homosexuality, 3*, 12–39.

Langhorne, M. C., & Secord, P. F. (1955). Variations in marital needs with age, sex, marital status, and regional locations. *Journal of Social Psychology, 41*, 19–38.

Lasswell, M., & Lobsenz, N. M. (1980). *Styles of loving*. New York: Ballantine Books.

Laws, J. L. (1971). A feminist review of the marital adjustment literature: The rape of the Locke. *Journal of Marriage and the Family, 33*(3), 483–516.

Lee, J. A. (1977). *The colors of love*. New York: Bantam.

Leik, R. K. (1963). Instrumentality and emotionality in family interaction. *Sociometry, 26*, 131–145.

Leslie, G. R. (1976). *The family in social context* (3rd ed.). New York: Oxford University Press.

Levinger, G. (1964). Task and social behavior in marriage. *Sociometry, 27*(4), 433–448.

Levinger, G., & Raush, H. L. (Eds.) (1977). *Close relationships: Perspectives on the meaning of intimacy*. Amherst: University of Massachusetts Press.

Levinger, G., & Senn, D. J. (1967). Disclosure of feelings in marriage. *Merrill-Palmer Quarterly, 13*, 237–249.

Lewis, R. A., & Spanier, G. B. (1979). Theorizing about the quality and stability of marriage. In W. R. Burr, R. Hill, R. I. Nye, & I. L. Reiss (Eds.), *Contemporary theories about the family* (Vol. 1). New York: Free Press.

Lloyd, C. B. (Ed.) (1975). *Sex, discrimination and the division of labor*. New York: Columbia University Press.

Lowenthal, M. F., & Haven, C. (1968). Interaction and adaptation: Intimacy as a critical variable. *American Sociological Review, 33*, 20–30.

Lu, Y. C. (1952). Marital roles and marriage adjustment. *Sociology and Social Research, 36*, 364–368.

Lynch, J. J. (1977). *The broken heart: The medical consequences of loneliness*. New York: Basic Books.

Mason, K. O., Czajka, J. L., & Arber, S. (1976). Change in U.S. women's sex-role attitudes, 1964–1974. *American Sociological Review, 41*(4), 573–596.

McCormick, N. B. (1979). Come-ons and put-offs: Unmarried students' strategies for having and avoiding sexual intercourse. *Psychology of Women Quarterly, 4*, 194–211.

McCormick, N. B., & Jesser, C. J. (1983). The courtship game: Power in the sexual encounter. In E. R. Allgeier & N. B. McCormick (Eds.), *Changing boundaries: Gender roles and sexual behavior*. Palo Alto, Calif.: Mayfield.

McNamara, M. L. L., & Bahr, H. M. (1980). The dimensionality of marital role satisfaction. *Journal of Marriage and the Family, 42,* 45–55.

Murstein, B. I. (1976). *Who will marry whom?* New York: Springer.

Napier, A. Y. (1978). The rejection–intrusion pattern: A central family dynamic. *Journal of Marriage and Family Counseling, 4,* 5–12.

Newcomb, T. M. (1981). *The acquaintance process.* New York: Holt, Rinehart, & Winston.

Olson, D. H. (1977). Insiders' and outsiders' views of relationships: Research strategies. In G. Levinger & H. L. Raush (Eds.), *Close relationships: Perspectives on the meaning of intimacy.* Amherst: University of Massachusetts Press.

Osmond, M. W., & Martin, P. Y. (1975). Sex and sexism: A comparison of male and female sex-role attitudes. *Journal of Marriage and the Family, 37,* 744–758.

Paloma, M. M., & Garland, T. N. (1971). The married professional woman: A study in the tolerance of domestication. *Journal of Marriage and the Family, 33,* 531–540.

Parelman, A. (1983). *Emotional intimacy in marriage: A sex-roles perspective.* Ann Arbor, Mich.: UMI Research Press.

Parsons, T. (1955). The American family: Its relations to personality and to the social structure. In T. Parsons & R. F. Bales, *Family: Socialization and interaction process,* Glencoe, Ill.: Free Press.

Pearlin, L., & Johnson, J. (1977). Marital status, life-strains, and depression. *American Sociological Review, 42,* 704–715.

Pearlin, L., & Schooler, C. (1978). The structure of coping. *Journal of Health and Social Behavior, 19,* 2–21.

Pepitone, A. (1981). Lessons from the history of social psychology. *American Psychologist, 36,* 972–985.

Peplau, L. A. (1976). Impact of fear of success and sex-role attitudes on women's competitive achievement. *Journal of Personality and Social Psychology, 34,* 561–568.

Peplau, L. A. (1983). Roles and gender. In H. H. Kelley et al., *Close relationships.* New York: Freeman.

Peplau, L. A. (1984). Power in dating relationships. In J. Freeman (Ed.), *Women: A feminist perspective* (3rd ed.). Palo Alto, Calif.: Mayfield.

Peplau, L. A., Bikson, T. K., Rook, K., & Goodchilds, J. D. (1982). Being old and living alone. In L. A. Peplau & D. Perlman (Eds.), *Loneliness: A sourcebook of current theory, research and therapy.* New York: Wiley-Interscience.

Peplau, L. A., & Rook, K. (1978, April). *Dual-career relationships: The college couple perspective.* Paper presented at the annual meeting of the Western Psychological Association, San Francisco.

Perlman, D., Gerson, A. C., & Spinner, B. (1978). Loneliness among senior citizens: An empirical report. *Essence, 2*(4), 239–248.

Perrucci, C. C., Potter, H. R., & Rhoads, D. L. (1978). Determinants of male family-role performance. *Psychology of Women Quarterly, 3*(1), 53–66.

Pietropinto, A., & Simenauer, J. (1981). *Husbands and wives.* New York: Berkeley Books.

Pifer, A. (1978). Women working toward a new society. *The Urban and Social Change Review, 11,* 3–11.

Pleck, J. H. (1975, November). *Men's role in the family: A new look.* Paper presented at the World Family Sociology Conference, Merrill-Palmer Institute, Detroit.

Pleck, J. H. (1976). The male sex role: Definitions, problems and sources of change. *Journal of Social Issues, 32*(3), 155–164.

Pleck, J. H. (1981a, August). *Changing patterns of work and family roles.* Paper presented at the annual meeting of the American Psychological Association, Los Angeles.

Pleck, J. H. (1981b). *The myth of masculinity.* Cambridge, Mass.: MIT Press.

Pleck, J. H., & Rustad, M. (1980). *Husbands' and wives' time in family work and paid employment in the 1975–1976 Study of Time Use.* Wellesley, Mass.: Wellesley College Center for Research on Women.

Rainwater, L. (1965). *Family design.* Chicago: Aldine.

Rapoport, R., Rapoport, R., & Thiessen, V. (1974). Couple symmetry and enjoyment. *Journal of Marriage and the Family, 36*(3), 588–591.

Raush, H. L., Barry, W. A., Hertel, R. K., & Swain, M. A. (1974). *Communication, conflict and marriage.* San Francisco: Jossey-Bass.

Raven, B. H., Centers, R., & Rodrigues, A. (1975). The bases of conjugal power. In R. E. Cromwell & D. H. Olson (Eds.), *Power in families.* New York: Wiley.

Renne, K. (1970). Correlates of dissatisfaction in marriage. *Journal of Marriage and the Family, 32,* 54–67.

Risman, B. J., Hill, C. T., Rubin, Z., & Peplau, L. A. (1981). Living together in college: Implications for courtship. *Journal of Marriage and the Family, 43,* 77–83.

Robinson, J. P. (1977). *How Americans use time.* New York: Praeger.

Robinson, J. P., Yerby, J., Fieweger, M., & Somerick, N. (1977). Sex-role differences in time use. *Sex Roles, 3*(5), 443–458.

Rollins, B. C., & Bahr, S. J. (1976). A theory of power relationships in marriage. *Journal of Marriage and the Family, 38,* 619–627.

Rollins, B. C., & Cannon, K. L. (1974). Marital satisfaction over the family life cycle: A re-evaluation. *Journal of Marriage and the Family, 36,* 271–282.

Rosenfeld, L. B., Civikly, J. M., & Herron, J. R. (1979). Anatomical and psychological differences. In G. J. Chelune et al. (Eds.), *Self-disclosure.* San Francisco, Calif.: Jossey-Bass.

Rubin, L. B. (1976). *Worlds of pain.* New York: Basic Books.

Rubin, Z. (1968). Do American women marry up? *American Sociological Review, 33*(5), 750–760.

Rubin, Z. (1970). Measurement of romantic love. *Journal of Personality and Social Psychology, 16,* 265–273.

Rubin, Z. (1973). *Liking and loving: An invitation to social psychology.* New York: Holt, Rinehart, & Winston.

Rubin, Z., Hill, C. T., Peplau, L. A., & Dunkel-Schetter, C. (1980). Self-disclosure in dating couples: Sex roles and the ethic of openness. *Journal of Marriage and the Family, 42*(2), 305–318.

Rubin, Z., Peplau, L. A., & Hill, C. T. (1981). Loving and leaving: Sex differences in romantic attachments. *Sex Roles, 7,* 821–835.

Rubin, Z., Peplau, L. A., & Hill, C. T. *Unpublished data from the Boston Couples Study.*

Safilios-Rothschild, C. (1970). The study of family power structure: A review 1960–1969. *Journal of Marriage and the Family, 32,* 539–552.

Scanzoni, J., & Fox, G. L. (1980). Sex roles, family, and society: The seventies and beyond. *Journal of Marriage and the Family, 42,* 743–756.

Scanzoni, L., & Scanzoni, J. (1976). *Men, women, and change: A sociology of marriage and the family.* New York: McGraw-Hill.

Soskin, W. M., & John, V. (1963). The study of spontaneous talk. In R. Barker (Ed.), *The stream of behavior.* New York: Appleton-Century-Crofts.

Spanier, G. B., Lewis, R. A., & Cole, C. L. (1975). Marital adjustment over the family life cycle: The issue of curvilinearity. *Journal of Marriage and the Family, 37*(2), 263–275.

Spence, J. T., & Helmreich, R. L. (1978). *Masculinity and femininity: Their psychological dimensions, correlates and antecedents.* Austin: University of Texas Press.

Staines, G., Pleck, J., Shepard, L., & O'Connor, P. (1978). Wives' employment status and marital adjustment. *Psychology of Women Quarterly, 3,* 90–120.

Steinmetz, S. K. (1978). Violence between family members. *Marriage and Family Review, 1*(3), 1–16.

Symons, D. (1979). *The evolution of human sexuality.* New York: Oxford University Press.

Thibaut, J. W., & Kelley, H. H. (1959). *The social psychology of groups.* New York: Wiley.

Tomeh, A. K. (1978). Sex-role orientation: An analysis of structure and attitudinal predictors. *Journal of Marriage and the Family, 40,* 341–354.

Troll, L. E., & Turner, B. F. (1979). Sex differences in problems of aging. In E. S. Gomberg & V. Franks (Eds.), *Gender and disordered behavior: Sex differences in psychopathology.* New York: Brunner-Mazel.

Wakil, S. P. (1973). Campus mate selection preferences. A cross-national comparison. *Social Forces, 51,* 471–476.

Walker, K. (1970). Time spent by husbands in household work. *Family Economics Review, 3,* 8–11.

Walker, K., & Woods, M. (1976). *Time use: A measure of household production of family goods and services.* Washington, D.C.: Home Economics Association.

Waller, W. (1938). *The family: A dynamic interpretation.* New York: Dryden.

Warheit, G. J., Holzer, C. E., Bell, R. A., & Arey, S. A. (1976). Sex, marital status, and mental health: A reappraisal. *Social Forces, 55*(2), 459–470.

Wills, T. A., Weiss, R. L., & Patterson, G. R. (1974). A behavioral analysis of the determinants of marital satisfaction. *Journal of Consulting and Clinical Psychology, 42*(6), 802–811.

Yankelovich, D. (1974). *The new morality: A profile of Americans in the 70s.* New York: McGraw-Hill.

10

Sex, Gender, and Groups: Selected Issues[1]

Kenneth L. Dion
University of Toronto

INTRODUCTION AND HISTORICAL BACKGROUND

This chapter is concerned with the relation of sex, both as subject variable and as stimulus or object variable, to small group processes. This general issue contains a variety of important questions for those interested in the psychology of women, gender, and social psychology. For example, how do women and men respond to others, and to one another in small group settings and gatherings? How does the sex composition of a group affect interpersonal processes within it, and the group's effectiveness at its task or function? How are groups of varying sex composition perceived by their members, and by observers outside the group? Do women differ from men in the ease with which they can attain and maintain leadership in groups and organizations?

One might expect questions like these to have received considerable attention by social psychologists over the years. After all, the study of groups dominated social psychology from the 1920s to the 1960s. Within this timeframe, research on sex differences and group sex composition also had a relatively good head-start, dating back at least 55 years to early studies comparing the relative effectiveness of mixed-sex to unisex committees of women and men on judgmental and problem-solving tasks (South, 1927).

Furthermore, sex composition is obviously a key structural dimension of small groups—a fact that has been recognized from time to time. For example,

---

[1]In this chapter, as in all the others in this volume, Unger's (1979a,b) recommendations for using the terms ''sex'' and ''gender'' are employed.

Hemphill and Westie (1950) identified "homogeneity" (i.e., the extent of similarity of group members on "socially relevant characteristics") as one of the dimensions necessary for describing and categorizing groups objectively, and included sex composition as a pertinent aspect of a group's homogeneity. Somewhat later, in reviewing the group problem-solving literature, Hoffman (1965, p. 126) urged researchers to attend to the sex composition of groups by saying: ". . . the oft-noted description of subjects as 'members of a class in introductory psychology' neglects the sex composition of the group . . . [and until] the characteristics of different populations relevant to problem solving have been systematically studied and identified, the comparative interpretation of different experimental results will remain obscure." Commenting in a similar vein, Kent and McGrath (1969, p. 438) concluded from their own exemplary investigation of sex composition and group performance that: ". . . sex composition . . . [is] a major group-structural factor . . . [and] an important determiner of the characteristics of written group products. Small group studies which employ groups of only one sex composition may very likely yield results of limited generality."

Yet, until recently, the study of sex and gender had been largely neglected in small groups research. This omission is easily documented by reference to periodic bibliographies and reviews of small groups research. For example, in the initial edition of the *Handbook of Small Group Research,* Hare (1962) sought to organize the large volume of groups research that had been produced between 1927 and 1958. Of nearly 1400 studies in the bibliography, only 10 listings dealt with sex as a "social characteristic" relevant to groups. In a follow-up a decade later covering small groups research between 1959 and 1969 (Hare, 1972), only 11 of 35 studies identified under research on "social characteristics" concerned the sex variable. More recently, in the second edition of the aforementioned handbook (Hare, 1976), approximately 30 studies were listed under the rubric of sex. Similarly, with some notable exceptions discussed below, assessments of the small groups literature in the *Annual Review of Psychology* (e.g. Davis, Laughlin & Komorita, 1976; Gerard & Miller, 1967; Steiner, 1964; Zander, 1979) have indicated little systematic research interest in either sex or gender.

Why has the sex variable been neglected by social psychologists studying small groups? One factor has probably been the emphasis in social psychology toward considering situational variables as more important than personality or individual differences for understanding social behavior. The situationist emphasis in social psychology reflects an experimental orientation and a preference for the experimental method in testing the effects of manipulable, situational, or environmental variables. From this perspective, individual differences such as the sex of the subject are simply an annoying source of error (Cronbach, 1957). This view was occasionally reinforced in small groups research by some studies which found few meaningful differences in the behavior or performance of groups of women versus groups of men (e.g., Cattell & Lawson, 1962).

Lack of attention to the sex variable undoubtedly also reflected a reluctance by small group researchers to include women as subjects in their investigations.

Both Carlson and Carlson (1961), as well as Holmes and Jorgenson (1971) convincingly demonstrated that men were disproportionately represented as subjects in the fields of personality and social psychology during the 1950s and 1960s. In the case of small groups research there were even instances where, although the sample contained subjects or groups of both sexes, only the data for males were presented and discussed. This occurred, for example, in Festinger, Pepitone, and Newcomb's (1952) classic study of "deindividuation" (i.e., a lessened sense of personal identity that sometimes occurs in group settings). The female groups in the latter investigation, largely excluded from the published report, were mentioned only in a footnote. (Fortunately, however, subsequent investigators have rectified this particular omission, by taking account of sex differences and the sex composition of the group in influencing the occurrence of deindividuation and its consequences [Cannavale, Scarr, & Pepitone, 1970; Diener, Westford, Dineen, & Fraser, 1973; Maslach, 1974].)

The bias against female subjects probably stemmed from the almost exclusive predominance of male researchers in the small groups area. Then too, small groups research in the U.S. has often been funded by military agencies and has been conducted in military contexts in which men predominated. At the present time, U.S. Government policies of integrating women more fully into the military academies and armed forces are serving to reverse these past biases, and to facilitate small groups research in which sex and gender are primary dimensions (see Adams & Hicks, 1980; Larwood, Glasser, & McDonald, 1980; Rice, Bender, & Vitters, 1980).

Leadership Differentiation and Gender-roles.   Most of the studies of small groups that did focus on the sex variable during the 1950s and 1960s were strongly influenced by role differentiation theory and gender-role explanations for the behavior of women and men in groups. The notion of leadership role differentiation emerged from the research and theorizing of Bales and Slater (Bales, 1953, 1956, 1958; Bales & Slater, 1955; Slater, 1955). These investigators observed small groups of previously unacquainted people in weekly sessions as they discussed human-relations case studies for a month or so. Interactions during these sessions were observed and classified according to Bales' (1950) Interaction Process Analysis (IPA) system for assigning communicative acts into task-oriented categories (e.g. attempt answers, questions) or socioemotional categories (positive and negative reactions). After each meeting, the group members ranked one another on their respective contributions toward helping their group solve the problem and also indicated their liking for each member.

From this information, Bales and Slater found that leadership often tended to differentiate into separate task and socioemotional specialties or roles adopted by different group members. The "task specialist" was oriented primarily to directing the group to meet its assigned objectives, whereas the "socioemotional specialist" focused predominantly on maintaining solidarity in the group and reducing tensions among group members. To account for these observations,

Bales and Slater theorized that leadership differentiation occurs because the task specialist incurs costs (e.g., becoming disliked) and creates interpersonal stresses in pressing the group toward its goal. Presumably to keep the group from disintegrating, another group member is needed to restore harmony and support the task leader, and this person becomes the socioemotional specialist. (Subsequent research has shown that leadership differentiation into task and socioemotional roles occurs primarily when the group's task activity has relatively low legitimacy [Burke, 1972].)

Although Bales and Slater's studies were completed with exclusively male groups, an analogy between leadership role differentiation and gender-role differentiation in groups was soon created. In their influential book *Family, Socialization, and Interaction Process,* Parsons and Bales (1955) drew attention to the apparent similarity between leadership differentiation in small laboratory groups and the nuclear family structure, with the husband playing the role of the instrumentally-oriented "task specialist" and the wife-mother as the "socioemotional specialist" responsible for expressive concerns and supporting the task leader. This conceptual link between leadership role differentiation and gender-role differentiation was strengthened at the time by studies exploring the interaction pattern between women and men in family groups and ad hoc (i.e., newly formed) groups (Heiss, 1962; Kenkel, 1957; Strodtbeck, 1954; Strodtbeck & Mann, 1956).

Strodtbeck and Mann's well-known investigation, for example, focused on gender-role differentiation in mock jury deliberations. People from both the Chicago and St. Louis jury pools deliberated and rendered a verdict upon a recorded trial, with the resulting interactions classified according to Bales' IPA system. The analysis of the interaction patterns revealed that men excelled in the task-oriented categories of "attempted answers," whereas women excelled in the socioemotional categories of "positive reactions." From these findings, Strodtbeck and Mann (1956, p. 9) concluded that: ". . . men *pro-act,* that is, they initiate relatively long bursts of acts directed at the solution of the task problem, and women tend more to *react* to the contributions of others." They also suggested that their findings of women and men adopting different interaction roles in jury deliberations were related to gender-role differentiation in the nuclear family; together, they presumably reflected a "persistent continuity" in the "structural differentiation" of gender roles across different types of groups.

More recently, Kanter (1977) has alternatively suggested that the marked gender-role differentiation observed by Strodtbeck and Mann was due to the under-representation of women in the mock jury groups. In a separate vein, Nemeth, Endicott, and Wachtler (1976) re-examined the issue of gender-role differentiation in mock jury deliberations with college student samples in two investigations. One study conceptually replicated Strodtbeck and Mann's findings, in that men initiated more task-oriented acts than women. A second study failed to find any sex differences in interaction behaviors. Nemeth and her associates attributed these different outcomes to variations in the presentation and availability of evidence during deliberations. The notably smaller sample size in the second study, as compared with the first, however, is another factor that needs to be considered when evaluating the results. In any case, the question of gender-role differentiation in groups remains controversial and pertinent today.

Coalition Formation.   Another important exception to the neglect of the sex variable in previous group research was Vinacke's studies of coalition formation. A coalition is defined as ". . . the joint use of resources to determine the outcome of a decision in a mixed-motive situation involving more than two persons" (Gamson, 1964, p. 82). Vinacke and Arkoff (1957) devised an experimental paradigm for studying coalitions by having groups of three play a board game in which participants advanced toward the goal by moving the number of spaces indicated on a tossed die multiplied by weights assigned the different individuals. Moreover, the individuals could ally with one another to pool their weights and increase their chances of winning the game. Once a coalition was formed, its members had also to decide how to divide the winnings between or among themselves.

With this general paradigm, Vinacke and his colleagues subsequently demonstrated in a series of studies that women and men exhibit quite different coalition behaviors (Amidjaja & Vinacke, 1965; Bond & Vinacke, 1961; Chancy & Vinacke, 1960; Vinacke, 1959, 1964). As compared to men, women were consistently observed to form triple alliances involving all three members of the group more frequently, to divide winnings equally rather than in proportion to individual weights, to form coalitions even when unnecessary to win, and to be less likely to take advantage of "weak" partners. Vinacke and his associates took these findings to be indicative of different strategies of coalition formation: Women presumably adopt an "accommodative" strategy characterized by concern for others and a desire for fairness in distributing outcomes. The behavior of men, on the other hand, was said to reflect an "exploitative" strategy aimed primarily at winning the game, exercising power, and maximizing one's own payoff. Vinacke (1959) has further suggested that these different behaviors are reflective and reminiscent of the respective gender-roles of women and men in the nuclear family.

Retrospect and Prospectus

To summarize the preceding, the dimensions of sex and gender had been relatively ignored in small groups research until the 1970s. Two notable exceptions to this neglect were the investigations into gender-role differentiation in group interaction, and sex differences in coalition formation. In these particular cases, the different behaviors of women and men in group contexts were taken as an expression of gender roles generalized from the nuclear family group. However, no attempt was made to test the adequacy of the gender-role explanations, perhaps because the observed differences were consistent with the then prevalent ideology of what women and men were supposed to be like. As we shall see, traditional gender-role explanations have come to be increasingly questioned in groups research of the 1970s and 80s. The number of studies focusing on the group behavior of women and men has also markedly increased in this period. As a reflection of a problem endemic to groups research generally, however, much of the recent literature is piecemeal, unintegrated, and often atheoretical in its orientation.

An exhaustive survey of this recent literature is not the aim of this chapter. Instead, as suggested by its title, this chapter focuses in depth on selected issues concerning sex, gender, and groups. The issues, however, are *key* ones for two reasons. First, they draw upon theoretical viewpoints from both the psychological and sociological traditions of social psychology (Stryker, 1977). These theoretical viewpoints are given special emphasis in this chapter because of their utility for organizing past findings and, more importantly, for generating new research. Also, the issues selected for attention include ones that have or should have figured prominently in the social psychological study of groups.

Specifically, five general issues are dealt with in this chapter. First, Tiger's (1969) controversial theory of male bonding in groups is assessed, along with the related questions of sex differences in social-political participation and interpersonal involvement, in the light of available evidence. Second, group sex composition is considered with regard to its effects upon sex discrimination and its impact upon the processes of self-perception and person-perception. Third, the effects of group sex composition upon verbal interactions in groups and the interplay of group sex composition with individual differences in dominance and gender orientation, respectively, are highlighted. Finally, the topic of leadership receives extended consideration, with particular attention to theories of emergent leadership (e.g., idiosyncrasy-credit theory and status characteristics theory), as well as theories of leadership and group effectiveness (viz., Fiedler's contingency theory and status consistency theory, respectively).

Having presented an overview of the chapter, we proceed to the first issue.

"BONDING" IN GROUPS

Male Bonding

In his controversial book, *Men in Groups,* Tiger (1969) has suggested that a unique and intense attraction develops between and among men in exclusively male relationships, which he calls "male bonding." To Tiger, male bonding is a presumed tendency for men to join together cooperatively in all-male groups carrying out political, military, and economic functions and actively excluding women from these organizations. Male bonding in humans was postulated to be a genetically transmitted and biologically based, "species-specific" form of behavior having its origins in hominid inheritances from primates, evolutionary pressures toward male exclusiveness in primordial, human hunting parties, and a breeding advantage for "bonded" men. The predominance of men in positions of leadership in the spheres of politics and war was, according to Tiger's analysis, one of the consequences of male bonding. In his own words: ". . . human nature is such that it is 'unnatural' for females to engage in defence, police . . . and high politics" (Tiger, 1969, pp. 198–199).

Not surprisingly, Tiger's notion of male bonding has been seriously criticized on numerous grounds. Briefly, these include: (a) questions about the difficulty or impossibility of testing aspects of the theory; (b) its reliance upon anecdotes, naive analogies between human and primate behavior, and selective, limited samplings of the anthropological and ethological record as evidence; and (c) its apparent justification of anti-female discrimination, especially in the political arena, on the dubious grounds that it reflects male-male attraction rather than misogyny per se (Deaux, 1976; Lips & Colwell, 1978; Rosenblatt & Cunningham, 1976; Weisstein, 1971).

Yet Tiger's theory may not be entirely lacking in merit. For example, despite awareness of its failings, Rosenblatt and Cunningham nevertheless considered Tiger's ethological perspective worthy of "attention," perhaps as a foil for alternative interpretations of cross-cultural sex differences. In a different vein, Wolman and Frank (1975) invoked male bonding to account for the rejection and isolation in social interaction that women encountered in T-groups of graduate students and psychiatric residents, respectively, in which they were the only female members. Their case descriptions of these "professional peer" groups suggested that excluding the "solo woman" reflected attempts by the predominantly male memberships to protect the group's cohesiveness from the threats of female sexuality and the potential sexual rivalry among themselves introduced by her presence. Perhaps most notable, however, Tiger's notion of male bonding has provoked research into sex differences in social participation by social psychologists of both sociological and psychological persuasions.

Social Participation. Booth (1972) attempted to test Tiger's male bonding thesis by relying on systematic survey methods to select 800 middle-aged (i.e., 45 yrs.) or older noninstitutionalized residents of two Nebraska cities and interviewing these respondents concerning their participation in voluntary associations, friendships, and kin ties. Neither sex consistently exceeded the other in the extent of their "social" participation. On the one hand, proportionally more men than women affiliated with, and occupied positions of leadership in, voluntary associations classified as "instrumental" in their objectives (i.e., economic, political, or military-oriented)—findings compatible with Tiger's theory though, of course, not necessarily for the reasons stated by the theory.

Other facets of Booth's (1972) data, however, were at variance with Tiger's perspective, in that they indicated women's superiority in social participation and stronger affective bonds between females than between males. For example, women predominated in both the membership and leadership of "expressive" associations oriented toward education, religion, recreation, health, and welfare. Moreover, women reported more same-sex relationships; these friendships were "affectively richer" in that they reportedly engaged in more spontaneous and frequent interactions with one another and also shared more confidences. Women also reported more kin-relations than men.

The "affective richness" Booth found in women's friendship patterns has been alternatively attributed to their lesser mobility than men, presumably leading them to focus on fewer, albeit "richer," relationships (Wheeler & Nezlek, 1977). In fact, the women and men in Booth's sample did *not* differ significantly in the number of close friends they reported.

For his part, Tiger (1972) criticized Booth's research for: (a) having an age bias toward older people in the sample; (b) failing to test sufficiently for the differential focus of affiliation hypothesized by male bonding theory to exist in women's versus men's groups; and (c) lacking a comparative (i.e., cross-cultural) reference in the sampling of people. These criticisms are, in good part, vitiated by other cross-cultural data.

In the political domain that Tiger does stress as a male prerogative, for example, recent survey studies of children's political interest and orientation in countries including the U.S., Great Britain, and Finland are finding much less evidence of sex differences relative to earlier research (Orum, Cohen, Grasmuck & Orum, 1974). With regard to participation in voluntary associations, Curtis (1971) analyzed sample surveys conducted in six different countries representing North America (i.e., Canada, Mexico, and the U.S.) and Europe (i.e., Great Britain, Germany, and Italy). In the U.S. and Canada—where women enjoy comparatively greater personal autonomy—rates of affiliation in voluntary organizations and multiple affiliations with such organizations are very similar for women and men and are virtually identical when membership in labor unions is excluded from consideration. Rosenblatt and Cunningham's (1976) review of the cross-cultural literature on sex differences deserves particular mention in this context. These authors have argued that sex differences in work and warfare might be better explained in terms of interpretations emphasizing the role of division of labor than by Tiger's ethological perspective.

Although they focus on smaller samples of convenience than the preceding survey research, social psychologists of the psychological ilk have also contributed a body of consistent and interrelated findings, indicating that women's friendships and interactions with others of their sex are more intense and rewarding than are men's. For example, women have consistently reported greater self-disclosure, especially to same-sex friends, than men (Cozby, 1973; Jourard & Lasakow, 1958). Compared to men, women obtain higher love scores when completing the Rubin love scale with regard to a close, same-sex friend (Rubin, 1970). Similarly, Gibbs, Auerbach, and Fox (1980), using indirect sentence-completion items, found that respondents of both sexes attributed greater friendliness, empathy, and altruism to the same-sex friendships of women and only more companionship to men's friendships with one another.

Similar findings have also emerged from psychological studies focusing on reported or observed social interactions rather than relying only on self-report, questionnaire measures. From a study in which first-year undergraduates kept daily diaries of their social interactions, Wheeler and Nezlek (1977) reported that women were consistently more satisfied with their same-sex best friends and relied more heavily upon them in their initial adjustment to the social stimulation of a university environment. Aries (1976), for her part, systematically observed and analyzed the interactions of women and men in both same- and mixed-sex groups. She found that women displayed greater interpersonal affection in same-sex rather than mixed-sex groups, and that women in same-sex groups also looked forward more to subsequent meetings of their groups. Men, in contrast, preferred mixed-sex over same-sex groups, exhibiting a more interpersonal orientation in the former. Likewise, in studies in which the initial, unstructured interactions between two persons of the same sex were unobtrusively observed, Ickes and his colleagues obtained consistent and convergent evidence, with measures of verbal as well as nonverbal interaction, of greater friendliness and involvement in interaction within female dyads as opposed to male dyads (Ickes & Barnes, 1978; Ickes, Schermer & Steeno, 1979).

Overall, relatively little evidence supporting Tiger's (1969) theory of male bonding exists. Recent survey data from several nations suggest that whatever gap may have existed between women and men in political or social participation is rapidly narrowing, or will probably do so in the future. Furthermore, several kinds of data, independently gathered by different investigators, point to a conclusion that is the opposite of Tiger's: Female bonds are stronger than male bonds.

The notion that sex differences interact with the sex composition of a group to determine the nature of the interpersonal relationships that develop among group members is implicit in Tiger's theory. As we have seen, the available research evidence substantiates this premise, though in a direction opposite to that predicted by the theory itself. In the next two sections, we explore more fully the effects of group sex composition, dealing first with its impact in the absence of verbal interaction between or among members of the group.

EFFECTS OF GROUP SEX COMPOSITION I: SEX
DISCRIMINATION AND PERCEPTUAL PROCESSES

The diverse studies discussed below share an interest in the following question: What influence does the numerical proportion of women and men in a group or setting have on the individuals assembled? While we are obviously unable to answer the question definitively at this point, the different lines of research discussed strongly suggest that the impact of sex composition of groups is one of the more important and provocative issues in the area.

Discrimination and Sex-Role Attitudes

An interesting but somewhat complicated line of research concerns discrimination against women as a function of testing in groups varying in their sex composition. Falling in this category are studies using the well-known paradigms Goldberg has devised for assessing sex discrimination, such as having subjects judge professional, journal articles or artistic works attributed either to a woman or to a man, or having the subject guess which women are active feminists from their facial photographs.

Before presenting the research on sex composition, it is worth emphasizing that findings with the aforementioned paradigms have proven difficult to replicate. For example, Goldberg (1968) reported that female undergraduates at a women's college were "prejudiced against women," in that they rated articles in a variety of fields as being more valuable and competently done when they were attributed to male rather than female authors. Pheterson (1969), however, who subsequently asked middle-aged, noncollege women to judge articles in child discipline, special education, and marriage, found an *opposite* tendency to favor articles written by women over those written by men. Attempting to reconcile discrepant findings like these, Pheterson, Kiesler, and Goldberg (1971) demonstrated a pro-male bias in undergraduate women's judgments of the merits of artistic paintings they thought to have been entered in a competition. Unfortunately, according to Toder (1980, p. 298), Deaux and Farris (1973) later failed to replicate Pheterson et al.'s findings of discrimination against women.

Similarly, Goldberg, Gottesdiener, and Abramson (1975) reported "another put-down of women" when they found university men and women prone to select unattractive women as apparent supporters of the women's liberation movement. More recently, however, Unger, Hilderbrand, and Madar (1982) were unable to replicate this latter finding, as they had anticipated on the basis of the greater acceptance of the women's movement, but found considerable evidence that minor social deviants, including political radicals, homosexuals, and individuals with nontraditional occupational aspirations, were likely to be perceived as being physically unattractive.

In light of these developments, it is perhaps not surprising that research on the effects of group sex composition, with these various paradigms, has yielded results that are not entirely compatible with one another. Starer and Denmark (1974) first drew attention to the importance of group versus individual testing, as well as the sex composition of the group testing situation. Subjects read two equivalent poems attributed to aspiring student authors of each sex and indicated their preferences between the poems and the authors. Subjects were tested individually or in groups of four and these groups were either homogeneous or heterogeneous in sex composition. Within the heterogeneous groups, women and men were represented in equal numbers.

The most interesting findings involved comparisons between female subjects tested individually versus those in groups. Females tested individually revealed a pro-male bias in their preference for the male author over the female one. In contrast, females in groups, especially mixed-sex groups, favored the aspiring female poet over her male counterpart by a margin of nearly 2 to 1. The authors concluded that perhaps the presence of others deters women from discriminating against their own sex.

Toder (1980) also explored the effect of group sex composition on discrimination against women, as well as gender-role attitudes. To assess sex discrimination, she employed condensed versions of several of Goldberg's (1968) essays, which were attributed either to female or to male authors. Female experimenters tested subjects in groups of 6–12 persons, half of them mixed-sex with approximately equal numbers of women and men, and the other half composed exclusively of women. In the mixed-sex groups, both women and men felt the articles by female authors were generally less worthy than those by male authors. Women in all-female groups, on the other hand, showed no evidence of discrimination toward either sex in their judgments of the articles and their authors.

Toder (1980, p. 304) interpreted the lack of discrimination in the latter case as due to the greater sense of femaleness and sisterhood that women in all-female groups presumably experienced. The adequacy of this explanation is somewhat undercut by the fact that, contrary to Toder's prediction, women in all-female groups did not endorse pro-feminist attitudes more strongly than those in mixed-sex groups. Instead, the strengthening of pro-feminist sentiment was dependent on a more complex and unanticipated interaction of the variables in the experimental design of this study. Toder found that the additional experience of reading articles allegedly authored by other women was necessary to lead those in all-female groups to espouse a more staunchly pro-feminist stand than their female counterparts in other conditions.

Finally, let us consider a study by Berman, O'Nan, and Floyd (1981), who focused on the attractiveness attributed to middle-aged women by younger adults of both sexes. Subjects rendered their attractiveness judgments of people portrayed on slides who had been selected for their perceived maturity and average attractiveness, either privately or in groups. The four-person groups were composed of either all women, all men, or two people of each sex. In the group conditions, the attractiveness judgments of members were made public with each stimulus presentation. As the authors predicted, downgrading the attractiveness of middle-aged women relative to men was observed among those in all-male groups. In contrast, no sex bias in the attractiveness appraisals of middle-aged women vs. men was manifested either by the women in all-female groups, or by the women and men in the mixed-sex groups and private conditions.

The preceding studies reveal an intricate puzzle whose ultimate solution remains for future researchers to discover. To date, this research yields some discrepant and apparently contradictory conclusions as to the type of group testing situation that would lessen women's tendencies to discriminate against other women. Whereas Starer and Denmark (1974) would point to a mixed-sex group for this purpose, Toder's (1980) results clearly suggest that an all-female group is the setting that elicits less anti-female discrimination on the part of women. To further complicate matters, it should also be remembered that the original findings of "women prejudiced against women" by Goldberg and his associates (Goldberg, 1968, p. 29; Pheterson et al., 1971) were obtained by testing women in all-female groups of various sizes. Similarly, Toder (1980) and Berman et al.'s (1981) studies also appear to disagree with one another regarding the apparent utility of mixed-sex groups for mitigating men's tendencies to downgrade and discriminate against women.

What underlies these contradictory findings? First, secular trends may be crucial in influencing results with sex discrimination paradigms. Second, researchers should not assume that different procedures for assessing sex discrimination are equivalent or equally sensitive to a given treatment. Third, but no less important, when different investigators obtain discrepant findings with the same induction, it strongly suggests that the dimension of interest may be interacting with other variables that have been intentionally or unintentionally incorporated into the experimental design.

The sex of the experimenter should also be taken into account when considering the effects of group sex composition or anti-female discrimination and gender-role attitudes. Shomer and Centers (1970) tested the hypothesis that the salience of group membership could be aroused implicitly by such subtle features of the situation as the sex composition of the group being tested (without verbal interaction among the individuals assembled) and the sex of the experimenter. They found that males' responses to a feminism scale were influenced by both of these dimensions in a complex pattern that they interpreted as reflecting a conflict in conformity to norms of chivalry vs. male chauvinism. By the same warrant, in the case of women today, pro-feminist attitudes should be especially strong under the conditions Toder (1980) implemented in her study: Group membership cues are implicitly made salient by testing in an all-female group, subjects are exposed to female achievement models by reading professional articles by other women, and the situation is presided over by female experimenters. Berman et al. (1981), on the other hand, matched the experimenters' sex to the different experimental conditions. Thus, paying attention to sex of the experimenter and perhaps the nature of the testing materials may well help to clarify findings concerning sex discrimination and the role of group sex composition.

Discrimination in the Group Context.   Other research has focused on the conditions and consequences of sex discrimination within the context of the group itself. In an especially thought-provoking study, for example, Hagen and Kahn (1975) demonstrated the conditions under which men are prone to discriminatory behavior toward female comembers. Female and male subjects performed a prediction task individually, believing they were either competing with, cooperating with, or merely observing two other people of the same or opposite sex, one of whom was more competent than they at the task; the other, less competent.

Men's liking for the female partners varied as a function of the type of relationship and their relative level of competency at the task. Specifically, they liked the competent woman more when observing her than when they thought they were cooperating or competing with her. Indeed, the competent female was preferred by the male subjects over her incompetent counterpart *only* in the observation condition. Moreover, the competent females were more often selected for exclusion from anticipated group performance of the task. Hagen and Kahn concluded that men do not like competent women in competitive contexts, and thus both discriminate and attempt to punish them by exclusion from the group.

In an independent study, Dion (1975) experimentally probed the complementary issue of women's reactions to discrimination in a situation of interpersonal competition with members of the same or opposite sex. In this experiment, the female subjects believed they were competing against several unseen individuals and that they failed either mildly or severely compared to their opponents. Different sets of photos served to vary the alleged sex of the opponents. For half the female subjects, photos of three individual women led them to think that their opponents were other females. The other half were provided photos of three men and thus thought their competitors were men.

The hypothesis that women's self-esteem may be more vulnerable to interpersonal rejection and discrimination by males than by females was confirmed, especially when the failure experienced was severe. However, whether the female subjects attributed this discrimination to perceived prejudice on the part of their opponents, as assessed by post-competition ratings, made an important difference in their self-esteem and personal identification with the traditional female stereotype. The women who attributed their severe failure at the hands of their putative male opponents to prejudice on their part exhibited stronger self-regard and also identified more closely with positive aspects of the traditional female stereotype than did those who did not attribute their failure to the men's

sexist bias. Using the same experimental paradigm with methodological improvements, Goldberg (1981) also found that women confronting failure at the
hands of several men in a small group situation exhibited greater self-esteem if
they explicitly appraised it as due to a discriminatory bias than if they did not.
Thus, in the face of failure induced by men, the attribution of prejudice appears
to help sustain the self-images of women. Because they depersonalize the experience (Dion, Earn & Yee, 1978), attributions such as these may have a salutary
effect.

In summary, within the context of a small group, men may be more apt to
discriminate against a competent woman and women's self-esteem seems vulnerable to rejection by men. However, women who attribute discriminatory acts
by men toward them to prejudice seem better able to preserve their self-image.

In the next section, research indicating that a group's sex composition influences self-perception and person-perception is reviewed. As with the sex discrimination research, some self-perception studies involve situations in which
subjects are tested in groups varying in sex composition without verbal interaction among the participants. Other studies of sex composition and self-perception, however, have focused on intact groups (e.g., family households, classroom groups) with past interaction histories. Although it somewhat violates the
general rubric for research in this section, both types of studies on self-perception
are considered here in order to permit a more coherent presentation of distinctiveness theory—a conceptual framework that has interesting implications
for gender salience. Distinctiveness theory provides a useful, organizing framework for understanding the effects of group sex composition upon person-perception as well.

Self-Perception

Viewed from the integrating perspective of McGuire's distinctiveness theory of
perception (see McGuire, McGuire, and Winton [1979] for a recent, complete
statement of the theory), group sex composition should have consequences for
the perception of the self as well as of others. According to McGuire's distinctiveness postulate, a person taking a complex stimulus such as the self as an
object of perception more readily notices and focuses upon her/his *distinctive*
traits or personal characteristics because of their greater informational richness
and value for discriminating self from others. Thus, for a red-haired person in a
family or group otherwise composed exclusively of brunettes, the relatively
distinctive quality of ''redheadedness'' should be a salient feature of that individual's self-perceptions and spontaneous self-concept.

In testing this theoretical perspective, McGuire and his colleagues have analyzed the content of children's written or oral answers to the request to ''tell us
about yourself.'' Evidence from several studies to date confirms the distinctiveness postulate in that children are apt to cite their more distinctive charac-

teristics relative to others when spontaneously describing themselves. The hypothesis that sex will be salient in an individual's self-perceptions and self-concept to the extent that it is distinctive in regard to *chronic* or habitual reference groups has been addressed in two of these studies.

McGuire and Padawer-Singer (1976) explored both general self-concept (as assessed by responses to the "tell us about yourself" probe) as well as physical self-concept (as indexed by children's self-descriptions of what they look like) as a function of the sex composition of children's classrooms. These classrooms varied slightly—by one to five people—as to which sex happened to be in the majority. Despite the relative subtlety of this variation, school children were much more prone to indicate sex as an element of their physical self-concept when their sex comprised the minority in the classroom rather than the majority, as distinctiveness theory would predict.

McGuire et al. (1979) subsequently investigated the impact of household sex composition on childrens' general self-concept. Once again, the implications of distinctiveness theory were borne out. Sex was considerably more salient as an element of spontaneous self-concept for children whose sex was, numerically speaking, the minority in the household, and therefore more distinctive. This effect was observed in boys and girls, respectively. Thus, girls from households with males in the majority were more likely to spontaneously refer to their femaleness in describing themselves and vice-versa for boys from predominantly female households. Further analyses have suggested that it is the number of males in the home that is principally responsible for the effects of household sex composition upon children's self-perception.

The preceding studies have dealt with the effects of the sex composition of chronic reference groups, to which the individual has repeated and habitual exposure over time. However, McGuire has also implied several times that group sex composition should influence one's self-perception even if the reference group is "momentary" or transient (McGuire et al., 1979; McGuire & Padawer-Singer, 1976). For example, McGuire and Padawer-Singer (1976, p. 573) state: ". . . it would be predicted that by testing children in ad hoc groups constructed to have different percentages of males and females, we could manipulate the relative salience of sex in the girls' and boys' self-concepts."

Logically, though, the impact of sex composition with exposure to a momentary, transient reference group should be rather less potent and more difficult to demonstrate than for chronic reference groups. Indeed, research reported by other investigators suggests that the effects of sex composition in ad hoc groups may perhaps be more subtle and complex than originally envisioned by McGuire's distinctiveness theory. Ruble and Higgins (1976), as well as Higgins and King (1981), have described a laboratory study in which the spontaneous self-concepts of college undergraduates were assessed while they were in noninteracting groups whose sex composition was systematically varied. Rather than coding whether or not a given characteristic is mentioned by a respondent, as

McGuire and his colleagues have typically done, however, subjects' responses were scored for the frequency with which traditional female and male stereotypic traits were cited.

Interestingly, members of both sexes in the position of being a "token" in the group (i.e., a lone female together with two or three males, and vice-versa) were more prone to indicate traits traditionally associated with the *opposite* sex in their self-descriptions than those in groups whose sex composition was more balanced. Ruble and Higgins (1976) explained these findings by making the following assumptions: (a) most people are, to some extent, androgynous; (b) androgyny is positively valued by liberal-minded undergraduates; and (c) the increased gender-role awareness arising from token status in a mixed-sex group leads these individuals to perceive themselves as possessing traits of the opposite sex. These authors also reported additional, developmental data to bolster the argument that the perceived value or personal desirability of traditional vs. modern gender-role orientations needs to be taken into account in order to predict the consequences of sex composition in ad hoc groups upon self-perception and self-presentation. Higgins and King (1981), for their part, have cited studies which suggest that the heightened salience of sex arising from unbalanced sex composition in ad hoc groups determines person-perception as well as self-perception by influencing the accessibility of social constructs. Alternatively, Unger (personal communication) has proposed that being the only member of one's sex in a group is threatening and may thus elicit in the token a tendency to "identify with the aggressor."

Thus, research by Ruble, Higgins, and their associates suggests, in accord with the distinctiveness postulate, that being in the minority sex, even of a temporary group, increases the salience of sex to its members. However, these findings also appear to contradict McGuire's theory, in that members of the minority sex of an ad hoc group seem to perceive themselves in terms of the stereotypic characteristics of the majority sex. It is thus left to future research to decide whether Ruble and Higgins' research and conceptualizing concerning sex composition in ad hoc groups reflects a challenge or an extension of McGuire's distinctiveness theory. Subsequent studies should also explore whether Ruble and Higgins' findings are readily replicable; and if so, what social psychological processes underlie them.

Person-Perception

According to a recent version of McGuire's theory, the distinctiveness postulate presumably explains, in principle, how any object is perceived and thus readily applies to the perception of people as well as of oneself (McGuire et al., 1979). As regards person-perception, the distinctiveness postulate implies that in a group setting, the person(s) with the more distinctive characteristics would be more apt to be noticed by other group members and/or external observers. This prediction, however, has been independently generated and extended by other theorists more specifically to the area of sex composition and groups.

Kanter (1977), in particular, has developed an important theoretical framework for understanding how highly imbalanced or "skewed" sex ratios in groups can condition the interaction between women and men, one based on field observations in a prominent, industrial organization. As a key feature of her conceptual analysis, she emphasized that token women in skewed groups were prone to suffer the consequences of three perceptual processes directed at them: (1) greater *visibility* to others; (2) *polarization* of their distinctiveness and exaggeration of the perceived similarities of the numerically dominant men; and (3) *assimilation* to familiar stereotypes.

Taylor, Fiske, Etcoff, and Ruderman (1978) also derived very similar predictions from cognitive perspectives emphasizing the importance of categorization processes and salience for the perception and memory of individuals' behavior in mixed-sex and biracial groups. Further, they reported a series of elegantly designed experiments to test their predictions. Two of these experiments demonstrated that race and sex, respectively, are employed by external observers as categorical cues for encoding and organizing information about individuals in groups. The third experiment is more immediately pertinent, however, to the line of thought developed here concerning group sex composition.

Specifically, Taylor and her colleagues presented subjects with "slide and tape" group interactions of six stimulus persons, in which sex composition was parametrically manipulated—and ingeniously so. Three of the seven hypotheses evaluated in this experiment deserve particular mention. One predicted that observers would attend more—and make clearer discriminations within—a sex subgroup as an inverse function of its size. Consistent with this hypothesis, the smaller the sex subgroup, regardless of whether it consisted of females or males, the more prominent its members were perceived to be by observers. In addition, the fewer the representatives of a given sex in a group, the less favorably they were regarded on measures of general evaluation.

The other two hypotheses concerned perceivers' tendencies to stereotype individuals within the group, and even the group itself, as a function of sex composition. The hypothesis that individuals would be perceived in gender stereotypic terms the more numerically distinctive their sex subgroup was, was weakly supported. The hypothesis that a group as a whole would be stereotyped in line with the relative proportion of the two sexes represented was more successful. Indeed, the greater the number of females in a group, the stronger was the tendency for observers to perceive the group as less competent, unorganized, and disharmonious.

To briefly recapitulate this section, the preceding studies, taken together, clearly indicate that group sex composition has considerable impact upon self- and person-perception. The numerical distinctiveness of one's sex, in particular, plays a crucial role. In general, the fewer the members of one's sex in a group or setting, the greater the salience of gender and the stronger the proneness to perceive self, others, and the group itself in terms of gender categories.

An interesting study by Grady (1977; also cited in Unger, 1979a, pp. 20–21) deserves mention in this context. Grady gave subjects the task of describing one person selected from a set of ten photos using as few cues as possible. The relative distinctiveness of various cues (e.g. eyeglasses, hair color, lightness of clothing, etc.) was varied. Although sex of the stimulus persons was less distinctive than other cues, in that women and men were represented in equal numbers in the photos, sex was still chosen 60% of the time by the subjects. In this and other demonstrations, Grady has shown that sex is so prominent a cue that it is apt to be noticed by perceivers even when it is not especially distinctive or functional.

EFFECTS OF GROUP SEX COMPOSITION II:
INTERACTION IN GROUPS

The preceding section on group sex composition has generally not considered member-to-member interaction in groups varying in sex composition. Most of the studies discussed involved situations in which individuals were tested on measures of discrimination (Starer & Denmark, 1974), gender-role attitudes (Toder, 1980), or self-perception (Ruble & Higgins, 1976) in multiperson contexts varying in sex composition but providing little or no opportunity for overt interaction among the people assembled. On one hand, research of this ilk may be seen as relatively "pure" tests of the effects of group sex composition, uncontaminated by interaction between group members. On the other hand, one could perhaps question whether such research deals with *group* processes at all. In fact, investigations of both types are probably necessary for a complete understanding of sex composition effects. In any event, the studies considered in the present section all focus directly on the processes and consequences of interaction in groups constructed to vary in sex composition.

Aries' (1976, 1977) study is a prototypical example of research into the quantitative and qualitative aspects of social interaction in groups whose sex composition was systematically manipulated. The social interactions and conversational content of same-sex and mixed-sex groups of white college women and men were observed and recorded as they met on five separate occasions with the task of becoming acquainted with one another. Analysis of these interaction patterns highlighted the differential effects of group sex composition on individuals' interpersonal styles. Interactions of the exclusively male groups, for example, principally reflected concerns for status, power, and interpersonal competition, as reflected by members' tendencies to evolve a stable dominance pattern, to focus on themes of aggression and superiority, and to communicate to the group as a whole rather than to individuals. Members of all-female groups were more open and intimate with one another as well as more democratic in sharing speaking time, with no stable dominance hierarchy developing over time.

The interactions in mixed-sex groups, on the other hand, revealed clear status differences between women and men. In the mixed groups, men both gave and received more interactions than did women. Women's interactions were addressed primarily to the male comembers rather than to one another; moreover, men adopted a more positive, interpersonal orientation with female comembers present in the group.

In essence, Aries (1976) demonstrated that the interpersonal styles of women and men differ markedly in same-sex versus mixed-sex groups. She interpreted the changes in interaction patterns from same-sex to mixed-sex groups as reflecting individuals' adjustment of their interpersonal styles to fit the gender-role pressures of the situation.

Eskilson and Wiley (1976) investigated the gender-role pressures on women and men in positions of leadership over two females, two males, or one female and one male. Leaders guided followers in solving a complex geometric puzzle to which they alone had access to part of the unique solution. Essentially, both women and men found the leadership role easiest and performed it most effectively with followers of the same sex. Notably, women found directing the activities of two male followers most difficult, as they permitted little opportunity for the woman to exercise her authority. A male leader encountered greatest difficulty with mixed-sex followers because the single male follower tended to challenge his suggestions and compete with him—a phenomenon aptly dubbed the "rooster effect." Thus, group sex composition can affect leader–follower interactions in groups.

Piliavin and Martin (1978) have also conducted an extensive study of small group interaction (see also Piliavin, 1976). Using Bales' (1970) revised category system, the interactions of four-person groups composed of one or both sexes were analyzed as they discussed three different problems in succession. During the second discussion period, an operant conditioning procedure was instituted whereby red and green signal lights were presented to individual members so as to encourage a given target person to participate more in the interaction and the others to do so less.

Let us consider the results for the first discussion period, where no attempt was made to alter the group's interaction pattern. Assuming that the presence of men as comembers might act to suppress task behaviors on the part of women, Piliavin and Martin had predicted that women would exhibit more task behavior and less socioemotional behavior in an all-female group as compared to a mixed-sex group. Similarly, they expected men in all-male groups to show less task behavior and more expressive behavior than in mixed-sex groups. In other words, the behaviors of women and men in mixed sex groups were hypothesized to be more congruent with gender stereotypic expectations than in same-sex groups.

The results clearly disconfirmed these predictions. For example, the interaction profiles showed the single-sex groups to be the ones more prone to behave in line with gender stereotypes. Although both women and men in same-sex groups focused the majority of their behavior in the task-oriented categories of social interactions, women in exclusively female groups exhibited a greater percentage of their interactions in the socioemotional spheres. Mixed-sex groups, in contrast, showed a less pronounced tendency to center their activities exclusively in either the task or the expressive categories of interaction. Moreover, other analyses suggested that mixed-sex groups provided opportunities for cross-sex modelling of behavior rather than heightening conformity to gender stereotypes.

As for the experimental manipulation of group interaction, the most interesting findings arose in attempts to increase the participation of a female target person relative to her comembers in a mixed-sex group. Women in this position markedly augmented their production of task behavior, whereas their male comembers expressed more socioemotional behaviors while sustaining the same level of task contributions. Notably, in those mixed-sex groups in which a woman had been singled out and encouraged to increase her participation in the group interaction, both women and men became equivalent in the extent of task and socioemotional behavior that they manifested. Piliavin and Martin (1978, p. 294) phrased it especially well when they concluded from these findings that: "... a concerted effort to encourage task-oriented participation on the part of females . . . can increase behavioral options for both sexes."

Interaction studies such as these yield a fascinating but complex picture of the impact of sex composition on group processes. The evidence to date does not suggest a simple relationship between group sex composition and the strength of the gender-role pressures that confront group members. Rather, same- and mixed-sex groups differ principally in the *type* of gender-role pressures that they exert. For example, as Ickes and Barnes (1978) have insightfully observed from their own research as well as from other studies, sex differences in behavior reflecting gender-role expectations are far less in mixed-sex groups than in groups composed exclusively of only one sex. The cross-sex modelling of behavior, where men adopt a more interpersonal orientation in the company of women, and women adopt somewhat more of a task orientation, further mutes such sex differences.

In other regards, though, mixed-sex groups bring to the fore issues of the relative status and power of women and men. As we have seen, men tend to dominate interaction in mixed-sex groups, and women often defer to them. Furthermore, "hidden agendas" of heterosexual attraction are additional issues obviously more likely to occur in mixed-sex groups.

Interaction of Group Sex Composition and Personality

The sex composition of a group also interacts with certain personality characteristics of members, creating gender-role conflicts that affect social interaction (Aries, 1976). This phenomenon is best illustrated by research on trait dominance and gender-role orientation, which follows, to which we turn.

Dominance.   Megargee and his associates have conducted several studies in which an individual who had a high score on the Dominance Scale of the California Personality Inventory was paired with one whose score was lower. These pairs were then given a task in which they had to select which one was to lead and direct the activities of the other. Megargee, Bogart, and Anderson (1966) found that when men differing in their need for dominance were left to resolve who would play the superordinate role on a simulated industrial task, the male high in dominance adopted the leadership role 90% of the time, thereby providing some evidence of construct validity for the Dominance Scale itself.

In what has become a classic in the area of gender, sex, and social psychology Megargee (1969) subsequently tested the hypothesis that gender-role conflict would inhibit highly dominant women from seeking leadership over another person in certain conditions of dyadic sex composition. Four types of dyadic relationships were explored in which subjects differing in their need for interpersonal dominance (i.e. high vs. low) were paired with a partner of either the same or the opposite sex. For both women and men with same-sex partners, the individual scoring higher in dominance emerged as the leader approximately 3 out of 4 times. Not surprisingly, a highly dominant man assumed leadership functions 90% of the time when paired with a woman relatively lacking in need for dominance. The interesting case, however, is what happens when a woman otherwise high in dominance is paired with a low dominance man. In such a case, the woman's ordinary proclivities toward assertiveness and dominance over others conflicts with traditional gender-role norms proscribing that women should not exercise influence or authority over men. As a result, according to a gender-role conflict hypothesis, a high dominance woman would be expected to relinquish her prerogative for being directive when her partner happened to be male, even though he was low in dominance and presumably submissive.

Indeed, for this pairing, the high-dominance woman became the leader only 20% of the time over the low-dominance man. To show that these findings were not merely a consequence of having employed a masculine-oriented task, Megargee replicated this study with a simulated clerical task that was presumed to be relatively neutral in gender-role connotations and obtained identical results. Moreover, further analyses suggested that the high-dominance women's inhibition in adopting the leadership role was due not to the low-dominance man's greater assertiveness toward her, but to her tendency to actively abdicate leadership and nominate her partner for this role, despite the fact that he was ill-suited for it.

Using a similar paradigm and a simulated clerical task, Fenelon and Megargee (1971) subsequently found a similar tendency for dominant, white women to defer their personal claims to leadership to less dominant, black women. In this case, the former's deference reflected a combination of reluctance on her part to assume leadership as well as greater assertiveness on the part of an ordinarily submissive, black woman. Notably, when this biracial situation was reversed, a black woman high in trait dominance successfully claimed the leadership role over her white, less dominant, female partner nearly 3 times out of 4.

In an interesting extension of this research, Bartol (1974) has explored the effects of having a female or a male leader of varying need for dominance on followers' satisfaction. In her study, the leaders were appointed to direct the activities of several all-male or mixed-sex followers as they performed a simulated business game over several weeks as part of a management course. Two findings were especially notable. First, male leaders high in need for dominance were more readily appreciated for their efforts at structuring the task in the all-male groups than in the mixed-sex groups. Indeed, it was the female members who were disenchanted with the dominating male leader in the mixed-sex groups. Second, but perhaps more interesting, groups of all-male followers with a female leader expressed greater satisfaction with team interaction when her need for dominance was high rather than low. Thus, the dominant female leader, who presumably took a directive stance vis-à-vis exclusively male followers, was more appreciated than her submissive counterpart.

The preceding research suggests that women possessing the trait of dominance fail to exhibit their usual interpersonal assertiveness in dyadic interactions with men. Megargee and his associates have attributed these findings to a conflict between personality and gender-roles in which the latter win out. A similar inhibition of dominance behavior by an otherwise high-dominance white woman occurs when she interacts with a black woman on a one-to-one basis. Bartol's (1974) research, however, suggests that when placed in a position of leadership and legitimized in that role, high-dominance women respond more adroitly with regard to men and more consistently with respect to their own motivational orientation than in the unstructured type of situation explored by Megargee, in which who will lead is the primary issue.

Androgyny.   Several investigators have focused on individuals' gender-role orientation, indexed by Bem's Sex-Role Inventory (BSRI), as a personality dimension that they hypothesized would correlate with interaction in groups of varying sex composition. For example, Ickes and his colleagues performed laboratory studies of same-sex dyads (Ickes & Barnes, 1978; Ickes et al., 1979) and mixed-sex dyads (Ickes & Barnes, 1977) and also suggested a theoretical model of gender-role influences in dyadic interaction (Ickes, 1981).

According to their model, gender-role orientations reflect different orientations to social behavior, with masculinity associated with an instrumental orientation, femininity with an expressive orientation, and androgyny with a combination of both. Social systems, Ickes and his colleagues assume, function most effectively to the extent that both instrumental and expressive functions are performed and integrated. Because androgynous individuals are presumably capable of exhibiting either or both of these orientations (cf., Spence & Helmreich, 1978), they should be better able than their gender-typed counterparts to adapt their behavior and mesh it with the capacities of the person with whom they interact. As a result, social interactions with androgynous individuals should be more optimal in various regards than those in which traditionally gender-typed individuals take part.

Ickes and his collaborators have tested this general prediction and a host of more specific ones in studies of initial, unstructured interactions in dyads whose composition varied in terms of their members' gender-role orientations and sex. They have demonstrated that social interaction in pairings of androgynous individuals are indeed better in terms of behavioral measures of involvement and reported satisfaction and liking than those between people with other combinations of gender-role orientation. Moreover, the superiority of the interaction in androgynous dyads appears to endure somewhat beyond a brief, initial interaction of two strangers and is not attributable to differential self-esteem or physical attractiveness of the individuals. The principal difference between same- and mixed-sex dyads occurs in pairings of an androgyne and a gender-typed individual. In such cases, interactions are more optimal between an androgynous individual and a gender-typed person of the opposite sex rather than the same sex, as, in the former case, the androgyne is less constrained to adopt gender-role consonant behavior.

Other research into gender-role orientation and group sex composition involves groups larger than dyads and lengthier, more structured interactions than those studied by Ickes and his associates. Korabik (1982), for example, explored the effects of androgyny in the context of triads given a human relations problem to discuss. Based on the premise of greater adaptability by androgynous persons (Bem, 1974, 1976), she expected androgynous persons to modulate their output of task and socioemotional behaviors so as to complement that of their comembers, especially in mixed-sex groups. Three-person groups were composed of two sex-typed individuals paired with an androgynous person of the same or opposite sex. The results revealed reliable but complex interaction effects between members' gender-role orientation and group sex composition. Korabik's expectations, however, were not confirmed—perhaps because the androgyne was outnumbered 2 to 1 by the gender-typed persons.

Spillman, Spillman, and Reinking (1981) fared somewhat better in their study of androgynous and gender-typed persons in mixed-sex groups of five to eight members that met four times over several weeks. Using a novel matrix-rating procedure for indexing task and social leadership behavior, Spillman and her colleagues confirmed their predictions that androgynous persons would obtain higher task and social leadership scores than feminine persons, and that these differences would decrease over time sessions. Their sample may be somewhat unique, though, in that many of the women qualified as androgynous or masculine in their BSRI classification and also excelled the men on a measure of autocratic tendencies.

Thus, androgyny *appears* to have some benefits at the interpersonal level. Perhaps by virtue of their more extensive behavioral repertoires, androgynes are better able to adapt to different group contexts and situations, as predicted by Ickes' (1981) model of gender-role influences. The preceding research gains added interest because of the theoretical controversy raised by Sampson (1977) as to whether it is better to synthesize masculine and feminine qualities within the individual or in an interdependent system of persons. Ickes and his colleagues have countered Sampson's contentions with results indicating that androgyny at the personal level would enhance interaction possibilities in groups.

Yet it seems questionable that it is inevitably better for instrumental and expressive functions in a group to be fulfilled by a single, androgynous person rather than separate "specialists." Indeed, future research might profitably explore the possibility of integrating androgyny theories with role differentiation theory (see, for example, Korabik, 1982), rather than assuming they are necessarily antithetical to one another. Such a conceptual integration could be organized around the fact, stressed by several authors (Burke, 1972; Dion, 1978), that leadership role differentiation is fostered under certain situational conditions.

For example, when group members are relatively unmotivated to accomplish the group's task and reject it, an instrumental "specialist" is disliked as group members are goaded toward achieving the group goal, and another person typically emerges in the role of socioemotional specialist to relieve the resulting interpersonal stress. In such cases, differentiation into instrumental and expressive roles, with different persons performing them, is clearly adaptive for group functioning. On the other hand, when group members are positively oriented and accept their task, leadership differentiation generally does not occur and an androgynous person would be likely to emerge as leader and facilitate group effectiveness by performing both types of functions. In any case, this comprehensive viewpoint seems promising and worth exploring.

THEORIES OF EMERGENT LEADERSHIP

As a consequence of their interactions with one another, people in a group gradually become differentiated from one another in several regards. Certain individuals acquire more status and influence over the others; thus, they "emerge" as leaders. This process of emergent leadership is the focus of the present section. Two influential theories of emergent leadership—idiosyncrasy-credit theory and status characteristics theory—are each considered in turn.

Idiosyncrasy-Credit Theory

Hollander (1958) proposed the idiosyncrasy-credit theory to account for some otherwise conflicting observations and beliefs concerning leaders' perceptions of—and conformity to—group norms. "Idiosyncrasy-credits" are positive impressions of an individual that are held by her/his group comembers and are acquired, principally, by demonstrating competence on the group's focal task activity and by conforming to the common expectations or norms for group members, at least initially. These idiosyncrasy-credits define one's emergent status in the group and permit one to offset any debits arising from idiosyncratic departures from common group norms that would otherwise incur sanctions. As an individual's status rises, a threshold for accumulated idiosyncrasy-credits may be reached whereupon she or he becomes subject to new, different expectancies by group members, which permit and may even prescribe greater latitude in behavior, including innovations aimed at altering the group's norms.

This notion of shifting expectancies over time as a group member gains status, emerges as a leader, and begins to assert influence over comembers is the key element of Hollander's (1958, 1964) idiosyncrasy-credit model, which has received most of the attention in experimental tests. Hollander (1960) himself provided strong experimental support for this aspect of his model. In the context of four-to-five person groups composed entirely of male engineering students, a confederate was made to appear highly competent on an ambiguous matrix task by suggesting the correct choice on 11 of 15 trials and claiming special adeptness on mathematical tasks. The occurrence and timing of the confederate's nonconformity to previously agreed upon rules of conduct (e.g. talking out-of-turn, questioning majority rule for decision-making, suggesting unequal division of winnings) over the course of the trials constituted the key manipulation. Using the number of trials on which the group followed the confederate's suggestion on the matrix task to index influence acceptance, Hollander (1960) demonstrated that, as predicted by the idiosyncrasy-credit model, nonconformity by a highly competent individual led to maximal acceptance of influence only if it was preceded by some prior conformity to group norms in the early or early and middle trials.

Using very similar experimental procedures as well as all-male groups, however, Wahrman and Pugh (1972) failed to replicate Hollander's (1960) findings. Specifically, on the critical "acceptance of influence" measure, the "early" nonconformer (who violated group norms beginning in the first block of five trials) had the greatest influence on the group's decisions, as compared to those who delayed their nonconformity until the second and third trial blocks (i.e., the "middle" and "late" nonconformers, respectively). Wahrman and Pugh (1972) attributed these discrepancies to sample differences. Whereas Hollander's sample of male engineering students from a technical institute had been reputedly challenged by the matrix task, the liberal arts students who served as the subjects in Wahrman and Pugh's investigation were apparently intimidated by the same task and thus eager to accept the suggestions of anyone who seemed knowledgeable in their choices or claimed mathematical expertise. In any event, the idiosyncrasy-credit model fared better on a measure of resentment that Wahrman and Pugh devised themselves. Specifically, despite his greater influence, the early nonconformer was markedly disliked by the other group members—a finding that accords with the idiosyncrasy-credit model.

To explore the additional effects of low ascribed status (i.e., female sex) upon status attainment and leadership emergence in groups, Wahrman and Pugh (1974) subsequently collected additional data from groups of males confronted with a female confederate who deviated from procedural norms either early, middle, late, or never in the course of the problem-solving trials. Wahrman and Pugh's introduction of an ascribed status dimension also addressed Hollander's (1958, p. 121) original contention that an individual's "status in a broader group," or external status, influences one's potential for acquiring idiosyncrasy-credits within the group. The investigators assumed that when a woman deviates from a group's established procedures and does so in an assertive or aggressive manner, she violates gender-role norms as well as internal group norms and would thus be at a disadvantage relative to her male counterpart. A comparison of the reactions of male subjects in exclusively male or predominantly male groups to a male versus female confederate bore out these expectations. For the male confederate, influence increased directly with the extent of nonconformity, with the greatest influence being found for early nonconformity. Quite a different picture emerged for a woman in a similar circumstance. The earlier that a competent woman deviated from procedural rules in a group otherwise composed of men, the *less* influence she came to have over her male comembers and the more likely they were to report being pleased at the prospect of her expulsion from the group.

Nor, apparently, would a woman in the role of a competent nonconformer fare much better were her fellow group members all female rather than all male. In a carefully designed and executed study, Ridgeway and Jacobson (1977) explored the reactions of female groups to a male or a female nonconformer, respectively, taking special care to present the matrix task as a puzzle or common game rather than a mathematical exercise. Consistent with the view that a low ascribed status constrains idiosyncratic behavior in a group context, a woman in the role of a competent nonconformer was less influential and was also perceived as a less worthy groupmate by *female* comembers than was a man in the same position. As with the Wahrman and Pugh (1972, 1974) studies, however, it was previous *non*conformity rather than prior conformity that enhanced influence.

Ridgeway and Jacobson explained this finding with the provocative suggestion that early nonconformity serves as a "perceptual marker," drawing comembers' attention to an individual's competency and thus hastening her or his attainment of achieved status and leadership. Further, this notion of a "perceptual marker" is conceptually similar to Moscovici's stress upon the behavioral style of consistency as a necessary condition for a minority to persuade a majority toward its viewpoint (Moscovici & Faucheux, 1972; Moscovici & Lage, 1976; Moscovici, Lage & Naffrechoux, 1969; Moscovici & Nemeth, 1974).

Nevertheless, as Bray, Johnson, and Chilstrom (1982) have insightfully observed, the formulations by Hollander and Moscovici, respectively, suggest quite different strategies in the use of nonconformity as a means of attaining influence over one's group members. As just noted, Moscovici's minority influence formulation encourages the nonconformist to be consistent and resolute from the outset in pressing her or his minority viewpoint upon any comembers who disagree with it. Hollander's idiosyncrasy-credit viewpoint, in contrast, urges the would-be influence agent to conform initially to the majority position and to demonstrate competency prior to attempting to persuade other group members to take a discrepant stand on another topic.

Bray and his colleagues experimentally tested these divergent predictions in studies varying the strategy adopted by an opinion deviate (viz. à la Hollander vs. Moscovici) and whether or not this nonconformist demonstrated exceptional competence on a word task. Additionally, in one of a pair of studies, homogeneous groups of females as well as males were exposed to these manipulations. Although both strategies proved effective when compared to a baseline control condition, in two separate studies the Hollander strategy elicited greater acceptance of the nonconformist's influence in groups of males than did the Moscovici strategy. Groups of women, on the other hand, were not differentially influenced by one strategy or the other.

To recapitulate, Hollander's idiosyncrasy-credit model originally gave little explicit attention to sex. Ironically, the original thrust of the theory, concerning the importance of demonstrating initial conformity and competence as a means to status attainment and the acceptance of one's influence, currently seems questionable (at least with regard to its generality) in the light of recent evidence. Ridgeway and Jacobson (1977), in particular, have suggested that this model may be limited to specific conditions characterizing Hollander's (1960) original study; namely, high perceptual task clarity and equal status relationships among group members. Along similar lines, the results of Bray and his colleagues could be taken as implying that with regard to opinion change, the Hollander strategy might be more effective in groups of males rather than females, though whether this effect is due to the sex of the subject and/or the sex composition of the group awaits further investigation.

With one notable exception discussed below, studies of the idiosyncrasy-credit model are consistent in pointing to femaleness as a deterrent to the acceptance of a person and her influence. These findings raise questions whose importance is difficult to overemphasize: What does it take for a woman to emerge as a leader in a group? How does the sex composition of the group affect her chances? How can obstacles to attainment of high status and leadership be overcome? Before questions like these can be answered, we need to know more clearly than at present the precise nature of the obstacles that arise from being female.

As we shall see in the next section, one possibility noted by several theorists is that femaleness reflects low ascribed status. Yet there are other, albeit interrelated, possibilities that should also be considered. For example, given the gender-stereotyping literature indicating that competence is a masculine characteristic (Broverman et al., 1972), a woman in a small group setting may find it more difficult to demonstrate high levels of competency to other members of the group than would a man. Exceptional competence may not be as readily perceived or as positively evaluated in the case of a woman.

Another possibility concerns the nonconformer's interpersonal style. In the Hollander paradigm, the nonconformer adopts a somewhat obnoxious, aggressive manner toward comembers. Although some evidence suggests that a masculine orientation in competency is regarded as desirable by and for persons of both sexes (Spence & Helmreich, 1972), it is very doubtful that this extends to the domain of assertiveness and aggressiveness. In a series of studies by Costrich, Feinstein, Kidder, Maracek, and Pascale (1975), a woman who behaved assertively and aggressively toward others in a group or a dyadic relationship was markedly unpopular and prone to being considered psychologically maladjusted.

Finally, the female nonconformer in the Hollander paradigm exhibits greater competency than her fellow group members and thus strongly violates stereotypic gender-role expectations, especially when excelling male comembers. Hagen and Kahn's (1975) research suggests that a competent woman is apt to experience a complex and pernicious pattern of discrimination that competent men do not confront. They have shown that a woman who is more capable at a certain task than other group members may be liked less by them and is prone to being ousted from the group at their request, but is still selected for group leader. As Hagen and Kahn (1975, p. 372) have emphasized, it is obviously awkward and difficult to live up to one's potential as a leader under such circumstances.

On the other hand, recent research by Bradley (1980) offers a more hopeful outlook for the competent woman. In her study, a female or male confederate took a stand on an issue provided for group discussion that was markedly discrepant from the opinions of four male comembers. In addition, the confederate was either clearly more competent than the other group members, by virtue of previously acquired knowledge, or no more competent than the others. Reactions to the "opinion deviate" were assessed, as well as any changes in attitude occasioned by the dissenter. The highly competent woman was found to have considerable influence in changing her comembers' opinions. Moreover, her competency appears to have shielded her from the hostility, dominance, and unreasonableness directed by the male group members toward the less competent female confederate.

In closing, the literature on the idiosyncrasy-credit model illustrates well the importance of considering sex as an important dimension in small groups research. Obviously, we cannot necessarily assume that a social psychological theory derived and/or tested solely with male subjects or all-male groups will also apply to women. Such a theory or model runs the serious risk of being male-specific and thus inevitably limited in its generality. The preceding research also indicates the conceptual fertility that comes from introducing the dimensions of sex and gender. Indeed, the issues introduced by considerations of sex and gender clearly constitute one of the more worthwhile aspects of the idiosyncrasy-credit model to explore in future research. A study of the conditions that determine when a highly competent woman will be treated well or badly by male comembers in a small group would seem to be a particularly important goal in this line of research.

The Theory of Status Characteristics and Expectation States

The theory of status characteristics and expectation states, proposed by Berger and his colleagues (Berger, Cohen & Zelditch, 1972; Berger, Conner, & Fisek, 1974; Cohen, Berger & Zelditch, 1972), bears some similarity to the idiosyncrasy-credit model in that it also deals with the interrelationship of status, competency, and acceptance of influence. It differs, however, in focusing on observable differences in "external" or visible status dimensions (e.g. age, sex, or race), which individuals bring with them to a newly formed group, rather than on the attainment of achieved status via early conformity and demonstrated competency.

Essentially, status characteristics theory is concerned with task-oriented groups, whose members differ from one another on an external status dimension and work together cooperatively on a collective, valued task. Because success at the task is assumed to require competency or ability relevant to that task, each individual presumably attempts to gauge the abilities of the others relative to themselves in the hope of maximizing personal as well as group success at the task. In the absence of direct information on the differential competency at the specific task, the group members rely on knowledge of one another's external status to form expectations of their own and others' likely task-competency. These self–other expectations, in turn, serve as self-fulfilling prophecies whereby individuals higher in external status expect themselves, and are expected by other group members, to be more competent at the task and act accordingly. As a result, the distribution of members' task activity and influence within the group comes to parallel the rank order with regard to the external status characteristic, even though the latter may have little or no actual relationship to task-competency. More succinctly, in the theorists' own statement of the key postulate underlying status characteristics theory: "When a task-oriented group is differentiated with respect to a diffuse status characteristic external to the task situation, this differentiation determines the observable power and prestige order within the group, whether or not the diffuse status characteristic is related to the group task" (Cohen, Berger & Zelditch, 1972, p. 476).

This latter statement refers to two concepts—the "power and prestige order of the group" and "diffuse status characteristics"—that require definition. The power-prestige order of a group refers to the theorists' conceptualization of the task-relevant aspects of social interaction among group members and its operationalization in terms of four kinds of observable behavior: action opportunities, performance outputs, the evaluation of these outputs, and influence. These classes of task-related behavior in the group are seen as being interrelated correlates of "total participation" reflecting an individual's overall power and prestige among her or his group comembers.

A diffuse status characteristic is defined in terms of three properties. First, the states of a diffuse status characteristic are differentially evaluated, and these are generalized or "diffuse." Sex is an excellent example of a diffuse status characteristic, in part because maleness is broadly considered to be better than femaleness in our society, as is shown from studies of gender stereotypes (e.g. Broverman, Broverman et al., 1970; Broverman, Vogel et al., 1972) and discrimination against women (Goldberg, 1968). Second, expectations of performance at specific tasks are associated with each state of a diffuse status characteristic. The beliefs from gender stereotypes that "men like science and math more than women do" and that "men are more skilled in business than are women" are examples of specific performance expectations. Finally, generalized beliefs are also associated with the states of a diffuse status characteristic. In the case of sex, gender-role stereotyping research by Broverman and her colleagues (1972) indicates that maleness is strongly associated with perceived competency, whereas warmth and expressiveness are the underlying dimensions believed to characterize femaleness.

A number of authors have proposed that sex be viewed as a status characteristic. Unger (1975) concluded from a literature review that male–female interactions bear a striking similarity to interactions between people of differential status. Unger (1976) also documented the socialization process underlying status inequality between the sexes. In a similar vein, Lockheed and Hall (1976) conceptualized sex as a diffuse status characteristic to which the theory of status characteristics would apply. They also conducted separate studies to test the prediction that males are more apt to initiate task-oriented acts and emerge as leaders than are females in mixed-sex groups. In both cases, the videotaped interactions of four-person groups were analyzed to index each individual's rate of task-oriented behavior and to rank group members relative to one another.

Hall (1972) focused on mixed-sex groups of teacher trainees composed of two males and two females. Group members, who had been matched for their training and experience in teaching, were told beforehand that this matching should facilitate equal contributions to the group decision-making task. Despite this, men were more task-oriented than women in several senses: They were four times more likely to rank first in task-oriented behaviors initiated, they initiated more task-oriented acts overall, and they both contributed and supported proportionally more of the ideas that were incorporated in the group's final decisions.

In groups of high school students matched for verbal ability and cognitive style, Lockheed (1975) found an even stronger differentiation of task-oriented activity in favor of the males in newly-formed, mixed-sex groups performing a collective decision-making task. To contrast the view of sex as a status characteristic with gender-role explanations, she included another experimental condition in which subjects first performed the task in single-sex groups. Counter to a gender-role explanation implying "true" or natural sex differences for behavior in groups, Lockheed found no differences in verbal or task activity between members of all-male and all-female groups.

The subjects in this latter condition also completed another round of the decision-making task in mixed-sex groups. This additional feature was designed to test the prediction, derived from status characteristics theory, that females who have first developed self-expectations for performance and task-competency in an all-female group would subsequently be more task-oriented in a mixed-sex group than females lacking this opportunity. Consistent with theoretical prediction, women whose sense of personal competency had been initially established in groups exclusively composed of other females were indeed more likely to rank higher in initiated task behaviors in mixed-sex groups, especially with regard to increased percentages of second and third ranks. This enhancement of task-oriented activity by females with initial task experience in all-female groups showed some evidence, albeit weak, of "task-specific" generalization: i.e. generalization on the same task with different group members.

Although Berger et al.'s (1972) statement of status characteristics theory did not address how a diffuse status characteristic becomes activated, Lockheed (1977) has speculated that the cognitive style of group members perhaps mediates the activation of sex as a diffuse status characteristic in a task-oriented group. Specifically, she hypothesized that field-dependence might serve as such a mediator, altering the power and prestige order of a group in line with sex differences, owing to the greater influenceability, sensitivity to social context, and reliance on stereotypic cues known to be associated with it, relative to the dimension of field-independence. As a test of this hypothesis, high school students who scored high, medium, or low on field-dependence measures were respectively assigned to mixed-sex groups of two females and two males and given the collective decision-making task, previously used. As expected, sex differences in activity, influence, and attributed leadership were observed in field-dependent groups but not in groups of field-independent persons. Only in field-dependent groups did males initiate more activity and influence than females, as well as being accorded the top leadership ranks and considered by comembers as having the best ideas and doing the most to guide and direct the group. Moreover, females who were field-dependent initiated fewer acts and exercised less influence than did other females in the medium and field-independent groups.

Although it was not designed as a test of status characteristics theory, Messé, Aronoff, and Wilson's (1972) research reinforces Lockheed's contention that personality and individual difference characteristics are pertinent to activating sex as a diffuse status characteristic in small task groups. These investigators focused on individuals' needs for safety versus their need for esteem. Lacking ability, skill, and experience in interpersonal relationships, safety-oriented people are presumed to judge and evaluate others in terms of superficial, external status such as sex. In contrast, esteem-oriented people are concerned with assessing their own personal worth and competence and use social comparison of their own and others' performance toward this end. Indeed, males in three-person (2 females and 1 male), mixed-sex safety-oriented groups were much more apt to initiate a variety of task behaviors reflecting leadership than those in esteem-oriented groups. In this latter type of group, women emerged as group leaders precisely as often as one would expect from their proportional representation in the group, that is, two-thirds of the time. Accession to leadership in esteem-oriented groups was also more closely tied to the observed task competency of its members than in safety-oriented groups.

Status characteristics theory has also been tested in an experimental paradigm in which individuals first privately choose which one of pairs of pictures previously rated as neutral is the more attractive, and must then defend their selections against a confederate's challenges in cases of discrepant choices. In an initial study with white subjects of both sexes assigned either to same-sex or mixed-sex dyads, Adams and Landers (1978) confirmed the prediction from status characteristics theory that males would be more dominant than females in this situation. Regardless of the challenger's sex, males were more steadfast than females in defending their opinions against a partner's challenges.

Adams (1980) subsequently investigated the race (i.e., white vs. black) as well as the sex of both the subject and the challenger. From status characteristics theory and the literature concerning race and gender stereotyping, Adams expected white males and black females to be more dominant in sustaining challenges from another person than either white females or black males. Although her findings generally corresponded to this pattern, Adams took them as partially supporting status characteristics theory, in that the predictions were sustained only under certain conditions involving the race and/or the sex of the challenger. Because the boundary conditions of the original theory specified a situation in which individuals differ on only one status characteristic (Berger et al., 1972; Lockheed & Hall, 1976), status characteristics theory should perhaps not be faulted unduly for failing to anticipate the complexities introduced by the simultaneous operation of multiple status characteristics.

An interesting conceptual analysis by Meeker and Weitzel-O'Neill (1977) also deserves mention in this context. These authors propose combining status characteristics theory with elements of exchange theories and status consistency theory into a more general theory of status processes. They begin by assuming that an individual's contribution to the group's task may be seen as having competitive as well as cooperative elements. By making a valuable task contribution, the individual is obviously being cooperative in furthering the group toward attainment of its goal; in addition, however, the contributor may also be perceived as engaging in "competitive status enhancement": i.e., enhancing their position in the power and prestige order of the group at the expense of other group members. Meeker and Weitzel-O'Neill further suggest that external status defines the *legitimacy* of the group's power and prestige order, as well as establishing performance expectations. As a consequence, when an individual with high external status also attains high status within the group, it is considered just and deserving. Such a person, then, is permitted by group members to contribute to the group's task and so earns a privileged position in the power and prestige order. An individual with low external status who makes a similar attempt, however, is seen as engaging in competitive status enhancement, which is not considered legitimate for someone of that lesser station.

Applying this theoretical extension to the domain of female–male relations, Meeker and Weitzel-O'Neill (1977) propose the following: (1) Gender-role expectations make it legitimate for men, but not women, to engage in competitive status enhancement, and (2) women are permitted to make task contributions provided (a) they are seen as being cooperatively motivated and/or (b) status enhancement has been legitimized for them (by being appointed leader by an outside authority, for example). According to these authors, these expectations hold for women and men in both same-sex and mixed-sex groups. Although they do not themselves test the merits of this formulation and theoretical extension, the utility of considering the legitimacy of competitive status enhancement is insightfully illustrated by a review and reinterpretation of findings in sex differences in a number of areas of small groups research.

Ridgeway (1982) recently tested experimentally an hypothesis derived from Meeker and Weitzel-O'Neill's analysis of the importance of being perceived as cooperatively motivated toward the group. She predicted that a competent person with low external status could attain higher status and influence within a group by exhibiting a group orientation and thus acquiring legitimacy for her or his task contributions. This prediction was confirmed by findings indicating that a competent woman in a mixed-sex group did indeed attain higher influence and greater status with male comembers when she adopted a "group orientation" (i.e., one emphasizing cooperativeness and supportiveness) rather than a "self-orientation" (i.e., being distant, critical, and hostile).

In a related vein, Fennell, Barchas, Cohen, McMahon, and Hildebrand (1978) proposed an organizational perspective stressing the concepts of legitimacy and division of labor to account for sex differences in groups otherwise unexplained by status characteristics theory—most notably, women's and men's behavior in single-sex groups. Their theoretical extension deals principally with the issue of how a task group in a formal organizational setting determines the procedure to follow in solving a problem that has been delegated to them by "a representative of a legal-rational authority system."

According to Fennell and her colleagues, legitimacy for deciding issues of task procedure in single-sex groups is determined by what is "empirically usual" in the group's organizational context. Within the highly differentiated divisions of labor of formal organizations in North American societies, white males typically occupy the positions of authority. Thus, for all-male groups, task procedure issues are apt to be settled by creating a division of labor, in which all the "white males" are equal contenders for the authority role(s). On the other hand, because it is unusual to find a woman in a position of authority in a formal organization, and because women's incumbency in authority roles within a differentiated division of labor is "equally questionable," women in all-female groups would presumably be unlikely to develop a differentiated division of labor when organizing (themselves) to deal with a delegated task.

This formulation helps to understand a variety of previously obtained sex differences, such as Maslach's (1974) finding that men nominate themselves for the leadership position in a same-sex group more often than women do. Hoffman (1965), as well as Meeker and Weitzel-O'Neill (1977), both observed that the ineffectiveness of single-sex groups, as compared to mixed-sex groups, is due to excessive competition for leadership in the case of the all-male groups and to a failure for anyone to come forward and coordinate task activities in all-female groups.

Fennell and her associates (1978) support this formulation in a study of the interactions of male and female groups as they attempted to solve a problem (viz., the "Desert Survival Problem") at which women typically excel more than men. Using the frequency and type of verbal statements concerning procedure to index different divisions of labor, Fennell et al. confirmed their prediction that a differentiated division of labor, in which one person is consistently more active in settling procedural issues, was more characteristic of all-male than of all-female groups. Single-sex groups of women were more prone to develop a division of labor that was optimal for producing group gains over members' individual efforts at problem solution: viz., a "specialist" pattern, where members took responsibility for different facets of the group's procedural organization. Taken together, these initial results make Fennell et al's formulation seem promising.

Let us now take stock of the strengths and weaknesses of status characteristics theory. On the positive side (of the ledger), its emphasis on the self-fulfilling nature of stereotypic and status-derived expectations in biasing interaction in a group context complements current theorizing and research by experimental social psychologists. Status characteristics theory also provides a strong, competing explanation of sex differences in small group behavior that are often otherwise attributed to gender-role interpretations (Lockheed & Hall, 1976; Meeker & Weitzel-O'Neill, 1977).

Perhaps most important, status characteristics theory also suggests tactics for improving women's effectiveness and leadership potential in mixed-sex groups. Procedures for countering negative expectations directed at people with low external status and bolstering their sense of competency by reinforcement, role modelling, and direct assignment to positions of competence have proven effective in promoting "equal status" interaction in groups whose members differ on a diffuse status characteristic (Lockheed & Hall, 1976). Lockheed (1977, p. 164) has reported that demonstrating the task-competency of females in front of males was efficacious for field-dependent girls. Similarly, other investigators have provided experimental confirmation of the effectiveness of the public acknowledgment of a women's competency on an issue for improving her leadership potential in a mixed-sex group (Bradley, 1980). For women with low scores on the ability and performance aspects of self-esteem (Stake, 1979; Stake & Stake, 1979), providing them with positive information to heighten confidence in their ability to contribute to the group's task can increase their leadership behavior, provided the information is conveyed to both parties of the mixed-sex interaction some time before it actually occurs (Stake, 1981).

As suggested previously, however, advocates of status characteristics theory emphasize that such "expectation training" needs to be aimed at the high status members of a group as well as those of low status in order to successfully overcome the latter's "interaction disabilities" (see Cohen & Roper, 1972). The underlying reasoning is that focusing only on the behavior and expectations of the low-status individuals would not lessen the resistance of the high-status group members and might merely heighten "status conflict." However, as Ridgeway (1982) has recently noted, it is sometimes difficult to change the expectations of individuals with high external status outside the laboratory. As an alternative, she recommends heightening the group-orientation of women in mixed-sex groups—a seemingly more efficient procedure that they may effect by simply changing their own behavior.

On the negative side, too, the conceptualization of sex as a diffuse status characteristic would be more convincing if investigators assuming or attempting to test that premise would assess the expectations held by women and men in mixed-sex groups rather than merely assuming the existence of these expectations. The notion of expectations serves as the central construct of status characteristics theory. As Lockheed (1977, p. 159) has so aptly put it, the essence of the theory is that it ". . . describes the process and conditions under which stereotyped beliefs lead to stereotyped behavior."

Yet in none of the tests of status characteristics theory regarding sex did the investigators actually measure the subjects' self–other expectations of performance and/or their actual proneness to gender stereotyping. Nor have the adherents of status characteristics theory apparently considered exploring the impact upon group processes of composing mixed-sex groups so that members' adherence to gender stereotypes, or their tendency toward gender stereotyping of self and others was systematically varied.

It is perhaps also an auspicious time to implement the technology for assessing expectations and stereotypes regarding gender in this line of research. In the past, stereotyping on the basis of gender was sufficiently widespread so that status characteristics theory could be reasonably accurate in predicting the pattern of female and male behavior in mixed-sex groups without assessing members' expectancies. In future, one can (hopefully) be less confident in assuming that gender stereotyping beliefs are as broadly shared, at least by women. The emerging literature reveals cases in which the usual pattern of men's dominance of activity, influence, and leadership in mixed-sex groups no longer obtains or is reversed in favor of women. In a study of mixed-sex, graduate seminar groups, for example, Kennedy and Camden (1981) found the women showing "communication dominance" over the men, as indexed by the number of speeches they made and their interruptions of other speakers. Without expectancy assessments, we are unable to tell whether such instances reflect a failure of prediction or an inadequacy of the theory, or if it has exceeded its boundary conditions.

The "scope" or boundary conditions of status characteristics theory also require consideration for appreciating its limits. With regard to sex, it would apply only to temporary, ad hoc groups of women and men who are unacquainted with one another and possess no prior expectations about the task. From one perspective, this limitation is quite desirable, because it implies that sex would not bias activity, influence, and leadership processes in more established groups, whose members are familiar and affectively involved with one another.

This line of thought essentially squares with research exploring the impact of leader's sex in field studies of actual organizations. Traditional gender stereotyping, with its negative characterizations of women, has been extensively documented among businessmen, male managers in private and public organizations (Bass, Krusell & Alexander, 1971; Bowman, Worthy & Greyser, 1965; Schein, 1973, 1978), and even female managers (Schein, 1975). Yet attempts to find evidence of reported sex differences in leader behavior, motivation, and effectiveness, or in subordinate satisfaction in actual organizations, have typically met with failure (see Bartol & Wortman, 1976; Day & Stogdill, 1972; Osborn & Vicars, 1976; Veiga & Yanouza, 1978; Wexley & Hunt, 1974).

In summary, status characteristics theory has served as an explanation of sex differences in mixed-sex groups that is an alternative to gender-role interpretations. Moreover, a number of authors have suggested extensions of the theory, focusing on the issue of legitimacy, which should extend its domain. Perhaps the most important contribution of status characteristics theory is its suggestion of improving women's leadership potential in mixed-sex groups by heightening their sense of competency and demonstrating it before the other group members. This is a plausible recommendation with solid experimental support. However, whether expectation training needs to be directed at the high status group members as well as those with low external status is beginning to be questioned. Future research should also attempt to assess the gender-stereotypic beliefs of group members in order to permit more direct and probing tests of status characteristics theory. Nevertheless, at the present time, status characteristics theory is perhaps the best *single* theory for understanding the task and interpersonal behavior of women and men in mixed-sex groups.

LEADERSHIP AND GROUP EFFECTIVENESS

In this section, the focus shifts to theories concerning group effectiveness. Two issues are discussed in this context. First, Fiedler's well-known contingency theory deals with how a leader's style interacts with situational variables to influence the group's performance at its assigned task. Second, research and theorizing concerning the phenomenon of status congruence are also presented. Status congruence refers to the consistency of members' rank-orderings on different status dimensions within a group. According to various conceptualizations, including Sampson's (1969) expectancy theory, the extent of status congruence within a group determines both its task-effectiveness and the members' satisfaction with their roles.

Fiedler's Contingency Theory of Leadership Effectiveness

Reviewing the literature concerning styles of leadership with particular reference to women, Denmark (1977, p. 104) observed that: ". . . insufficient attention has been addressed to how situational factors may help determine the effectiveness of different leadership styles." Fielder's (1964, 1967, 1971, 1972, 1978) contingency theory of leadership effectiveness deals precisely with this issue. This viewpoint also commands attention because it is generally considered the currently dominant theoretical perspective concerning leadership in social psychology; of the several contingency models of leadership that emerged in the 60s and 70s, it is easily the best known to social psychologists. Unfortunately, of the several hundred studies that have been conducted to test various aspects of Fiedler's theory, only a mere handful have focused on the dimension of sex. This neglect currently appears to be in the process of being remedied and, as is documented below, interesting issues relating to sex await further exploration.

Essentially, Fiedler's contingency theory of leadership effectiveness maintains that the relationship between leadership style and group performance is contingent upon situational favorability. It focuses on task-orientation and relationship-orientation as alternative leadership styles. Situational favorability refers to the extent to which the situation permits the leader to control and influence the group and is operationally defined in terms of three dimensions: (1) position power (high vs. low); (2) leader–member relations (good vs. poor); and (3) group task (structured vs. unstructured). Permuting all the combinations of these variables yields eight different situational variations that Fiedler terms "octants" and for which his contingency model predicts the nature of the relationship between leadership style and group performance. In general, the theory specifies that task-oriented leaders will perform better in stimulating or maintaining group performance under either relatively favorable or relatively unfavorable situations, whereas relationship-oriented leaders are presumed to be more effective under situational conditions of intermediate favorability.

Leadership style is indexed in terms of the leader's evaluative ratings of her or his "Least Preferred Coworker" (LPC)—i.e., the one person of all those they have known with whom they have had the greatest difficulty as a coworker. Typically, a low LPC score indicates that the least preferred coworker is evaluated very negatively by the leader and is presumed to reflect a task-oriented leadership style. A high LPC score, on the other hand, means that the person views the least preferred coworker positively in some regards and is taken as an indication of a relationship-oriented style of leadership.

Sex, Leadership Style, and Group Composition.   In the leadership literature, one frequently encounters the notion that the sexes differ in their approach to leadership: women supposedly focus on socioemotional concerns and being supportive to comembers, while men take a more task-oriented approach. Various studies, such as Strodtbeck and Mann's (1956) classic jury study and Vinacke's (1959, 1964) research on sex differences in coalition formation, have reinforced these beliefs concerning putative sex differences in leadership and group orientation.

Fiedler's LPC measure may be considered a self-report index of leadership style that is indirect and not especially obvious to the respondent. With that well-validated instrument, several studies suggest that sex and leadership style are independent of one another. In a field survey investigation, Chapman (1975) administered leadership and biographical questionnaires to managers of both sexes drawn from a civilian and a military organization. In order to insure that the situations confronting the female and male managers were reasonably comparable, the sample was stratified and included as respondents only those women and men whose jobs were similar in responsibility and formal authority. As

Chapman had anticipated, the LPC scores of these men and women did not differ from one another in either organization. Thus, these women were neither more nor less task-oriented as practicing managers than their male counterparts. In a related laboratory study, Eagly (1970) found no sex differences in the LPC scores of the women and men who emerged as task leaders in same-sex groups. Likewise, in a field experiment of emergent leadership, Schneier (1978) both predicted and obtained no difference in the LPC scores of emergent female and male leaders identified from members' sociometric choices. The percentages of emergent leaders of each sex were also not notably discrepant.

Thus, it does not appear that women and men differ in leadership style. There is some reason to believe, however, that the sex composition of a group may influence the leadership style score of the leader, especially in the case of women. Chapman's (1975) comparison of the leadership styles of practicing female and male managers in a civilian as well as a military organization suggests this possibility. In that study the LPC scores of the female managers were negatively correlated with the number of males they supervised, particularly in the military organization. Specifically, as the number of males supervised increased, the LPC scores of the female managers declined, denoting a tendency toward a greater task-orientation. For the male managers, no relationship was found between the number of males or females supervised and their leadership style scores.

Recent research by Offermann (1984) further suggests that this finding may be neither idiosyncratic nor only a product of lengthy supervisory experience in established groups. Offermann explored the effects upon individuals' leadership style scores of a relatively brief episode in which female and male leaders supervised a group of followers on Maiers's Change of Work Procedure task, modified so as to be more neutral regarding gender-role connotations. The sex composition of the supervised groups was systematically varied so that the followers were either (a) all of opposite sex from the leader; (b) all of the same sex as the leader; or (c) two opposite-sex persons and one individual of the leader's sex. Group sex composition interacted with leader sex in influencing the leader's post-supervision LPC scores.

Specifically, female leaders with three followers of the opposite sex obtained *lower* LPC scores, indicative of a stronger task orientation, than did either male leaders with all opposite-sex followers or female leaders of mixed-sex or same-sex groups. Male leaders with wholly opposite-sex followers scored *higher* on the LPC measure, reflecting a more pronounced relationship orientation than did their male counterparts in charge of mixed-sex or same-sex groups. The leadership style scores of male and female leaders of mixed- and same-sex groups did not differ.

These results, along with Chapman's, are provocative, pointing toward the possibility that one's leadership style may be influenced by simply supervising a set of individuals exclusively or preponderantly of the opposite sex. Offermann

(1984) sees her own findings as questioning the LPC measure as an index of a presumably stable leadership orientation on the part of the individual. However, her findings could also be viewed as reflecting the impact of group sex composition upon the leader's self-perception and/or the followers' perceptions of the leader, as discussed earlier in this chapter. Specifically, the effects reported by Offermann (1984) are strongly reminiscent of Ruble and Higgins' (1976) findings that both females and males describe themselves in terms of the opposite-sex stereotype when in an ad hoc group composed largely of persons of the opposite sex. Analogously, Offermann (1984) has shown that when supervising a group of opposite-sex members, female leaders obtain lower LPC scores (indicative of a stronger task orientation); male leaders obtain higher LPC scores. In any case, these intriguing findings deserve to be followed up.

Sex, Leadership Style, and Group Performance. As noted earlier, the core of Fiedler's theory concerns the relationship of leadership style to group effectiveness. How, then, does leadership style relate to group effectiveness when the leader's sex and the group's sex composition are taken into account? Eagly (1970) suggests that the relationship of leadership style to group effectiveness may be quite different in groups of females as compared to groups of males. In her study, same-sex groups of five people were convened to discuss a human relations problem. Each group consisted of one individual who scored high on the LPC scale, one who scored low, and three others whose scores fell in the middle of the scale. The group's effectiveness was indexed by the length and detail of the resulting report that was presented under time-limited conditions.

Some predictions, which were derived from a joint consideration of Fiedler's contingency theory and the Bales–Slater theory of leadership role differentiation, failed to be sustained. However, serendipitous findings concerning sex did emerge. Specifically, the LPC scores of the best-liked persons were found to be related to group effectiveness, but in opposite directions for role-differentiated groups (i.e., groups in which the task leader and the best-liked person were different individuals) composed of males versus females.

In the male groups, the LPC score of the best-liked person was *positively* related to group effectiveness. That is, the more interpersonally oriented the best-liked person was in the male groups, the more effective was the group's performance at its task. Further analysis suggested that this relationship was due to the best-liked person's function as a socioemotional leader, reducing interpersonal tensions in the groups. On the other hand, within the female groups, the LPC score of the best-liked person was *negatively* related to group effectiveness. Unlike her male counterpart, the best-liked person in the all-female groups apparently directed her interpersonal orientation toward becoming better liked by her comembers rather than attempting to lower tensions and thus facilitating group effectiveness.

Thus, Eagly's (1970) study illustrates once again the vulnerability of assuming that a conceptualization based on members or groups of one sex will necessarily apply to the other sex, or to mixed-sex groups, for that matter. As mentioned earlier, Bales and Slater's formulation of leadership role differentiation was based on groups composed exclusively of men. Eagly found that the best-liked person performed the role of socioemotional leader, much as had been previously suggested by Bales and Slater, but *only* in groups of males. Perhaps not surprisingly in retrospect, the best-liked person in all-female groups responded quite differently. This pattern of findings, then, is another illustration of the utility and importance of taking sex differences and group sex composition into account in formulating theories of small group processes.

Fiedler's contingency theory fared somewhat better in Schneier's (1978) field experiment on emergent leadership and sex. Schneier had anticipated that with experimental tasks neutral regarding gender (viz., experiential learning exercises), the leader's sex would not interact with leadership style in influencing group performance. The situation confronting the groups and their leaders fell in Octant II of Fiedler's model—i.e., it was characterized by good leader–member relations, highly structured tasks, and weak leader power. For such a relatively favorable situation, Fiedler's model predicts a negative correlation between leader's LPC scores and group performance, such that task-oriented leaders would tend to facilitate group performance. Consistent with Fiedler's model as well as his expectations for sex differences, Schneier found significantly negative LPC-group performance correlations with no difference between female and male leaders.

Bullard and Cook (1975) also attempted to test Fiedler's theoretical predictions for an Octant II situation with appointed leaders, but in the context of a single laboratory session in which leaders guided groups that were composed of members entirely of the same or opposite sex and that were homogeneous in their task- or relationship-orientation. Group performance on a modified T-group exercise did not differ as a function of leaders' style, though it is not unusual for laboratory tests to fail to sustain contingency theory expectations for Octant II (Fiedler, 1971). More notably for our purposes, group performance was unaffected by whether or not the leader's sex matched the otherwise homogeneous sex composition of the group.

Thus, for the relatively favorable situation represented by Octant II, the experimental evidence suggests that the relationship between leadership style and group effectiveness does not appear to depend on either the leader's sex or the sex composition of the group.

Gender-role Expectations and Situation Unfavorability.   Paymer and Dovidio (1981) found evidence that a leader's sex interacted with leadership style and group size. They assumed that a woman may find it more difficult than a man to become accepted as a group leader, owing to traditional gender-role expectations. Thus, the same situation that is highly favorable for a male leader would, on this count, be only moderately favorable for a female leader. Increments in group membership beyond an optimum size of five people were also assumed to lower situation favorability. Fiedler's suggestion that leadership effectiveness is promoted by having low LPC leaders for very favorable and very unfavorable situations and high LPC leaders for situations moderate in situation favorability should be noted here. Taking these assumptions together, Paymer and Dovidio expected that: (a) in 5 -person groups, low LPC male leaders would be more effective than their high LPC male counterparts, while high LPC female leaders would have greater effectiveness than the female leaders with a low LPC orientation; and (b) in 9-person groups, the low LPC female leaders were expected to be more effective than high LPC female leaders.

To test these hypotheses, individuals with extreme LPC scores were selected to be group leaders—purportedly by chance—and directed mixed-sex groups with nearly equal numbers of male and female members in the performance of two tasks. Although there were no effects on group task performance, the predicted pattern of results was obtained for leader effectiveness perceived by group members. As expected, for example, in the 9-person groups led by a male, the high LPC leader was more favorably regarded for his effectiveness than was the low LPC leader. For the females, on the other hand, the high LPC leader was perceived as more effective than the low LPC leader in the 5-person groups.

The premise that traditional gender-role expectations decrease the favorability of the situation for a female leader is echoed and reinforced by other research relating to Fiedler's contingency theory. Taking an organizational perspective, Arnett, Higgins, and Priem (1980) have also suggested that traditional gender-roles make the leadership situation of a female leader less favorable than that for a male leader, especially when she is required by a superior to adopt a more assertive, directive stance toward her subordinates, who may consequently resent her for behaving contrary to traditional expectations for a woman. According to Fiedler's (1972) reconceptualization of the LPC construct, leaders rely on their primary style when the situation is unfavorable for them. Taking these considerations jointly into account, Arnett and his colleagues predicted that under pressure to act directively, appointed female leaders would be more prone to employ their primary styles than would their male counterparts. This prediction was strongly supported in a study of business students taking part in a simulated business exercise· in which a manager was required to mediate between a superior's demands and subordinates' reactions.

In sum, although relatively little research on Fiedler's model has dealt with the dimensions of sex or gender, the existing studies raise several provocative issues. First, women and men who serve as leaders in traditional groups, or who emerge as leaders in ad hoc groups of varying duration, do not differ in leadership style as indexed by LPC scores. However, perhaps indicating a reciprocal influence between the leader and the led, some studies suggest that group sex composition may influence its leader's style. Second, but perhaps more important, introducing a consideration of sex and gender appears to complicate the ability of Fiedler's model to predict relationships between leadership style and group effectiveness, in some circumstances at least. On one hand, in the relatively favorable situation represented by Octant II of the model, the relationship between leadership style and group effectiveness does not appear to depend on the leader's sex or on the group's sex composition. On the other hand, however, there is data suggesting that the relationship of leadership style and group effectiveness is fundamentally different in groups of women versus groups of men. Moreover, other studies indicate that traditional gender-role expectations can lower the favorability of a situation confronted by a female leader as opposed to a male leader.

One implication of this latter research is that the concept of situation favorability in Fiedler's contingency model may well have to be expanded to include gender-role expectations as an element with adverse impact on women in leadership roles. We can also speculate as to the circumstances in which traditional gender-role expectations are apt to be problematic: viz., When the female leader is under pressure from superiors to act assertively toward subordinates, the group's sex composition is mixed or predominantly of the opposite-sex, and the task is one over which men rather than women have typically exerted dominance or authority.

Fiedler's theory of leadership effectiveness was derived largely, if not exclusively, from studies of all-male groups, especially in military contexts. By expanding the theory to include issues of sex and gender, its applicability to mixed-sex groups and all-female groups can be enhanced and its overall domain of relevance increased.

Status Congruence

Within a group or social system, individuals are typically differentiated from one another according to one or more dimensions involving ascribed or achieved characteristics. Sex, for example, is an ascribed characteristic, commonly regarded as conveying status, where 'maleness' is associated with greater power, prestige, and social value than 'femaleness' (Cohen et al., 1972; Linton, 1966; Sampson, 1969). When individuals' rank relative to one another on a dimension defining status is incommensurate with their standing on other status dimensions, the group is said to be in a state of status incongruence and the individuals comprising the group are, theoretically, motivated to "equilibrate" their various status rankings. Status incongruence is presumed to disrupt interpersonal interaction and the smoothness of group functioning because it renders individual expectations for one another's behavior unstable and conflicting.

Studies of small groups support these theoretical assumptions by demonstrating that status incongruence can undermine group effectiveness and morale within the group (Adams, 1953; Exline & Ziller, 1959). For example, in a laboratory investigation in which groups of women were given two successive problems to solve, Exline and Ziller (1959) found that status incongruence between alleged task ability and relative power to influence the group decision led to increased interpersonal conflict and lower positive affect and congeniality, as well as some evidence of less effective task performance.

Sex has figured as a variable in several studies of status congruence. Consider, first, those investigations with men and women in groups whose sex composition was homogeneous. Using the same general paradigm as that just described, Ziller and Exline (1958) explored age heterogeneity in problem solving groups of men and women, respectively, and obtained quite different findings as a function of sex composition. The prediction of a direct relationship between age and power in the groups, as indexed by the percentage of total interaction accounted for by the person, was validated only in the case of the all-male groups. Further, within the groups of males, age heterogeneity was associated with more effective group problem-solving. For the all-female groups, it was the *youngest* member who exhibited the greatest power and there was some evidence that group effectiveness was associated with age homogeneity rather than heterogeneity. These unexpected findings were interpreted to reflect differences in status congruence by the assumption that a person's power in a group context increases with age for men but decreases with age for women. Following this reasoning, groups heterogeneous in members' age and with the oldest person exerting the greatest influence would be characterized as status congruent for men and status incongruent for women. As status congruence should also facilitate group functioning, this post hoc explanation would also account for the findings of greater problem-solving effectiveness in heterogeneous-age male groups, as compared to homogeneous-age male groups or to heterogeneous-age female groups.

Somewhat more recently, Johnson, Goodchilds, and Raven (1972) have explored the effects of status congruency-incongruency and ambiguity in a communication network paradigm that, they suggest, has promise for studying sex differences in responsiveness to status in a small group context. Johnson and his colleagues hypothesized that women would be more sensitive than men to status incongruency, owing to the differential socialization pressures for each sex in the American culture. As a consequence of such socialization, women are presumably responsive to status in interpersonal settings, whereas men orient toward being autonomous and independent of others. To test this hypothesis, university men and women assembled in sex-homogeneous groups were given several anagram problems to solve in a highly centralized communication network consisting of one central position and three peripheral positions. Similar to a technique devised earlier by Sampson and his associates (some of whose research is described below), status congruency and incongruency were experimentally manipulated by providing differential feedback to subjects as to the comembers' alleged year in school and majors. Status congruency and incongruency, respectively, were effected by feedback indicating that either the highest status or the lowest status person present had been assigned to the single central position in the network. Some groups of subjects were provided no information about their comembers' ostensible status and comprised a no-feedback condition.

Males in the status-congruent and no-feedback groups showed greater improvement in task efficiency over trials, as well as more satisfaction with the peripheral role than did those in status-incongruent groups. For groups of females too, status congruency in the group similarly promoted both task effectiveness and peripheral role satisfaction, as compared to status incongruency. In contrast to the men, however, women responded to the absence of status feedback with the *lowest* level of task efficiency and satisfaction with the peripheral role, leading the investigators to conclude that the no-feedback condition represented a state of status ambiguity for the women. The replicability of this sex difference in response to apparent status ambiguity and its generalizability to less restricted communication settings deserves further exploration.

Unlike the preceding studies, Sampson (1969) and his associates have focused on groups whose sex composition was heterogeneous, and have incorporated the sex variable itself as an integral element of their status congruence manipulations. These investigators assumed that within the university community, "personal" status is determined principally by age, year in school, and sex. An older graduate student, for example, presumably possesses greater personal status than a somewhat younger, upper level undergraduate (i.e., a senior or junior), whose personal status in turn exceeds that of an even younger, lower-level undergraduate (i.e., freshman or sophomore). Furthermore, men were also believed to enjoy greater personal status than women within the university community at large. Thus, relative to one another, a group composed of (1) an older, male graduate student, (2) a male, upper-level undergraduate, and (3) a young, female undergraduate would be considered high, medium, and low in personal status, respectively.

Brandon (1965) formed her laboratory groups in precisely this manner for a study that tested Sampson's expectancy theory of status congruence. According to Sampson, inconsistency in status rankings per se will not necessarily produce status incongruence or result in attempts to restore congruence. Rather, one must additionally take into account whether or not the discrepant status dimensions are expected to be relevant to one another. Sampson (1963, 1969) suggested that only when group members expect the status dimensions to be related and consistent with one another will discrepancies in status ranks elicit status incongruence.

Brandon devised a laboratory situation that introduced two other status dimensions in addition to personal status. Specifically, on a group production task, subjects performed jobs varying in difficulty and responsibility and were also assigned positions of leadership within the task group. Brandon provided evidence to validate her assumptions that personal status was expected to be linked to job difficulty and leadership position, respectively, while the latter dimensions were not considered particularly relevant to one another. Thus, by assigning people of different personal status to an appropriate job difficulty level and leadership position, it was possible to create experimental conditions in which (a) expectations of consistency between pairs of status dimensions were confirmed (expected consistency conditions); (b) dimensions perceived as unrelated were consistent with one another (unexpected consistency condition); and (c) the three status dimensions were either all consistent or unrelated to one another (the complete consistency and no consistency conditions, respectively).

The results nicely illustrated the heuristic value of taking expectations of consistency into account when attempting to predict the occurrence of status congruence and incongruence. As predicted from Sampson's (1963, 1969) expectancy congruence model, subjects in the expected consistency conditions reported more positive attitudes toward their groups, indicated less tension in the group or felt by them personally, and showed more interest in the group's productivity than did those in either the unexpected consistency or the no consistency conditions. Notably, the no consistency condition, which scored lowest of all conditions on positivity of affect and concern for productivity, was one in which patterns of status expectancy were violated by having the single, female group member occupy the highest leadership position. Although sex of subject was not incorporated as a separate factor in the analyses, it is nevertheless tempting to speculate that the negative affect arising from the no consistency condition was due, at least partly, to the expressed displeasure of the two male group members toward the 'low status' female's appointment as the key leader and potential supervisor over them. Conceivably, the lone woman herself may have also felt uncomfortable in being the group's leader under these circumstances and may similarly have disliked the situation.

Another aspect of Brandon's (1965) results deserves mention. Theories of status congruence, including Sampson's model, concur in predicting that of Brandon's various conditions, the complete consistency condition—in which all three forms of status are congruent with one another—should produce the greatest amount of positive affect. Counter to this prediction, however, the complete consistency condition elicited a somewhat less positive affect than either one or both of the expected consistency conditions across affect measures, but a somewhat more positive affect than the unexpected consistency and no consistency conditions, without differing significantly from either set of conditions. Brandon (1965) interpreted these results as due to opposing and countervailing forces: On one hand, pressures toward positive affect arose from the confirmation of expectancies concerning consistency in status ranks; on the other hand, pressures toward negative affect arose from the violation of a principle of equality suggesting that certain resources or rewards be distributed equally among group members without regard to their "inputs" or "investments." This interpretation, however, may not place sufficient stock on the potentially critical role of sex. In the completely consistent condition of Brandon's study, the older male held all the highest status desirable positions, while the female occupied lowest status on all counts. Perhaps the female's dissatisfaction with her lot in this situation was principally responsible for the failure to find the most positive affect in the complete consistency condition.

A final aspect of Sampson's research program that is pertinent to our concerns with sex involves the consequences of making one of the status dimensions contributing to status incongruency more salient by endowing the status holder with reward-and-punishment power. Sampson and Bunker (unpublished study cited in Sampson, 1969) addressed this issue and created variations in status congruency in a manner similar to Brandon's by having either a male accomplice (i.e., the Status Congruent condition) or a female accomplice (i.e. the Status Incongruent condition) supervise two upper-level undergraduate men on an alternative uses task. The accomplice was also given power to award monetary rewards and levy fines, the size of the rewards and punishments being varied so as to result in high versus low power. Status congruency was found to have generally weaker effects than "previous studies of a similar nature," especially as regards task performance. In contrast, task performance was clearly influenced by job role power, with high power leading to greater improvements in performance. There is an intriguing implication here: It appears that the impact of status congruency that is introduced when a "low status" woman enacts a leadership role over "higher status" men can be markedly mitigated, at least as regards the important dimension of task effectiveness, by endowing her with reward and punishment power. (In their chapter in this volume, Eagly and Wood deal with the related issue of the elimination of sex-related influencibility when work roles are taken into account.)

In summary, then, the sex variable has typically been implicitly rather than explicitly considered in studies of status congruence in small groups. Yet the research reviewed here suggests that it would be worthwhile to take the sex variable more systematically into account. For example, some studies suggest that women and men in same-sex groups respond quite differently to status incongruence and status ambiguity. Likewise, from studies of status congruence in mixed-sex groups, the sex variable may well have played a more prominent role than was previously appreciated, and may help to account for some otherwise unexplained findings.

SOME CONCLUDING THOUGHTS

It is now time to rest my case regarding the merits of this line of work. Throughout this chapter, I have focused on theoretical viewpoints concerning groups whenever possible. I have done so in the belief that progress in understanding the behavior of women and men in groups will be best fostered by conceptual perspectives that serve as frameworks for organizing past findings and generating new knowledge. A related aim has been to illustrate the mutual benefit to be gained from the joint consideration of the literatures of the social psychology of groups and the psychology of women, along with the research that constitutes the interface between them. Perhaps the sections on leadership best exemplify how traditional theories of social psychology can be enriched conceptually and empirically by paying attention to the dimensions of sex and gender. In turn, the psychology of women can profit from the insights of social psychological theories concerning interpersonal behavior in groups.

The sections on the effects of group sex composition provide another case in point. To the investigator primarily interested in the psychology of women, small groups can be viewed as microcosms for studying gender-role pressures and conflicts, as well as sex differences, more easily and clearly than in larger social units. Moreover, by exploring the interaction of women and men in both same-sex as well as mixed-sex groups, it is possible to determine the extent to which the interpersonal behavior reflects the impact of group sex composition versus sex differences per se (see Kahn, Nelson, & Gaeddert, 1980). On the other hand, to the researcher for whom groups are the primary focus, group sex composition is an obviously important contextual variable whose effects appear to be potent and worth documenting.

Finally, there is an entirely pragmatic reason for being informed about sex, gender, and groups. Small groups are responsible for much of the problem-solving, policy-making, and decision-making in business, government, and academia. As women increasingly gain membership and leadership in the decision-making groups of these organizations, it behooves us to understand as well as possible the interrelations among sex, gender, and groups.

ACKNOWLEDGMENT

The thoughtful comments of Rhoda K. Unger and Karen K. Dion are gratefully acknowledged. Of course, responsibility for the final product is mine alone. Correspondence to the author should be directed to the Department of Psychology, University of Toronto, Toronto, CANADA M5S 1A1.

REFERENCES

Adams, J. (Maj.), & Hicks, J. M. (1980). Leader sex, leader descriptions of own behavior and subordinates description of leader behavior (Project Athena: West Point). *International Journal of Women's Studies, 3,* 321–326.

Adams, K. A. (1980). Who has the final word? Sex, race, and dominance behavior. *Journal of Personality and Social Psychology, 38*, 1–8.

Adams, K., & Landers, A. (1978). Sex differences in dominance behavior. *Sex Roles, 4*, 215–223.

Adams, S. (1953). Status congruency as a variable in small group performance. *Social Forces, 32* (October), 16–22.

Amidjaja, I., & Vinacke, W. E. (1965). Achievement, nurturance, and competition in male and female triads. *Journal of Personality and Social Psychology, 2*, 447–451.

Aries, E. (1976). Interaction patterns and themes of male, female, and mixed groups. *Small Group Behavior, 7*, 7–18.

Aries, E. (1977). Male–female interpersonal styles in all-male, all-female, and mixed groups. In A. G. Sargent (Ed.), *Beyond sex roles.* New York: West, pp. 292–299.

Arnett, M. D. Higgins, R. B., & Priem, A. P. (1980). Sex and least preferred coworker score effects in leadership behavior. *Sex Roles, 6*, 139–152.

Bales, R. F. (1950). *Interaction process analysis: A method for the study of small groups.* Reading, Mass.: Addison-Wesley.

Bales, R. F. (1953). The equilibrium problem in small groups. In T. Parsons, R. F. Bales, & E. A. Shils (Eds.), *Working papers in the Theory of Action.* New York: Free Press

Bales, R. F. (1956). Task status and likeability as a function of talking and listening in decision-making groups. In L. D. White (Ed.), *The state of the social sciences.* Chicago, Ill.: University of Chicago Press.

Bales, R. F. (1958). Task roles and social roles in problem-solving groups. In E. E. Maccoby, T. M. Newcomb, & E. L. Hartley (Eds.), *Readings in social psychology.* New York: Holt, Rinehart, & Winston.

Bales, R. F. (1970). *Personality and interpersonal behavior.* New York: Holt, Rinehart, & Winston.

Bales, R. F., & Slater, P. E. (1955). Role differentiation in small decision-making groups. In T. Parsons & R. F. Bales (Eds.), *Family, socialization, and interaction process.* New York: Free Press, pp. 259–306.

Bartol, K. (1974). Male versus female leaders: The effect of leader need dominance and follower satisfaction. *Academy of Management Journal, 17*, 225–233.

Bartol, K. M., & Wortman, M. S. (1976). Sex effects in leader-behavior self-descriptions and job satisfaction. *Journal of Psychology, 94*, 177–183.

Bass, B. M., Krusell, J., & Alexander, R. A. (1971). Male managers' attitudes toward working women. *American Behavioral Scientist, 15*, 221–236.

Bem, S. L. (1974). The measurement of psychological androgyny. *Journal of Consulting and Clinical Psychology, 42*, 155–162.

Bem, S. L. (1976). Probing the promise of androgyny. In A. G. Kaplan & J. P. Bean (Eds), *Beyond sex-role stereotypes: Readings toward a psychology of androgyny.* Toronto: Little, Brown.

Berger, J., Cohen, B. P., & Zelditch, M., Jr. (1972). Status conceptions and social interaction. *American Sociological Review, 37*, 241–255.

Berger, J., Conner, T. L., & Fisek, M. H. (Eds.) (1974). *Expectation states theory: A theoretical research program.* Cambridge, Mass.: Winthrop.

Berman, P. W., O'Nan, B. A., & Floyd, W. (1981). The double standard of aging and the social situation: Judgments of attractiveness of the middle-aged woman. *Sex Roles, 7*, 87–96.

Bond, J. R., & Vinacke, W. E. (1961). Coalitions in mixed-sex triads. *Sociometry, 24*, 61–75.

Booth, A. (1972). Sex and social participation. *American Sociological Review, 37*, 183–192.

Bowman, G. W., Worthy, N. B., & Greyser, S. A. (1965). Are women executives people? *Harvard Business Review, 43*, 14–28 and 164–178.

Bradley, P. H. (1980). Sex, competence and opinion deviation: An expectation states approach. *Communication Monographs, 47*(2), 101–110.

Brandon, A. C. (1965). Status congruence and expectations. *Sociometry, 28*, 272–288.

Bray, R. M., Johnson, D., & Chilstrom, J. T., Jr. (1982). Social influence by group members with minority opinions: A comparison of Hollander and Moscovici. *Journal of Personality and Social Psychology, 43,* 78–88.

Broverman, I. K., Broverman, D. M., Clarkson, F. E., Rosenkrantz, P., & Vogel, S. R. (1970). Sex-role stereotypes and clinical judgments of mental health. *Journal of Consulting Psychology, 34,* 1–7.

Broverman, I. K., Vogel, S. R., Broverman, D. M., Clarkson, F. E., & Rosenkrantz, P. S. (1972). Sex-role stereotypes: A current appraisal. *The Journal of Social Issues, 28* (2), 59–78.

Bullard, P. D., & Cook, P. E. (1975). Sex and workstyle of leaders and followers: Determinants of productivity. *Psychological Reports, 36,* 545–546.

Burke, P. J. (1972). Leadership role differentiation. In C. G. McClintock (Ed.), *Experimental social psychology.* New York: Holt, Rinehart, & Winston.

Cannavale, F. J., Scarr, H. A., & Pepitone, A. (1970). Deindividuation in the small group: Further evidence. *Journal of Personality and Social Psychology, 16,* 141–147.

Carlson, E. R., & Carlson, R. (1961). Male and female subjects in personality research. *Journal of Abnormal and Social Psychology, 61,* 482–483.

Cattell, R. B., & Lawson, E. D. (1962). Sex differences in small group performance. *Journal of Social Psychology, 58,* 141–145.

Chaney, M. V., & Vinacke, W. E. (1960). Achievement and nurturance in triads varying in power distribution. *Journal of Abnormal and Social Psychology, 60,* 175–181.

Chapman, J. B. (1975). Comparison of male and female leadership styles. *Academy of Management Journal, 18,* 645–650.

Cohen, B. P., Berger, J., & Zelditch, M., Jr. (1972). Status conceptions and interaction: A case study of the problem of developing cumulative knowledge. In C. McClintock (Ed.), *Experimental social psychology.* New York: Holt, Rinehart, & Winston.

Cohen, E. G., & Roper, S. S. (1972). Modification of interracial interaction disability: An application of status characteristics theory. *American Sociological Review, 37,* 643–655.

Costrich, N., Feinstein, J., Kidder, L., Marecek, J., & Pascale, L. (1975). When stereotypes hurt: Three studies of penalties for sex-role reversals. *Journal of Experimental Social Psychology, 11,* 520–530.

Cozby, P. C. (1973). Self-disclosure: A literature review. *Psychological Bulletin, 79,* 73–91.

Cronbach, L. J. (1957). The two disciplines of scientific psychology. *American Psychologist, 12,* 671–684.

Curtis, J. (1971). Voluntary association joining: A cross-national comparative note. *American Sociological Review, 36,* 872–880.

Davis, J. H., Laughlin, P. R., & Komorita, S. S. (1976). The social psychology of small groups: Cooperative and mixed-motive interaction. *Annual Review of Psychology, 27,* 501–541.

Day, D. R. & Stogdill, R. M. (1972). Leader behavior of male and female supervisors: A comparative study. *Personnel Psychology, 25,* 353–360.

Deaux, K. (1976). *The behavior of women and men.* Monterey, Calif.: Brooks/Cole.

Deaux, K., & Farris, E. (1973). *Re-evaluating the performance of women: Two replications.* Unpublished paper, Purdue University.

Denmark, F. L. (1977). Styles of leadership. *Psychology of Women Quarterly, 2* (2), 99–113.

Diener, E., Westford, K. L., Dineen, J., & Fraser, S. C. (1973). Beat the pacifist: The deindividuating effects of anonymity and group presence. *Proceedings of the 81st Annual Convention of the American Psychological Association, 8,* 221–222.

Dion, K. L. (1975). Women's reactions to discrimination from members of the same or opposite sex. *Journal of Research in Personality, 9,* 294–306.

Dion, K. L. (1978). Small group processes. In W. H. Holtzman (Ed.), *Introductory psychology in depth: Social topics.* New York: Harper & Row.

Dion, K. L., Earn, B. M., & Yee, P. H. N. (1978). The experience of being a victim of prejudice: An experimental approach. *International Journal of Psychology, 13* (3), 197–214.

Eagly, A. H. (1970). Leadership style and role differentiation as determinants of group effectiveness. *Journal of Personality, 38,* 509–524.

Eskilson, A., & Wiley, M. G. (1976). Sex composition and leadership in small groups. *Sociometry, 39,* 183–194.

Exline, R. V., & Ziller, R. C. (1959). Status congruency and interpersonal conflict in decision-making groups. *Human Relations, 12,* 147–162.

Fenelon, J. R., & Megargee, E. I. (1971). Influence of race on the manifestation of leadership. *Journal of Applied Psychology, 55,* 353–358.

Fennell, M. L., Barchas, P. R., Cohen, E. G., McMahon, A. M., & Hildebrand, P. (1978). An alternative perspective on sex differences in organizational settings: The process of legitimation. *Sex Roles, 4,* 589–604.

Festinger, L., Pepitone, A., & Newcomb, T. (1952). Some consequences of deindividuation in a group. *Journal of Abnormal and Social Psychology, 47,* 382–389.

Fiedler, F. E. (1964). A contingency model of leadership effectiveness. In L. Berkowitz (Ed.), *Advances in experimental social psychology.* New York: Academic Press.

Fiedler, F. E. (1967). *A theory of leadership effectiveness.* New York: McGraw-Hill.

Fiedler, F. E. (1971). Validation and extension of the contingency model of leadership effectiveness: A review of empirical findings. *Psychological Bulletin, 76,* 128–148.

Fiedler, F. E. (1972). Personality, motivational systems, and behavior of high and low LPC persons. *Human Relations, 25,* 391–412.

Fieldler, F. E. (1978). Recent developments in research on the contingency model. In L. Berkowitz (Ed.), *Group processes.* New York: Academic Press.

Gamson, W. A. (1964). Experimental studies of coalition formation. In L. Berkowitz (Ed.), *Advances in experimental social psychology* (Vol. 1). New York: Academic Press.

Gerard, H. B., & Miller, N. (1967). Group dynamics. *Annual Review of Psychology, 18,* 287–332.

Gibbs, M., Auerbach, D., & Fox, M. (1980). A comparison of male and female same-sex friendships. *International Journal of Women's Studies, 3,* 261–272.

Goldberg, J. O. (1981). *Defensive styles and women's reactions to discrimination.* Unpublished Master's Thesis, University of Waterloo.

Goldberg, P. (1968). Are women prejudiced against women? *Transaction, 5(5),* 28–30.

Goldberg, P. A., Gottesdiener, M., & Abramson, P. R. (1975). Another put-down of women? Perceived attractiveness as a function of support for the feminist movement. *Journal of Personality and Social Psychology, 32,* 113–125.

Grady, K. (1977, April). *The belief in sex differences.* Paper presented at the meeting of the Eastern Psychological Association, Boston.

Hagen, R. L., & Kahn, A. (1975). Discrimination against competent women. *Journal of Applied Social Psychology, 5,* 362–376.

Hall, K. P. (1972). Sex differences in initiation and influence in decision-making among prospective teachers. *Dissertation Abstracts International, 33(8),* 3952-A.

Hare, A. P. (1962). *Handbook of small group research.* New York: Free Press.

Hare, A. P. (1972). Bibliography of small group research, 1959–1969. *Sociometry, 35,* 1–150.

Hare, A. P. (1976). *Handbook of small group research* (2nd ed.). New York: Free Press.

Heiss, J. S. (1962). Degree of intimacy and male–female interaction. *Sociometry, 25,* 197–208.

Hemphill, J. K., & Westie, C. M. (1950). The measurement of group dimensions. *The Journal of Psychology, 29,* 325–342.

Higgins, E. T., & King, G. (1981). Accessibility of social constructs: Information-processing consequences of individual and contextual variability. In N. Cantor & J. F. Kihlstrom (Eds.), *Personality, cognition, and social interaction.* Hillsdale, N. J.: Lawrence Erlbaum Associates.

Hoffman, L. R. (1965). Group problem solving. In L. Berkowitz (Ed.), *Advances in experimental social psychology* (Vol. 2). New York: Academic Press.

Hollander, E. P. (1958). Conformity, status, and idiosyncrasy credit. *Psychological Review, 65,* 117–127.

Hollander, E. P. (1960). Competence and conformity in the acceptance of influence. *Journal of Abnormal and Social Psychology, 61,* 365–369.

Hollander, E. P. (1964). *Leaders, groups, and influence.* New York: Oxford University Press.

Holmes, D. S., & Jorgensen, B. W. (1971). Do personality and social psychologists study men more than women? *Representative Research in Social Psychology, 2,* 71–76.

Ickes, W. (1981). Sex-role influences in dyadic interaction: A theoretical model. In C. Mayo & N. Henley (Eds.), *Gender, androgyny, and nonverbal behavior.* New York: Springer.

Ickes, W. & Barnes, R. D. (1978). Boys and girls together—and alienated: On enacting stereotyped sex roles in mixed-sex dyads. *Journal of Personality and Social Psychology, 36,* 669–683.

Ickes, W., Schermer, B., & Steeno, J. (1979). Sex and sex-role influences in same-sex dyads. *Social Psychology Quarterly, 42,* 373–385.

Johnson, E. B., Goodchilds, J. D., & Raven, B. H. (1972). Male and female differences in response to status congruency–incongruency and ambiguity in a restricted communication network. *Proceedings of the 80th Annual Convention of the American Psychological Association, 7,* 215–216.

Jourard, S. M., & Lasakow, P. (1958). Some factors in self-disclosure. *Journal of Abnormal and Social Psychology, 56,* 91–98.

Kahn, A., Nelson, R. E., & Gaeddert, W. P. (1980). Sex of subject and sex composition of the group as determinants of reward allocations. *Journal of Personality and Social Psychology, 38,* 737–750.

Kanter, R. M. (1977). Some effects of proportions on group life: Skewed sex ratios and responses to token women. *American Journal of Sociology, 82,* 965–990.

Kenkel, W. F. (1957). Differentiation in family decision making. *Sociology and Social Research, 42,* 18–25.

Kennedy, C. W., & Camden, C. T. (1981). Gender differences in interruption behavior: A dominance perspective. *International Journal of Women's Studies, 4,* 135–142.

Kent, R. N. & McGrath, J. E. (1969). Task and group characteristics as factors influencing group performance. *Journal of Experimental Social Psychology, 5,* 429–440.

Korabik, K. (1982). Sex-role orientation and leadership style. *International Journal of Women's Studies, 5,* 329–337.

Larwood, L., Glasser, E., & McDonald, R. (1980). Attitudes of male and female cadets toward military sex integration. *Sex Roles, 6,* 381–390.

Linton, R. (1966). *The study of man.* New York: Appleton-Century-Croft.

Lips, H. M., & Colwill, N. L. (1978). *The psychology of sex differences.* Englewood Cliffs, N.J.: Prentice-Hall.

Lockheed, M. E. (1975). The modification of female leadership behavior in the presence of males. *Research in Education* (Abstract). (Eric Document Reproduction Service No. ED 106 742).

Lockheed, M. E. (1977). Cognitive style effects on sex status in student work groups. *Journal of Educational Psychology, 69,* 158–165.

Lockheed, M. E., & Hall, K. P. (1976). Conceptualizing sex as a status characteristic: Applications to leadership training strategies. *The Journal of Social Issues, 32* (3), 111–124.

Maslach, C. M. (1974). The social and personal bases of individuation. *Journal of Personality and Social Psychology, 29,* 411–425.

McGuire, W. J., McGuire, C. V., & Winton, W. (1979). Effects of household sex composition on the salience of one's gender in the spontaneous self-concept. *Journal of Experimental Social Psychology, 15,* 77–90.

McGuire, W. J., & Padawer-Singer, A. (1976). Trait salience in the spontaneous self-concept. *Journal of Personality and Social Psychology, 33,* 743–754.

Meeker, B. F., & Weitzel-O'Neill, P. A. (1977). Sex roles and interpersonal behavior in task-oriented groups. *American Sociological Review, 42,* 91–105.

Megargee, E. I. (1969). Influence of sex roles on the manifestation of leadership. *Journal of Applied Psychology, 53,* 377–382.

Megargee, E. I., Bogart, P., & Anderson, B. J. (1966). The prediction of leadership in a simulated industrial task. *Journal of Applied Psychology, 50,* 292–295.

Messé, L. A., Aronoff, J., & Wilson, J. P. (1972). Motivation as a mediator of the mechanisms underlying role assignments in small groups. *Journal of Personality and Social Psychology, 24,* 84–90.

Moscovici, S., & Faucheux, C. (1972). Social influence, conformity bias, and the study of active minorities. In L. Berkowitz (Ed.), *Advances in experimental social psychology* (Vol. 6). New York: Academic Press.

Moscovici, S., & Lage, E. (1976). Studies in social influence III: Majority versus minority influence in a group. *European Journal of Social Psychology, 6,* 149–174.

Moscovici, S., Lage, E., & Naffrechoux, M. (1969). Influence of a consistent minority on the responses of a majority in a color perception task. *Sociometry, 32,* 365–380.

Moscovici, S., & Nemeth, C. (1974). Social influence: Minority influence. In C. Nemeth (Ed.), *Social psychology.* Chicago: Rand McNally.

Nemeth, C., Endicott, J., & Wachtler, J. (1976). From the '50s to the '70s: Women in jury deliberations. *Sociometry, 39,* 293–304.

Offermann, L. R. (1984). Short-term supervisory experience and LPC score: Effects of leader sex and group sex composition. *The Journal of Social Psychology, 123,* 115–121.

Orum, A. M., Cohen, R. S., Grasmuck, S., & Orum, A. W. (1974). Sex, socialization, and politics. *American Sociological Review, 39,* 197–209.

Osborn, R. N., & Vicars, W. M. (1976). Sex stereotypes: An artifact in leader behavioral and subordinate satisfaction analysis? *Academy of Management Journal, 19,* 439–449.

Parsons, T., & Bales, R. F. (1955). *Family, socialization, and interaction process.* Glencoe, Ill.: The Free Press of Glencoe.

Paymer, L. D., & Dovidio, J. F. (1981, April). *Effects of leader sex, leader orientation, and group size on leadership effectiveness.* Paper presented at the Eastern Psychological Association convention, New York City.

Pheterson, G. I. (1969). *Female prejudice against men.* Unpublished manuscript, Connecticut College.

Pheterson, G., Kiesler, S., & Goldberg, P. (1971). Evaluation of the performance of women as a function of their sex, achievement, and personal history. *Journal of Personality and Social Psychology, 19,* 144–148.

Piliavin, J. A. (1976). On feminine self-presentation in groups. In J. I. Roberts (Ed.), *Beyond intellectual sexism: A new woman, a new reality.* New York: David McKay.

Piliavin, J. A., & Martin, R. R. (1978). The effects of the sex composition of groups on style of social interaction. *Sex Roles, 4,* 281–296.

Rice, R. W., Bender, L. R., & Vitters, A. G. (1980). Leader sex, follower attitudes toward women, and leadership effectiveness: A laboratory experiment. *Organizational Behavior and Human Performance, 25,* 46–78.

Ridgeway, C. L. (1982). Status in groups: The importance of motivation. *American Sociological Review, 47,* 76–88.

Ridgeway, C. L., & Jacobson, C. K. (1977). Sources of status and influence in all-female and mixed-sex groups. *Sociological Quarterly, 18,* 413–425.

Rosenblatt, P. C., & Cunningham, M. R. (1976). Sex differences in cross-cultural perspective. In B. B. Lloyd & J. Archer (Eds.), *Exploring sex differences.* New York: Academic Press, pp. 71–94.

Rubin, Z. (1970). Measurement of romantic love. *Journal of Personality and Social Psychology, 16,* 265–273.

Ruble, D. N., & Higgins, E. T. (1976). Effects of group sex composition on self-presentation and sex-typing. *The Journal of Social Issues, 32,* 125–132.

Sampson, E. E. (1963). Status congruence and cognitive consistency. *Sociometry, 26,* 146–162.

Sampson, E. E. (1969). Studies of status congruence. In L. Berkowitz (Ed.), *Advances in experimental social psychology*, vol. 4. New York: Academic Press.

Sampson, E. E. (1977). Psychology and the American ideal. *Journal of Personality and Social Psychology, 35,* 767–782.

Schein, V. E. (1973). The relationship between sex-role stereotypes and requisite management characteristics. *Journal of Applied Psychology, 57,* 95–100.

Schein, V. E. (1975). Relationships between sex-role stereotypes and requisite management characteristics. *Journal of Applied Psychology, 60,* 340–344.

Schein, V. E. (1978). Sex-role stereotyping, ability, and performance: Prior research and new directions. *Personnel Psychology, 31,* 259–268.

Schneier, C. E. (1978). The contingency model of leadership: An extension to emergent leadership and leader's sex. *Organizational Behavior and Human Performance, 21,* 220–239.

Shomer, R. W., & Centers, R. (1970). Differences in attitudinal responses under conditions of implicitly manipulated group salience. *Journal of Personality and Social Psychology, 15,* 125–132.

Slater, P. E. (1955). Role differentiation in small groups. *American Sociological Review, 20,* 300–310.

South, E. B. (1927). Some psychological aspects of committee work. *Journal of Applied Psychology, 11,* 348–368 & 437–464.

Spence, J. T., & Helmreich, R. (1972). Who likes competent women? Competence, sex-role congruence of interests, and subjects' attitudes toward women as determinants of interpersonal attraction. *Journal of Applied Social Psychology, 2,* 197–213.

Spence, J. T., & Helmreich, R. L. (1978). *Masculinity and femininity: Their psychological dimensions, correlates, and antecedents.* Austin, Texas: University of Texas Press.

Spillman, B., Spillman, R., & Reinking, K. (1981). Leadership emergence: Dynamic analysis of the effects of sex and androgyny. *Small Group Behavior, 12,* 139–157.

Stake, J. E. (1979). The ability/performance dimension of self-esteem: Implications for women's achievement behavior. *Psychology of Women Quarterly, 3,* 365–377.

Stake, J. E. (1981). Promoting leadership behaviors in low performance–self-esteem women in task-oriented mixed-sex dyads. *Journal of Personality, 49,* 401–414.

Stake, J. E., & Stake, M. N. (1979). Performance–self-esteem and dominance behavior in mixed-sex dyads. *Journal of Personality, 47,* 71–84.

Starer, R., & Denmark, F. (1974). Discrimination against aspiring women. *International Journal of Group Tensions, 4,* 65–70.

Steiner, I. D. (1964). Group dynamics. *Annual Review of Psychology, 15,* 421–446.

Strodtbeck, F. L. (1954). The family as a three-person group. *American Sociological Review, 19,* 23–29.

Strodtbeck, F. L., & Mann, R. O. (1956). Sex-role differences in jury deliberations. *Sociometry, 19,* 3–11.

Stryker, S. (1977). Developments in "Two Social Psychologies": Toward an appreciation of mutual relevance. *Sociometry, 40,* 145–160.

Taylor, S. E., Fiske, S. T., Etcoff, N. L., & Ruderman, A. J. (1978). Categorical and contextual basis of person memory and stereotyping. *Journal of Personality and Social Psychology, 36,* 778–793.

Tiger, L. (1969). *Men in groups.* London: Thomas Nelson and Sons, Ltd.

Tiger, L. (1972). Comment on "Sex and social participation." *American Sociological Review, 37,* 634–637.

Toder, N. L. (1980). The effect of the sexual composition of a group on discrimination against women and sex-role attitudes. *Psychology of Women Quarterly, 5,* 292–310.

Unger, R. K. (1975, May). *Status, power, and gender: An examination of parallelisms.* Paper presented at the conference "New Directions for Research on Women," Madison, Wisconsin.

Unger, R. K. (1976). Male is greater than female: The socialization of status inequality. *The Counseling Psychologist, 6,* 2–9.

Unger, R. K. (1979a). *Female and male. Psychological perspectives.* New York: Harper & Row.

Unger, R. K. (1979b). Toward a redefinition of sex and gender. *American Psychologist, 34,* 1085–1094.

Unger, R. K. (1982, September). Personal communication.

Unger, R. K., Hilderbrand, M., & Madar, T. (1982). Physical attractiveness and assumptions about social deviance: Some sex by sex comparisons. *Personality and Social Psychology Bulletin, 8,* 293–301.

Veiga, J. F. & Yanouza, J. N. (1978). What women in management want: The ideal vs. the real. *Academy of Management Journal, 19,* 137–143.

Vinacke, W. E. (1959). Sex roles in a three-person game. *Sociometry, 22,* 343–360.

Vinacke, W. E. (1964). Puissance, stratégie, et formation des coalitions dans les triades dans quatres conditions expérimentales. *Bulletin du Comité d'Études et Recherches Psychologigues, 13,* 119–144.

Vinacke, W. E., & Arkoff, A. (1957). An experimental study of coalitions in the triad. *American Sociological Review, 22,* 400–414.

Wahrman, R., & Pugh, M. D. (1972). Competence and conformity: Another look at Hollander's study. *Sociometry, 35,* 376–386.

Wahrman, R., & Pugh, M. D. (1974). Sex, nonconformity, and influence. *Sociometry, 37,* 137–147.

Weisstein, N. (1971). Psychology constructs the female, or the fantasy life of the male psychologist In M. H. Garskof (Ed.), *Roles women play: Readings toward women's liberation.* Belmont, Calif.: Brooks/Cole.

Wexley, K. N., & Hunt, P. J. (1974). Male and female leaders: Comparison of performance and behavior patterns. *Psychological Reports, 35,* 867–872.

Wheeler, L., & Nezlek, J. (1977). Sex differences in social participation. *Journal of Personality and Social Psychology, 35,* 742–754.

Wolman, C., & Frank, H. (1975). The solo woman in a professional peer group. *American Journal of Orthopsychiatry, 45,* 164–171.

Zander, A. (1979). The psychology of group processes. *Annual Review of Psychology, 30,* 417–451.

Ziller, R. C., & Exline, R. V. (1958). Some consequences of age heterogeneity in decision-making groups. *Sociometry, 21,* 198–211.

Epilogue: Toward a synthesis of women, gender, and social psychology

Rhoda K. Unger
Montclair State College

It is clear from reading the articles collected for this book that the study of the interface between women, gender, and social psychology has gone beyond mere theoretical and methodological critique. These articles form the basis for a model for looking at sex and gender[1] effects across content areas. They also provide a rich source of theory and research ideas for social psychology.

SEX AND GENDER IDENTITY

First, recent research (Spence & Sawin) indicates that concepts about sex and some aspects of gender identity develop so early that they come to represent a psychological "given" below the level of conscious awareness. From open-ended questions about the bases for these beliefs about the self and others, Spence and Sawin have identified some intriguing sex-related similarities and differences. Thus, both sexes appear to use physical appearance as the basis for

[1]Although we asked contributors to maintain a consistent terminology with respect to sex and gender (Unger, 1979), it is indicative of the conceptual complexity of the area that this terminology is not always used in the same way in various articles. Terminological problems are compounded by the fact that earlier historical resources do not make as many or the same distinctions as we do at present. For the purposes of this epilogue, sex refers to the biological or stimulus aspects of being male or female and gender refers to the characteristics ascribed and prescribed to the sexes—masculine or feminine. Gender-identity refers to one's beliefs about one's own characteristics. It is recognized that these various components of sex and gender may not be highly related to each other or to sexuality or sexual preference. These terminological distinctions are used to facilitate research into such questions.

perceptions of the masculinity or femininity of others, but are unlikely to use this criterion when making judgments about their own identity. The bases of self-image appear to differ for males and females. Males are more likely to include some instrumental characteristics when evaluating their masculinity, than females are to include expressive ones when evaluating their femininity. Females are more likely to use role descriptions—wife or mother—in self-evaluations than are males.

These findings also indicate that there is little relationship between individuals' self-images about their own masculinity or femininity and their perception of the extent to which they possess instrumental or expressive characteristics. These results extend previous findings (Spence & Helmreich, 1978), indicating that the degree of instrumentality/expressiveness one perceives oneself to have has little relationship to what one perceives about others' characteristics in these dimensions, or to what one perceives should be the relationship between the sexes within political, economic, or social spheres. In sum, these data indicate that there is no global attribute that one can identify as "gender" and that one must identify the various ways components of gender operate for the self in its interactions with others. We have probably been misled as to the unitary nature of sex and gender identity because (except for a few individuals) these identifications represent unproblematic tautologies.

Because sex and gender can operate at a multitude of levels does not mean that they will always have an effect. The conditions under which people label themselves and others are at least as important as the labels themselves. The conditions under which sex may become a salient label for the self and produce gender-related effects have begun to be explored. One important contribution is McGuire's distinctiveness theory (McGuire, McGuire & Winton, 1979; McGuire & Padawer-Singer, 1976). These studies indicate that when people are asked to describe themselves they focus on the ways that they are different from others who form a majority in their family or classroom. Thus, individuals who are part of the "minority" sex will include sex in their self-descriptions more often than will those who are part of the majority in their social context.

A distinction appears to be necessary in terms of the impact of customary versus transient groups to which an individual may belong (Dion). When individuals are in a minority in transient groups, they appear to minimize their differences from the majority and use more traits associated with the majority sex in their self-descriptions than do individuals in more sex-balanced groups (Higgins & King, 1981; Ruble & Higgins, 1976). A number of factors discussed later may be responsible for this phenomenon.

SEX AND GENDER AS SOCIAL LABELS

The conditions under which sex is a significant label for others have also begun to be explored. Virtually all the contributors to this book have discussed the theory that sex as a stimulus variable functions as a diffuse status characteristic; e.g., it confers differential value on individuals of each sex as well as particular assumptions about their traits and behaviors (Unger, 1976; 1978). There are remarkably few subject sex differences in perceptions based on stimulus sex (Wallston & O'Leary, 1981). And, sex is noticed even when it is not particularly distinctive or functional (Grady, 1977).

Besides noting the apparent universality of sex labels, researchers have begun to explore the way they are used to explain sex-related effects (Hansen & O'Leary). The sex of stimulus persons seems to be particularly salient in attributions about differential competence and achievement. Attributions about why an achievement results may be particularly important in mediating differential rewards to women and men in our society. Thus, identical outcomes for men and women appear to be attributed to the greater effort and intrinsic motivation of the latter than of the former. These attributions have two major consequences. Women's achievements may not be considered indicative of their competence and women may be seen as not requiring as much external reinforcement as men to maintain their performance. Hansen and O'Leary note that these attributional patterns could be responsible for the fact that women are promoted less rapidly within organizations than men are.

Perceptions may maintain as well as reflect sex and gender distinctions. A number of contributors to this volume (Eagly & Wood; Macaulay; Peplau & Gordon; Piliavin & Unger) have noted the pervasiveness of various stereotypic sex differences when the evidence does not warrant them. Eagly and Wood note that stereotyping has begun to be viewed as a normal cognitive process—one used to simplify the person perception process. Sex stereotypes, in particular, may be viewed as manifestations of the fundamental attribution error—assigning traits to the individual that are actually an aspect of environmental contingencies (role). Under usual environmental circumstances, an individual's sex and role are often confounded. Men and women are differentially distributed into different work and family roles in our society. Eagly and Wood's research indicates that when role and status are clearly stated, sex ceases to be a basis for predicting differential influence and conformity.

Conditions Under Which Sex and Gender Labels Influence Behavior

Again, recent researchers have stressed the need to explore the conditions under which sex is a relevant "trigger" for differential perceptions and behaviors. It is clear that this is a formidable undertaking. For example, Dion notes that the sex composition of the group determines relative biases for or against the identical products of women and men. These effects are inconsistent, but frequently present. Dion suggests that together with the sex of the experimenter, the sex of even noninteractive others may make norms about sex and gender salient. Similarly, Macaulay cites a recent study (Richardson, Bernstein & Taylor, 1979) that explicitly manipulated norms about aggressiveness—through the provision of an audience—and significantly altered women's retaliatory behavior.

Piliavin and Unger indicate that specific environmental conditions (possibly as a result of sex stereotypic socialization from childhood on) may also make norms about sex and gender salient. A systematic investigation of the field conditions in which help was requested indicated that consistent sex differences in who is helped are found mainly in areas involving travel of some kind. Women are more likely to be helped than men when they require travel directions, need assistance with their automobiles, or need someone to phone a garage for them. Deviation from appropriately normative feminine modes of presentation (as when attractiveness or attire is manipulated) appears to reduce the amount of assistance women are given. A number of specific stereotypes involving females and travel away from their domestic domain have been identified.

The public versus the private nature of the behavior investigated may be a particularly important variable when sex and gender effects are explored (Unger, 1981). A number of studies have indicated that traditional sex of subject effects tend to disappear when the individual is assured anonymity for his or her behavior. For example, it has long been known that sex differences in achievement are more likely to occur under conditions involving interpersonal competition than when individuals are concerned with personal mastery (Sutherland & Veroff). Men are likely to deviate from their customary equity and women from equality when allocating rewards in private rather than in public (Kidder, Belletirie & Cohn, 1977). Perhaps the most interesting recent study in this area is that by Eagly, Wood, and Fishbaugh (1981), which showed that males are much more nonconforming in public than they are in private although there is little change in females' behavior in terms of whether or not it is scrutinized. Eagly and Wood suggest that we look at societal rewards and punishments for nonconformity. Dion's discussion of idiosyncrasy credit theory and the treatment of nonconforming men and women certainly suggests that the rewards are greater for men and the punishments greater for women who deviate from the group.

SEX, GENDER, AND SOCIAL NORMS

Analysis of public versus private behavior is also useful because it allows us to discriminate between behaviors that are a result of personality traits and those that are primarily a response to situational demands. It is unlikely that sex-related differences in conformity have an intrapsychic origin when they appear to be so responsive to the effect of surveillance. It is important to analyze the social function of sex-related behaviors. For example, nonconformity attracts attention within a group (Eagly & Wood). Such attention may be positive for a male or for a majority member of a group, but not for a female or a minority member. Of course, such effects are closely linked with the way that sex functions to carry information about status. Thus, it may be socially desirable for women (usually lower status members of groups) to allocate rewards equally and to so present themselves in public (Kahn & Gaeddert).

The above discussion focuses on the role of social norms in the construction of gender related behaviors. Social norms have been little studied by psychologists, possibly because they cannot be easily manipulated within the laboratory (Wallston & Grady; Macaulay). However, researchers on sex and gender have begun to specify some issues that may lead to greater precision in determining the effects of norms. These issues include that of legitimacy—especially in terms of aggression. Macaulay asks us to consider such questions as what is defined as an approprite level of aggression? By whom? Against whom? Peplau and Gordon remind us that appropriate levels of aggression are perceived and defined differently depending on whether the participants are married or otherwise involved in a relationship. Kahn and Gaeddert suggest that equity as a basis for justice was unquestioned as a behavior within groups as long as both the investigators and their subjects shared beliefs in self-individuation, legitimate hierarchies of achievement, and the fair relationship between output and outcome. The dominance of such beliefs in our society (whether or not they were acted upon by most females) is suggested by the connection between high need for achievement and conformity with stereotypic sex roles in both females and males noted by Sutherland and Veroff. Ignoring social norms does not make them go away—it just leaves them as unpredictable confounds.

GENDER AND THE SELF-FULFILLING PROPHECY

A number of contributors to this volume have used the concept of the self-fulfilling prophecy to analyze how gender roles are constructed and maintained. For example, Hansen and O'Leary note that beliefs about the intrinsic motivation of women and, therefore, their decreased need of external rewards, may lead women to expect lower payoffs and behave accordingly. Piliavin and Unger suggest that widespread beliefs about female helplessness may lead women to perceive themselves as powerless, making them less likely to engage in self-helping instrumental activities that would enhance their self-esteem. Some of this behavior may involve compliance rather than acutal changes in behavior, but self-perception theory (Bem, 1972) would suggest that people acquire at least some of their beliefs about themselves by looking at their own behavior.

An interesting model of the self-fulfilling prophecy for gender may be generated from the current literature on physical attractiveness (Unger, in press). Thus, more attractive women are perceived to be less competent in instrumental but more competent in social skills than are less attractive women. Interactions with unseen partners who are labeled as attractive produce more socially facilitative cues than do interactions with supposedly less attractive women (Snyder,

Tanke & Berscheid, 1977). Random women labeled as attractive respond in a more socially skilled way in such an interaction, as compared to those who do not receive such labels. Indeed, those who are judged as more physically attractive in our society are seen to possess more social skills by themselves and others, although they do not see themselves as more intellectually competent than less attractive women. Physical attractiveness distinctions are made more strongly by those who are more sex-typed themselves. And, finally, physical attractiveness is associated with perceived gender for both men and women; e.g., attractive women are considered more feminine. Similar effects may be documented with sex as a stimulus variable, but all these steps have not been documented in various behavioral domains.

WHY SOCIAL PSYCHOLOGY IGNORED SEX AND GENDER

One may ask why it has taken social psychology so long to consider seriously the impact of sex and gender on behavior. Various contributors have offered a number of different responses to this question. Wallston and Grady and Macaulay have pointed to the existence of implicit theories. An older implicit theory involves the belief that sex-related effects require only biological explanations due to a confusion between sex and gender (Unger, 1979). A more recent implicit theory that has continuing implications in the widespread use of androgyny as an explanatory variable, is the belief that there is a strong connection between gender identity—masculinity and femininity—and other sex-related attributes, such as instrumentality and expressiveness (Spence & Sawin).

Social psychology is also only beginning to recognize the value of the self, probably because of the influence upon the discipline of the behaviorist positivist view of science (Macaulay; Wallston & Grady). Self-perceptions about sex and gender may be particularly difficult to operationalize because they lie so far below the level of everyday awareness. It is interesting that they begin to emerge when researchers use open-ended instruments to investigate them (Spence & Sawin; Peplau & Gordon).

Psychology, in general, has had difficulty dealing with complex multi-dimensional interactive processes. We have had difficulty incorporating into our research the fact that sex and gender labels are only evoked sometimes. We appear to be having particular difficulty with the use of one gender-relevant self-label—androgyny—as a predictor of an individual's behavior. Although some researchers (Eagly & Wood) note no connection between androgyny and conformity, others note connections with leadership behavior (Dion) and attributional processes (Hansen & O'Leary). Although the concept is clearly controversial, it appears that at least one aspect of gender identity is more important for predicting the behavior of some people under some conditions than is biological sex. It has

become increasingly clear, however, that although instrumentality and expressiveness are important dimensions in the evaluation of women and men, they
are not necessarily well-connected to other aspects of sex and gender (Spence &
Sawin).

Social psychology has also been unwilling or unable to deal with large socio-
cultural realities. In this respect it can gain much from the methodology of
developmental psychology, particularly with reference to cohort effects. Thus,
Sutherland and Veroff indicate that in 1979 males had lower values about
achievement than did a group of the same age measured in 1972. The reverse was
true for the females in their samples. Something critical happened in late 1960s
and early 1970s that changed the achievement orientation of adolescent boys and
girls. They note that one cannot talk about levels of achievement motivation as
being consistently tied to one age or sex group or another. Social psychologists,
however, conduct few intergenerational studies.

Social psychologists conduct few cross-cultural studies as well. Thus, Piliavin
and Unger point to the existence of anthropological evidence suggesting that
societies that value chivalry as a social norm also have more extreme and un-
egalitarian views about appropriate behaviors for the two sexes. We may have
difficulty separating ourselves from our cultural matrix and defining issues and
problems as well as operationalizing them (Wallston & Grady). Thus, Macaulay
points to social psychology's customary definition and examination of aggression rather than response to provocation, and Piliavin and Unger point to the
earlier and more extensive study of helping rather than recipients' requests for or
response to help as indicative of difficulty in overcoming the predominant male
bias in science and society.

SEX, GENDER, AND SCIENTIFIC BIAS

There is no reason to believe that social psychology has not been limited by
forms of scientific exclusiveness other than the sex of the investigators (Wallston
& Grady; Kahn & Gaeddert). Most questions have been generated from a narrow
healthy white male, middle-class, heterosexual perspective. A sociology of
knowledge framework is particularly useful in elucidating how science works
(Macaulay; Sherif, 1979). Macaulay perceptively notes that the control of stimuli
was important for publication in psychology, whereas the generalizability of
results was not. Therefore, concern with issues of internal validity and methods
of control have been much more central to the concerns of social psychology than
have issues involving external validity (Wallston & Grady). There is no reason to
believe, however, that female psychologists are any more immune to cognitive
bias than are males. Eagly and Wood note possible biases in the research on
conformity of male and female investigators, with each sex reporting results
more favorable to their own sex. Wallston and Grady note that our science will

only be improved by a consideration of the investigator's characteristics as well as those of his or her subjects.

It is clear that many of the phenomena involving sex and gender require clarification and redefinition. But it is also important to recognize the impact of who does the naming. In a society that defines many stereotypically masculine characteristics as more socially desirable, it is easy to fault women for their lack of such characteristics. This process of "blaming the victim" has been documented in the areas of instrumental competence (Sutherland & Veroff) and equity (Kahn & Gaeddert). It is important to look at our levels of explanation and examine them for nonconscious assumptions and biases (Kahn & Gaeddert).

A recognition of how the "real world" impinges at every level of social psychology—from how one views oneself privately and publicly and the effect of group context with or without participant interaction (Dion), through the way relational concerns influence both affectional and cognitive behaviors (Peplau & Gordon; Sutherland & Veroff)—is clearly critical. Real world concerns seem to imply relinquishing control over subjects. It is important, nevertheless, to remember that in the real world, people select their own circumstances (Macaulay; Eagly & Wood); people have relationships (Peplau & Gordon); and people exist in organizations and groups with habitual affective bonds (Dion). All of these factors probably alter the extent to which sex- and gender-related effects appear.

SEX AND GENDER, PERSONALITY, AND SOCIAL PSYCHOLOGY

These chapters point to specific research directions in many of the traditional areas of social psychology. The study of sex and gender in each of these areas also helps to remind us of the importance of individual difference variables. Much lip service is given to Lewin's notion that behavior is a function of the person and the environment. But social psychologists have tended to focus on environmental factors and to consider personality factors as error variance. As we become more comfortable with the importance of sex or gender—considered as individual difference variables—and are more able to explicate the mechanisms by which they operate, we may be able more comfortably to investigate other individual differences. The investigation of behavior focusing on both the situation and the person will be enhanced by the recognition of the centrality of sex and gender.

SEX, GENDER, AND THE COGNITIVE "REVOLUTION"

One of the major consequences of the cognitive revolution within social psychology is the recognition that we cannot control the individual's subjective reality. For many reasons, identical objective realities may produce different subjective responses in different individuals. Sex and gender are integral parts of that subjective reality. They impinge at many levels, beginning with different bodily structures and reproductive processes: continuing with long-term socialization of gender-related characteristics which, in turn, reflect and produce sex-related normative perceptions of and expectations about sex and gender. Salient sex and gender-related characteristics (including self-labels) are probably activated by critical social conditions and labels (especially in areas and domains where society trains us to respond in terms of stimulus sex). The nature of the socio-structural rewards and punishments for the sexes as classes is as important as a cost-benefit analysis at the level of the individual. In terms of rewards and punishments for gender-acceptable and deviant behaviors in men and women, sex is a central feature in all of our lives.

However, we will probably not find universal laws of behavior that predict for *all* males or *all* females, let alone for *all* human beings. Sex and gender are probably more important to some people some of the time depending on their perceived deviance in terms of the group or society, their need to present themselves in a socially desirable manner and how they interpret what is desirable, and the actual costs and benefits operating in particular situations. Sometimes these aspects will conflict with each other and the individual may engage in a complex equation to determine his or her appropriate behavior. It will be very useful for social psychology to develop situations that maximize gender incongruence. Some of the work discussed in this book points some directions by which to do so.

In sum, the study of sex and gender has been compared to the study on an onion. We continue to peel the onion, only to find that there is no central core. We cannot say that one layer is better than another, and sometimes these layers are difficult to distinguish from one another. And, like an intact onion, unexamined, sex and gender appear to form an integral whole. But both form the basis for culinary and intellectual exploration. One never knows where they will appear or in what guise.

REFERENCES

Bem, D. J. (1972). Self-perception theory. In L. Berkowitz (Ed.), *Advances in experimental social psychology* (Vol. 6) New York: Academic Press.
Eagly, A. H., Wood, W., & Fishbaugh, L. (1981). Sex differences in conformity: Surveillance by the group as a determinant of male nonconformity. *Journal of Personality and Social Psychology, 40*, 384–394.
Grady, K. (1977). *The belief in sex differences.* Paper presented at the meeting of the Eastern Psychological Association, Boston.
Higgins, E. T., & King, G. (1981). Accessibility of social constructs: Information processing consequences of individual and contextual variability. In N. Cantor & J. F. Kihlstrom (Eds.), *Personality, cognition, and social interaction.* Hillsdale, N.J.: Lawrence Erlbaum Associates.

Kidder, L. H., Bellettirie, G., & Cohn, E. S. (1977). Secret ambitions and public performance: The effects of anonymity on reward allocations made by men and women. *Journal of Experimental Social Psychology, 13*, 70–80.

McGuire, W. J., McGuire, C. V., & Winton, W. (1979). Effects of household sex composition on the salience of one's gender in the spontaneous self-concept. *Journal of Experimental Social Psychology, 15*, 77–90.

McGuire, W. J. & Padawer-Singer, A. (1976). Trait salience in the spontaneous self-concept. *Journal of Personality and Social Psychology, 33*, 743–754.

Ruble, D. N., & Higgins, E. T. (1976). Effects of group sex composition on self-presentation and sex-typing. *Journal of Social Issues, 32*, 125–132.

Sherif, C. W. (1979). Bias in psychology. In J. Sherman & E. Beck (Eds.), *The prism of sex.* Madison: University of Wisconsin Press.

Snyder, M., Tanke, E., & Berscheid, E. (1977). Social perception and interpersonal behavior: On the self-fulfilling nature of social stereotypes. *Journal of Personality and Social Psychology, 35*, 656–666.

Spence, J. T., & Helmreich, R. L. (1978). *Masculinity and femininity: Their psychological dimensions, correlates, and antecedents.* Austin: University of Texas Press.

Unger, R. K. (1976). Male is greater than female: The socialization of status inequality. *The Counseling Psychologist, 6*, 2–9.

Unger, R. K. (1978). The politics of gender: A consideration of relevant literature. In J. Sherman & F. Denmark (Eds.), *Psychology of women: Future directions of research.* New York: Psychological Dimensions.

Unger, R. K. (1979). Toward a redefinition of sex and gender. *American Psychologist, 34*, 1085–1094.

Unger, R. K. (1981). Sex as a social reality: Field and laboratory research. *Psychology of Women Quarterly, 5*, 645–653.

Unger, R. K. (in press). Personal appearance and social control. In M. Safir, M. Mednick, D. Izraeli, & J. Bernard (Eds.), *Women's worlds: The new scholarship.* New York: Praeger.

Wallston, B. S., & O'Leary, V. E. (1981). Sex makes a difference: Differential perceptions of women and men. In L. Wheeler (Ed.), *Review of personality and social psychology* (Vol. 2). Beverly Hills, Calif.: Sage.

Author Index

Numbers in *italics* denote pages with bibliographic information.

Subject Index

A

Achievement, *see also* Achievement motivation, Attributions
  and affect, 86–88
  assumptions about and gender, 68, 104
    105, 171, 177
  beliefs about in the U.S., 131, 353
  cohort effects, 118–125, 355
  and group sex composition, 323–324
  and learned helplessness, 175
  sex-related differences
    in attitudes about, 78–81, 132–133, 138
    in attributions, 176, 351
    in incentives for, 115–118
  and status, 85, 321–322
Achievement motivation, 101–128, *see also*
    Fear of success
  age differences in, 120–125
  definition of, 101
  review of studies of, 102–110
  sex-related differences in, 103–110
  and sex roles, 110–126
  stability of, 118–120
Affiliation, 133, 298–301
  need for and female achievement, 105–
    109
  need for and male achievement, 114–115
Agency, *see* Instrumentality

Aggression, 19, 168, 191–224, *see also* Violence against women
  and cultural norms, 199–200
  definitions of, 196–198, 353
  and frustration, 208
  research issues
    bias in research design, 201–207
    dominant paradigms, 208–211
    history, 198–200
    laboratory versus real-life, 193
    recent changes, 214–219
    the structure of academia, 211–214
  sex-role ideology, effect on, 172
  unanswered questions about, 193–194
Altruism, *see* Helping
Androgyny, 5, 18, 43, 156, 283, 308, 354,
    see also Gender, Masculinity-femininity
  and achievement, 81–82, 118, 121, 125
  and group interaction, 314–316
Anger, 196–197, 200, *see also* Aggression
Arousal, *see also* Attention
  and achievement, 103–104
  and helping, 153, 168
Assertiveness, 197, 216–217, 246, 320,
    334
Attention, 83–85, 153, 203–204, *see also*
    Arousal
Attraction, *see* Affiliation, Physical
    attractiveness

Gender (*cont.*)
  confounding of, with sex, 82, 192, 349
  constancy, 59
  and equity, 135–138
  as a construct, 62–63
  and person perception, 60
  as a personality trait, 250
  in persuasion experiments, 232
  in roles and situations, 64
  as a stimulus variable, 133
Gender identity, *see also* Androgyny, Gender
  and consciousness, 349
  definition of, 59–60
  development of, 62–63
  disturbances in, 59
  and group interaction, 314–316
  and the perception of others, 350
  and the prediction of behavior, 250
Gender-roles, *see also* Gender, Sex-roles
  and achievement, 105–110, 111–113
  and conformity, 112, 236–239, 318
  and the division of labor, 37, 326
  and group processes, 325, 333–334
  and group sex composition, 311–312
  and helping, 160–161
  and influence tactics, 275–276
  and love relationships, 262–263
  and marriage, 279–280, 281
  perceived costs and rewards of, 55
  problems of measurement, 57–58
  sex-related differences
    in attitudes about, 259
    as explanations of, 228–230
  and small group behavior, 295–297
  socialization of, 240
  and status, 241–245, 318
  theories of, 35–41
Gender-role identification, *see also* Androgyny, Femininity, Masculinity, Sex-roles
  definition of, 36
  and instrumentality/expressiveness, 40
  and mental health, 37–38
  and perceptions of helplessness, 177–178
  salience of, 308
  significance of, 56–64
  and sympathy, 156
Gender schema, 39, 42, 57, 84–85
Group processes, 238–239, 293–347
  group sex composition, effect on, 293–294, 302–316, 323–329, 351–352

Group processes (*cont.*)
  history of study of, 293–294, 297–298
  and sex as a label, 350
  status manipulation, effect on, 141

H

Helping, 149–189
  and cross-sex interactions, 159–160
  definition of, 150
  and gender-role expectations, 159–161
  model of, 152–154
  and norms, 169–170, 171–172
  perceptions about the recipient of, 172–174
  and physical strength, 158
  and pre-attentive processing, 153–156
  recipient dependency, effect on, 163–166
  situational factors in, 170
Homosexuality, 59, 61, 62
Husbands, *see* Marriage

I

Identification, *see* Gender identity
Idiosyncrasy credit, 238, 317–321, *see also* Conformity, Social deviance
Individual differences, 149, 294
  in gender identity and conformity, 237–238
  and sex as a social variable, 179
  in small group behavior, 323–324
  and the study of sex and gender, 5
Influenceability, 225–256, *see also* Conformity, Group processes, Power
  and conformity with group norms, 317–321
  sex-related differences in, 228–234
  stereotypes about sex differences in, 239–245
Instrumentality, 36, 229, *see also* Androgyny, Expressivity, Gender identity, Masculinity
  and achievement, 131
  and group processes, 316
  and leadership, 300
  and masculinity/femininity, 40, 355
  and reward allocation, 137
Interaction
  between persons and situations, 149, 218, 356
  between sex of helper and sex of recipient, 151
  between sex and the variable of interest, 210
  between subject sex and gender, 156, 218